ENGAGING

THE

JUBILEE

ENGAGING

THE

JUBILEE

Freedom and Justice Papers of the
Baptist World Alliance
(2010-2015)

Edited by Raimundo C. Barreto Jr.,
Kenneth L. Sehested and Luis N. Rivera-Pagán
and Paul Hayes

CONTENTS

Recovery of Sight to the Blind

To Let the Oppressed Go Free

To Proclaim the Year of the Lord's Favor

DEDICATION

This work is dedicated posthumously to the lives and memory of Dr. Samuel K. Roberts, Dr. J. Deotis Roberts, and Dr. Glen H. Stassen, Baptist scholars whose erudition is evident in the pages of this book. These men have made significant contributions to the global Baptist community over the years and have impacted the work of the BWA Division of Freedom and Justice by advancing the Christian faith through teaching, writing, and their personal example. *Ad majorem Dei gloriam.*

PREFACE

The Baptist World Alliance, through its Division on Freedom and Justice, is delighted to present the first volume of the *BWA Freedom and Justice Papers*, a collection of papers representative of the work of the diverse BWA Freedom and Justice Commissions during the past quinquennium (2010-2015). It reflects the completion of the F&J Division's first full quinquennium of work. This new series follows the footsteps of *Faith & Witness*, although with its peculiarities.

The Freedom & Justice Division is a dream come true, emerging out of and expanding the BWA's long time advocacy for religious liberty and human rights. From its inception in 1905, the BWA has been an international voice for Baptist concerns with human rights and justice. In the words of William Brackney, the founding of the BWA was "part of the drive toward greater cooperation among Christians at the end of the 19th century and the beginning of the 20th century." Eight major Christian World Communions were formed between 1880 and 1930 (Brackney, 2005:8). Early on, BWA presidents and secretaries took on religious liberty and human rights advocacy as an important aspect of their portfolio. Edgar Y. Mullins (BWA President, 1923-1928), for instance, traveled extensively to Eastern Europe to meet with political authorities and advocate on behalf of Baptist communities in the region, as well as to "present the BWA case for freedom of conscience and democratic government" (Brackney, 2005:8). Subsequent to the Baptist World Congress in Stockholm (1923), Baptists have used the BWA international platform to issue statements in support of many significant causes (persecution of religious minorities, world peace, condemning racism, supporting the Universal Declaration of Human Rights, etc.).

The Commission on Religious Liberty was born at the BWA Congress in Copenhagen in 1947 (McDormand, 1975), just one year prior to the adoption of the Universal Declaration of Human Rights (UDRH) by the United Nations. Thirty years later, Thomas McDormand identified some relation between what was happening in the context of the BWA and what was taking place in the larger society. In words delivered at the 1975 Congress, McDormand observed the UDRH "included a statement on religious liberty which coincided remarkably with that of our Commission" (McDormand, 1975). In 1961, the mandate of the Commission was broadened, explicitly adding the concern for human rights. According to McDormand, this addition was made "because of the unquestionable relationship between religious liberty and human rights generally—all basic human rights stemming from religious liberty" (McDormand, 1975). The expanded commission had five areas of concern: (1) Positive approaches to problems of discrimination in human relations; (2) positive contributions to religious liberty and church-state relations.; (3) positive approaches to the formation of Christian character; (4) positive approaches to the exercise of Christian influence on public policy; and (5) positive elements in our approach to international tensions (McDormand, 1975). Since then, the BWA concern for freedom and justice has remained broad, having expanded even more to include ecological concerns, and interfaith relations in the past decades.

Baptist public witness took another important step towards more consistent advocacy in the international realm when in 1974, through the agency of Carl Tiller, the BWA obtained special consultative status with the Economic and Social Council of the United Nations. The formation in 1992 of the Special Commission on Baptists against Racism was another catalyst to build support for the creation of the Division on Freedom and Justice, which took place in 2008. The new Division became responsible for the coordination and articulation of all the above areas of concern. In accord with the BWA Freedom and Justice Charter, "through F&J, the BWA promotes both respect for human rights, especially religious liberty, and due regard for justice in human affairs as values that are grounded in Scripture and therefore in the faith of the church."

Since 2010, the work of the Division of Freedom and Justice has been assisted by five commissions: (1) Religious Freedom; (2) Peace; (3) Human Rights Advocacy; (4) Social and Environmental Justice; and (5) Baptist-Muslim relations. In 2014, the BWA General Council meeting in Izmir approved a slight reordering of these commissions, which for the next quinquennium will become seven instead of five. This book reflects the work of the five commissions above. They met once a year during the BWA Annual Gatherings between 2011 and 2014, and supported initiatives throughout the year between annual gatherings. The Commissions contributed to training sessions on conflict transformation and trauma awareness, supported human rights visits, helped to raise awareness of human rights abuses in different places, wrote letters of solidarity to victims of abuse and violence, and collaborated in several ways with the advocacy work coordinated by the F&J Division. They assisted in the coordination of advocacy visits to political offices, UN state missions, and the office of the UN High Commissioner for Human Rights, and in the preparation of white papers for BWA advocacy at the UN Human Rights Council.

In keeping with the 2010-2015 Ministry Plan, the F&J Commissions gathered under the general theme *In Step with the Spirit*, which united the overall work of the BWA throughout the past quinquennium. In order to fit the particular nature of its work, F&J Commissions adapted the overall theme, which for them became *In Step with the Spirit of Freedom, Justice, and Peace*. This theme was developed throughout the quinquennium with the following annual emphases: consecration, proclamation, liberation, transformation, and dedication. Each of these emphases was related to one of the areas of work of the F&J Division: peace (2011); religious freedom (2012), social justice (2013), and environmental justice (2014). The element of interfaith relations represented by the Commission on Baptist-Muslim relations was present throughout the F&J gatherings.

The editorial team organized the papers around the biblical idea of the jubilee, based on Luke 4:18-19, the thematic verse for the BWA Ministry Plan.

The Spirit of the Lord is upon me, because he has anointed me to proclaim good news to the poor. He has sent me to proclaim liberty to the captives and recovering of sight to the blind, to set at liberty those who are oppressed, to proclaim the year of the Lord's favor. (ESV)

The reference to the jubilee reminds us of the centrality of freedom and justice to Jesus' ministry, and consequently to his followers. The programmatic character of this passage is generally acknowledged. (Willoughby, 1995:41). Freedom is understood in liberational terms, as the Day of the Lord's favor. These verses are more than a declaration of a hopeful future. They lay out a program of action for Jesus' disciples based on his own priorities. The Gospel of Jesus is more than wishful thinking. It is a call for action. *Engaging the Jubilee* is, therefore, the challenge before us. It is one, however, which we cannot take on our own. We have to be in step with the Spirit, empowered by the Spirit of Jesus, to continue the ministry he started. "The Spirit of the Lord is upon me," is what each Baptist around the world is called to say. It is moved by the Spirit of the Lord that we will be able to "bring good news to the poor" (part 1), "proclaim release to the captives" (part 2), "recovery of sight to the blind" (part 3), "let the oppressed go free" (part 4), and "proclaim the year of the Lord's favor" (part 5).

The areas of action are established by the text itself. The fact that they fit so well the work coming out of the F&J Commissions speaks of the holistic understanding of freedom and justice themes, constantly noticed in the many papers and conversations held by these commissions in the past five years. That also explains the overlap in the work of the different commissions, a theme that came up several times in our annual meetings. We recognized the benefits of overlapping, since it is not the same as duplication. International advocacy is a cross- and interdisciplinary endeavor. Those concerned with religious freedom will naturally address other sorts of slavery and oppression, as well as talk about interfaith relations. Similarly, topics related to peace will lead to conversations about social injustice, religious intolerance, or environmental sustainability.

Finally, for those who are not well acquainted with the nature and work of the BWA, it is important to reinforce that the thoughts and ideas expounded by the diverse Baptist pastors, leaders, activists, and scholars in this book do not represent any official position of the BWA. They are simply representative of the healthy diversity that characterizes Baptist life locally, nationally, regionally, and globally, and proof that in spite of our differences, we can do greater work together in the spirit of collaboration, mutual respect, and joint learning.

Bibliography

Brackney, William. "The BWA: Making of an International Identity." *Baptist Quarterly*. No. 1. March 2005.

McDormand, Thomas B. "The Work of the Study Commission on Religious Liberty and Human Rights." Delivered at the Baptist World Congress, 10 July 1975.

Willoughby, Robert. "The Concept of Jubilee and Luke 4:18-30." *Mission and Meaning: Essays Presented to Peter Cotterell*. Antony Billington, ed. Paternoster. 1995.

ACKNOWLEDGMENTS

This book is a collection of testimonies reflecting the important work Baptists worldwide have done over the past five years in the field of freedom and justice. It is an expression of a deep commitment to the love of God and neighbor, which is characteristic of Baptist life. It is impossible to name all people who contributed to this publication, but there are some whose generous contribution to this work requires acknowledgement.

We express thanks to all those who served as members of the Freedom and Justice Advisory Committee and of the several Freedom and Justice commissions during this past quinquennium. Their great work is an expression of the collaborative spirit that one can see in Baptist life around the world. Deepest gratitude goes to Solomon Ishola (chair of the F&J Advisory Committee) and to commission chairs: Alan Marr (Chair of the Commission on Peace); Karen Bullock (Chair of the Commission on Religious Freedom); Jeffrey Haggray (Commission on Social and Environmental Justice); Olu Menjay (Commission on Human Rights Advocacy); and Nabil Costa (Commission on Baptist-Muslim Relations. We are aware They were supported by vice-chairs and commission members who shared the burden of their responsibilities.

The papers selected for this volume reflect the collaborative work between the BWA office, members and chairs of F&J commissions, national and regional Baptists leaders, BWA representatives at the United Nations, and Baptist individuals and churches resisting oppression, promoting human rights, and advocating for peace and justice in different localities around the world. In many cases, papers presented during the Annual Gatherings resulted from particular efforts to respond to the needs of brothers and sisters in situations of distress, which had mobilized a number of people for collaboration between different annual meetings of the commissions.

We are grateful also to each person who positively responded to the invitation to present on the different meetings of the F&J Commissions. Some chapters in this book have appeared in other publications. We acknowledge all the authors, institutions, and journals, which authorized those texts to be reprinted. Specific information on those authorizations can be found at the end of particular chapters, where applicable.

A note of special gratitude to those who voluntarily spent many hours editing the manuscripts of this book. No one devoted more time and did more rigorous editorial work than Paul Hayes. Thanks to his editing skills and incredible availability for this project, we have completed it in time. A busy pastor, with many responsibilities, Paul contributed significantly to make it possible for this work to be completed in a timely manner. Ken Sehested and Luis Rivera-Pagan also generously gave a significant amount of time and expertise to this project. Without them, this book would not be in your hands.

Finally, we acknowledge the editorial assistance provided by Steve dos Santos Belo, M. Div. Student at Princeton Theological Seminary. Princeton Theological Seminary has contributed with the resources for this editorial assistantship.

The editorial team is grateful for the opportunity to work on this project. We have been richly blessed to experience this process from such a privileged perspective.

The Baptist World Alliance (BWA) expresses its sincere appreciation to Raimundo Barreto who served as Director for the BWA's Commission on Freedom and Justice for the period, 2010-2014, and who voluntarily coordinated the work of the editorial team after demitting office on the staff of the BWA.

INTRODUCTION

Raimundo C. Barreto Jr.

In the early decades of this century, one thing has become certain: the world is crying out for peace. The 20th century, considered one of the most violent periods in human history, left a legacy of two world wars, many regional conflicts, and several gruesome and costly genocides. The hope of a new millennium was quickly overshadowed by horrific events that launched a global war on terrorism, military assaults in Afghanistan and Iraq, and political revolutions and militant battles throughout the Middle East, Asia, and Africa. According to experts (Goldstein, 2015), there are currently 10 mass-scale wars and 22 other armed conflicts, resulting in more than a million casualties in 2015 alone, most of them innocent civilians.

As alarming as this reality is, armed conflicts are responsible for only 10% of violent deaths around the world. According to UNICEF, urban violence and structural oppression caused by an imbalance of political and economic power are directly related to the deaths of more than 6 million children annually. Behind these statistics are human lives needlessly traumatized or lost—a fact that sears the moral consciousness of humankind and challenges the global Church to work harder for justice and meaningful peace.

The Baptist World Alliance, from its inception, has vowed to be an agency of peace and reconciliation. Since World War I, Baptists have materially and spiritually assisted victims of war as they reconstructed their lives; they have also supported initiatives and programs to promote and protect human rights and religious freedom, while waging peace and justice. Doing this good work has accompanied our proclamation of the Gospel message for over a century; building peace and protecting freedom has been integral to our efforts to fulfill the objectives of the Great Commission.

The chapters of this book will acquaint readers with the work of Baptists from different parts of the world to promote freedom, justice, and peace in their immediate contexts, but also on the national, regional and international level. The writers exemplify the variety of practical and theoretical contributions Baptists are making for a fuller understanding and commitment to peace and justice in the world. Likewise, this book is a testament to the conviction that Baptists can make a unique and significant contribution to Christianity and to the larger society in the 21st century in two specific ways.

First, Baptists have known suffering and oppression as religious minorities in different parts of the world. Many have experienced firsthand discrimination, slavery, religious persecution, imprisonment, and cultural marginalization as persecuted minorities. Forged through 400 years of history, Baptists have developed a deep conviction for religious freedom for all, which has often translated into a strong advocacy for human rights and to the promotion of just and peaceful relations. So, in times of great civil strife and violence, Baptists share stories of hope, solidarity, and unselfish commitment to the wellbeing of others inspired by the public witness of many Baptists around the world. These storied lives help equip us to work in solidarity with other victims of injustice and violence, in order to promote tolerance, mutual respect, freedom of religion and belief, just relationships, and peaceful coexistence.

Secondly, in the past century there has been a drastic shift in the epicenter of Christianity. For the first time in a millennium, there are more Christians living in the "Global South" than in the Northern hemisphere. Historians, anthropologists, missiologists, and theologians are beginning to grasp and understand the consequences of this new reality for the future of Christianity, not only institutionally, but also for what it means to the missionary enterprise. Some scholars have framed this in terms of a non-Western Christianity meeting a post-Christian West (Granberg-Michaelson, 2013). Others have a more nuanced perception, identifying the polycentric nature of Christianity today. In any case, new forms of Christianity are emerging around the globe, particularly in Africa, Asia, and Latin America, and in their "diasporas" in European and North American societies.

The Baptist World Alliance was born in 1905 as part of the Christian mission enterprise, and the search for denominational cooperation and unity. It was one of several ecumenical initiatives which emerged in the modern missionary era. Most ecclesiastical structures of that time, however, face a crisis of identity today, as does the ecumenical movement as a whole, with the shift toward the Global South. The BWA is not immune to it. Yet, of all the ecumenical structures created in the late 19th and early 20th centuries, the Baptist World Alliance has remarkable potential to renew itself and remain relevant in the 21st century. No other World Christian communion is as deeply rooted in the local realities of churches as is the BWA. The primary identity for Baptists worldwide is at the grassroots level, with associations that are inherently committed to diversity.

As the pages of this book will make clear, Baptists hold different views on a variety of important matters, doctrines, theology, and worldviews. Baptists recognize religious freedom is experienced substantially through mutual respect and tolerance for diversity among themselves. Member bodies of the BWA understand and protect the freedom of their brothers and sisters to worship and express their faith in different ways, thus fostering a sense of unity rather than uniformity. This places the Baptist World Alliance in an advantageous position to appreciate Christian diversity, enculturation, and contextualization, as compared to maintaining rigid ecclesiastical structures. Such potential, based on the respect for diversity and autonomy, is inscribed in Baptist identity and heritage.

Furthermore, in the pages that follow authors from each of the six regions of the Baptist World Alliance shed light on how particular tenets of Baptist identity are interpreted in the light of specific histories and cultures. One of the narratives shows, for instance, how Jamaican Baptists have developed their interpretation of religious freedom through the historical lens of their own experience as a nation and people. Such a historical review demonstrates well how even a marker of Baptist identity is never static. Tenets of faith are dynamically renewed in the particularities of Baptist churches around the world.

Another perspective from the Caribbean offers a thoughtful read on human rights in the context of educating for peace, in conversation with the liberating pedagogy first expounded by Brazilian, Paulo Freire. Another chapter, by a seasoned and renowned North American scholar-peacemaker, argues how the English Baptist, Robert Overton, developed the first comprehensive theory of human rights traced to the teaching of Jesus rather than to the humanist theories of the Enlightenment. Additional contributions focus on important Baptist historical figures, such as Thomas Helwys, Sam Sharpe, and J. Deotis Roberts, who are highlighted as exemplars for those engaged in advocacy for peace and justice in the 21st century. These are just some examples of the richness of backgrounds and experiences shared by each of the authors in this book.

One of the most valued contributions made by the Baptist World Alliance has been the creation of safe space for scholarly discussion through its diverse commissions, where members from a variety of backgrounds and cultures reflect together on topics of interest and concern. The BWA commissions create a unique opportunity for Baptist pastors, laypersons, and scholars to interact and appreciate the variety of perspectives in the field of freedom and justice. Typically, scholars and activists relate mainly to their own peers and guilds, opting for either strategy-making or theoretical reflection. Pastors frequently value only what can be translated into sermons and congregational initiatives. The work of Christ through each of these agencies is enriched when it takes place in a dialogical engagement, where all these approaches are held in collaborative tension with each other. This has been the goal over these past five years of work among the various F&J commissions, which is well represented in this book.

At the same time, this book reflects a collaborative effort between the BWA office through its Division on Freedom and Justice, the F&J Commissions, and other areas of ministry of the Baptist World Alliance. Some of the chapters were presentations revised by commission discussions that further evolved into resolutions before the governing body. Some reflect a pattern of collaboration between the BWA F&J Division, BWA representatives at the United Nations, and F&J Commissions resulting in important advocacy efforts, such as, contributing to the release of prisoners, raising awareness of oppressive situations in certain regions, organizing delegations for visits of solidarity, and providing training sessions in conflict transformation. Most of the stories told could not be shared publicly or published. But those that could appear in the pages of this book.

Finally, this volume represents the public witness of Baptists on the international level. Baptists value freedom and justice ministries in different ways. I like to see it as an important aspect of our collaborative public witness. In the past five years, such public witness involved a number of initiatives. In July 2012, for instance, the BWA passed a resolution expressing "concern about the discriminatory bombing of places of worship," the slaughtering of Nigerian people and the "abuse of human rights in the name of religion." This resolution called for advocating for religious liberty and for efforts in peacemaking. Baptists worldwide were urged to voice their concerns to "their governments, religious leaders, and persons of influence."

In the same year, the BWA co-sponsored side-events during the United Nations Conference on Sustainable Development in Rio de Janeiro and, along with other Christian organizations, put forward a statement calling on world leaders to consider the ethical implications of sustainable development when discussing the principles guiding the United Nations agenda for the next 20 years. Those instances of public witness led to further self-reflection on each of these situations—some of which are included in this text.

In other cases, we were simply asked to stand in solidarity with others. During the Annual Gathering in Santiago, Chile (2012), Pablo Moreno, the president of the Baptist University in Cali, spoke at one of the sessions of the Peace Commission regarding the situation in Colombia and the urgent need for international support in the work for peace and justice in his country. He urged the BWA to witness firsthand the violations of human rights in the country, as well as the churches' work for peace and justice. A BWA delegation visited Colombia and reported back to the Peace Commission the following year in Jamaica (2013), sharing the impressive work of the Peace and Justice Commission of the Evangelical Council of Churches in Colombia (CEDECOL), and calling for ways Baptist worldwide can support the work done by the Colombian churches in the area of peacebuilding and theological education.

Stories like the peace and justice programs at the Baptist University, Cali, need to be heard around the world (e.g., a Diploma Course on "Social Action and Peace building," for pastors and other Christian leaders). Baptists are involved in similar innovative approaches to theological education in places such as the Peace Studies Centre in Yangon, Myanmar, or in the Arab Baptist Theological Seminary in Beirut, Lebanon. Such stories are important to share as great examples of Baptist public witness around the world.

This book intends to be a contribution to enrich that narrative. Its pages are filled with an emphasis on transforming Christian practices based on the programmatic agenda proposed by Jesus in Luke 4:18-19. It is a challenging agenda, which requires from us a humble attitude of dependence upon the power of the Holy Spirit. As Denise Forrest, one of the speakers on the Commission on Social and Environmental Justice in Jamaica (2013), said, as basis for these transforming practices we need "to discern the Holy Spirit as a source of guidance into the virtues that will lead to renewal of life with direct impact on the whole creation."

Many of the presentations made on the different F&J Commissions were not included in this book. In the appendices, a full agenda of the meetings, with all topics and presenters, is offered, along with a couple of documents produced by the Division on Freedom and Justice during the past quinquennium. The selected essays, which you will see in the following pages, are meant to offer only a taste of the vibrant work done by the global Baptists on Freedom and Justice in the past five years. It is also a testimony of our commitment to be witnesses to all the things "Jesus began to do and to teach until the day he was taken up to heaven" (Acts 1:1-3).

Bibliography

Goldstein, Joshua. "Wars in Progress." http://www.internationalrelations.com. 2015.

Granberg-Michaelson, *From Times Square to Timbuktu: The Post-Christian West Meets the Non-western Church*. Eerdmans. 2013.

THE
SPIRIT OF THE LORD
IS
UPON ME

1 | MARTIN LUTHER KING, JR. IN LATIN AMERICA

Francisco Rodés González

In the part of Latin America from which I come, one day was heard the sound of the "drum major for justice"—Martin Luther King, Jr.—waking up the Christian conscience to see the need for Christians to take part in efforts for social justice.

The Awakening of Social Conscience

However, no one thought that this awakening of social conscience was an easy process. Rather, it was (and still is) slow, with both advances and set-backs. In our particular case, the island of Cuba, the churches in the 60s and 70s were living through a complex and difficult stage due to the predominance of dogmatic Marxism with its strong pressures and discrimination against believers. For the outside world, this generated a perspective that everything in Cuba, even the churches, should be suspected of atheism and Satanism. On the other hand, the inherited missionary presence in Cuba proposed the rejection of any participation in the social activism of the day since it was considered worldly and tainted by political militancy.

So the younger generation who wanted to live out a Christian commitment to a better world had to face two obstacles: on one hand, the incomprehension of our society's atheistic leaders and, on the other hand, the narrow vision of Christian pastors and leaders.

But the example of the African-American pastor, who was marching at the head of the multitudes leading the quest for civil rights, facing powerful enemies while surrounded by indifferent white churches, was a powerful inspiration for us. King came to be our hero. His actions reminded us of the prophets of Israel with their denouncing of powerful oppressors, who free from the fear of their retaliations, preached a message of justice for the poor. And even more with his martyrdom, King confirmed to us that the way of social redemption is marked by sacrifice and blood. "Oppressors will never voluntarily give up their power, conflict is inevitable," he said.

It is necessary to recognize that Marxism held a particular attraction for the generations of young people who were aspiring to construct a society without class exploitation. They found in this ideology a tool to understand the economic and ideological mechanisms that support the system of domination and exploitation. Many Christians in Latin America utilized this economic analysis and at the same time they rejected its atheism.

Latin America

Latin America has a long history of abuses and oppression. There is the violence carried out by the Spanish and Portuguese conquerors in the name of evangelization, as Luis Rivera-Pagán shows us in his work (Rivera-Pagán, 1992). Added to that is the exploitation of Latin America's natural and human resources in order to serve the interests of the First World's transnational companies that create a planet with major social inequality.

How could we be missionary churches in a continent plagued with violence, corruption and injustice? How could we announce to the poor a gospel of love and simultaneously allow them to live in misery, illiteracy, and dying of curable illnesses? These were the pressing questions of those turbulent years.

The era of revolutions arrived to the doorsteps of Latin America's Christian churches. The Catholic churches, with their presence and service among the poor, became the place that first developed a theological basis for Christians wanting to accompany the poor and help create change. It was called, Liberation Theology. The evangelical churches with their missionary legacy (which restricted the evangelizing task to proselytism) centered on the numerical growth of church membership. They were much more resistant to the commitment that the times demanded.

The task of creating this social awareness among evangelicals required a strong biblical basis. And Martin Luther King Jr. appeared like a powerful symbol. He was a pastor with his Bible in hand and from the pulpit he carried out his prophetic ministry. It was the model that the evangelical people of Latin America needed, even though the missionaries were promoting other projects and other goals.

Biblical-Theological Essentials

What were the Biblical essentials on which Martin Luther King, Jr. stood that allowed evangelical Latin Americans to take up a social commitment? We were educated in a form of evangelization that consisted of preaching the salvation of souls and forgetting that the center of Jesus' message was the Kingdom of God.

Helping us rediscover the centrality of the Kingdom of God was one of the contributions of the Social Gospel teaching. Among other teachers was the Baptist pastor, Walter Rauschenbush, who undoubtedly contributed to the vision of Martin Luther King, Jr. He proclaimed that there is no dichotomy between material and spiritual needs (Rauschenbush, 1907). He preached a full salvation, which consisted of announcing the dignity of life in this world and not just life after death. As Jesus said, "I have come so that you may have life and have it abundantly." The signs of the Kingdom became clear through Jesus' ministry of healing the sick, the casting out of demons, the restoration of life, the feeding of the hungry and many other actions on behalf of the marginalized and the despised.

The Biblical concept of the Kingdom of God, with its indisputable sense of community, of inclusive space, holistically defines the horizons of Church mission as something that evangelicals in Latin America still need to reclaim today. It is a revolutionary message that proclaims the possibility of a radically different world.

A very important aspect of this concept of the Kingdom of God is its eschatological dimension. The Kingdom is perceived in the present only through its signs which are apparent when human life is promoted. These signs point toward a future fully realized—that final consummation when the goal of God's people is reached and rests in perfect harmony with creation and with God. This is the utopia, the dream glimpsed by the prophets, always looking towards a future with the challenge of a greater vision. As someone said, "if we can never reach utopia: what does it serve?" And one responded, "To help us to walk."

This was the heart of the famous speech of King in Washington when he famously proclaimed "I have a dream" and offered his vision of the Promised Land in which white children and black children play together and live in an integrated and new society free of prejudice and discrimination. This utopia is expressed in Latin America in radical terms which include a new economic model, a just redistribution of natural resources, equal opportunities for all to receive education and healthcare, as well as the care of creation.

Principalities and Powers

Another challenge that evangelical Latin Americans had to face was the question: how do we send a message to the structures and ideologies that govern society if our mission is to preach only to persons about their individual sin?

With this question, we were again helped by the example of Martin Luther King, Jr. as he launched his struggle against the power of racism. He made us remember the Biblical language of struggle against the "principalities and powers"

(Eph. 6:12). It refers to forces that attempt to rule over humanity, the assumption of control and domination over the lives of human beings. In the time of Paul, the power of Jewish tradition was very serious and threatened the integrity of the Christian community. It is a legitimate interpretation that can also be applied to the different current powers that in some way determine the reality for millions of human beings, as Walker Wink has demonstrated in his famous works about the principalities and powers (Wink, 1984, 1986, 1992).

For Martin Luther King, Jr., racism exercised control over the entire country, but was most pronounced in the South. His strategy for change required not only public actions but a spiritual formation capable of resisting the violence and the hate that such racism generates. This discipline of nonviolence was the spiritual weapon to prevail over such principalities and powers, which sadly still persist in segments of North American society.

Evangelicals of Latin America have to wake up to the structural forms of sin in our society. Sin is also in political systems and economic structures that favor wealth for a few to the detriment of the majority. To enter this terrain, of course, creates conflict. It creates division in our communities because these principalities and powers have a place in the consciousness of the people who have been shaped for generations and therefore justify present situations and accept them as the will of God. That's why, if King struggled against the power of the racism, why can't we face the structural sin in our continent?

The Incarnation

The story of the "empty pulpit" is an important one. When Dr. King was invited to present a sermon at an ecumenical meeting in Geneva, Switzerland, it happened to be at a critical moment in the struggle for racial justice. He decided to remain next to his people and sent a recorded version of his sermon. Many listened with great reverence to this "empty pulpit" and it was powerful inspiration for those thinking about how to do mission on our continent. Because King was present at all the important moments of the struggle, it was not possible for others to remain comfortably behind the walls of the Church. He showed us the way of full incarnation in the movements for justice and peace.

The recovery of the idea of "incarnation" meant a turn in our way of understanding God's work in the world. In the text, "As the Father has sent me, so I send you" (Jn. 20.21b), the word "as" is important. It demonstrates a specific model for carrying out the evangelizing task in a way that is incarnated. It calls us to be the physical presence, the body and soul of Christ in the world with Jesus as our example. As evangelical Christians, we have understood evangelization more as conveying effective words, as if the gospel was merely a product to offer or goods for sale. It is not a question of now despising such verbal proclamation, but of affirming the principle that only life can transmit life. There are times in which gestures and deeds are much more valuable than words.

In Latin America, we understood that acts are more important than words. As when Jesus answered John's disciples who were investigating if he really was the awaited Messiah: "Go and tell John what you hear and see: the blind receive their sight, the lame walk, the lepers are cleansed, the deaf hear, the dead are raised, and the poor have good news brought to them" (Mt. 11:4-5). Jesus was not trying to scorn the power of words, but he emphasized the redemptive acts of God on behalf of human beings.

The Present Impact of Martin Luther King Jr. in Latin America

These are some of the Biblical-Theological perspectives that nourished a social practice committed to a new order of social justice in Latin America. In this period, many hoped that dramatic changes in political power and socio-economic structures would take place. In many ways, they did not. We are left with the question: where do we find ourselves and where are we going? What about the dream and message of Martin Luther King, Jr. is pertinent to our new reality?

There is not enough time to speak about the current context of Latin America. I want only to affirm that the utopia of a new order has not died even though we no longer think in the old language and worldview of achieving political power through revolution and the implementation of socialism. The situation is more complex than it was in those years.

But the inability to satisfy the basic needs of so many and the social alienation of large groups have given birth to grass-roots movements which respond to the urgent problems that affect people. They have also acquired strong new concepts of popular mobilization as it is expressed in social forums. This is especially true in the World Social Forum which gathers diverse groups in a very inclusive way. I will briefly mention some of the participants. There are Sin Tierra ("Without Land") of Brazil, indigenous movements, women, the urban marginalized, the religious ecological movements and the religious involved in the reclaiming of a new world. These are movements independent of political parties. Instead, they have arisen spontaneously like the movement for civil rights that Martin Luther King, Jr. led, and they carry great energy and mobilizing capacity.

A New Spirituality

If the movement for overcoming racism in the United States needed disciplined followers and a spiritual formation that prepared them to transcend the anger and the spiral of violence, the same is needed in Latin America. There has been a growing awareness of this need for a deeper spirituality for those working to build a new world. Many hold the conviction that the necessary changes that are longed for will not be reached without a transformation that radically alters personal conscience in a way that bares the fruit of ethical values.

Numerous literary works account for this new spirit. It is interesting that the founding father of the Theology of the Liberation, Gustavo Gutiérrez, was one of the first to demonstrate this in a very respected work called, *We Drink From Our Own Wells* (Gutiérrez, 1984). In Brazil, the Dominican friar, Frey Betto, veteran of many social struggles, is inspiring a movement of mysticism and revolutionary spirituality. And among the Baptists, the theologian, Harold Segura, has written an important work of spirituality. We could keep on mentioning authors and works that highlight this concern for a spirituality that nourishes the walk towards a new social order—a Latin-American spirituality, to clarify—that avoids the postmodern style of self-fulfillment manuals, new age, etc.

It is not possible to speak about spirituality without mentioning the resurgence of native spiritualities of our America's indigenous people. The Spanish and Portuguese conquerors did not respect the ancestral traditions of the indigenous peoples, considering it to be like a satanic disease that needed to be exorcised. They did not appreciate the values that these traditions held but viewed them only as negative. Nevertheless, these religious forms survived in different ways, be it through syncretism with Christian practices or by maintaining original purity. These were forms of resistance and affirmed indigenous self-dignity. These native spiritualities have in common a deep respect for nature as well as a deep sense of community solidarity. These values today are recovered and through interreligious dialogue, they become contributions important to all spiritualities.

Latin-American spirituality is strongly resistant to globalization which tries to impose consumer and individualistic models for living. In addition, the religious transnational companies, with their style of religious emotional entertainment, must be challenged with an authentic spirituality.

Of course nonviolence requires a deep spirituality. The current situation of Latin America demands a spirituality with its own roots.

The Martin Luther King, Jr. Center

Perhaps, the most important legacy that we have in Latin America, which honors the memory of Martin Luther King, Jr., is the center that takes his name in Havana, Cuba. Through the work they have been doing over the last 20 years, the Martin Luther King, Jr. Center has transcended national borders, becoming an essential part of the web of Latin American civil society organizations. In fact, it is one of the most active promoters of the World Social Forum.

But the fundamental contribution the Center makes is its effort in Popular Education. It recognizes that nothing is more important than capacity building work with communities, co operatives and unions for the flourishing of democratic participation. This participatory methodology was created by the Brazilian educator, Paulo Freire, and was primarily utilized with the marginalized poor farmers and the humble so that they begin to make their own decisions, become creators of their own agenda, learn to critique the domineering power and begin exercising their own liberation.

The demand for Popular Education extends to all sectors of Cuban life and it develops many popular educators i n different sectors. Already, the network of popular educators in Cuba includes hundreds of Cubans throughout the whole Island.

Certainly, this is a grass-roots movement, trying to create a culture of authentically democratic participation in all sectors of society. It receives neither support nor official recognition, though more and more leaders in different positions of authority are taking notice of the importance of this education. In our judgment, it is one of the most interesting things that is happening in current Cuban society and plants a powerful seed of transformation.

Another major contribution of the Martin Luther King, Jr. Center is its "popular, critical, liberating, and contextual theology," which reflects the influence of the Latin-American theology of liberation. The articulation of this theological education is done jointly with the LatinAmerican Biblical University of Costa Rica and with numerous theologians who regularly offer workshops at the Center.

In the area of communications, the Center offers a wide selection of books and periodical publications. They make significant contributions to the fields of sociology, theology and biblical studies that are enormously valuable to the evangelical community. Of particular note is its prestigious magazine, Caminos (Ways). It has earned itself a unique place in Cuba for its high quality and validity.

Conclusion

The influence of Martin Luther King, Jr., in spite of the apathy of religious institutions, has been earning its own place. Today, I join with many evangelical Christians who are committed to a world filled with peace and justice and who find inspiration and treasure in his life witness. Every day, more and more will march to the rhythm of this "drum major for justice."

Bibliography

Gutiérrez, Gustavo. *A Theology of Liberation*. Orbis. 1988.

_____. *We Drink From Our Own Wells: The Spiritual Journey of a People*. Orbis. 1984.

Rauschenbush, Walter. *Christianity and the Social Crisis*. Hodder & Stoughton. 1907.

Rivera-Pagán, Luis. *A Violent Evangelism: The Political and Religious Conquest of the Americas*. Westminster John Knox. 1992.

Wink, Walter. *Engaging the Powers: Discernment and Resistance in a World of Domination*. Fortress.1992.

_____. *Naming the Powers: The Language of Power in the New Testament*. Fortress. 1984.

_____. *Unmasking the Powers: The Invisible Forces That Determine Human Existence*. Fortress. 1986.

2 | Thomas Helwys: Unlikely Prophet of Universal Religious Freedom

Tony Peck

Introduction

We do not know much about the life of Thomas Helwys. Neither the date of his birth, possibly in the 1570s, of that of his death, probably in Newgate prison around 1615, is certain. We know that he was born and lived as an English gentleman in Nottinghamshire and trained as a lawyer. But there are periods of his life about which we know nothing. But two factors have assured Helwys' place in the history of Baptists around the world and in the history of religious toleration and religious freedom. The first is that Helwys, together with John Smith, were leaders of the earliest Baptist Church begun in exile in Amsterdam in 1609, and Helwys went on to found the first Baptist church in England, in Spitalfields in London, exactly 400 years ago in 1612. So Helwys is the original Baptist pioneer.

And the second factor is that, in the middle of a rather polemical book attacking nearly every other religious group in England at that time, Helwys made what is usually considered to be the first plea for universal religious freedom in the English language, and since then religious freedom for all, not just themselves, has been a core conviction of Baptists in every part of the world. It is this second aspect on which I want to mainly focus in this paper.

I will say something about the religious and political background of the turbulent times in which Helwys lived; then focus on his book, *A Short Declaration of the Mystery of Iniquity,* and especially its plea for religious freedom. Then I want to inquire as to what possible influences came to bear on Helwys to formulate such a radical idea in the England of his time. I will especially concentrate on his interaction with Anabaptism from his contact with Dutch Mennonites when he was part of John Smyth's church in Amsterdam. Finally I will ask about Helwys' legacy, both immediately in the later seventeenth century, and also for us in the twenty-first century.

In June 2011, the Archbishop of Canterbury's Annual Lambeth Interfaith Lecture was delivered by Malcolm Evans, Professor of International Law at the University of Bristol. The lecture was entitled, "Advancing Freedom of Religion or Belief: Agendas for Change." (Evans, 1997) Professor Evans happens to be a Baptist, and has become a widely respected expert in the interaction of law and human rights, and specifically European law and Religious Freedom. This is part of the conclusion of his lecture:

> What should Christians – and indeed those of other faiths and none – do to further the freedom of religion or belief? As people of faith it is up to us to champion the cause of others rather than ourselves. And we must do this based on a better understanding of what the religion of belief entails, including what practical steps we should take. As a Christian myself, I suggest that when Christ commanded us to love our neighbour as ourselves, he meant us to do exactly that...along with all people of goodwill. For if religious believers will not stand up for the right of other believers, irrespective of their faith, why in heaven's name should anyone else? (Evans, 2002)

I would suggest that in his plea for Christians not to be partisan in their concern for religious freedom, but to be active campaigners for religious freedom for all, Professor Evans is the latest to pick up the challenge thrown down by the first English Baptist leader, Thomas Helwys, 400 years ago. Helwys lived in a different age and very different world but his words addressed to the all-powerful King James of England have the same passion and fire of conviction:

> For our Lord the King is but an earthly king, and he has no authority as a king in earthly causes. And if the king's people be obedient and true subjects, obeying all human laws, our lord the king can require no more. For men's religion to God is between God and themselves. The king shall not answer for it. Neither may the King judge between God and men. Let them be heretics, Jews or whatsoever, it appertains not to the earthly power to punish them in the least measure (Groves, 1998:53).

This is widely considered to be the first plea for universal religious freedom in the English language (Bebbington, 2002:15). It comes in Helwys book, *A Short*

Declaration of the Mystery of Iniquity, which is not primarily about religious freedom, but about identifying the errors of the State Church, The Church of England, and other churches. So Helwys, with an uncompromising polemic, identifies the first, second, third and fourth beasts of the Book of Revelation as the Roman Catholic Church, the Church of England, the Puritans and the Separatists (out of which he had come). It is not a book famed for its ecumenical sensitivity, or indeed its literary grace. It was also written in a somewhat feverish state of apocalyptic expectation. In his own opening summary of the book, Helwys describes it as "the Declaration with proof that these are the days of greatest tribulation spoken of by Christ (Matthew 24) wherein the abomination of desolation is set in the holy place" (Groves, 1998:4). Helwys saw certain religious events around him that he thought were leading to an imminent apocalypse (Early, 2009:456-463). His response, though, is to engage with the powers of England rather than take the other option of withdrawing and waiting for the End. In this polemical and apocalyptic context his plea for universal religious freedom is perhaps all the more remarkable.

The early twentieth century British Baptist scholar, Henry Wheeler Robinson, comments in this way in his Introduction to the facsimile edition of Helwys' book, published in 1935:

> The strong terms in which Helwys denounces those who differ from him, even on points that that may seem to most men today immaterial, and the rather appalling use of Scripture which men then made to characterise the position of their opponents, must not be allowed to obscure from us the fact that the principle of unlimited liberty of religion is here unmistakably asserted. Helwys clearly was ready to give the liberty for which he asked to all these opponents, even the Roman Catholics – a fact which shows us how much ahead of his times he was. He knows it is his duty to convince these opponents of their errors, their deadly errors, but the task must be achieved by reason and prayer, and not by physical force (Robinson, 1935:xiv).

Unlike Professor Evans, Helwys would certainly not have been allowed to deliver a lecture based on such thoughts at Lambeth Place, the home of the Archbishop of Canterbury, leader of the English State Church! In fact, Helwys addressed one edition of his book to King James with a bold, some would say foolhardy, preface to "despise not the counsel of the poor" and a plea to the King not to take the place of God in determining the way the English people would worship. We do not know whether King James read it, though we could probably imagine his reaction if he did. As a result, Helwys was put in prison and probably died there around 1615-1616.

But the words from his book about religious freedom for all have continued to justify the judgement of many, like the U.S. Baptist historian, H. Leon McBeth:

> For (almost) four centuries Baptists have insisted upon complete religious liberty not only for themselves but also for others. In no other area has Baptists witness proved clearer or more consistent than in their struggle for the right of persons to answer to God and to government for religious beliefs and behaviour (McBeth, 1987:252).

And so Thomas Helwys holds an honoured place among us. My study of theology for ministry took place at Regent's Park College, Oxford, where the name of Helwys was carved in stone outside the dining hall that also bears his name. In the International Baptist Theological Seminary in Prague where my office is, there is a building known as the Helwys Pavilion, and also there is based the Thomas Helwys Centre for the study of Religious Freedom. A U.S. Christian publisher (which has literary freedom as its chief value) has taken the name of Helwys, alongside that of his mentor and leader of the first Baptist church in Amsterdam, John Smyth.

In this paper I too want to celebrate Helwys as the source of our continuing commitment to religious freedom for all. At the same time I want to suggest that in many ways in background and temperament he was an unlikely advocate for this. But in spite of that he achieved a unique synthesis of influences and ideas in his views on church and state. I am sure that some of the consequences of what Helwys wrote are ones which he was not able to work out or foresee. In all this it may be that we discover that the situation is not quite as "clear and consistent" as that quote from Leon McBeth would seem to suggest!

The Political and Religious Context

Thomas Helwys was born into the age of the English Queen Elizabeth, who had achieved the final settlement of the Church of England as the State Church established by law, and which allowed for no other lawful religion. During her reign came the growth of Puritanism, which as its name implies ought to "purify" the State Church by recalling it to what the Puritans saw as the authentic biblical faith. They wanted limits set on the power of the bishops and a greater place given to preaching. The more radical of the Puritans become so disillusioned with the Church of England that they separated from it completely to form their own congregations, on the basis of a covenant. These Separatists, as they were called, included among their number John Smyth, who had been trained as an Anglican clergyman, and Thomas Helwys, then a lawyer and a member of the English gentry, who joined Smyth's Separatist congregation in Lincolnshire in east England.

When King James VI of Scotland succeeded Elizabeth as King James I of England as well there were high hopes among the Separatists that James, coming from Presbyterian Scotland, might allow some kind of religious toleration in England. These high hopes were dashed at the Hampton Court Conference of 1603 in which, although James conceded some moderate puritan demands, he reaffirmed conformity with the Church of England as the only religious option. Law required the attendance of the whole population at the Anglican parish church. It is important to note that religious freedom (or the lack of it) was inextricably linked with political loyalty, following the doctrine of *cuius regio eius religio* (the religion of the state is that of its ruler) that was common in Europe at that time.

Persecution against Separatists increased and this resulted in the Separatist congregation led by John Smyth and including Thomas Helwys escaping to Amsterdam in around 1608. Amsterdam was then a free city practising religious toleration, and it had already received a number of separatist-type groups. And it was here that the Separatist congregation led by John Smyth adopted what we would see now as a Baptist way of being the church.

As is well known, Helwys and Smyth had serious theological disagreements and agreed to separate. Smyth's church applied to join the Mennonites and Helwys returned to England to start the first Baptist church on English soil, at Spitalfields in London in 1612.

Helwys' Plea for Religious Freedom

Helwys' plea for religious freedom is truly remarkable because nobody was really discussing it at that time in England. It is important to see that someone putting this forward in that context would not only be guilty of spreading dangerous religious ideas, but would also be seen as threatening the security of the state, which was understood to depend on religious uniformity.

Thirty years later in the 1640s he situation was very different. England for the only time in its recorded history rid itself of its monarchy and experienced a "commonwealth" republic led by Oliver Cromwell where the Puritans were in control and Presbyterianism was favoured.   In that context many different political ideas flourished, including religious freedom, both for and against.   One of the Presbyterian opponents of what he saw as dangerous sectarians, especially Baptists, was Thomas Edwards. He wrote in 1646 lamenting that within five days as many books came out for religious toleration. One of them was Roger Williams' famous defence of religious freedom, *The Bloody Tenet of Persecution*.   Edwards state his belief that all such books should be delivered to the hangman for public burning. "Oh what a burnt offering, a sweet smelling sacrifice this would be to God!" he exclaimed (George, 1984:30-31).

The influence of this intense debate about religious toleration would be felt first of all in the New World, rather than in England where the Restoration of the monarchy in 1660 meant nearly 30 years of severe legal restrictions for Baptists and other dissenters. But from this ferment of religious ideas in the 1640s, Roger Williams would later go to the New World to found a colony at Providence, Rhode Island, based on religious freedom for all (though he himself moved from being a Baptist to being a Seeker). The same period would later influence John Locke to be instrumental in drawing up the Constitutions of Carolina, and William Penn the Constitution of Pennsylvania, all on the premise of a plural society which guaranteed religious freedom. The link of all this with Helwys may well come through John Murton, a member of Helwys' church and his successor as leader of the first Baptist church in England. Murton was also imprisoned for some time. But, influenced by Helwys, he wrote two works on religious freedom, one of which was later read by Roger Williams.

But back in 1612 none of these discussions were taking place. King James believed in his "divine right" to rule his subjects, including determining their religion and ensuring religious conformity. Standing in direct opposition to this is Helwys' unqualified plea for religious freedom: "Let them be heretics, Jews or whatsoever, it appertains not to the earthly power to punish them in the least measure."

Influences on Helwys

What were the influences on Helwys to develop this conviction? It may be a combination of a number of factors. We must remember that Helwys was an educated layman, with no formal theological training. He was very influenced by John Smyth, and his earlier writings reveal the closeness of his thought to Smyth. But as we have heard he later broke with Smyth on a number of theological issues, and also differed with him on a crucial aspect of the church-state relationship;

whether a Christian believer could also be a magistrate. Helwys emerges as something of a free thinker and perhaps this enabled him to achieve the unique synthesis of thought that we see in his views on religious freedom and the relationship of church and state.

We will come in a moment to the undoubted influence on Helwys of Anabaptist thinking. But other factors may well have been present too. Helwys was a lawyer, having trained for the law at Grays Inn, London. In legal circles on the continent of Europe notions of religious freedom were being debated and written about, supremely of course by Hugo Grotius. But an interesting example for our purposes would be the Italian Protestant, Alberico Gentili (1552-1608), described as the "father of religious toleration under law" (Evans, 1997:35-37). Gentili emigrated to England in 1580 where he later became Regius Professor of Civil law at Oxford University. In 1600 he was admitted to the legal fraternity of Grays Inn where Helwys had studied just a few years earlier. Despite the lack of direct evidence, it is a reasonable conjecture, I think that, as a lawyer, Helwys might have been familiar with the thinking of this prominent jurist.

In a passage written around 1590, Gentili wrote what in many ways is a legal equivalent of what Helwys would write from a more theological perspective 20 years later. Gentili wrote not only to oppose European wars in the name of religion but also to justify toleration of religious differences between states.

> Religion is a matter of the mind and the will, which is always accompanied by freedom...Our minds and whatever belongs to the mind are not affected by any external power or potentate, and the soul has no master save God only, who alone can destroy the soul...Religion ought to be free. Religion is a kind of marriage of God with man. And so, as liberty of the flesh is resolutely maintained in the other wedlock, so in this one freedom of the spirit is guaranteed (Evans, 1997:6).

I note here that the creative interaction between law and theology continues to be a key relationship in considering questions of religious freedom today.

Then in examining possible influences on Helwys we should not ignore the situation of the Separatists in England, whose ranks Helwys had so recently left. Their desire to see the true church emerge through separatism had clearly not occurred. They were beginning to see those opposed to the State Church and its excesses fragmenting into different groups. It might seem a logical step as a persecuted minority to accept this situation of religious pluralism and envision a society where religious freedom was guaranteed to all. This could probably not come from anywhere else but a marginalised group rejected by mainstream society (Coggins, 1991:128-132). The challenge for this view of religious freedom has always been what you do with it if you ever become the powerful majority.

Helwys also had the experience of living for a few years in the free city of Amsterdam where the English separatists had worshipped in freedom. He observed the prosperity and security of the Netherlands and made the connection with religious liberty, declaring "Behold the Nations where freedom of Religion is permitted, and you may see there are not more flourishing and prosperous Nations under heaven than they are" (Coffey, 2000:70-71).

And of course Helwys' own reflection on Scripture, especially the New Testament, also played its part. In his book he speaks of the Christ who in the Gospels refuses to force himself on anyone. This went along with the free will that characterised the Arminian understanding of salvation which Helwys had by this time embraced. (Arminius was developing his ideas in the Netherlands at the same time as the various separatist congregations were there, including that of Smyth and Helwys).

In spite of all these influences it remains an intriguing question as to what precise combination of factors brought together contributed to Helwys' radical understanding of the relationship of church and state and of religious freedom. James Coggins, in his work on Smyth's congregation in Amsterdam, says "there is no obvious place Helwys could have learned such an understanding of church and state other than his own experience interacting with his theology and understanding of scripture" (Coggins, 1991:132). But Coggins goes on to admit the possibility (I would say probability) of influence by the Waterlander Mennonites in Amsterdam; and it is this contact with Anabaptists thinking on which I want to focus now, along with its creative interaction with other influences of the Reformers.

Interaction with Anabaptism

In Amsterdam the Separatist group led by John Smith made contact with the Waterlanders, a branch of the Mennonites. Eventually the church split on doctrinal and other issues and half the congregation led by Smyth joined the Waterlanders, the other led by Helwys returning to England. Like other Anabaptist groups, the Mennonites would put forward a view of religious toleration.

The founder of the Mennonites in the sixteenth century, the Anabaptist Menno Simons, famously said that to "throttle the truth" or to defend "lies" "with the sword" is not the way of Christ. He said, "For this is the real disposition and conduct of Antichrist: to employ slander, arrest, torture, fire and murder against the spirit and the Word of God" (Wenger, 1956:66).

Indeed, the Anabaptist movement, beginning in Zurich in the 1520s, could be seen as having been primarily founded on this principle that the ruling authorities cannot determine the faith and religious practice of their people, or enforce conformity to it with the sword. Only reflection on the Word of God in Scripture and a listening to the Spirit of God could do this. "We must obey God rather than men" was a watchword of the early Anabaptists. And much was made in their writings (and indeed those of the early Baptists writing about religious toleration) of Jesus' parable of the wheat and the weeds (tares) to demonstrate that those regarded as heretics should not be subjected to premature judgement by worldly rulers (Klassen, 1981:292).

We can perhaps assume that other Anabaptist writing on the subject would be known to the Waterlander Mennonites. For example, the Swiss Anabaptist Hans Denck had written in 1527 about what he called the "practice of the true Gospel" being that "each will let the other move and dwell in peace – be he Turk or heathen, believing what he will…That is to say, no one shall deprive another – whether heathen or Jew or Christian – but rather allow everyone to move in all territories in the name of his God. So may we well benefit in the peace which God gives" (Klassen, 1981:292). Denck's is a remarkable vision of a truly religiously plural society, living in peace, which perhaps goes even further than Helwys.

As has been said about the various strands of Anabaptism, "ideas have legs," and it seems to me in the way he expresses such an unqualified plea for religious liberty for all that Helwys must have imbibed something of the Anabaptist spirit here. In the same year, John Smyth had also written his own plea for religious freedom, if not quite as far-reaching as Helwys.

> That the magistrate is not by virtue of his office to meddle with religion, on matters of conscience, to force or compel men to this or that form of religion, or doctrine; but to leave Christian religion free, to every man's conscience and to handle only civil transgressions (Rom xiii), injuries and wrongs of man against man, in murder, adultery, theft, etc., for Christ is the only king and lawgiver of the church and conscience (James iv.12) (Lumpkin, 1969:140).

Note the emphasis here and in Helwys on the universal Lordship of Christ as the starting point for arguing for universal religious freedom. "The crucial matters for Helwys are the sovereign right of Christ the king and the consequent holy nature of the human conscience before God" (Cross and Wood, 2010:69).

In locating religious freedom in this view of the all-embracing Lordship of Christ, Helwys and the Anabaptists would be in agreement. However, in exploring further the relationship between Helwys' thought and Anabaptism, there are some crucial distinctions to be made.

Both make a distinction between material and spiritual concerns. But for the Anabaptists the division was between the people and institutions of the true church, and the people and institutions of the world, the latter to be avoided wherever possible. So the pacifist Mennonites would not allow that a member of the church could also serve as a Magistrate to wield the "earthly sword" of justice. I do not think it is too sweeping a statement to say that the Anabaptists came to their judgement on these matters by distancing themselves so far as possible from "the world" (Wright, 2006:73-74). This was a situation often forced on them physically and geographically as mainstream society hunted them down as threats to both the religious and the political order.

In bringing together his views on the relationship of church and state and religious freedom, for Helwys the division is not so much between the church and the world as that each human life divided in to its material and spiritual aspects. "The body was subject to the world, subject to earthly kings, and able to use the physical sword. The spirit was subject only to spiritual authorities and spiritual penalties" (Coggins, 1991:130). On this reading, as Helwys writes in the preface of the copy of his book given to the king, "The king hath no power over the immortal souls of his subjects. Contrast this to the view of King James himself who famously said that it would only be half a king who controlled his subjects' bodies but not their souls" (Coggins, 1991:130).

One element that was shared by Helwys and the Anabaptists was the idea of a radical separation of Old and New Testament, corresponding to this dualism of body and spirit. Christendom had mainly relied on the Old Testament model of Israel for the view that the state should enforce religious conformity and have a right to intervene in their subjects' relationship to God. Helwys and the Anabaptists focused on the "spiritual" nature of the New Testament and the church, and that the wheat and the weeds (tares) must be allowed to grow together. This is the view that Christianity, as Roger Williams famously commented, "fell asleep in Constantine's bosom."

Nevertheless Helwys is interested in a full participation and engagement with English society acknowledging the fact that its executive authority was then invested in its King. He was a patriotic Englishmen and a member of the English gentry; and he wanted to show that in the matters that God has entrusted to him, the King deserved the unswerving loyalty of his subjects. The state was worthy of godly and patriotic support.

So in his book he pours lavish praise on the king and goes on, "Let us declare what power and authority God has given to him, whereunto his subjects ought of conscience to obey." Helwys goes on to list these areas before making it clear that whilst the king enjoys this power in the earthly kingdom, the Lord has reserved to himself a heavily kingdom whose people are not subjects of the kingdom of the world.

Altogether in the thought of Helwys we find an interesting creative fusion of Anabaptist influence, the Two Kingdoms doctrine of Luther and the Calvinist conviction of all things being under the sovereignty of God and the sovereign rule of Christ.

Nevertheless the plea of Helwys and the early English Baptists for universal religious liberty distances them not only from the pacifist position of Anabaptists but also from the magisterial reformers. Their version of Luther's two kingdoms doctrine went far beyond Luther in secularising the state, so that it had no coercive power over religion. And though Helwys was influenced by the Calvinist concept of an elect nation with a Godly Prince as it applied to England, he denied the king any power over men's consciences.

But in this one sense Helwys does indeed behave like a classic Protestant, in that he addresses the king as the Godly Prince. Rather than address his book to society at large, he is specific about directing it to the king. Whereas government for the Mennonites and Anabaptists was an impersonal rather distant force to be shunned, for Helwys it was close and personal and he wanted to be a critical friend to it.

But at the same time Helwys denied the king his earthly power to rule the heavenly realm, and in particular to appoint the bishops of the Church of England. It is in this context of a discussion about the king's rule in relation to the state church that Helwys make his famous statement about religious freedom. In the wake of the Gunpowder Plot of 1605, when a Catholic group tried to blow up the English King and Parliament, Helwys also argues that the Catholics would be more peaceable and the state itself was more secure if they had freedom of worship and were not forced to be behave like political insurrectionists.

General Baptist Leonard Busher, writing in 1614, commented on the *milet* system of limited religious toleration in the region ruled by the Ottomans commented that "Even the Turks in Constantinople 'force no man to believe in Mahomet's law' but leave Christians and Jews to the peaceful practice of their own religions. 'Shall we be less merciful than the Turks, or shall we learn from the Turks to persecute Christians?'" (George, 1984:46).

The differences between Helwys and the Anabaptists can be particularly focused on their differing views on the possibility and role of a Christian magistrate (for which read: a Christian believer involved in government, especially in dispensing justice). With the notable exception of Balthasar Hubmaier, the usual Anabaptist stance was a radical apoliticism and non-resistance, with the result that no Anabaptist believer could participate in society by becoming a magistrate and dispensing justice. Government, according to the Anabaptist Schleitheim Confession, was "outside the perfection of Christ."

The American Baptist historian and theologian, Timothy George, identifies three crucial points in the positive position on magistracy taken by Helwys and the early English Baptists: 1) a defence of the ethics of war, 2) a recognition that coercion was the necessary pre-condition of social order and religious toleration, and 3) a willingness to admit magistrates to church membership. On the first point, in his writing Helwys showed himself ready to defend his king and country. "Our Lord the king hath power to take our sons and daughters to do all his service of war, and of peace, yea, all his servile service whatsoever" (George, 1984:38).

On the second point, Helwys criticises the Dutch Mennonites for considering the office of magistrate "a vile thing" yet had benefited from the security, freedom and peace that the magistrate by using the sword had won for them.

On the third point about the possibility of a Christian magistrate, Helwys, unlike John Smyth declared that "Kings, Princes and Magistrates, ruling and governing by the power of God, with the sword of justice, may be members of the church of Christ retaining their magistracie" (George, 1984:39). They could punish the criminal whilst praying for his soul.

Timothy George concludes that in these three aspects Helwys and the early English Baptists "remained faithful to the Calvinist-Puritan-Separatist tradition from which they had sprung."

The effect of all this is that the concept of universal religious freedom, which is certainly a radical departure from this tradition, is not affirmed "from a distance" from government and political power. It is brought as an argument right into the centre, in this case to the King himself, so that it might challenge the existing order in a direct way. And in many ways from the most unlikely of people, Helwys was probably what we would call a natural "social conservative," originally a member of the educated privileged class of England. He cared passionately about the peace, security, good law and order of his country He perhaps did not see that in taking this stance he did he was laying the ground for Christian political involvement in society (Wright, 2006:73-74). A Baptist magistrate was in fact very unlikely under King James, but if such a one existed, then sooner or later there surely would have come the challenge to actively oppose unjust policies such as state compulsion in religion. As Stephen Wright concludes, Helwys' stance "amounted to a theoretical foundation for political activism."

Helwys' Legacy

It is time to conclude this discussion and ask what the legacy of Thomas Helwys is, both in the immediate aftermath of his life and then some challenges for us in the twenty-first century.

As the seventeenth century went on, Baptist defenders of religious freedom (or at least, religious toleration) began to think seriously about what kind of society this might produce, and therefore what limits needed to be set on religious freedom within it (Coffey, 2006:21-22). Helwys' cry of "heretics, Turks, Jews or whatever" was somewhat modified by the Particular Baptist Confession of 1677, which professes liberty to all opinions *not contrary to Scripture* and the General Baptist Confession of 1678, which advocated only a limited religious freedom (Lumpkin, 2011:275, 344-345). Individual Baptists wrote that magistrates must prevent the spread of heresy (Bebbington, 2002:22), or that Protestant, Jews and papists should only be allowed in their writings to appeal to Scripture and not to the Fathers (Bebbington, 2002:22). Other Baptists who defended religious toleration also wished to assure puritan society that toleration need not mean licentious anarchy. They appealed to the concept of "natural law" or "the light of nature" and then set about trying to define what did or did not come under those headings. For instance, there was a common view among some that the entire second table of the ten commandments could be deduced by natural reason, and therefore could be enforced by law (Bebbington, 2002:23). Some argued from Romans 1 that natural reason led to belief in a Deity who ought to be reverenced, and therefore atheism and blasphemy should be punished in all societies.

So from the immediate period following Helwys' book Baptists were greatly exercised about the implications of the radical tolerationist view so eloquently argued by Thomas Helwys and later by Roger Williams. They were already having to think seriously about the moral code of society and where the boundary lines might be drawn. The fact that no clear consensus emerged on this issue only serves to indicate the difficulty of holding together a commitment to religious freedom for all in a religiously pluralist nation, alongside a desire to see society ordered according to Christian principles. I believe that this has continued to be a point of tension for Baptists and other Christians as they have taken their stance on religious freedom.

The historian John Coffey, from his study of seventeenth century religious life in England has identified three "political visions" that Baptists have adopted in their history on this question religious freedom and its limits (Bebbington, 2002:34). The first is what he calls a radical separationist view, as espoused by Helwys and Williams. The state is a purely civil institution and "its purpose is not promote a particular faith but to govern and order a multi-faith society, in which protestants Catholics, Muslims, pagans and even atheists enjoy the full rights of citizenship and dwell together in peace" (Bebbington, 2002:34). Coffey estimates that this position has only been held by a substantial minority of Baptists over the centuries.

The second political vision is of a theocratic apocalypticism with very little religious tolerance, as espoused by the Fifth Monarchists of the seventeenth century. Believing that God was about to establish his millennial kingdom on earth accompanied by the rule of the saints, they wanted to move quickly from pluralism to unity with no room for religious diversity. Only a minority of Baptists have ever been attracted to this; but Coffey concludes, "Insofar as there are Baptists today who endorse the theocratic blueprint of Christian reconstructionism, a movement partly inspired by dreams of the millennium, this second vision survives" (Bebbington, 2002:35).

But Coffey sees the greatest proportion of Baptists as being firm upholders of what he calls the "Christian nation" position, with its assumption that Christianity should be at the heart of the political nation. The holders of this view "have not been averse to supporting systematic discrimination against 'outsiders' who did not share the orthodox Protestant faith." It is not difficult to see how this has worked out in different ways in the concepts of "Christian England" or "Christian America." I believe that in England it has led to some reluctance of Baptists to be true to their roots in full religious freedom because there are times when they have been very happy to hang on to the coat tails of the established Church of England in its more ready access to the State on crucial issues.

Each of these positions leads to a different view of religious freedom and its limits. The first allows full religious freedom and encourages dialogue about the collective morality of a society, but begs the question about how and where that moral consensus is to be achieved. The second is hardly tolerant at all of other religious beliefs and practices because of its imminent expectation of the full establishment of the Kingdom of God. The third tries to see everything through a consensus around the concept of a Christian society, a consensus which may be more wishfully imagined than real; and its proponents might use it to discriminate against divergent religious views, especially of other faiths.

So despite our Baptist rhetoric on this issue, if we are to accept Coffey's thesis, the outworking of our Baptist commitment to religious freedom is not as straightforward as it might first appear. I believe that is still the case today.

Conclusion

In this year of the 400th anniversary of Helwys' book you would expect me to want to call and challenge us in the twenty-first century to embrace the full scope of Helwys' radicalism. So in conclusion I have selected just three ways in which we might do this.

First, as the quote from Malcolm Evans at the beginning of this lecture reminds us, a real commitment to religious freedom for *all* is still a challenge in the twenty-first century. Recently I have been to too many consultations and conference on the subject of human rights and religious freedom where different confessional groups are manoeuvring for their own advantages and rights, and not speaking up for the religious rights of all, especially those of other faiths, and especially those who may be suffering oppression. As the Baptist World Alliance (BWA) General Secretary so succinctly put it in a recent article about the early Baptists, in his attitude to other Christian traditions Helwys does not come across as a tolerant man. He seems to have fully imbibed the polemical religious spirit of his time, fuelled by an imminent apocalypticism. But as I have argued, this aspect of his character and writing, somewhat repugnant to us in this irenic ecumenical age, makes his central conviction about religious freedom all the more remarkable. And for us today, Helwys reminds us that we can speak up for the rights of religious people everywhere to live and worship in freedom without necessarily agreeing with their ideas and beliefs or compromising our own faith. Article 18 of the United Nations Declaration on Human Rights, on religious freedom, enshrines this principle, and we go on supporting it however others may treat us in return. A recent example would be the statement of the Swiss Reformed Church, supported by the Swiss Baptists, among others, defending the right of Muslims to build their mosques with minarets, after a referendum in Switzerland had opposed this.

Second, religious freedom can never be seen in isolation from other freedoms. Whether he fully appreciated it or not, Helwys' radical stance of religious freedom had implications for the wider question of rights and responsibilities in society – implications which radicals such as Richard Overton, a member of the Amsterdam congregation of Smyth and Helwys, was to draw out in the 1640s when he laid some of the foundations of the modern concept of human rights (Stassen, 1992:137-163). There have been some tragic examples of Baptists being granted their freedom to worship unhindered, and then their gratitude for this preventing them being prophetic concerning the other injustices and evils around them in society. Recently this has been documented in relation to the situation of the German Baptists during the Nazi era. But in less obvious ways this can still be a weakness on our emphasis on religious freedom – that it can prevent us from speaking prophetically into our society about the abuse of other freedoms.

Third, Helwys encourages us to have a positive view of the state as the civil society guaranteeing religious freedom for all. Not only that, but he encourages us to actively engage with it for the common good. One way to understand this might be to see the State as "secular" and "neutral." But the experience in many countries in Europe is that a secular state with consigns religion to the private sphere is not morally neutral. And in fact, it increasingly threatens religious belief and freedoms in its espousal of secularism as an ideology.

Helwys was not prepared to accept the consigning of religious ideas to the private sphere, but instead directly addresses the king and the powers. Based on this, my own preferred model in our time would be of a stakeholder society, where people of all faiths and none are in the public space with a unique contribution to make to the life, prosperity and transformation of society as a whole. In this respect Helwys' stance implies an acceptance of a multi-faith plural society in which he encourages active engagement rather than a withdrawal to the margins, or, indeed, any attempt to re-establish Christendom.

One example of such an engagement is the Baptist World Alliance response to "A Common Word," the letter from moderate Muslim scholars to the leaders of the world Christian communities. It urges Muslims and Christians to seek to find ways of leaving at peace in the same geographical space, a peaceful co-existence based on love of God and love of neighbour. The BWA made a much-praised response (found on the website of "A Common Word"), in which it sought to both support such an initiative and also to make it clear that in the Helwys tradition we stand for religious freedom both for ourselves and all religions, whether in Islamic States, secular Europe or elsewhere.

Thomas Helwys would no doubt struggle to exist in the secular world which most of us now inhabit. For instance, I doubt whether he conceived of atheists in his plural society. But in these three ways and others I believe we can celebrate his courage and his achievement and yet remain true to his legacy and the rich heritage in which we stand 400 years later. May his bold words continue to inspire us!

Bibliography

Coffey, John. "From Helwys to Leland: Baptists and Religious Toleration in England and America, 1612 -1791". *The Gospel in the World*. David W. Bebbington, ed. Paternoster. 2002.

_____. *Persecution and Toleration in Protestant England 1558-1689*. Longmans. 2000.

Coggins, James R. *John Smyth's Congregation: English Separatism, Mennonite Influence and the Elect Nation*. Herald. 1991.

Cross, Anthony and Nicholas J. Wood, eds. *Exploring Baptist Origins*. Regent's Park. 2010.

Early, Joe, "The Apocalyptic Nature of Thomas Helwys' Writings." *American Baptist Quarterly*, Vol. XXVIII. Winter 2009.

Evans, Malcolm D. Annual Lambeth Inter Faith Lecture delivered on 8 June 2011.

http://www.archbishopofcanterbury.org?cgi-bin/parser.pl.

_____. *Religious Liberty and International Law in Europe*, Cambridge: Cambridge University. 1997.

George, Timothy. "Between Pacifism and Coercion: The English Baptist Doctrine of Religious Toleration." *Mennonite Quarterly Review*. Vol. 50, Issue 1. January 1984.

Groves, Richard, ed. *A Short Declaration of the Mystery of Iniquity: Thomas Helwys (ca. 1550-ca 1612)*. Mercer University. 1998.

Klassen, Walter. *Anabaptism in Outline*. Herald. 1981

Lumpkin, William, ed. *Baptist Confessions of Faith*. Philadelphia: Judson Press, Second Revised Edition, 2001.

McBeth, H. Leon. *The Baptist Heritage: Four Centuries of Witness*. Broadman. 1987.

Robinson, H. Wheeler. *Introduction to Helwys, The Mystery of Iniquity*. Facsmile Edition. Kingsgate. 1935.

Stassen, Glen, "The Christian Origin of Human Rights." *Just Peacemaking*. Westminster/John Knox. 1992.

Wenger, John Christian, ed., Preface to "Meditation on the Twenty-Fifth Psalm" (c. 1537). *The Complete Writings of Menno Simons, c. 1491-1561*. Leonard Verduin, trans. Herald. 1956.

Wright, Stephen. *The Early English Baptists 1603-1649*. Boydell. 2006.

3 | WHAT BAPTISTS NEED TO KNOW

Glen Harold Stassen

What Baptists need to know is that Richard Overton is the father of the tradition of human rights and that he was also a Baptist.

Richard Overton was a member of the group of the very first Baptists who, with John Smyth, joined the Waterlander Mennonite Church in Holland in 1615. He wrote out his confession of faith with themes that later led him to become the father of human rights:

- All humankind is created in the image of God;

- Jesus Christ died for *all* humankind; and,

- Christ, not the traditions of the hierarchy, is the norm for the church.

With the Baptist confession of 1612, other tenets were likewise formalized, such as the freedom of conscience, independence of church from state, religious liberty, love for enemies, nonviolence, and serving the needs of the poor. Later in England, Overton was a member of Thomas Lambe's Church in London.

As those very first Baptists had done, Overton, as well, wrote that Jesus made disciples by teaching, not by religious persecution and not by torture. And he, too, wrote that Jesus taught we should let the "wheat" and the "weeds" grow side by side and not uproot them by force and violence. So his doctrine of the human right of religious liberty was deeply grounded in Jesus, in the Bible, and in Baptist tradition from the start. Richard Overton was deeply grounded in Jesus Christ as Lord of all of our life.

During the Puritan Revolution in England, Overton gained fame as the best writer of the Leveller Movement, championing the human right to religious liberty. He also was a printer and publisher. At the time, it was illegal to print books not approved by the government, resulting in his arrest and confinement. Nevertheless, his wife kept up the printing until even she was jailed along with her tiny baby. So, freedom of the press became part of the Overton doctrine of human rights. (*As an aside, it was a religious experience for me to read Overton's books in the rare books archive of Union Theological Seminary, to hold the very books in my own hands that Overton had written and printed and held in his own hands.*)

Overton was a biblical Christian—a Baptist—so he had a strong commitment to justice for the poor, as did Jesus. He based the right to basic needs of life for all people, including the poor, on many teachings of Jesus and the biblical emphasis on justice for the poor. And while he was in jail, he got to know poor people who were starving in jail because they could not pay their debts. So he advocated not only for religious liberty, freedom of the press, and the right not to be tortured, but for the right to life itself and to basic human needs being met.

Overton's comprehensive doctrine of human rights, published in 1647, remarkably still fits what most church denominations have said when they have affirmed human rights. These are the basic human needs:

- The right to religious liberty and civil liberty—freedom from coercion in religion, from governmental establishment of religion, and from taxation for religion; freedom of the press; the right of prisoners not to be tortured, starved, or extorted; the right not to be arbitrarily arrested nor forced to incriminate oneself; the right to a speedy trial; the right to understand the law in one's own language; and equality before the law.

- The right to life, including basic needs of life—a free education for everyone; housing and care for poor orphans, the widowed, the aged, and the handicapped; the right of the poor to maintain their portion of land and not be imprisoned for debt; the right to trade internationally without restrictions by monopolies. This is a consistent life ethic with justice that delivers people from what kills them or deprives them of life's requirements. (Gushee, 2012)

- The right to dignity in community, with rights of participation for all in a church of their choice, in voting for a government that is responsive to the people and the common good, and participating in government regardless of one's beliefs; and the right to petition Parliament.

Strikingly, Overton argued for religious liberty for Baptists and all Protestants, Catholics, Jews, and for "Turks," of which he meant Muslims. He was the British friend of Roger Williams in Rhode Island, who argued similarly in his *Bloudy Tenent of Persecution*.

Baptists need to know that Overton, an Anabaptist Baptist, wrote the first comprehensive doctrine of human rights, as cited by historians, Richard Tuck

(Tuck, 1979: 147-50) and William Haller, who wrote: "The task of turning the statement of the law of nature into a ringing declaration of the rights of man fell to Richard Overton" (Haller, 1934: 111). More recently, Michael Westmoreland White has written of Overton's role (White, 1995: 75-96) as have I (Stassen, 1992, 2008). Overton's own *An Appeal to the Free People* (of 1647) with his comprehensive doctrine of human rights is also available in print. This inspirational role for Overton cannot be denied.

However, Germans were not aware that human rights were the product of Baptists in the 17th century. They thought that the source of human rights was the secular French Enlightenment in the 18th century. So the fallacy of confusing the source of human rights arose in pre-fascist Germany. Therefore, German churches rejected human rights and rejected Germany's effort to form a constitutional democracy in the Weimar Republic. Germany then fell under the vicious dictatorship of Adolf Hitler, who massacred six million Jews and caused World War II. Without loyalty to human rights, the German churches had no articulate basis for opposing Hitler's massive violations of human rights.

The exceptions were Dietrich Bonhoeffer and Karl Barth, who advocated human rights in their theology and ethics and led opposition to Hitler and the Nazis. After World War II, in revulsion to the human rights violations by Hitler, Germans and the world corrected this error and adopted the UN's Universal Declaration of Human Rights (Tödt, 1978).

Baptists more than anyone else should reject the fallacy of confusing the source that unfortunately we can find in Alasdair MacIntyre and Oliver and Joan O'Donovan. They assume supporters of human rights claim their source is universal reason (or Occam's nominalism). In fact, their source is particular, not universal: the biblical teaching of the image of God in all humankind, and Jesus' teaching that God shines sun and rains rain on the just and unjust alike, so we are to be complete in our love as God is complete in God's love—for all humankind. The source comes from a particular tradition—initially the Bible and our Baptist tradition; and the intent is universal—human rights belong to all humankind, loved by God. Other religions base human rights in their own particular traditions, but also intend them to apply to all persons.

These opponents of human rights did not participate in the civil rights movement, or the struggle of former colonies or others who have struggled against domination and oppression and for human rights. We should not give our support to any elitist or status-quo-supporting theological ethicists who oppose human rights because they make the pre-fascist German error (Wolterstorff, 2008). We need to know and teach that human rights came from Baptist Richard Overton with solid biblical grounding as a follower of Jesus, and not from the French Enlightenment a century later.

The justice that God cares about deeply, and that many of us care about deeply in our own contexts, requires developing congregations that care about and serve people who need justice and human rights and it requires governments that support human rights for all people.

What Baptists also need to know is that it was Baptists in Virginia who persuaded James Madison to write the human right to religious liberty as the first article in the Bill of Rights of the U.S. Constitution, and who acted as Madison's troops, his political movement, to drive for adopting the religious liberty amendment to the U.S. Constitution (Miller, 1986).

What Baptists need to know is that president Abraham Lincoln, who advocated the human right to your own body, and the human right to fair pay for your work, and therefore abolished slavery, was raised a Baptist (Stassen, 1997).

What Baptists need to know is that Martin Luther King, Jr., whose powerful advocacy of human rights for all persons regardless of race by nonviolent action has spread around the world, was a Baptist. King said "they call it a civil rights movement. But it is actually a human rights movement" (Garrow, 1988:563).

What Baptists need to know is that president Jimmy Carter learned to advocate human rights for all persons regardless of race in his own Baptist church in Plains, Georgia, and during his governorship of Georgia. And it was Jimmy Carter who got the law passed that U.S. economic aid would depend on assessing the human rights of recipient nations, and that this was a powerful influence for freeing Latin American nations from the tyranny of dictatorship and for becoming democracies with human rights. And it is the Carter Institute that works for human rights and democracy for persons in many nations throughout the world, including human rights for Palestinians now. Jimmy Carter is a faithful, Bible-teaching Baptist.

What Baptists need to know is that no democracy with human rights made war on another democracy with human rights during the entire twentieth century. Political scientists call this "the iron law of international relations"—democracies with human rights do not make war on other democracies with human rights. Therefore, when nations turn from dictatorships to democracies with human rights, it prevents many wars. This is why "Advance Democracy, Human Rights, and Religious Liberty" is practice number six in the new paradigm of the ethics of peace and war, Just Peacemaking, which the BWA endorsed last year (Stassen, 2008).

What I would also like people to know is that my father, as president of the American Baptist Convention, helped lead American Baptists to support Martin Luther King. King then joined the American Baptist Convention. Dad grew up in a family tradition of strong commitment to human rights. My grandparents emigrated away from Bismarck's authoritarian and militaristic Germany, looking for human rights in Minnesota. Dad's biography will be published this fall as, *Harold E. Stassen: The Life and Perennial Candidacy of the Progressive Republican* (Kirby, 2012).

Dad was a founder of the United Nations. As U.S. delegate to the conference that wrote the UN charter in 1945, Dad worked especially hard to develop the Trusteeship Council, which worked to free colonial nations around the world so they could achieve their human right to freedom and self-government. When the UN Charter-writing Assembly finished, the reporters from all over the world voted on who did the most for the success of that UN Charter-writing Assembly. My father won--in a tie with the ambassador from Australia. He was a faithful Baptist.

We are now in a time when proponents of an ideology of neoliberal laissez-faire ideology want to replace the tradition of human rights and the common good with advocacy of "my selfish rights and let others fend for themselves." We are in an international struggle for the obligation, the duty, to defend the tradition of the human rights and the common good of all persons loved by God, including especially those whose human rights are being violated, as they were being violated in Richard Overton's time, against an individualism of greed.

What Baptists need to know is that human rights are our baby. Let us defend our baby!

Bibliography

Garrow, David J. *Bearing the Cross: Martin Luther King, Jr. and the Southern Christian Leadership Conference*, Vintage. 1988.

Gushee, David. *Sanctity of Life*. Wm. B. Eerdmans. 2012.

Haller, William. *Tracts on Liberty in the Puritan Revolution, 1638-1647*. Columbia. 1934.

Kirby, Alec, David G. Dalin, & John F. Rothmann. *Harold E. Stassen: The Life and Perennial Candidacy of the Progressive Republican*. MacFarland. 2012.

Miller, William Lee. *First Liberty*. Knopf. 1986.

Stassen, Glen. "Baptist Presidents in the White House." *Baptist History and Heritage*. January, 1997.

_____. "Human Rights." *Global Dictionary of Theology*, William Dyrness and Veli-Matti Kärkkäinen, eds. InterVarsity. 2008.

_____, ed. *Just Peacemaking: The New Paradigm for the Ethics of Peace and War*. Pilgrim. 2008.

_____. *Just Peacemaking: Transforming Initiatives for Justice and Peace*. Westminster John Knox. 1992.

_____. "Religious Roots of Human Rights." *Religious Faith, Torture, and Our National Soul*, David Gushee, ed., Mercer. 2009.

Tuck, Richard. *Natural Rights Theories: Their Origin and Development*. Cambridge. 1979, 1981.

Tödt, H. E. and Wolfgang Huber, *Menschenrechte*. Broschiert. 1978.

Westmoreland-White, Michael. "Setting the Record Straight: Christian Faith, Human Rights, and the Enlightenment." *Annals of the Society of Christian Ethics*. 1995.

Wolterstorff, Nicholas. Justice: *Rights and Wrongs*. Princeton. 2008.

4 | RELIGIOUS LIBERTY IN THE U.S. POLITICAL EXPERIENCE

A. Roy Medley

First, to our Muslim hosts, I bring you greetings of peace, *As-salaam alaikum*, and to our Christian hosts, grace and peace to you from God the Father and our Lord Jesus Christ. We are deeply indebted to you for your kind hospitality and to Dr. Riad Jarjour, especially, who has arranged this opportunity for us to be with you and to Dr. Daouk who so graciously agreed to host us.

As American Baptists we have been involved in fostering Baptist-Muslim dialogue with the Islamic Society of North America for the past several years in order to build bridges of understanding between Baptist Christians and Muslims in the United States. For us it is a response of obedience to our Lord Jesus who taught, "Blessed are the peacemakers, for they shall be called the children of God" (Mt. 5:9). We are convinced that the world cannot live in peace until Christians, Muslims and Jews have learned to live in peace with respect for one another, working for the common good of all humankind.

As a member of the Executive Committee of the Baptist World Alliance, let me say that we received with joy and gratitude the Muslim missive to the Christian world, "A Common Between Us and You." As our response says, "In adding our voice to [others], we want to embrace your conviction that it is only the movement of human hearts and minds towards love and worship of the One God, creator of us all, that will begin to resolve the huge needs for peace, justice and love of neighbors in our world today." We welcome the gift of this sacred space where our two faiths can meet and dialogue.

Let me introduce to you my colleagues who are with me. We are pleased to have two officers of the denomination with us: Mrs. Patti Stratton is the vice-president of American Baptist Churches USA (ABCUSA), and with her is her husband Jonathan who pastors the Baptist church in Bowdoinham, ME; Mr. Jim Ratliff is the other officer and he serves as our budget review officer. In addition we have Dr. Leo Thorne, Associate General Secretary for Mission Resource Development and his wife, Yvonne, who is a counselor. We are also pleased to have with us several heads of regions of our denomination: the Rev. Alan Newton, Executive Minister of ABC/Rochester-Genesee, where there has been extensive relations between local Baptists and Muslims; the Rev. Marshall Peters, Executive Minister of ABC/Mid-America (Iowa and Minnesota) and his wife, June (Marshall and June served many years with the Baptist churches in Thailand); and Dr. Riley Walker, executive minister of ABC/Dakotas, and his wife, Joyce, who is a nurse; and my wife, Patricia, who is an ordained Lutheran pastor serving in New Jersey.

Let me now turn to the assigned topic, "Religious Liberty in the U.S. Political Experience."

The place of religious liberty in the political life of the United States cannot be divorced from the life and convictions of the early Baptist community in America. The emphasis of Baptist Christians upon religious liberty is rooted in both biblical doctrine and experience.

At the heart of our commitment to religious liberty is a key scriptural principle: we are created in the image of God (*imago dei*, cf. Gen. 1:27) for relationship with God. In addressing the 400th Anniversary Celebration of Baptist Life and Witness in Amsterdam, the Netherlands in 2009, the Rev. Van der Leer reminded us that the Baptist argument for religious liberty is also eschatological and Christological in focus, having as its base the fact that each shall stand before God who shall judge us all. Because we are the creation of God who desires to know and be known by us and because God has invested us with genuine moral choices for which we will stand accountable, we believe that God alone is sovereign in matters of faith.

It therefore follows that Baptists believe that faith cannot be compelled by any external force. Faith that is not freely chosen and freely embraced is not faith. I am delighted to note that "A Common Word between Us and You," also reaffirms the importance of religious liberty in matters of faith. For Baptists, religious liberty means the freedom to accept, deny or change one's religious faith. Apart from these basic rights, liberty is a lie.

This theological conviction that faith is genuine only if freely embraced is the organizing principle of Baptist life and thought. Consequently, Baptists have consistently sought to safeguard the encounter of the creature with her/his Creator, of the beloved with the Lover. The Baptist emphases upon what we call soul freedom/soul competency and religious liberty are all means of safeguarding the holy encounter between the soul and its sovereign Lord. Not without reason, Baptists have preferred the term "religious liberty" to the alternative language of "religious tolerance" as the more robust statement of the freedom of each to believe or not believe as they will.

Because of this core theological conviction about the necessity of freedom for faith to be faith, Thomas Helwys, one of the founders of the Baptist movement, in 1612 wrote the following to English King James in protest of religion imposed by the state: "For men's religion to God is between God and themselves. The King shall not answer for it. Neither may the king be judge between God and man. Let them be heretics, Turks, Jews, or whatsoever, it appertains not to the earthly power to punish them in the least measure" (Helwys, 1998 ed.). Given the circumstances of his day, what is truly amazing in his plea for liberty is that he plead not only for the rights of dissenting Christians, but also for the rights of Muslims, Jews and even heretics to practice their faith or lack of faith without fear of punishment by the state.

Baptist experience is another source of our conviction concerning the importance of religious liberty. As a minority group, Baptists suffered persecution in both England and the American colonies at the hands of the state. In England, Baptist worship services were often raided and closed down. Baptist preachers were jailed. For his defense of religious liberty, Thomas Helwys was thrown into prison where he died.

Helwys was not the only Baptist advocate for religious liberty. As a persecuted people, such liberty was sacred to them and they risked even their lives in defiance of state-imposed faith. I think you will especially appreciate the argument of Leonard Busher. In 1614 he, too, wrote to King James: "I read that a bishop of Rome would have constrained a Turkish emperor to the Christian faith, unto whom the emperor answered, 'I believe that Christ was an excellent prophet, but he did never, so far as I understand, command that men should, with the power of weapons, be constrained to believe his law; and verily, I also do force no man to believe Mohamet's [sic] law.' Also I read that Jews, Christians, and Turks, are tolerated in Constantinople, and yet are peaceable, though so contrary the one to the other. If this be so, how much more ought Christians not to force one another to religion? And how much more ought Christians to tolerate Christians, when as the Turks do tolerate them? Shall we be less merciful than the Turks?" (Busher, 1614).

In the emerging American colonies, Baptists were forbidden to exercise their faith, to hold public worship, or to practice believer's baptism as opposed to infant baptism. Here, too, Baptists were jailed, publicly whipped, and persecuted for their faith by the state and the state-established church. Roger Williams, the founder of Baptist life in America, was exiled from the Massachusetts Bay Colony in the dead of winter because of his beliefs and would have perished except for the hospitality of Indian tribes whom he had earlier befriended. Roger Williams would then go on to found the colony of Rhode Island where religious liberty was guaranteed by the charter of the colony.

But in most of the early colonies in New England and the South, religious liberty was curbed. Therefore, Baptists from both theological conviction and experience, sought to secure the blessings of religious liberty for all persons. Baptists such as Isaac Backus and John Leland led the effort to place religious liberty in the founding documents of our nation. Hence, the first ten amendments to the Constitution of the United States, which we call the "Bill of Rights," enshrine key principles of religious liberty for our country.

The first two principles are contained in the first amendment and are known respectively as the "Establishment Clause" and the "Free Exercise Clause." The "Establishment Clause" states, "Congress shall make no law respecting an establishment of religion." This clause has been interpreted consistently by the courts of the United States to mean that the federal government has no authority to establish a national church such as is the practice in Europe. And it also means that it does not have the authority to establish one faith over another in public life. If America can in any way be termed a Christian nation, which, by they way, many of us as Christians would quickly challenge, it can be so only by heritage and culture but not by law.

The Constitution itself provides that "No religious test shall ever be required as a qualification of any office or public trust under the United States." Unlike in England where the sovereign holds as one title – "defender of the faith" – among others, the president of the United States has no such charge or authority.

Baptists and others have referred to these provisions as "separation of church and state." The origins of this phrase lie with that early Baptist, Roger Williams, of whom we spoke earlier, who referred to a "hedge or wall of separation." Likewise, both James Madison, the father of our constitution, and Thomas Jefferson spoke of the separation of church and state. The Baptist Joint Committee for Religious Liberty, an organization founded by the Baptists of America to serve as a watchdog for religious freedom, notes in one of its articles, "… the separation of church and state serves both religion clauses in the First Amendment. It operates not only to insist upon non-establishment, but also to ensure the free exercise of religion. … Properly understood, separation calls for 'neutrality' – even, to use Chief Justice Warren Burger's words, 'benevolent neutrality' – toward religion, not in any sense hostility."

Some would argue that separation of church and state hinders the public role of faith and its values. However, the Baptist Joint Committee notes that "the separation of church and state does not require a 'segregation' of religion from public life. In fact, even John Leland and Isaac Backus, for all their insistence upon the principle of separation, were thoroughly involved in public policy debates and attempts to influence legislation in their day." None of us as citizens are required to leave our faith or our religious values at the door when we enter the political realm. In fact, there is a strong presence of the religious community – Christian, Jewish, and Muslim – in Washington, D.C. and our goal is to advocate for government policies that reflect our religious values. But "advocate" is the operative word. We as religious bodies and people have every right to speak for or against any proposed legislation before Congress. The National Council of Churches, the Islamic Society of North America, the National Association for Evangelicals and the Roman Catholic Bishop's Conference all have been active in advocating for immigration laws that are fair and just and reflect our religious values of love, mercy, and justice. What no religious group has is the right to mandate a particular law. Our voices mingle with those of others and decisions are made in light of the will of the citizenry to whom the politicians are accountable through regular elections. Certainly, our elections over the past few decades speak to the ability of religious people to dramatically influence the course of legislation as evidenced in the power of the religious right in the Republican Party base.

So, negatively, the government is constrained by our Constitution from imposing faith demands upon the citizenry, but, positively, it is charged to protect the religious rights of each person. The protection of the individual's religious rights is contained in the second clause, the "free exercise clause" we spoke of earlier which states that Congress can not "prohibit the free exercise" of religious practices. This clause coupled with the "freedom of speech" clause also contained in the First Amendment provides strong protection for the practice of religious faith in the United States.

Working in tandem with the "free exercise clause," the Fourteenth Amendment secures the "equal protection of the laws" for every person and prevents the singling out of any person or group for discrimination due to religion or other factors such as race or gender. This amendment guarantees equality before the law for every citizen. The protection provided by these two provisions is robust. For example, the U.S. Congress could never, unlike the French legislature, outlaw the wearing of the hijab in public. But on the other hand, neither could it require it of women, either. Likewise, businesses must reasonably accommodate the religious practices of employees. Not long ago, Somali Muslims who work in the meat cutting industry sued their employer and won because the employer was not allowing time for them to pray according to the dictates of their faith.

On the other hand, in the 1960s the Supreme Court struck down state-mandated prayer in public school systems as unconstitutional. The law cannot forbid students from praying on their own, nor can student-organized religious clubs be forbidden from acts of prayer in their gatherings. The law is designed to protect students from state-imposed prayer that might violate their religious or non-religious conscience. Needless to say, this ruling has stirred controversy within the U.S. public.

Many of us would argue that the separation of church and state and the strong support of the religious liberty of all has been a manifest blessing to our society. Again, to quote the Baptist Joint Committee for Religious Liberty,

> The institutional and functional separation of church and state has resulted in a vibrant religion, a plush pluralism and a vital democracy. History teaches and contemporary geo-politics reveals that nations that abjure a healthy separation of church and state wind up with tepid, attenuated, majoritarian religion, at best, or a theocracy, at worst.

"Vibrant religion, a plush pluralism, and a vital democracy," are three significant blessings to our country. Americans by and large rank among the most religiously active of any western democracy. Likewise, the separation of church and state has allowed people of many faiths and no-faith to live in harmony with one another in community where each is free to practice his or her faith but not free to restrict the practice of the other of their faith.

Now, as indicated above in the discussion of the unconstitutionality of state-mandated prayer in school, there are areas of tension around the exercise of religious liberty. Let's examine briefly just two more.

First, is the place of religious symbols displayed on government (not private) property. This issue is especially heightened at this time of year when we begin the seasons of Advent and Christmas. Over the past several decades, the courts have placed restrictions upon the display of manger scenes or other Christian symbols on government property as contrary to the separation of church and state. The cultural history of the U.S. has obviously been heavily influenced by the Christian faith and for many the presence of nativity displays and Christmas carols in government settings has been a part of the public celebration of Christmas. However, as we have become increasingly pluralistic in religious demographics, such displays have become problematic, hence the court rulings.

Other forces have been at work as well, primarily economic ones, that have undermined apart from any court decrees the religious nature of these religious festivals and made of them feasts of consumption. So we find two Christmases and, for that matter, two Easters celebrated in the States. One is religious where the Christian faithful gather to celebrate the birth of Jesus as the Son of God and his resurrection, and the other secular/materialistic which focus on Santa and the Easter Bunny. For many Christians this has been a wrenching shift from a culture that reinforced their faith and they point with anger to the court rulings. My own perspective is that while the court rulings have rightfully sought to make government "benevolently neutral" in the matter of such displays on government property, that which has most seriously compromised the meaning of these religious observances has been the corrosive impact of unabated materialism. The court rulings do not restrict the right of display on private property; hence, our house is adorned with Christian symbols at Christmas and Easter while our Jewish neighbors display the Star of David and the Menorah during their holidays. Likewise, our Muslim neighbors are free to mark their holidays in appropriate ways on their property.

A second controversial issue is the matter of the controversy around the proposed Islamic Center at Ground Zero in New York. This firestorm, stoked by the media, burned around the time of the observance of the terrorist attacks of 11 September 2001. The "equal protection clause" and the "free exercise of religion clause" in the end guarantee that the Muslim community, like any other religious community, has the right to build a house of worship in any locale they please as long as they meet the same zoning and other standards that are imposed upon all apart from religious faith. Legally, there was never a question about their right, and I was pleased to join in a national press conference with many other faith leaders from the Jewish, Christian and Muslim traditions during the height of the controversy to reinforce the importance of religious liberty in our nation's laws and practices.

The debate was never a legal one, but one of appropriateness in the face of the sensibilities it raised. Even the Muslim community in America was divided over whether building in that locale was appropriate. Some in the Muslim community in my own county issued a statement that while they believed the supporters had every right to build in the proposed locale, they did not think it was wise to do so given the feelings of the victims' families. But in this matter, there is legal recourse for the proponents.

In spite of these tensions and others which could be named, the constitutional guarantees have by and large provided the robust protection of religious liberty that Baptist Christians long sought and worked for in the United States. Separation has been good for both state and religion. The personal guarantees of the exercise clause and equal protection under the laws have afforded Americans of every religious tradition the right to practice their faith without fear or interference by the forces of the state. And at the same time we have retained every right to advocate for our faiths and their values in the public square while not being able to command any regarding them. There is a robust public presence of many faith traditions in our nation, and yet we are able to live together in relative peace and security.

As Baptists we would contend that in an era when religious conflict threatens the peace of many nations, religious liberty is a gift of mercy that provides common ground for the common good.

Bibliography

Baptist Joint Committee for Religious Liberty. http://www.bjconline.org.

Busher, Leonard. "Religions Peace: or, A Plea for Liberty of Conscience" [London 1614]. *Tracts on Liberty of Conscience and Persecution, 1614–1661.* ed. by Edward B. Underhill, J. Haddon. 1846. 1, 17-22.

Helwys, Thomas. *A Short Declaration of the Mystery of Iniquity.* Richard Groves, ed. Mercer. 1998.

To Bring
Good News
to the Poor

5 | ON ADVOCACY FOR PEACE AND JUSTICE IN TODAY'S WORLD: A LOCAL PASTOR'S PERSPECTIVE

Amy Butler

Introduction

The fact is, most people in the United States do not turn to the church when they are looking for meaningful perspective on issues of peace and justice, or even faith, for that matter. The church, once a social institution of great meaning and stature, has become another option in a varied list of recreational activities each weekend. Gone is the concept of investing in community, of being 100% sold out to the message of the Gospel.

Where do historic, institutional churches in the United States find themselves in this social trend? It's a difficult place to be, because churches have generally worked so hard to build institutional presence that very often their attention to issues of mission and purpose wane. There's no doubt that becoming an "institution" has had a detrimental effect on a church's mission. After all, Jesus modeled for us a radical movement of people organized to stand in opposition to the structures of the world. What happens when this radical movement begins to build buildings and participate in mainline social structures?

What happens is a conflict between the stability of an institution and the risk of raising a radical voice. Since society holds the keys to most symbols of security, church folk who speak out for change of societal norms stand in danger of losing their institutional security. But, without a strident voice of advocacy motivated by faith, the church runs a high risk of becoming irrelevant.

And here is where we find ourselves: asking how we make the church relevant, how we reclaim the alternative voice in society that Jesus modeled for us, and how we live showing the world Jesus' dream of Gospel community.

Being Baptist

As Baptists, we hold very dear the principle of the separation of church and state. Integral to our very identity is the determination that freedom to worship is essential, and that no government should ever endorse, support, or prohibit the free exercise of faith.

Because of this basic Baptist value, however, we can run the risk of interpreting the separation of church and state to mean that we should never participate in politics or work for changes in laws, even when the values of our faith mandate a call to change. This interpretation of the separation of church and state, however, is flawed.

Brent Walker, head of the Baptist Joint Committee for Religious Liberty writes: "The metaphorical wall of separation does not block one's religion from playing a role in public life. Religious people have the same right as others to communicate their convictions in the marketplace of ideas and to convert their religious ethics into public policy by preaching, teaching, lobbying, and even running for office. People of faith need not limit their piety to houses of worship or to acts of private devotion; nor do they have to concede the public square to others. They should speak out, become involved, and transform culture through this public witness, including political involvement" (Walker).

I would argue that it may be even more critical that Baptists get involved, speak out, become advocates in the political arena because of our Baptist identity. After all, we have a long history of suffering persecution ourselves, and a proud heritage of advocacy since our inception. Further, the church has often been the place where movements for social change begin. In the United States, movements to express the "Social Gospel" in the early twentieth century and later to campaign for Civil Rights both began in churches, specifically Baptist churches. One might even say that advocating for those who are suffering is a holy calling for us as Baptists, and certainly if we call ourselves followers of Jesus Christ.

So how might the local Baptist church actually engage in advocacy around issues of peace and justice in the political arena without sacrificing the separation of church and state? Walker comments: "Humility is called for when one enters the public debate or political arena armed with religious motivation. Moreover, any attempt to elevate one view of an issue to 'the Christian' position, to the exclusion of others, should be held in check. Religious persons of goodwill often disagree over how their religious convictions play out in the public arena. As has been observed, there is no direct line from the Bible to the ballot box" (Walker).

Following Jesus

As followers of Jesus Christ, we are called to live lives that are modeled after the human life he lived. We know from reading the gospel texts that Jesus was ever and always an outspoken advocate for people living on the margins of society. He determinedly reached out, over and over again, to women, lepers, tax collectors, the sick, the hungry ... anyone who was marginalized, who suffered; these were the ones Jesus intentionally included in his life and ministry. He did this in two ways that seem very significant.

First, Jesus identified those who were living on the margins, those who had no voice in society. He then spoke on behalf of them—he challenged the authorities and questioned the order of things; he identified injustice and he worked to change it. Jesus talked often about a concept he called The Kingdom of God—a way of living in community with each other so that God's best dreams for our world are actually coming to be. When he saw people behaving in ways that worked against the coming of God's kingdom, he was never afraid to speak out and challenge them, to insist on change.

Secondly, Jesus went a step further than just speaking for those who could not speak for themselves; he actually lived the principles of the Kingdom of God in relationships; he invited everyone into life transforming relationship with him, even those who were outcasts. He did this by illustrating what he knew to be true—that Gospel can be lived and expressed in community, in relationship. Jesus was constantly inviting people to eat with him, walk with him, talk with him, even die with him; he seemed to know that relationships change us, they change the way we think about others. Jesus put actions behind his words. He engaged in life-giving relationship with people who were dying to know a different reality than the one they were living.

In all these ways Jesus demonstrated a commitment to being an advocate who changed the way society understood certain issues or people. He demonstrated that Christian faith was never empty religious practice, but rather a powerful, transformational way of life.

Finding a Voice

I spoke about the growing danger of the church's irrelevance. In the United States, this is not just perception. Recent studies have shown that even evangelical leaders themselves are aware of the church's waning influence in society. A recent Religion News Service article reports: "A new poll released June 22, 2011 from the Pew Forum on Religion & Public Life seems to say just that, with the vast majority—82 percent—of U.S. evangelical leaders saying their influence on the country is declining" (Banks).

Depending on the geographical setting of the community, people in general are becoming less and less inclined to attend church regularly and invest in a faith community. Social pressures to conform to what was once a widely accepted standard are waning significantly and, in some cases, do not exist anymore. Messages in society promote the idea that one can be a good person—a solid, contributing member of society, and a happy and fulfilled individual—without faith or religion featuring prominently in one's life.

In addition to these growing social messages, society in the United States is saturated with the principle of consumerism. That is, there's no need to sacrifice to be part of something. Churches, like every other institution in American culture, have been relegated to the ranks of Wal-Mart and any other institution serving consumers, and themselves ceded to pressures to "give people what they want." The end result of this approach is the creation of an attitude of a "consumer faith," one where people will quickly lose interest or surrender true commitment if they don't feel that their needs or desires are being met.

The general response of the church is reflected in the previously referenced Pew study, showing the strong decline in the relevance of the church in society. The church changes so radically to try to meet the expectations of a consumer-based society that it quickly loses—almost without noticing—the strong, prophetic voice that reflected Jesus' advocacy of the least of these among us and his insistence on the creation of a new world order, i.e., the Kingdom of God. Banks reports, "The Rev. S. Douglas Birdsall, executive chair of the Lausanne Movement, which worked with Pew on the survey, said: 'What can happen is that the minister becomes the communications marketing guru who knows how to appeal to various markets and so you attract people,' he said. 'When you do that, you lose your prophetic voice of what it means to challenge people to be in the world but not of the world'" (Banks, 2011).

It is very true that the church runs the risk of losing popular appeal if leaders intentionally and persistently forego the approach of consumer satisfaction and cling, instead to the radical, uncomfortable gospel message of Jesus. It's time for churches to regain the radical voice of Jesus, to risk marginalization themselves, because we know from the example of the one we follow, showing us that even a voice on the fringes—when it rings prophetic and true—will long outlast any attempts to imitate an approach of the world.

Pitfalls of the Advocate Church

Becoming a faith community that regularly advocates for systemic change, however, is not without potential problems. If the church is truly reaching out to the society in which it functions, there will be people from all different walks of life in the pews on Sunday mornings. With them these people bring different life experiences, diverse passions and convictions, and even varied faith stories. There is no such thing as uniformity in the body of Christ, so how do we decide which issues to adopt? How can we know what Jesus would do if he were here, living in our world at this time?

Surely each person of faith would have a different answer to these questions. Herein lies the struggle and potential danger of the church as advocate. Imagine, for example, if one or two strong voices within a community insist on taking a certain political or social position, and use the church's name and influence to advocate for this issue, all the while there are some within the community who do not share the same convictions and who, in fact, even feel that their faith would not promote such a position?

It is precisely in this situation that the church as advocate runs the very high risk of becoming a social advocacy organization rather than a community of faith. When the issues become the central focus of the church's life, gathering, and identity, sometimes communities forget the central reason for which they gather: to be followers of Jesus Christ. This risk can be highly destructive to a faith community, ironically pushing the loss of relevance to new levels at an accelerated pace. There are many nonprofit, advocacy organizations in which people may invest their time, energy, and resources, and these organizations do not bear the "trappings" of religion that put so many off from the start. If a church allows its advocate voice to be commandeered by issues—no matter their relevance or urgency—the church risks losing sight of the gospel that motivates its existence in the first place.

Avoiding this pitfall is tricky, especially if there is a strong level of shared conviction for a certain issue within a faith community. The avoidance of this danger is found, however, in two important safeguards. First, a faith community must articulate and know the principles around which its people gather and exist. Why are we here? What do we believe? When we are torn by controversy or uncertainty, what is the defining principle on which we can all gather together? We must repeatedly remind ourselves and each other of Jesus' gospel message, that which has redeemed each of us individually and can redeem our community and our world. Articulating this shared position of faith, representing it clearly to world, reminding ourselves and each other of what we believe, and repeatedly coming back to revisit the fundamentals of our identity as a community of faith is an essential quality of being an advocate church.

It is from this point—from the bedrock foundation of shared faith in Jesus Christ—that we can now step out into the world together, find issues about which we share conviction and can make significant difference, remembering together that it is our shared faith that motivates our advocacy.

Advocacy at Calvary

At Calvary Baptist Church in Washington, D.C., advocacy has always been part of the community's faith expression. Perhaps this comes from its geographical location in the center of the nation's capital. Issues that most people read about in the newspaper happen blocks from Calvary's sanctuary; in its history the church's members included some of American history's most influential politicians and government bureaucrats, including presidents, Supreme Court justices, members of Congress, elected City Council officials, and prominent business leaders.

The Calvary congregation shares an institutional memory that recalls advocacy for slaves and abolitionists; support for military personnel during world wars while simultaneously supporting conscientious objectors; radical advocacy before and during the Civil Rights Movement as the first white Baptist church in the city of Washington, D.C. to admit an African American member in 1954; outspoken advocacy for peace during the Vietnam war; advocacy on behalf of homeless women in the city of Washington, D.C., when they were not being served at all; commitment to the church's role in the city when many were leaving during urban blight of the 1980s and 1990s; the support of women and minorities in leadership and ministry positions; and a radical voice that welcomes people who are generally excluded from modern church life.

Given its location and history, perhaps this congregation sees advocacy and faith as inextricably intertwined. This does not mean, however, that internal controversy and the pitfalls of an advocate church do not threaten its expression of the gospel. Issues come and go; Calvary's challenge is to perpetually identify the issues to which God is calling the congregation to respond in this time and place, all the while holding fast to its primary calling: building and living gospel community as followers of Jesus Christ.

In the past eight years, since I came to Calvary as Senior Pastor in 2003, some of the issues of advocacy motivated by faith have been:

Environmental

Calvary's congregation, led by lay people who feel a passion and calling to address issues of environmental justice, have taken on projects as diverse as creating a "Green Team" to help congregation members learn environmentally sound strategies for their homes, connect with government and private resources to weather-proof their houses, and learn more about how faith and environmental justice are linked. Church members and pastors have led Bible Studies on environmental justice; written grants to help the church purchase electricity more effectively and plant trees around the building; helped congregation members replace energy sapping light bulbs in their homes; and lobbied the City Council to secure safe, green play space in the Penn Quarter neighborhood for the increasing number of families with children living in our neighborhood. Faith-inspired environmental efforts around the world included learning about and supporting efforts to create clean, safe drinking water in Haiti; relief during various tragic events, such as tsunamis and earthquakes, and efforts to support small scale farmers toward independence and self-sustaining farming in Africa and other parts of the world.

Immigration

With the conviction that everyone is welcome, the Calvary congregation has worked very hard in the last years to create a safe, welcoming worship environment for people who come to our country seeking opportunity. Efforts to support and encourage immigration reform in the United States as a reflection of our faith convictions include hiring diverse staff and ministry leaders who can speak different languages and who come from other cultures. The congregation has worked to create a worship experience that reflects diversity and offers welcome even to those who struggle to speak English. As advocates outside of Sunday mornings, Calvary has asked those who are immigrants among us to share their stories of resettlement and help us understand the mandate our faith offers us to welcome the stranger. Politically, Calvary members have lobbied City Council to oppose the "Secure Communities" act in Washington, D.C., marched in protests for immigration reform, worked to lobby political leaders on behalf of the Dream Act, organized to help change laws around driver's license restrictions in the District of Columbia, and provided actual sponsorship and support for some of the immigrant community worshipping with us. Despite differing political opinions on issues of immigration, the Calvary congregation has worked very diligently to find efforts in which we can work together with the motivation of our faith to speak for those who have no voice and to become advocates for those on the margins of our own society.

Peace

Prayers for those who suffer the ravages of war and conflict are a regular part of Calvary's worship expression. Among our own community, we work very hard to practice healthy conflict resolution, attempting to offer each other love and respect as we live with our own immediate differences. Even in the face of conflicting political positions, the church regularly marches together in public demonstrations for peace. Along with the World Council of Churches, Calvary became involved in promoting nuclear disarmament by lobbying congress, writing letters, and attending meetings. Joining in advocacy efforts with organizations like Bread for the World and the Heifer Project, Calvary has readily advocated for hunger relief around the world; regular food collections aid hunger relief in our local setting as well. Each year on the anniversary of the assassination of Archbishop Oscar Romero in El Salvador, Calvary sponsors a prayer service open to the community. This service, "Prayers for Peace," recalls Romero's dogged commitment to seeking justice and remembers all who offer their lives to advocate for peace and justice.

Neighborhood revitalization

With the firm conviction that the presence and participation of the church is essential to the life and vitality of any community, the Calvary congregation made a very conscious decision to remain in its downtown neighborhood even when the surrounding community became blighted, depressed, and dangerous. For decades, the dwindling congregation remained in the Penn Quarter neighborhood with little prospect of revitalization until the late 1990s, when the neighborhood began to radically change. Advocacy efforts then transitioned from serving homeless populations with feeding programs, for example, to partnering with new neighbors to provide nurture and opportunity for youth of the city; joining neighborhood associational groups to monitor area developers and make sure they kept a commitment to making the neighborhood livable; opening our building to four nonprofit partners serving youth through music and the arts, and continuing to be a vocal voice at City Council meetings, neighborhood discussions, and interfaith advocacy efforts to insure a safe, thriving neighborhood that makes room for everyone who lives here, even the most marginalized.

Calvary is only one example of a faith community that holds the conviction of advocacy as a natural expression of Christian faith. Any faith community reaching out to those who are marginalized by using the strategy Jesus used, speaking for the voiceless and inviting the marginalized into community, is an advocate community of faith.

The Future of the Church: Keeping Advocacy a Priority

It is clear that the influence of the church is waning in the United States and surely in other places around the world. It is my conviction that one reason for the church's lessening influence is our increased need to please a consumer-minded society that demands comfort and ease even in communal expression of the gospel. Unless the church is willing to hold the tension of prophetic gospel expression, even at the risk of losing popular appeal, this trend of waning influence and participation will continue. Worst of all, the institution intended to reflect the gospel message will not effectively communicate the radical nature of Jesus' message.

Will pastors and churches have the courage to build advocacy into their expressions of gospel truth? There is no doubt cost is involved. Beyond the loss of popularity lies the risk of internal division and the threat of marginalization ourselves. Perhaps, then, as we consider the challenge and risk of advocacy and radical faith expression in the world around us, we would do well to remember the one whose name we bear, Jesus Christ, the crucified.

Conclusion

The Church of Jesus Christ must retain the priority of advocacy as an expression of faith. Built into our Christian and even Baptist traditions lies the mandate to live as relevant and vocal expressions of Jesus' call to create the Kingdom of God, to insist that God's dreams for the world indeed become reality. Our world is filled with pain; there are so many who have lost sight of God's hope for salvation and restoration. It's our calling and mandate to rediscover the advocate's voice, to articulate the rigorous challenge of the gospel, and to be a prophetic voice in a world dying to even catch a glimpse of God at work.

Bibliography

Adele Banks. *Religious News Service (RNS)*. June 22, 2011.

Brent Walker. "Political Discourse." www.bjconline.org.

6

Prophetic Witness: The Church's Role in Advocating for the Poor and Speaking Truth to Power and Principalities

Samuel Escobar

Late in March I was asked to teach an intensive course about Christian mission in the Baptist Church at Montequinto, located in the Spanish city of Seville. The course was organized by a Brazilian missionary who leads an extension theological center for the region. It was hosted by a church where the pastor is a lady from Argentina who has been serving as a Baptist missionary in Spain for thirty-three years. During the course we prayed for a missionary team of Spanish Baptists that serve in Equatorial Guinea in Western Africa under the European Baptist Mission. We were hosted by a lady from El Salvador, an immigrant, and one of the hundreds of Latin American volunteers who are active in Spanish churches these days. Just before going to Seville I was a speaker in Torrox, Malaga, for a conference of Latino missionaries in Europe, attended by over a hundred of them from some fifteen countries.

This is the reality of the global church in the twenty-first century and we as Baptists are part of it. It is a result of two centuries of missionary work. First, we must humbly praise the Lord for the Baptist contribution to this new reality. As we review our history we must read it with new eyes because the way in which this history has been researched, presented and understood is going through a process of revision. Second, we witness the rise of a missionary spirit in the Southern hemisphere, which is expressed in a new sending activity from the younger churches that were planted in the two centuries that preceded us. This is what missiologists have called the shift of Christianity to the south—"the south" meaning in this case not only Asia, Africa and Latin America, but also the enclaves of poverty and marginalization in the rich nations of Europe and North America—places all in which churches are growing. That "periphery" has become the base for mission in our century and we have not yet explored all the theological significance of this possibility.

In a way we have witnessed the end of the imperial age of mission in which the Gospel was presented "from above" by Spanish conquistadores or British merchants, sometimes following too closely the British or European colonial pattern. Now the younger churches are carrying on mission "from below" not only through intentional missionaries but also through Gypsies in Spain, Filipino maids in the Muslim countries, illegal immigrants in the United States, African university students in Europe. New partnerships are developing and new patterns are called for. This is the new situation within which we must consider the theme posed before us: the prophetic witness of the church that goes along with the evangelistic and church planting dimension that has been a high mark of Baptist mission.

In recent times I have been struck by a passage about Jesus' ministry that appears in the Gospels of Mark and Luke. In both Gospels two actions of Jesus are portrayed with the same structure and contents. We have it in Mark 12:38-44 and the parallel in Luke 20:45-21:4. Let me use Luke's version, though the unity of the passage is broken by our chapter and verse division:

Ch. 20

45While all the people were listening Jesus said to his disciples: 46"beware of the teachers of the law. They like to walk around in flowing robes and love to be greeted in the market places and have the most important seats in the synagogues and the places of honor at banquets. 47They devour widows' houses and for a show make lengthy prayers. Such men will be punished most severely."

Ch. 21

1As he looked up Jesus saw the rich putting their gifts into the temple treasury. 2He also saw a poor widow put in two very small copper coins. 3"I tell you the truth," he said, "this poor widow has put in more than all the others. 4All these people gave their gifts out of their wealth; but she out of her poverty put in all she had to live on."

First, we have Jesus' words of acidic denunciation of the religious hypocrisy of the scribes and the way in which they abused the poor widows. Craig Keener calls our attention to the fact that though not all scribes would be exploiters of the poor, there were some teachers, like there are nowadays, who used religion as a way of making money (Keener, 1993). There is irony in the way Jesus describes the exhibition of piety that these scribes practiced and the thirst for power and prestige that went along with it. Jesus *announced* the coming of the Kingdom of God, but he also *denounced* injustices in the social order that was the context of his ministry.

The story continues with a description of the intentional way in which Jesus observes the scene of people bringing their offerings to God's house. He praises the sacrificial offering of a poor widow whom he sets as an example by contrast with the rich. There is here a dignifying intention, which connects with the compassion for the poor, the despised, and the marginalized that was also a hallmark of his ministry. It is also part of the announcing of the Kingdom. I think that in this twofold dimension of Jesus' ministry we have a good basis for approaching the double agenda that is set before us by the organizers of this workshop: Prophetic witness: the church's role in advocating for the poor and speaking truth to powers and principalities.

In the final decades of last century two Baptists theologians have helped us to see anew the importance of the Christological paradigm for ministry found in the Gospels. It is incarnational and marked by a spirit of service. René Padilla from Argentina has expressed well this Evangelical perspective recovered from a fresh reading of the Gospels: "Jesus Christ is God's missionary par excellence, and he involves his followers in his mission" (Padilla, 1982). As we find it in the Gospels, Jesus' mission includes "fishing for the Kingdom," or in other words the call to conversion to Jesus Christ as the way, the truth, and the life. It is this conversion to Jesus, which stands as the basis upon which the Christian community is formed. Mission also includes "compassion" as a result of immersion among the multitudes. It is neither a sentimental burst of emotion nor an academic option for the poor, but definite and intentional actions of service in order to "feed the multitude" with bread *for* life, as well as Bread *of* life. Mission includes "confrontation" of the powers of death with the power of the Suffering Servant, and thus "suffering" becomes a mark of Jesus' messianic mission and a result of this power struggle and of human injustice. Through creative contextual obedience Jesus' mission becomes a fertile source of inspiration, it contains the seeds of new patterns being explored today through practice and reflection, patterns such as simple lifestyle, holistic mission, the unity of the church for mission, the pattern of God's Kingdom as missiological paradigm and the spiritual conflict involved in mission.

For Padilla, however, it is clear that biblical Christology also includes an unequivocal reference to the atoning work of Jesus Christ in the cross and the need of every person to respond to it. There cannot be an imitation of Christ in the biblical sense without a new birth. In response to liberation theologians who would stress the sociopolitical dimension of the death of Jesus, Padilla, for instance, accepts the truth based on examination of the texts of the Gospels that the death of Jesus was the historical outcome of the kind of life he lived, and that he suffered for the cause of justice and challenges us to do the same. But a warning is necessary, because "Unless the death of Christ is also seen as God's gracious provision of an atonement for sin, the basis for forgiveness is removed and sinners are left without the hope of justification . . . salvation is by grace through faith and . . . nothing should detract from the generosity of God's mercy and love as the basis of joyful obedience to the Lord Jesus Christ" (Samuel & Sugden, 1983:28).

Within the new situation of a global church and the missionary dynamism coming from the South, Orlando Costas, a Baptist theologian from Puerto Rico, provided a theological key when he focused on the significance of mission as coming from the "periphery," from the marginalized people. He considers carefully the Galilean base of Jesus' ministry in the Gospel of Mark and concludes that the deliberate choice of Galilee is a key "not only to understanding Mark but also to recovering and interpreting Jesus' evangelistic legacy" (Costas, 1982:49). In Costas' use the term "periphery" means not only the region of Galilee that was on the fringes of the Palestinian Jewish world, but also the kind of people who were the first disciples, not only from the respectable classes of Israel but especially from the outsiders and the marginals. Thus Mark's emphasis provides a clue of universal value when we look at evangelization and the Christian mission:

> If evangelization starts on the periphery of society, if it works from the bottom up, the good news of God's kingdom is vividly demonstrated and credibly announced as a message of liberating love, justice and peace. When the Gospel makes "somebody" out of "nobodies" of society, when it restores the self-worth of the marginalized, when it enables the oppressed to have a reason for hope, when it empowers the poor to struggle and suffer for justice and peace, then it is truly good news of a new order of life" (Costas, 1982:62).

In the history of Baptist missionary practice there are fascinating examples of the way in which prophetic witness was carried on along the lines here proposed. Let me take one that has been researched by Frederick S. Downs, a Professor in the United Theological College in Bangalore, India. Miles Bronson was for forty-three years an American Baptist missionary in Assam, North East India. He was an evangelist but he also became a social agitator. Downs tells us "When the British annexed Assam in the fourth decade of the nineteenth century they began to use the Bengali language in the courts and government schools of the new territory. They needed to justify this action as the stated British policy was to use vernaculars in the lower courts and non English medium government schools" (Downs, 1989:251). This imposition of another language on the people of Assam was convenient for the British that had trained Bengalis to assist in the administration of the colony. A small Assamese elite that had learned the Bengali language benefitted from the colonial situation. However, "[t]he great majority of Assamese people did not benefit at all. In fact their condition was much worse than it had been previously. They found it difficult to learn the Bengali which they needed to function effectively under the new order. They were exploited in the courts and learned little in the government schools" (Downs, 1989:251).

Because of their immersion among the Assamese people and their identification with them the missionaries took up the defense of their rights. Downs continues: "Without significant assistance from any but a few members of the Assamese elite, the American Baptist missionaries began an agitation against the use of Bengali … Through their Assamese medium schools and publications sought to conscientize the Assamese people concerning their oppression. In due course they were able to convince a politically significant number of Assamese to support the agitation and the British gave in" (Downs, 1989:251).

Another inspiring example from our denominational history is the life and ministry of Gustavo Parajón, from Nicaragua (Slade, 2006:1-2; Deiros, 1986:331-341). The son of pastor and church planter Arturo Parajón, Gustavo graduated in Medicine and Public Health in the USA. He returned to Nicaragua as a medical missionary with his wife, Joan, and they were shocked by the poverty of the rural areas across the country. He founded PROVADENIC (Nicaragua Vaccination and Community Development Program) in 1967, in partnership with the Baptist Convention of Nicaragua, First Baptist Church of Managua, and First Baptist Church of Cleveland in the USA. It is a primary healthcare program that serves 25 rural communities by training local health promoters to treat and prevent common illnesses. His ministry as a pastor and a doctor gave him a strong vocation for social service and also an awareness of the corruption and abuse of the authoritarian military regime of the Somoza dynasty. An earthquake shook the country on 23 December 1972, leaving 10,000 persons dead, 40,000 houses destroyed and more than 200,000 persons displaced. Four days later evangelical churches under the leadership of Gustavo Parajón created CEPAD, a Committee to respond to the emergency.

Many countries sent help that was managed by the Somoza government. A good amount of foreign help went to the bank accounts of the Somozas and there was no accountability mechanism to control it. CEPAD requested to be given the responsibility of administering all help coming from Protestant and evangelical sources abroad. The transparency of their actions, their sacrificial dedication to service and their public accountability was an evident contrast with the way the government acted. CEPAD became an organization known and respected by most Nicaraguans. As the decade advanced, the opposition to the Somoza regime grew and revolutionary guerrillas appeared. Violence was tearing apart the nation. In such an atmosphere CEPAD and Parajón had the respect of both the government and the opposition. During the Sandinista Revolution and the war in the 1980s, CEPAD was the intermediary between the evangelical churches and the government and won the attention of Nicaraguan President Daniel Ortega, who appointed Parajón a member of the National Reconciliation Commission, together with Cardinal Miguel Obando y Bravo, former Roman Catholic Archbishop of Managua.

This appointment led to misrepresentation in some circles that CEPAD had become a communist organization working in tandem with the Soviet-backed government. As a result, CEPAD's clinics became targets for attacks from Contra rebels who sought to overthrow the government, placing doctors, nurses and patients at risk. Contra rebels were supported by the US government and reporting about this situation the evangelical periodical *Sojourners* published a provocative headline: "Ronald Reagan is lying about Nicaragua." An intervention by Eastern Baptist Theological Seminary (now Palmer Theological Seminary) professor and author, Ron Sider, who organized visits by conservative leaders from the USA to the sites served by the organization, helped to dispel the accusation. In fact, after on-site observation,

> ...the Rev. Gordon Kurtz, pastor of the First Baptist Church of Lewisburg PA, expressed the growing conviction of ABC pastors and churches: "As American Baptists we need to be informed about the impact of President Reagan's policies on American Baptists in that region. Indeed all American Baptists should

be protesting our government's arming of contras who invade Nicaragua leaving a trail of death and destruction" (Jennings, 1984:306,314).

At present CEPAD continues its ministry of service, representation of Evangelicals and reconciliation.

In receiving the 2006 BWA Human Rights Award, Parajón, who served as a BWA vice president from 2005-2010, was recognized for his outstanding relief and developmental work, his stand for reconciliation, as well as his contribution to the evangelical movement and Baptist witness in his country. BWA General Secretary Callam declared that Parajón's "dedication to reconciling people in situations of conflict has inspired us all. Gustavo has left us with a legacy of a loving and caring spirit which Baptists everywhere will seek to emulate."

Jesus' own ministry involved announcing the coming of God's Kingdom through preaching, teaching, healing the sick and feeding the hungry, and it also involved denouncing evil and injustice in the structures of society and pointing to corruption and religious hypocrisy. As we review the history of the Church with an attentive eye, we find that, in different ways and at different stages, believers in Jesus Christ have also followed this double agenda. The quality and dedication of their service among the poor as well as the socially redemptive effect of their evangelization have provided a platform that has allowed them to speak up against injustice and corruption at the power and government levels, or to show different ways of approaching human problems. Sometimes missionary projects of churches have become models that inspired governments to initiate far-reaching programs of social reform.

As we discuss this issue we must remember that we come from very different situations. Just to mention some of them I start in Europe where we are witnessing the slow or rapid collapse of Christendom. In most European nations there were established churches such as Roman Catholic, Lutheran, Reformed and Orthodox. Though the power and influence of these churches has been declining, there is still in society a measure of Christian ethics and values, and a possibility of appealing to them both for ways of service cooperating with the government in responding to the needs of the poor or raising a prophetic voice. Traditionally, Baptists have kept distant from the state but it is possible for them to raise their voice in defense of the human rights of the poor, especially immigrants from Eastern Europe, Africa and Latin America. In the case of Spain, for instance, Baptists have cooperated with other Evangelicals especially in Urban Mission that serves the poor, nowadays mostly immigrants. This practice of service has given them a measure of expertise that has helped sometimes in confronting government agencies or unjust legislation.

The Christendom situation was similar in Latin America in relation to the Roman Catholic Church. In some countries such as Mexico, Colombia, Peru and Argentina, the prophetic confrontation of the powerful had to be addressed to the Catholic Church that used its political clout to fight against religious freedom. The pioneers of Baptist work in Argentina, such as Swiss missionary, Pablo Besson, and Argentinian pastor, Santiago Canclini, became conversant with the political situation and fought long and hard battles to change legislation. Church growth in countries such as Brazil and Guatemala has opened the possibility of political participation for Protestant (Evangelical) churches. The sad experience in some cases has been that power has corrupted Evangelical politicians (Freston, 2008).

Very different is the situation in places where Christianity has never been in government. In some like the Muslim countries, where Christian minorities or missionaries are serving in a variety of ministries to the poor, it would be far more difficult for Christians (and for Baptists for that matter) to raise a prophetic voice confronting the powerful. In some cases the moral pressure coming from international bodies in which Christians take part is a possibility that should not be overlooked.

An important outcome of this workshop will be a better grasp of the variety of situations from which we come and the possibilities of mutual support and cooperation in the specific task of a prophetic confrontation of power structures and persons.

Bibliography

Costas, Orlando. *Liberating News*. Eerdmans. 1989.

Deiros, Pablo. *Los evangélicos y el poder político*. Nueva Creación. 1986.

Downs, Frederick. "Social Influences of Nineteenth Century Baptist Missionaries in India." *American Baptist Quarterly*. Vol. 8, No.4. 1989.

Freston, Paul, ed. *Evangelical Christianity and Democracy in Latin America*. Oxford. 2008.

Jennings, Raymond. "When President and Missionary Disagree: American Baptists Wrestle with a Basic Question." *American Baptist Quarterly*. Vol. III, No. 4. Dec. 1984.

Keener, Craig. *The IVP Bible Background Commentary*. InterVarsity. 1993.

Padilla, C. René. "Bible Studies." *Missiology.* Vol. 10, No. 3. 1982.

Samuel, Vinay and Chris Sugden, eds. *Sharing Jesus in the Two-Thirds World.* Eerdmans. 1983.

Slade, Stan. "Central America Celebrates Gustavo Parajón." *International Ministries Update.* Nov. 2006.

7 | PEACE AND HUMAN RIGHTS EDUCATION: CORE PEDAGOGICAL VALUES, PRINCIPLES, AND PRACTICES

Anaida Pascual Morán

"Human rights put flesh on the bones of the abstraction of peace, bringing the flesh to life" (Reardon, 2010).

"Human rights education is one of the most concrete and tangible expressions of critical pedagogy" (Magendzo, 2002).

"The principal aim of an education for peace, human rights, and democracy has to be the promotion of the universal values and types of behavior on which a culture of peace is based" (Tuvilla Rayo, 2004).

The centrality of Human Rights in Peace Education processes is not only evident, but also crucial. Peace Education and Human Rights Education are not only closely intertwined, but inseparable. In the following paper, I propose a pedagogical scaffold to educate for both peace and human rights in an articulated approach. The essence of this transformative framework is based on seven assertions and core principles, values and practices that derive from them.

1. Human rights provide the necessary normative and formative framework to contextualize peace education, thereby making peace relevant, real, and concrete. Xesús Jares, prominent for his remarkable work in Peace and Human Rights Education (Jares, 2002, 2004, 2005), underlines the centrality and transversality of social, economic, cultural and political human rights in peace education. Along

the same line, the internationally recognized peace researcher and educator Betty Reardon (Reardon, 1995, 1997, 2000) asserts that human rights standards, principles and values historically accumulated, configure the "ethical core" of an education for peace and human dignity.

As part of her argument, Reardon affirms that civil, political, economic, social, and cultural human rights provide us with a social, spiritual and moral ethics, since they constitute primary tools to detect manifestations of injustice, impunity, and violations to human dignity. In other words, Reardon asserts that human rights - as codified in pacts, covenants, conventions and international public policies - when denied, offer indicators of violence and vulnerability; yet when they are respected, provide indicators of progress and civility. Within this human rights framework, she indicates, we can make comprehensible concepts that otherwise would be abstract, such as: (a) the structural violence due to pervasive poverty and inequitable socio-economic relations; (b) the political violence, stemming from oppressive systems towards dissidence and marginality, and (c) the cultural violence that disdains and devalues particular identities and alternative styles of life through racism, sexism homophobia, ethnocentrism, colonialism, and other forms of exclusion that rationalize discrimination, domination and oppression (Reardon, 1995).

2. Both a culture of human rights and a culture of peace are essential for the defense of human dignity. Xesús Jares emphasizes the importance of promoting a culture of human rights, based on the values of solidarity, freedom, equality, justice, sustainability, and democracy. Moreover, in the face of a progressive weakening of democratic systems, the absence of citizen participation and the growing gap between technological and social advances, Jares affirms human rights education as a continuous formative process, permanently bound to the promotion of a positive peace. It is worth noting that Jares has identified the following as the fundamental educational challenges that we must assume in the 21st century in order to give life to this culture of peace and human rights (Jares, 2002, 2004 & 2005):

- More than reflect about human rights, we must live and practice human rights, democracy, conflict resolution and peace in every formative scenario;

- To counteract conformism, indolence, passivity, indifference, fatalism, defeatism, and resignation, it is necessary that we commit ourselves with an education that struggles against a single mindset, by means of a critical pedagogy and a "critical-conflictual-nonviolent model," recovering therefore, the value of utopia and hope;

- To embrace the values of peace and human rights it is necessary that we create "spaces of freedom and tenderness," where we can articulate the cognitive dimensions of learning with the affective and experiential dimensions;

- In order to liberate students from the "tension of competing," we must transit from a culture of competition, hostility, and disdain, to a culture of reciprocity, tolerance, sensibility, appreciation, and affirmation that propitiates cooperative strategies and group dynamics;

- We must dedicate time to examine daily problems and learn about the nonviolent confrontation of conflicts and how to contribute to the democratization and emancipation of those human beings that live side by side in the same shared space;

- In the global movement for a culture of peace, we can also find principles and guidelines to construct a genuine culture of peace and human rights. The concept culture of peace encompasses a style of life deeply rooted in a set of consensual values at a universal scale. This notion implies visualizing peace as the guiding thread and driving force across culture and education, in order to propitiate an ethics of reciprocity and responsible solidarity that confers dialogue, conciliation and human rights a protagonist role. In this context, education is conceived as the most valuable instrument to pursue a culture of peace. Therein, the urgency of a new educational paradigm geared towards civic principles and values vital for coexistence and the construction of a new global ethics (Mayor Zaragoza, 2004; Boulding, 2003; Hicks, 1993; Suliveres, 2008);

- The notion culture of peace exceeds the negative definition of peace, to make way for a positive content of peace, in terms of social justice, collective wellbeing, and absence of direct, cultural and structural violence. For example, we practice positive peace by fostering the reduction of asymmetries and inequalities; as we work to eradicate hunger, malnutrition, and poverty; when we struggle to bring to an end the exploitation of the marginalized; and, while we address problems, such as the rise of exacerbated ethnic conflicts, fundamentalisms, and nationalisms. In the context of a positive peace, an attempt is usually done to create the conditions for peace starting from four cornerstones: *human rights, disarmament, democracy,* and *sustainable development;*

- Moreover, close ties are established with issues of justice, solidarity, and democratic citizenship. The fundamental idea is to undertake a profound paradigmatic shift before actions and attitudes of domination and violence, ranging from daily relations to an international scale (Mayor Zaragoza, 2004; Boulding, 2003; Hicks, 1993; Suliveres, 2008). Along the same line, Reardon critiques that studies about peace are usually centered in the notion of negative peace, starting from the analysis about how to reduce and avoid war and violence, instead of creating the positive conditions for peace. This negative approach, Reardon affirms, constitutes a serious obstacle for the development of the necessary capacities to construct a positive and integral peace. To counteract this situation, she proposes the integration of human rights learning as a transversal perspective in all formal and informal curricula (Reardon, 1995, 1997 & 2000);

- From the point of view of the Movement/Vision for a Culture of Peace and Nonviolence, peace is conceived as a *construction,* as a *project* that involves us all. This movement is truly about, according to ex director of UNESCO Federico Mayor Zaragoza, assuring the promotion of values and rights that constitute "the leaven of peace": nonviolence, tolerance, democracy, solidarity, justice, dialogue, citizenship, and a spirit of openness towards diversity (Mayor Zaragoza, 2004). In this regard, the six principles in the Manifesto 2000 for a Culture of Peace and Nonviolence, agreed-upon by several Nobel Peace Prize laureates in the International Year for a Culture of Peace, and signed by over 75 million people worldwide, take on a crucial significance and constitute pillars for Peace and Human Rights Education (UN, 1999; UNESCO, 2000). Moreover, as peace educator and researcher José Tuvilla Rayo from Spain asserts, these six principles provide us with the minimal necessary ethical values in all formative peace spaces (Tuvilla Rayo, 1998, 2004);

- **Respect all life.** In adopting this principle, we commit ourselves to our co-existence and to safeguard human rights, both in terms of personal autonomy and shared responsibility. Educationally wise, we must work with experiential and relational knowledge, as well as with strategies of consensus building, mediation, conciliation, arbitration, and collaborative negotiation. This principle also requires that we explicitly undertake an education strongly oriented towards asserting diversity, alterity and interdependence among genders and generations. Likewise, we are also required to detect violent biases with overtones of racism, sexism, militarism, xenophobia, and homophobia (Tuvilla Rayo, 1998, 2004);

- **Reject violence.** According to this principle, we must adopt an ecological model for violence prevention, which addresses the social, communal, relational, and personal dimensions of learning in a formative environment of pertinence, justice, and security. It also demands that we channel aggressive behaviors towards creative, collaborative, and auto-affirmative activities, by means of students' active participation in change processes and social renewal projects. Moreover, on the basis of this principle we must acknowledge that we have been socialized in a model of interpersonal relations based on "anti-values," such as intolerance and the rejection of vulnerable populations (Tuvilla Rayo, 1998, 2004);

- **Share with others.** In line with this principle, it is our responsibility to assume teaching, research, and creative work as tools to delegitimize social disparities, within a liberatory framework of human rights and social justice. To this end, we must acknowledge democracy as a dynamic task and permanent challenge. It is also indispensable that we understand education as "democracy put into action" in a participatory learning atmosphere, where there is coherence between ends and means, theory, and practice. Ultimately, this principle is about constructing an informed citizenry that avoids exclusion and takes into account openness towards diversity as a determinant factor of social cohesion (Tuvilla Rayo, 1998, 2004);

- **Listen to understand.** To adopt this principle we must strongly believe in the importance of an authentic dialogue, based on active listening and due regard for the dignity of every human being. This requires that we create a dialogic climate of encounter, discovery, and reflection, centered in a sense of respect towards differences of opinions, values, and ways of life. Moreover, that we construct "learning spaces of trust" that enable the realization of human rights as a democratic practice. This principle should also lead us to uphold diversity and multiculturalism as an enriching social element, as well as to understand that uniformity entails the loss of liberty and intellectual poverty (Freire, 2006:11-18; Tuvilla Rayo, 1998, 2004);

- **Preserve the planet.** This principle connects education with sustainability, democracy, dignity, quality of life, and the exercise of human rights. This implies that we must sensitize ourselves about the ecological crisis and the urgency of equilibrium and peace with nature. Likewise, that we adopt certain goals established in international summits, as articulated in the Earth Charter, by the 2003 UNESCO General Conference: (a) improve the quality of human life; (b) preserve the vitality and diversity of the Earth; (c) remain within our Planet's endurance capabilities; (d) ensure a fair and just access to natural resources; (e) aim at a sustainable social and economic development; (f) promote human integrity, gender equality and social cohesion; and

(g) propitiate civil society's action-orientated participation (Tuvilla Rayo, 2004; Gadotti, 2006);

- **Rediscover solidarity**. The prior aim of this principle is that we reinvent solidarity. It summons us to rediscover those values that are inspired in a "culture of solidarity" that safeguards the human rights of the most vulnerable and unprotected. Thus, it requires us to rethink solidarity from the local to the global; from the educational sphere to communal spaces; from our "personal sovereignty" to distant places. In adopting this principle, we must confer this notion a new ethical meaning, as well as acknowledge that the value of human existence is based upon both each person, and society at large (Tuvilla Rayo, 1998, 2004).

According to Vicenç Fisas, titular professor of the Peace and Human Rights UNESCO Chair at the Universitat Autònoma de Barcelona, these six principles require us to adopt a critical and pro-social pedagogy based on ethical responsibility, interdependence, and creative conflict resolution. Ultimately, Fisas affirms, we are talking about a pedagogy that democratizes knowledge, based on citizen participation and human security, geared towards avoiding all types of exclusions, conducive to unlearning the prevailing culture of patriarchy, xenophobia and homophobia (Fisas, 2002).

3. Active nonviolence and conflict resolution jointly constitute the only possible route conducive to a culture of human rights and peace. Nonviolence is not only a philosophical ideal of life, but also a real and effective means to act and live. It announces the possibility of constructing peace through the creative resolution of conflict (Lederach, 2000), while at the same time, it denounces the failure of the violent ways as questionable and unacceptable modes of dealing with conflict (Lederach, 2000; Freire 1993, 2006).

In his seminal work, *My Faith in Nonviolence* (1930), Gandhi defines nonviolence as "the weapon of the strong" and affirms it as "the only way" conducive to a liberating and conciliatory social action. In the Gandhian perspective, "non-violence is the greatest force at the disposal of humankind;" so powerful, because every hierarchical system and authoritarian relation is contingent to our obedience, cooperation and submission (Gandhi, 1930; Pascual Morán, 2002, 2003). Moreover, it is a "law of life" since in the midst of war, destruction, and adversity, life persists thanks to actions without violence (ahimsa), and to our firm commitment to search for "the truth," in the context of our conviction of the sanctity of human dignity (*satyagraha*). Henceforth, the importance of a fundamental pedagogical task: to generate a nonviolent ethos, characterized by the liberation from fear, a spirit of resistance, a high moral tone, and a courageous testimony of coherence between preaching and practice, between word and action (Galtung, 1996, 2006, 2008; Pascual Morán, 2002, 2003).

Just as human rights and nonviolence, conflict is inherent to peace, since it is part of the human situation. On this basis, the notion of conflictual peace is recognized as valid. Johan Galtung, author of the Transcend Method, likens conflict to a "loop" that far from separating the "adversaries," unifies their destinies, because "they have their incompatibility in common." This method draws its premises from Hindu, Christian, Taoist, Islamic, and Judaic thought and creeds, which include among others: (a) conflict as a source of both violence and positive transformation; (b) respectful dialogue as a primary tool for peace; and, (c) the recognition of mutual causation and shared responsibility with respect to a conflict. In this regard, the well-known Norwegian peace researcher affirms that in conflict there are always diverse perspectives of "the truth," since we are dealing with a dialectic process of tension between forces; thus, the parties involved are called to: (a) maintain contact, rather than avoid it; (b) dialogue, and not just quarrel or isolate themselves; (c) think objectively, instead of fostering "destructive conflict;" (d) revise and suppress their "conflictive images" of the "adversary;" and, (e) offer nonviolent responses to "transcend conflict" and achieve reconciliation (Galtung, 1996, 2006, 2008).

Galtung defines violence as the failure to transform the creative potential of a conflict and thereby asserts peace as the emphatic and creative sum that emerges from dialogue and conflict management. Likewise, he describes "creating peace" as preventing violence before it appears and reducing it, once it manifests itself. The key idea is to surpass the never-ending spiral of violence, in order to transcend it. To these ends, Galtung convenes us to examine, not only the visible harm but also the invisible signs of conflict, resulting from a triangle of violence: *direct violence, cultural violence*, and *structural violence*. He also summons us to "trace maps" about the roots and evolution of conflicts, as well as to avoid "the metastasis of the conflict" into a "meta-conflict that eternalizes itself," by giving attention to three key phases of the life cycle of the conflict: before violence, during violence, and after violence (Galtung, 1996, 2006, 2008).

The *before violence phase*, requires channeling all energy and hostility towards the transformation of incompatible interests, to reach a "cease fire," prevent direct violence and resolve the conflict. In the *during violence phase*, the aggression that arises from a sense of frustration and revenge must be halted, in order to find pathways for violence cessation and conflict resolution. In the *after violence phase*, the roots of the conflict must be overcome, with emphasis on the parallel processes that Galtung refers to, as "the 3 R's to transcend conflict": Reconstruction, Reconciliation and Resolution. The reconstruction process aims at healing the open wounds in the parties involved, restoring damages, and addressing the resulting trauma. During the process of reconciliation, it is crucial to unravel the meta-conflict and assure reparation and restitution. In the resolution process, conditions must be created to solve the original conflict that escalated into a meta-conflict, unleashing the outbreak of violence. Unfortunately, since the whole process is so demanding, many parties tend to post-pone solving their meta-conflict (even forever), and go back sporadically to violent conflictive stages (Galtung, 1996, 2006, 2008).

- Martin Luther King, Jr. on the basis of the civil rights struggle in the United States, left us as legacy his philosophy of nonviolence, summarized in six key principles: (1) nonviolence is not passive and requires courage; (2) nonviolence must seek reconciliation, not the defeat of the adversary; (3) nonviolent action must be directed at eliminating evil, not the person that inflicts evil; (4) nonviolence requires willingness to accept suffering for a cause, but never allows inflicting it; (5) nonviolence rejects hatred, animosity and violence of the spirit, as well as direct violence; and, (6) it is essential to persevere and have faith that justice will always prevail (King, 1958). Based on these Six Principles of Nonviolence, the Martin Luther King, Jr. Center for Nonviolent Social Change in Atlanta has established Six Steps of Nonviolent Change, as a sequential process for nonviolent conflict resolution and social change: (1) research and gather information about the conflict to get the facts straight; (2) educate adversaries and the public about the facts of the dispute; (3) assume a commitment to nonviolent attitudes and actions; (4) negotiate with adversaries to correct injustices, in a spirit of goodwill; (5) carry out nonviolent direct actions, such as marches, boycotts, mass demonstrations, picketing, sit-ins, and paint-ins (Sharp, 1973); and, (6) propitiate a sense of community and reconciliation among adversaries (e.g., The Martin Luther King, Jr. Center for Nonviolent Social Change, Atlanta, GA, USA).

Since the ends are always contingent to the means, in active nonviolence and conflict resolution we certainly find the only possible route conducive to a culture of peace and human rights. Likewise, in a liberatory and critical framework, we find the pedagogical answer to propitiate this new culture.

4. Liberatory and critical pedagogies provide an emancipatory framework for Peace and Human Rights Education. María Montessori, world-renowned Italian

scientist and pedagogue, always visualized education as a "great armament for peace;" that is, as the ideal means to harness our "creative energy" and make tangible "the possibility of a better humanity" (Montessori, 1949). Likewise, Paulo Freire, one of the most influential pedagogues at the turn of the 20th century, reiterated that our educational work must be at the service of problematization, conscientization and humanization (Freire, 1993, 2006).

- According to Freire, "authentic liberation" is "humanization in process," and implies "the action and reflection of human beings upon the world to transform it." An emancipatory framework requires thus a historical commitment that incorporates both the <u>denunciation</u> of a dehumanizing reality, as well as the hopeful and prophetic <u>annunciation</u> of an alternative reality where, as always-unfinished human beings, we can constantly "become more" (Freire, 1993, 2006). Within this framework, education must be understood as "freedom in practice" and "thought for action" instead of "practice of domination" and "thought void of action." Since "no one teaches another, nor is anyone self-taught" but "humans learn and teach each other mediated by the world," emancipatory education affirms the dialogicity of theory, and coherently becomes dialogic in practice. Hence, from the Freirean perspective, three dialogical strands define liberatory education: dialogic pedagogy, dialogic environment, and dialogic method (Shor, 1987);

- A true **dialogic pedagogy** acknowledges and privileges the learners' democratic right of participation and opposes all authoritarian and elitist forms of teaching. For these purposes, it appeals to the learners' intrinsic motivation and thematic universe. It also contextualizes learning in their experiences and existential reality, both from their "reading of the world," as well as from their "reading of the word." The assumption is made that the more education is problematized, the more commitment and awareness the students will develop to respond to the challenges they identify (Shor, 1987);

- To construct a **dialogic environment**, a rupture with every authoritarian and power relationship that provokes a "culture of silence" in learners is essential. It is also necessary to create a climate of invention and impatient, permanent, and hopeful search. This calls for an elimination of all passive and oppressive relations, to give way to a democratic communication. Likewise, it requires recognizing that every educational act must start by overcoming the educator-educatee contradiction because, as educatees-educators and educators-educatees, we educate among ourselves, mediated by the world (Shor, 1987);

- The **dialogic method** constitutes a problematizing and participatory process, capable of illuminating the social, cultural, historical, political realities of our time, in order to transform them. It repudiates the act of depositing information and values, since it recognizes that authentic knowledge emerges, not from the discourse transmitted by the educator but from the experience and learning of the educatees. This method privileges inquiry, collaborative projects and listening to the diverse voices. Hence, it adopts dialogue as an essential process for deliberation and emphasizes the transformative power of the creative and action processes of the educatees as well as of the educators (Shor, 1987);

- As we have exposed, liberating and critical pedagogies are at the core of Peace and Human Rights Education. Nevertheless, in order to be coherent, these pedagogies must be accompanied by a differential and democratic approach towards teaching and learning;

5. It is essential to differentiate and democratize education, so that learners reach their optimal development and contribute to the construction of a culture of peace and human rights. This implies capturing and cultivating our personal and collective capacities, interests, and talents, so that we learn to be crafters of our own destiny (UNESCO, 1996). Notwithstanding, we are witnessing a vertiginous growth of girls, boys, and adolescents marginalized by the school system, and a tragic increase of youth that, having no real projections for the future, day by day literally survive, risk their lives and even die in drugs, arms, and vulnerable street scenarios. Our educational scenarios are no exception. Systemic violence in education is interwoven in many of the policies and practices that adversely impact students, "by burdening them psychologically, mentally, culturally, spiritually, economically, or physically" (Epp, 1997). These practices and policies of institutionalized violence often pretend to be neutral, but they are discriminatory and detrimental to learning. Among these educational policies and practices, we can find, for example: biases, prejudices and gaps in the curriculum; the imposition of controversial standards; the application of "interventions" and "treatments" from deficit-aware points of view; the use of typologies and labels that stigmatize; a lack of reasonable accommodations; authoritarian pedagogies; the formation of aggressive and antidemocratic traits of personality traits; and methods of teaching and evaluation that do not recognize diversity, bringing about a waste of talents and loss of potentialities (Pascual Morán, 2007).

- In the context of this violent institutionalized reality, according to the French researcher and pedagogue Philippe Perrenoud, we find the roots of inequalities in education. Ultimately, affirms Perrenoud, it is the "evaluative machinery" the one that arbitrarily determines the "success" of those "most favoured" and the "failure" of the "less favoured" (Perrenoud, 2007). This unilateral power to "judge, classify, and declare that a student is in a situation of failure," is usually exercised by means of obsolete and violent measures of differentiation, such as exams, standardized tests, and psychometric technics. And precisely these unjust and exclusionary "hierarchies of excellence" are the ones that often cause underachievement, grade repetition, dropout, and school failure. These inequalities in learning, which in turn derive from inequalities in cultural capital and developmental differences, are unacceptable, since they run contrary to human rights principles and democratic ideals. Therefore, asserts Perrenoud, we must bring to an end "the indifference before the differences," on the basis of a "pedagogy of the differences" and a "positive discrimination." It is urgent thus, that we respect the right of every learner to have the opportunity to learn within a pedagogical framework of "intentional differentiation."

As we differentiate education, we are also contributing to the democratization of education, so that students will not only be able to cultivate their interests and talents, thereby reaffirming their diversity and unity; but they will have the opportunity to reciprocally commit themselves to contribute their potentialities for the common good and a better quality of life. It is thus necessary to *differentiate* and *democratize* education, if our goal is to construct peace as a human right and edify a new culture (Pascual Morán, 2007).

6. The idea of peace as a human right of synthesis constitutes a key dimension for a new culture built upon the values of nonviolence, democracy, justice, and peace. It is worth noting that innumerable efforts are being made today, by means of international normative, geared to the acknowledgement of *peace as a human right of synthesis*. For example, we can mention two recent initiatives that resulted from the International Congress on the Human Rights to Peace, in Santiago de Compostela, Spain, in December of 2010: the creation of the International Observatory for the Human Right to Peace and the Santiago Declaration on the Human Right to Peace.

In the Santiago Declaration, a positive and holistic notion of peace is affirmed as an ethical value and force capable of harnessing the contributions of persons, nations and cultures, in attention to "human vulnerability." The eradication of all types of armed, structural and cultural violence is also claimed, for they are incompatible with the notion of "integral peace." Moreover, _the contents of peace as a human right_, are asserted - such as the right to an education for human rights; the right to human security; the rights to ecological equilibrium, disarmament, socioeconomic development, and migration; and the rights of persons and groups in situations of vulnerability. In the context of diverse international proposals for "human security," the negative and reductionist notion of peace is also questioned, as well as the prevailing concept of "national security," which incites "preventive wars" and "equilibrium of terror." As a viable alternative, a reconversion of the war fighting capabilities and the astronomic costs that militarism entails, in favor of social justice and ecological sustainability, is proposed.

In the long run, we are talking about a paradigm shift that requires us to transit, from the utopian vision of perpetual peace as a final state; to an imperfect peace, understood as a dynamic, always unfinished, evolutionary path. This paradigmatic change demands that we surpass the conception of negative peace, and aim at a multidimensional positive peace, that encompasses (a) direct peace attained through nonviolent conflict resolution; (b) the shared values of cultural peace; and, (c) policies of structural peace geared towards social justice (Fisas, 2002; Tuvilla Rayo, 1998, 2004). It also requires the vindication of democratic values and human rights, within the framework of a "democratic radicalism" (Freire, 1993) committed with actions, and particularly, with "projects of possibility."

7. The construction of "projects of possibilities" represents proposals for action within the framework of Peace and Human Rights Education. Envisioning a project constitutes a way of imagining the future, an interpellation to a given challenge, an option for change on the basis of an unwanted situation. Every project has its origin in an idea, whether to solve a problem, create something novel, or modify a specific reality (Ulla, 2006). Conceptualizing a project offers the possibility of constructing a piece of the future and giving it coherence through action (Ander-Egg, 2000; Ulla, 2006).

Paulo Freire has left us a challenging legacy in the notion of _lo inédito viable_ (the viable unknown) which designates what although does not exist, is not only desirable but also possible. At the heart of this approach is the conviction that destiny is not predetermined or inexorable. To build this uncertain future, Freire proposes the forging of _propuestas de posibilidad_ (proposals for possibility), since they constitute "the conjecture that is defined with clarity"; "the possible dream to be channeled by means of action;" the dream we fight for, even though it entails obstacles and counter-dreams." To these ends, Freire convenes us to dream with _proyectos de humanidad_ (projects of humanity) and to become bearers of the *sueño viable* (viable dream). He also summons us to reject the fatalist discourse that stands between our vision of history as possibility (Freire, 1993, 2006).

Out of the historical legacy of nonviolence, the pioneering imprints of Gandhi and Martin Luther King also point to the urgency of building links between civil nonviolent actions and prospective projects of cultural, ethical, political, and social transformation. In similar tuning, within the UNESCO Movement/Vision for a Culture of Peace and Nonviolence, peace is conceived as a construction, as a collective project for the promotion of peace values and human rights. It is also visualized as a trans-disciplinary initiative that require us to develop creative research and action-projects in a spirit of openness towards diversity, that transcend disciplines and institutional walls (Mayor Zaragoza, 2004; Pascual Morán, 2003, 2007).

From a pedagogical perspective, assuming this proposal implies propitiating project-based learning as the most authentic and democratic means of education. To these ends, I propose that we explore these seven premises as a pedagogical scaffold to construct a wide range of *proyectos de posibilidad*. Particularly, I refer to innovative justice, advocacy, service, and social reinsertion projects geared towards marginalized and excluded populations. The sum and synergy of these projects would have as primordial goal maximizing participatory democracy, human security, respect for human rights, and the transformation of the very fabric of our society.

Certainly, we live in uncertain times. We face times of violence and counter-violence; turbulent times of corruption and criminality in which life is devalued and faith in violence takes precedence over hope for peace; difficult times in which the "globalization of violence" prevails as fascination, addiction and tragedy (Pascual Morán, 2000). It is precisely in the context of this unprecedented spiral of violence that I call on all of you to dream with projects of possibility. Fortunately, there are many paths traveled upon which we can edify. I refer to innumerable peace and human rights formative projects all over the world that demonstrate that the *proyectos de posibilidad* are not only "viable dreams," but seeds that sown on fertile grounds can thrive into *proyectos de humanidad*. From this point of view, alongside the renowned Spanish singer/songwriter Joan Manuel Serrat, I invite you to vindicate "the realism of dreaming with a future where life is better and human relations more just, richer and positive, and always, in peace" (Serrat, 2006).

Bibliography

Ander-Egg, E. & Aguilar Idañez, M. J. *Cómo elaborar un proyecto: Guía para diseñar proyectos sociales y culturales*. Editorial Lumen/Humanitas. 2000.

Boulding, E. *Cultures of Peace: The Hidden Side of History*. Syracuse University. 2003.

Escola de cultura de pau. Cataluña. Created in Cataluña, Spain in 1999. http://escolapau.uab.cat/castellano/index.php.

Fisas, V. *La paz es posible: Una agenda para la paz del siglo XXI*. Intermón/Oxfam. 2002.

Freire, P. *Pedagogía de la indignación*. Ediciones Morata. 2006.

_____. *Pedagogía de la esperanza. Un reencuentro con la pedagogía del oprimido*. Siglo XXI. 1993.

Gadotti, M. & Antunes, A. "La ecopedagogía como la pedagogía indicada para el proceso de la Carta de la Tierra." *Cap. IV: Democracia, no violencia y paz, La Carta de la Tierra en Acción*. 2006.

Galtung, J. "La resolución de conflictos exige creatividad." [Interview by Ezequiel Moltó]. *El País*, España. 23 March 2008.

_____. "Trascender los conflictos: La perspectiva de Johan Galtung." *Futuros*, Revista Trimestral Latinoamericana de Desarrollo Sustentable. 2006.

_____. *Peace by Peaceful Means: Peace and Conflict, Development and Civilization*. Sage. 1996.

Gandhi, M. "My Faith in Nonviolence" (1930). *The Power of Nonviolence: Writings by Advocates of Peace*. Beacon. 2002.

Jares, X. *Educar para la verdad y la esperanza en tiempos de globalización, guerra preventiva y terrorismos*. Editorial Popular. 2005.

_____. *Educar para la paz en tiempos difíciles*. Ediciones Bakeaz. 2004.

_____. *Educación y derechos humanos*. Editorial Popular. 2002.

Hicks, D. *Educación para la paz: Cuestiones, principios y práctica en el aula*. Ministerio de Educación y Ciencia. Ediciones Morata. 1993.

King, M. L., Jr. *Stride Toward Freedom: The Montgomery Story*. Harper. 1958.

Lederach, J. P. *El abecé de la paz y los conflictos*. Catarata. 2000.

Magendzo, A. "Conversaciones y tensiones en torno a la educación en derechos humanos." Conferencia Magistral 2002-2003 Cátedra UNESCO de Educación para la Paz. Universidad de Puerto Rico. 2006.

_____, ed. *De miradas y mensajes a la educación en derechos humanos*. *Cátedra UNESCO de Educación en Derechos Humanos*, Universidad Academia de

Humanismo Cristiano, Fundación Ideas y Ediciones LOM. 2004.

_____. "Human Rights Education as Critical Pedagogy." *Human Rights Education listserv.* June 2002.

Mayor Zaragoza, F. & Á. Mateos García. "¿Por qué una cultura de paz?" *Polylog.* Foro para filosofía intercultural. 2004.

Montessori, M. *Educación y paz.* Errepar. 1949.

ONU *Declaración y Programa de Acción sobre una Cultura de Paz.* Resolución de la Asamblea General de las Naciones Unidas (A/RES/53/243). 6 October 1999.

Pascual Morán, A. "Liberar talentos, optimizar inteligencias, sobredotar potencialidades: ¿Paradigma vital para diferenciar la educación y propiciar los derechos humanos, la justicia y la paz?" *Pedagogía.* Revista Facultad de Educación, Universidad de Puerto Rico, Recinto de Río Piedras. 2007.

_____. *Acción civil noviolenta: Fuerza de espíritu, fuerza de paz.* Publicaciones Puertorriqueñas, Puerto Rico Evangélico y Cátedra UNESCO de Educación para la Paz. 2003.

_____. "La noviolencia: tiempos para una nueva mirada al pensamiento de Gandhi." *Signos de Vida, Revista Cristiana de Divulgación y Reflexión.* Consejo Latinoamericano de Iglesias, 24, 39-42. En A. Yudkin Suliveres & A. Pascual Morán, eds. Educando para la paz en y desde la Universidad: Antología conmemorativa de una década. 2002.

_____. "¿Fe en la violencia o esperanza de paz?" (2000). *Signos de Vida, Revista Cristiana de Divulgación y Reflexión.* Consejo Latinoamericano de Iglesias (CLAI), No 16, 16-19. En A. Yudkin Suliveres & A. Pascual Morán, eds. Educando para la paz en y desde la Universidad: Antología conmemorativa de una década. 2008.

Perrenoud, P. *Pedagogía diferenciada: De las intenciones a la acción.* Editorial Popular. 2007.

Reardon, B. "Human Rights Learning: Pedagogies and Politics of Peace / Aprendizaje en derechos humanos: Pedagogías y políticas de paz." Conferencia Magistral 2008-2009, Cátedra UNESCO de Educación para la Paz, Recinto de Río Piedras de las Universidad de Puerto Rico. 2010.

_____. "Human Rights as Education for Peace." *Human Rights Education for the Twenty-First Century.* J. Andrepoulos & Richard Pierre Claude, eds. University of Pennsylvania. 1997.

_____. *Educating for Human Dignity: Learning about Rights and Responsibilities.* University of Pennsylvania. 1995.

Ross Epp, J. & A. M. Watkinson. *Systemic Violence in Education: Promise Broken.* State University of New York. 1997.

Security Pax Forum: The International Network for the Promotion of Human Security and Peace. http://www.unesco.org/securipax/index.htm.

Serrat, J. M. Investiture address as Doctor "Honoris Causa." Universidad Complutense de Madrid. 15 March 2006.

Sharp, G. *The Methods of Nonviolent Action*. [3 vols]. Porter Sargent. 1973.

Shor, I. & Freire, P. "What is the dialogical method?" *A Pedagogy for Liberation: Dialogues on Transforming Education*. Bergin & Garvey. 1987.

Ulla, L. & Giomi, C. *Guía para la elaboración de proyectos sociales*. Instituto para la Cultura, la Innovación y el Desarrollo (INCIDE). Editorial Espacio. 2006.

Tuvilla Rayo, J. *Cultura de paz: Fundamentos y claves educativas*. Editorial Desclée de Brouwer, Colección Aprender a Ser / Educación en Valores. 2004.

_____. *Educación en derechos humanos: Hacia una perspectiva global*. Editorial Desclée de Brouwer, Colección Aprender a Ser. 1998.

UNESCO. *La educación encierra un tesoro. Informe a la UNESCO de la Comisión Internacional sobre la educación para el siglo XXI*. Santilla, Ediciones UNESCO. 1996.

UNESCO. *Manifiesto 2000 para una Cultura de Paz y No Violencia*. 2000. http://www3.unesco.org/manifesto2000/sp/sp_manifeste.htm

Yudkin Suliveres, A. & Pascual Morán, A. eds. *Educando para la paz en y desde la Universidad: Antología conmemorativa de una década*. Cátedra UNESCO de Educación para la Paz, Recinto de Río Piedras de la Universidad de Puerto Rico. 2008.

8 | Ethical Dimensions of Sustainability: Religious and Educational Perspectives

Mark Edward Greenwood

Introduction

Let us begin by thinking about two fundamental premises of Christian Ethics. These are:

- What we do has to be related to what we believe; and

- What we believe makes a difference to what we do.

The first denotes a deliberate seeking to live with integrity, a pro-active matching of words with actions. The second is recognition of the unseen forces which our cultural assumptions, worldview, religious beliefs, spiritual inheritance and personal spirituality exert on our actions.

Most of the time we live without stopping to reflect on why we are doing what we do or make the ethical decisions we make – they seem to be second nature, or common sense. This is an illusion, however (or delusion, perhaps). In fact, we have been molded to be the people we are, making the choices we make, by our social, cultural and spiritual context. These understandings are fundamental to the ethics of sustainability, because the destructive behaviours of humanity towards the ecosystem (and towards our very self) have been molded by our societies, cultures and spiritualities. Which also implies that if we can shift our social, cultural and spiritual concepts towards the environment, and seek deliberately to act towards the environment and fellow humans in accordance with those renewed concepts, then we may make some steps towards sustainable living.

Christian Understandings of Humanity's Relationship with the Planet

As Christian churches, then, we have to ask ourselves: What do we believe about the planet? Because what we do on or with the planet has to be related to what we believe about it, and what we believe about the planet will make a difference to what we do.

There are, in broad general terms, two ways Christians answer this question, both having a certain degree of biblical foundation. The first is to believe that as the world is embroiled in evil, the result of human sin, the earth is beyond redemption, awaiting a re-creation by God of a new perfect natural order. From this perspective, any action or intervention aimed at diminishing systemic human suffering or the suffering of the created order is, at best, irrelevant. From an extreme point of view such action is a diversion from the more important task of saving from perdition the greatest number of humans possible, so that in the future they might enjoy the new created order.

The second broad answer that is given, and I subscribe to this one, is that the planet is God's beautiful creation, and that one of the purposes of our very existence, as humans, is to look after God's handiwork, the environment in which we live. Indeed, according to the second chapter of the book of Genesis, God's plan included creating humans *in order to* care for the other things he had created. Now clearly, if our spirituality, religion and relationship with God have this idea as a fundamental concept, then our attitude and action in relationship to the planet will be radically different than for those who concur with the first answer above. We see a healthy relationship with God's creation as one of the fundamental means by which people can have a fulfilling relationship with God.

Now the first view, that the world is embroiled in evil, is based on a verse in 1 John (5:19). However, to understand this to mean that the physical world is unredeemable is to misunderstand Johannine Theology. The "world" in this verse signifies human society, and it is this world that God so loved, to which he sent his son, to be light in it (John 3). And although Jesus affirms that this world hates the followers of Christ, he nevertheless sends his disciples into the world to make a difference (Jn. 17). Indeed there is a clear stream in Johannine thought, and in Jesus' teaching, that it is actually possible to live a fulfilled life – in abundance – here on this earth, even before eventually benefitting from eternal life (Jn. 10:10, 17:13).

Furthermore, if we are to seek biblical thoughts on the relationship of God's people to the *physical* world (environment), then we can find the concept of the responsibility humanity has to care for creation and even alleviating its suffering – what has been called stewardship, or creation care. This is particularly clear in Genesis and the creation Psalms (e.g., 8, 104), but amazingly in Paul's drama of the ends of time, the created order is in pains akin to labour, anxiously awaiting the "sons of God" to bring liberation (Rom. 8:18-25). This is eschatological, and so does not preclude hope for a New Heaven and New Earth, nevertheless, the underlying principle in Paul's mind is that the sustainability of the physical created order is our responsibility as children of God.

Biblical Foundations for a Positive View of Humanity's Responsibilities Towards the Earth

Let us explore this positive view of humanity's relationship with the created world a little more. In Genesis 2:5-8 we can perceive that God did not wish to create the garden before having both water to irrigate it and someone to cultivate it. We have seen how part of God's purpose for creating humanity was for us to cultivate the garden, but note also, that the verb used in the Hebrew for the human's care for the creation is šmr (רמשׁ), the same as is used five times in Psalm 121 to refer to God's relationship with Israel, as their guardian. Our care for the created world, therefore, should reflect the nature of God's care for God's people.

Psalm 104 impresses with the richness of life which the author observes in the world, and the praise of God, as creator of the world, which this stimulates. There are three constant themes in the Psalm: 1. The greatness of God seen in the created universe. 2. The admiration and praise which the psalmist feels observing this greatness and beauty. 3. The interdependence between a human being, other living beings, and the world in which they live. Despite the vast differences between the principally rural world in which the author lived and our industrialised, principally urban society, everything we use or abuse still has its source – no, it's being – within the natural world, however distant it may seem as a result of human intervention. We are still interdependent with the incredible natural world in which we live. There is no technology without raw materials. When there are no more raw materials, there will be no more technology. Like the author of the Psalm, we should perceive the greatness of God in the world around us, gaze in awe upon its beauty, and understand the impossibility of our life (as we know it) without it.

In Leviticus 25:1-12 we encounter a revolutionary idea for our contemporary culture of unbridled production and consumption – the idea of a periodic rest for the earth, every seven years.

Commenting on this passage, René Padilla observes that:

> The earth's rest is not an end unto itself. ...[T]he rest is ... in honour of the LORD. ...These laws emphasize the importance of caring for natural resources...The ideology of unlimited economic growth does not leave space for rest, neither for humans, nor for creation. These laws call for an "economy of the sufficient." The economy of the sufficient prioritizes a simple lifestyle, leaving space for rest, because it puts the relationship with God, with one's neighbor and with the creation above material desires and needs. ... It questions the fundamental premises of the current economic system by which human life consists of the quantity of goods one possesses (Padilla, 2002).

Christian Ethics, the Green Economy, and Institutional Frameworks for Sustainability

So where does this reflection on Christian ethics leave us in relation to the *green economy*, and an *institutional framework for sustainable development* (the themes of United Nations Conference on Sustainable Development, *Rio* de Janeiro, Brazil, *20*-22 June 2012)? Well, clearly those who offer the first answer to the question "What do we believe about the planet" (i.e., that the world is embroiled in evil), will not be involving themselves with the debate. Their belief has determined their action, and they will want to be true to their belief.

On the other hand, those of us who believe that the planet is God's beautiful creation, in which we were placed to care for it, will be deeply concerned about institutional frameworks for sustainability, and the development of economic systems which respect and nourish the human societies and ecosystems of which we are a part. We will want to acknowledge that the evil in which the world is embroiled is, in fact, our sin; sins of selfish ambition, greed, exploitation and disregard, amongst others, which have so debilitated our relationships with each other and with the planet, in fact, destroying so much of them.

And we will want to turn from that sin and rediscover life in all its fullness in the garden of God, cultivating it, being its guardian.

We will want to challenge the fundamentally materialistic nature of the United Nations' philosophies and approaches which so very rarely reflect any understanding of the spiritual worldviews of its member states. Not only a truly biblical Christian ethic of creation, but many other spiritual worldviews would also draw us away from the materialistic economic systems which are behind most western development thinking, and in turn behind the U.N. To change the way our economies interact with the planet on which they depend, the basics concepts behind "economic growth" need to be challenged if we are to avoid a "greenwash" economy.

But to finish by looking at ourselves: As institutions, churches need to create frameworks, shapes of being and ways of living together, which denote a deliberate seeking to live with integrity and sustainability with God's creation. We need a pro-active matching of the words in our sacred book with our actions in the environment and human society.

What we do has to be related to what we believe, and what we believe must make a difference to what we do.

Bibliography

Brito, P. R. B. De, and Mazzoni-Viveiros, S. C. *Missão Integral: Ecologia e Sociedade*. A Rocha Brasil. 2006.

Damatta, R. *O que faz o brasil, Brasil?* Rocco, 1984.

Eade, D., ed. *Development and Culture*. Oxfam. 2002.

Freyre, G. *Homens, engenharias e rumos sociais*. Record. 1987.

Jones, J. *Jesus e a Terra: a ética ambiental nos evangelhos*. Ultimato. 2008.

Kaiser, O. *Isaiah 1-12: A Commentary*. Westminster Press. 1983.

Leite, A. C. L., Carvalho, G. V. R. de, and Cunha, M. J. S, eds. *Cosmovisão Cristã e Transformação*. Ultimato. 2006.

Padilla, C. René. *Economía humana y economía del Reino de Dios*. Kairos. 2002.

Pallister, A. *Ética Cristã Hoje: vivendo um Cristianismo coerente em uma sociedade emmudança rápida*. Shedd. 2005.

Peskett, H. and Ramachandra, V. *A mensagem da Missão: A Gloria de Cristo em todo o tempo e espaço*. ABU Editora. 2005.

PNUD. *Informe Regional sobre Desarollo Humano para América Latina y el Caribe 2010*. PNUD. 2010.

Queiroz, C. P. *Ser é o Bastante: Felicidade à Luz do Sermão do Monte*. Encontro, 2003.

Toombs, El. E. *The Psalms in Laymon: The Interpreter's One-Volume Commentary on the Bible*. Abingdon Press. 1971.

Wright, C. J. H. *The Mission of God: Unlocking the Bible's Grand Narrative*. InterVaristy. 2006.

9 | Impacting Public Policy to Achieve Educational Goals: A Civil Society Perspective

Peter J. Paris

I am greatly honored by your invitation to address you today on one of the greatest needs of the world, i.e., the United Nations' Millennium Goal, Education for All (EFA). Please know that I have the highest regard for all your endeavors to mobilize the non-governmental organizations of the world and provide them a place of visibility on this world stage. My purpose in this lecture is to reflect ethically on the moral value of your mission. Assuming that democracy is morally preferable to authoritarian governance, I will argue that the strength of a democracy depends on the quality of its civil society which in turn depends on the educational level of its citizenry. In short, civil society is an essential mark of any democracy and public education is a necessary resource for a sustained civil society.

It is a well known fact that the legitimacy of democratic governments is based on the consent of its citizens. That is to say, in every democracy those who rule are elected to their offices by the citizenry who, in turn, can vote them out of office whenever they choose to do so. In other words democratic governments belong to the people at large and not to any particular elite group. Consequently, citizens are duty bound to monitor their government regularly in order to ensure its proper functioning.

Such monitoring implies the need for a vibrant civil society which is the domain in which our ancestors fought tenaciously to reject their oppression by establishing and preserving their freedom through democratic processes of governance. In fact, the quality of any democratic society is determined by the extent to which citizens act collectively to achieve common goals. The aim of all such actions is to shape, transform, or repudiate existing public policies and identify new problems that require effective solutions.

Now civil societies occupy the space between the two natural communities into which all humans are born namely the family and the state. Since none of us choose membership in either of those natural communities, the sphere of individual freedom lies elsewhere, namely, in the civil associations that citizens choose to form. In those associations members choose whether to belong or not to belong; hence, the name "Voluntary Associations" that include such varied non-governmental associations as faith-based organizations, professional groups, labor unions, youth organizations, women's societies, advocacy organizations, social movements, political parties, to mention only a few.

Every school child in the western world is taught that democratic governance originated in the Greek city state of Athens during the fifth century BCE and gradually spread to Rome and a few other places in the ancient world. Unfortunately, those nascent democracies were relatively short lived because at that time direct governance by the people flourished best in relatively small republics and, hence, they were not able to survive in the broad geographical expanse of the Greek and Roman empires. Consequently, it was not until the eighteenth century revolutions in the United States and France that democratic governance gained firm grounding in the western world. Needless to say, perhaps, long arduous struggles and much bloodshed preceded that accomplishment.

I vividly recall visiting Nigeria while it was still under colonial rule and also visiting South Africa towards the end of the apartheid era. In both situations, the lack of vital civil societies was readily apparent. Neither country exhibited any evidence of citizens acting freely to criticize any law or public policy that had been established by its ruling authority. It seemed like a pall of fear pervaded those entire societies because their citizens did not enjoy the right of public dissent. In fact, all those who initially opposed either colonialism or apartheid were considered enemies of the state and quickly detained, imprisoned and sometimes even executed. Unfortunately, all of the so-called founding fathers of the various independence movements round the world faced a similar destiny.

Though many people in today's world view democratic government as the best of all possible alternatives, they also know that democracy does not guarantee morally good outcomes for its citizens. As a matter of fact, the earliest forms of democratic government excluded large sections of the population from exercising all the rights of citizenship. For example, the original constitution of the United States granted the franchise only to white male property owners. Both women and slaves were excluded from participation. That arrangement persisted until the 14th and 15th amendments to the constitution extended the franchise to the former males who had been enslaved. After the fall of Reconstruction in 1877, however, various states established their own laws that prohibited black men from voting and the Supreme Court eventually made racial segregation the law of the land in its 1896 Plesy v Ferguson decision. Thus, in this American democracy, the practice of racial discrimination produced a system of second class citizenship that endured until the Civil Rights Acts of 1964 and '65 were passed following a decade long life and death struggle by the Southern Christian Leadership Conference under the leadership of Dr. Martin Luther King, Jr.

Further, in the democratic societies of Europe and North America women waged long persevering struggles for the suffrage which they did not win until well into the twentieth century. In our day, most of those convicted of a felony in the United States are banned from voting for the rest of their lives. Paying their debt to society does not result in the restoration of full rights of citizenship.

As with democratic governments, the exercise of freedom by citizens in their various voluntary associations also does not guarantee morally good results. Yet, as a general rule the exercise of freedom is a greater moral good than its denial because the potentiality of human nature cannot be actualized apart from the experience of freedom. For example, the natural potential of humans to make rational choices evidences their capacity for practical reasoning which separates them from every other living species. Clearly, whenever humans are denied the exercise of that capacity their humanity is greatly diminished.

Nonetheless, both democratic governments and their respective civil societies have often joined forces to deny certain groups their full citizenship rights which invariably results in prohibiting or severely limiting their educational development. For example, in the American democracy universal education was denied enslaved Africans for two and one half centuries followed by another century of racially segregated educational facilities.

Clearly, one of the essential characteristics of authoritative political systems is that of preventing humans from acting freely and from developing their natural capacities for doing so. This is one of the primary reasons why such systems severely prohibit education among those whom they oppress while permitting it only for those selected few who are trained to serve in the administrative functions of the system. The following examples provide ample evidence of such practices: (a) the Bantu Education Act in South Africa that established an inferior educational system that prepared black Africans for a life of servitude; (b) the development of a colonial civil service system in Africa, India and elsewhere that permitted only a very small number of native peoples to receive an education that was equal to that of whites: (c) the denial of educational equality for women in both academe and the professions.

All of these endeavors demonstrate the deep fear that authoritarian rulers have for education among the people whom they choose to oppress. Now the term "education" derives from the Latin word *educere* which means to "lead out of." Thus education leads the learner out of ignorance and darkness into the light of knowledge. Thus, inevitably, the few who are permitted any measure of education in authoritarian systems soon discern that there are no innate differences between themselves and their rulers. That insight quickly motivates them to envision an alternative society where their freedom and dignity as subjects would be respected. This marks the first stage of the actualization of societal freedom.

Recent uprisings against authoritarian rulers in Tunisia, Egypt, Libya, Syria, Bahrain, and Yemen reveal the widespread discontent that has inspired educated young people to risk their lives by choosing to oppose systems that deny them their freedom. Thus, these contemporary revolutionaries are doing in our time what Americans and the French did in the latter part of the 18th century and what the peoples of Africa, India, Latin America, and elsewhere did in the twentieth century. Then and now, all such peoples engage in life and death struggles to give public expression to their desire for freedom and their endeavors to build institutions for its nurture, regulation, preservation, and expansion. Most important, this is a struggle for human dignity and self-respect. The combined endeavors of citizens provide the inspiration, legitimacy and encouragement needed for the development of legitimate civil societies where values like those specified in the United Nation's Declaration of Human Rights can be embraced, nurtured and preserved.

As stated earlier, the strength of any democracy is revealed by the quality of its civil society which, among other things, provides the conditions for citizens to evaluate the functions of their government and assess the health of their common life and destiny as a regular on-going practice. Most important, their freedoms of speech and of assembly enable them to organize freely for the redress of grievances by giving public visibility to various practices of social injustice and being strong advocates for social justice.

Apart from the advocacy of citizens there can be no major changes in their social condition because the perpetrators of injustice have no incentive to reform their practices as long as they receive benefits from them. Thus, we rightfully conclude that social change must come from the bottom up (so to speak) rather than from the top down. In other words, those who suffer injustice must become the agents of their own liberation. Others cannot and will not liberate them. Yet, this does not deny the assistance of empathetic allies which is always helpful as long as those allies do not increase the injustice by arrogantly seizing leadership from its principal agents. Doing so is always both a risk and a temptation as we presently see in the ten-year wars being fought in Iraq and Afghanistan.

As also mentioned earlier, in many democracies various groups have often been denied the freedom afforded to others because of their race, gender, religion, class, ethnicity, or some other characteristic. Undoubtedly, such inequalities create an imbalance of power in the social order between the privileged and the underprivileged. That imbalance can only be corrected by the coordinated actions of courageous men and women determined to be resolute and not shrink from the demands of the long, arduous, life-threatening struggle that confronts them. More often than not, however, such people comprise the heartbeat of civil societies. Though their actions may not always be effective, their voices of protest and cries for change nonetheless embolden all those who are treated unjustly. Martin Luther King, Jr. was altogether right when he said that "injustice anywhere is a threat to justice everywhere."

In my judgment, such empathetic people are likely to be active in various types of non-governmental organizations and especially those organizations that are affiliated with the United Nations. Invariably, such people have deep sympathies for justice in general and for all the moral concerns exemplified in the actions of the United Nations.

Now, in order for education to serve as a resource for social justice, one of its principal aims must be that of shaping the moral dispositions of those who learn. That can be done only by teachers who are moral exemplars; i.e., teachers who habitually act morally. Students must not only be encouraged to adopt the moral habits of their mentors but they should willingly desire to do so because that is the only way they can become morally good people. The culmination of good moral habits eventually results in the development of good moral character which is a settled state of moral excellence. In other words, people become moral by habitually acting in morally good ways which means embodying the moral habits of good moral exemplars. Thus, the primary moral excellences or virtues -- prudence, courage, temperance, and justice, are cultivated by habitually acting in prudent, courageous, moderate, and just ways. Whenever education is divorced from the type of moral excellence implied by the UN's Declaration of Human Rights, both individuals and the communities in which they were nurtured can become perpetrators of horrendous human oppression and injustice.

On a recent visit to New Orleans my wife and I toured the Lower Ninth Ward where thousands of its citizens suffered and died in the nation's worst flooding disaster when the levees broke in the aftermath of the 2005 Hurricane

Katrina. Sadly, those levees had been built by the Federal Government's Corps of Engineers. Thus, some had known from the beginning that they could never survive a Category #5 hurricane. Since most of the citizens of that ward were black and poor with limited education and very little leverage with the government, their situation was a disaster waiting to happen. Unfortunately, that section of the city seems to be almost forgotten in spite of all the promises to the contrary. Thus, it was not surprising to discover that much of the relief work and on-going rebuilding programs were initiated and in some cases completed by numerous non- profit organizations some of which have long-established traditions while many others are newly formed.

Since education is a *sine qua non* for improving the quality of human life, there can be no justification for denying it to anyone. Clearly, in our contemporary global world some measure of education is needed for every living person regardless of gender, race, ethnicity, economic status or any social circumstance. Its denial relegates humans to the confinement of an isolated world of privacy and destined never to contribute any enduring value to the wider community.

Thus, I greatly applaud your commitment to the UN's Millennium Goal, Education for All, and especially for the vast amount of creative thought and critical reflection you have given to this matter. While you rightfully acknowledge that governments must be the primary agency for realizing the agreed-upon goals, voluntary associations have key roles to play in mobilizing the good will of their respective nations to honor their commitments.

In my judgment, much more attention needs to be devoted to the possible role that youth organizations can play in persuading citizens and their governments to do the right thing. Let us not forget that youth have formed the vanguard of virtually every cultural and political reform movement in history as well as those presently taking place in many middle eastern countries and elsewhere. On a recent trip to South Africa I was greatly impressed by the many creative and effective strategies young people had devised for teaching their generation preventative measures against the HIV/AIDS epidemic. Thus, it seems altogether imperative that you mobilize the creative energies of young people for this important mission of impacting governments in pursuit of the Millennium Goal of Education for All. The youth of the world must be encouraged to use the most sophisticated instruments of technology with which they are well skilled to communicate the urgency of this message to governments round the world beginning with their own. The best educated and most talented among them must assume leadership in giving the widest possible publicity to this great need through visual and audible formats of videos, twitter, face book, and all other social media. Most important, they can inspire, organize and inform their own generation about the value of education more effectively than anyone else. Their imagination and energy must be harnessed for this important mission.

Further, those concerned about reaching the Millennium Goal of education by 2015 might do well to think about an idea similar to that of the Eight Goals for Africa music video composed by renowned Jazz musicians Hugh Masekela and Jimmy Dludlu of South Africa for the use of the United Nations' Millennium Goals to End Poverty by 2015. Since all of the millennium goals are interrelated, how wonderful it would be to find some famous pop artists willing to make similar contributions of their talents to this global enterprise of Education for All.

Finally, please know that there can be no more virtuous activity that that of working collectively to preserve our democracies by enhancing the quality of our civil societies and achieving the millennium goal of equal Education for All.

Delivered at the 2011 CoNGO/BWA Conference, United Nations, New York, USA

To
Proclaim Release
To
The Captives

10 | Addressing Domestic Violence in our Religious Communities

Nancy Murphy

As religious communities have long had an outstanding reputation for commitment to the sanctity of marriage and the sacredness of the family, the issues of violence and abuse in the home must be addressed! We must challenge the suffering that too many have been taught to endure within the family, or we risk supporting the message that God condones abuse.

The home is at the core of life, providing a foundation on which identity is developed, and meaningful relationships are formed with other people and with God. Violence, perpetrated in the very place intended for safety and security attacks the very design of life and outrages our Creator.

> Do you know that you are God's temple and that God's Spirit dwells in you? If anyone destroys God's temple, God will destroy that person. For God's temple is holy, and you are that temple" (1 Cor. 3:16-17).

Definitions of Domestic Violence

Laws vary in their description of domestic violence, but it is generally defined as:

- physical harm, bodily injury , assault, or the infliction of fear of imminent physical harm, bodily injury or assault of one family or household member by another; or
- sexual assault of one family or household member by another;
- stalking of one family or household member by another.

Domestic violence, family violence, partner violence, domestic abuse, spousal abuse, interpersonal partner violence – these are all terms used interchangeably to describe aspects of a similar dynamic: a pattern of assaultive or coercive behaviors that an adult or adolescent uses to gain and maintain power and control over an intimate partner, or someone in the household.

The behaviors can be physical, sexual, and psychological in nature yet all serve to establish the same thing. They serve to demonstrate who has the power and who has the control in the relationship. Once it is established, the behaviors switch in order to maintain this "understanding." A pattern emerges that while unique to each relationship is frighteningly similar to all abusive relationships.

Domestic Violence is a Learned Behavior

All those who "batter" have learned to use force through experience. When force to control a partner has been used, there have been few, if any negative consequences.

Through this experience, batterers have learned the family is a safe place to exercise their controlling behavior. Batterers often learn early in life how to gain and maintain power and control over others. Possible sources of learning include: family, peers, misinterpretations of religious teachings, media, pop culture and cultural norms. Therefore, an individual may justify battering behavior for several reasons:

- It is the right and responsibility of my "role;"
- I am entitled to use force;
- This is what I know;
- This is how I get people to listen;
- This works!

Domestic violence is not caused by:

- Anger;
- Problems in communication;
- Genetics;
- Jealousy;
- Something the victim did or did not do;
- Insecurity.

Factors that can heighten the violence or abuse:

- *Alcohol and Drug Abuse* – Both of these are highly correlated with battering, and violence appears to increase in severity when the auser is under the influence of certain drugs or alcohol.

- *Stress* – Stressors that can influence both the severity and the frequency of abuse include on-the-job tensions or unemployment, bereavement, severe illness, or other major losses.

- *Other Situational Factors* – The presence of infants or teenagers, pregnancy, and events associated with high levels of unpleasant emotions and frustation for the abuser, including holidays, doviorce and even televised sports, can also influence the severity and frequency of abuse.

Domestic violence is a choice. It is a means by which the abuser controls family members. Whether physically, sexually, emotionally, verbally or spiritually, the abuser chooses to use coercion and force to control.

The Language of "Domestic Violence" in the Bible

While the words "domestic violence" are not directly in the biblical text, there are many verses that describe abusive behaviors, commonly seen in domestic violence. These scriptures clearly call these behaviors sin.

- Jealousy, fits of rage, discord and dissensions, drunkenness, sexual immorality, impurity, debauchery, idolatry, witchcraft, hatred (Gal. 5:19-21);

- Lack of self-control, treachery, rashness, brutality, inability to acknowledge the truth (2 Tim. 3:1-5);

- Slander and verbal abuse (1 Cor. 5:11; Mk. 7:22; Mt. 5:22);

- Anger (Mt. 5:21-22);

- Lies, deceit, and falsehood (Mal. 3:5; Mt. 15-19; Rom. 1:29);

- Malice (Rom. 1:28-32; Mk. 7:22);

- Arrogance (Mk. 7:22);

- Taking advantage of others (Lev. 25:17);

- Impressing others while covering secret sin (Mt. 23:23, 28).

The Mandate of Micah 6:8

- *To act justly* – As Christians we have the responsibility to act on behalf of the oppressed;

- *To love mercy* – As Christians we are uniquely poised to provide protection for the abused and hope for change for the abuser;

- *To walk humbly with our God* – As Christians we walk with Him and care for His children as He has cared for us.

Getting Involved is Risky

"It is very tempting to take the side of the perpetrator. All the perpetrator asks is that the bystander do nothing. He appeals to the universal desire to see, hear, and speak no evil. The victim, on the contrary, asks the bystander to share the burden of the pain. The victim demands action, engagement, and remembering..." (Herman, 1997).

For the Church: Recommendations for Working with Victims and Perpetrators of Domestic Violence

"The fruit of the spirit is love, joy, peace, forbearance, kindness, goodness, faithfulness, gentleness and self-control. Against such things there is no law" (Gal. 5:22-23). In order for these fruit to be evident in the home, it is essential these goals be accomplished:

- Safety for the victim(s);

- Accountability for the abuser;

- Restoration of individuals and, IF POSSIBLE, relationships; *or*

- Mourning the loss of the relationships.

For Those Victimized by Abuse

- *Believe* the stories. The description of the violence is only the tip of the iceberg;

- *Reassure* them the abuse is not their fault; the abuse is not deserved nor is it God's will;

- *Give* referral information (i.e. domestic violence shelters and national helplines);

- *Support* and respect choices. Even if the victim is aware of the risks and chooses initially to return to the abuser, it is the individual's choice. The one who is being targeted has the most information about how to survive;

- *Encourage* to think about a safety plan;

- *Protect* confidentiality. Informing the abuser about the victim's whereabouts, discussing such matters with the congregation, prayer teams, etc., can compromise confidentiality and safety;

- *Help* with any religious concerns. Be prepared for theological questions;

- *Emphasize* that the marriage relationship God intended is shattered by domestic violence;

- *Assure* of God's love and presence, and of your commitment to walk through this valley of the shadow of death alongside the victim;

- *Help* the victim see that the abuser's violence has broken the marriage vows and that God does not want someone to remain in a situation where life and the lives of children are in danger. *If* the victim decides to separate and divorce, offer support and help to mourn the loss to the victim and the children;

- *Pray* together. Ask God for strength, courage and wisdom;

- *Prevent* from minimizing the danger. You can be a reality check. "From what you have told me, I am very much concerned for your safety;"

- *Give* information and support without telling the victim what to do;

- *Refrain* from reacting with disbelief, disgust, or anger. But don't react passively either. Let the victim know that you are concerned and that what the abuser has done is wrong and not deserved;

- *Reframe* for the victim that violence is the responsibility of the abuser. For example, if the victim is self-blaming, offer the following response: "I don't care if you did have dinner late or the house is a mess, there is no reason for someone to be violent with you;"

- *Avoid* recommending couples counseling or approaching the abusive partner to hear that person's side of the story. These actions may compromise the victim's safety;

- *Stay away* from recommending "marriage enrichment," "mediation," "communications workshop," or "anger management counseling." None of these will address the goals listed above;

- *Be aware* that sending the victim home with a prayer, a directive to be submissive, or suggestion to be a better Christian spouse can further perpetuate the abuse;

- *Avoid* prematurely encouraging the victim to forgive the abuser;

- *Do not* encourage the victim's dependence on you or become emotionally or sexually involved with the victim;

- Consult with colleagues in the wider community who may have expertise and be able to assist you in your response.

For Those Perpetrating Abuse

- *Meet* in a public place or in the church with several other people around rather than alone and/or in private;

- *Approach* the perpetrator only if you have the following: a) the victim's permission, b) the victim is aware that you plan to talk to the perpetrator and c) you are certain that the victim is safely separated from the perpetrator. Express your concern and support for the individual to be accountable and to deal with the violent behavior;

- *Address* any questions or theological rationalizations from the perpetrator;

- *Remind* the perpetrator there are no biblical excuses for abusive behavior;

- *Name* the violence as the perpetrator's problem, not the victim's. Encourage the abuser to seek help;

- *Refer* the abuser to a program which specifically addresses domestic violence intervention;

- *Stay away* from recommending "marriage enrichment," "mediation," "communications workshop," or "anger management counseling." None of these will address the goals listed above;

- *Warn* the victim if the abuser makes specific threats towards the victim;

- *Refrain* from couples' counseling with the abuser and the victim if you are aware that there is violence in the relationship;

- *Avoid* going to the perpetrator to confirm the victim's story;

- *Protect* the victim's confidentiality. Informing the abuser about the victim's whereabouts, discussing such matters with the congregation, prayer teams, etc., can compromise confidentiality and safety;

- *Watch out!* Be careful of the abusers potential for minimization, denial and/or lying about the violence. Accepting the victim is at fault or agreeing with other rationalizations for the abusive behavior can create collusion between you and the abuser;

- *Be aware!* The abusers "conversion" experience can be a way to manipulate you and the system and maintain control of the process to avoid accountability;

- *Encourage* forgiveness while honoring the goals of safety, accountability, restoration and/or mourning;

- *Stay away* from sending the abuser home with a prayer. Work with others in the community to hold the abuser accountable;

- *Be aware* that sending the abuser home with a prayer or suggestion to be a better Christian spouse can further perpetuate the abuse;

- *Encourage* the perpetrator. "You can change." "You need to follow the court orders." "You can get help;"

- *Pray* together. Ask God for strength, courage and wisdom;

- *Find* ways to collaborate with community agencies and law enforcement to hold perpetrator accountable and work together to end abuse.

Self-care Reflection

Above all, trust in the slow work of God.
We are quite naturally impatient in everything
to reach the end without delay.
We should like to skip the intermediate stages.
We are impatient of being on the way
to something unknown, something new.
Yet it is the law of all progress that is made
by passing through some stages of instability
and that may take a very long time.

And so I think it is with you.
Your ideas mature gradually. Let them grow.
Let them shape themselves without undue haste.

CHAPTER 10

Do not try to force them on
as though you could be today what time. . . .
Only God could say what this new Spirit
gradually forming in you will be.

Give our Lord the benefit of believing
that his hand is leading you,
and accept the anxiety of feeling yourself
in suspense and incomplete. ...

(Teilhard de Chardin, 2005).

Who We Are Matters!

We can be changed positively as we enter into the sorrow and heartache of domestic violence for the purposes of hope. We can also be changed negatively. In order to combat burnout, ward off apathy, and maintain your well-being:

- Trust in the slow work of God;
- Find and develop open, responsive, safe and supportive supervisory, consultative and collegial relationships;
- Create and maintain a program of self care that works and work it!

Bibliography

Herman, Judith. *Trauma and Recovery: The Aftermath of Violence—from Domestic Abuse to Political Terror.* Basic. 1997.

Teilhard de Chardin, Pierre. *Hearts on Fire: Praying with Jesuits.* Michael Harter, ed. Loyola, 2005.

11 | Reading the Hebrew Bible in Solidarity with the Palestinian People

Luis N. Rivera-Pagán

"The Bible...unlike the books of other ancient peoples, was...the literature of a minor, remote people – and not the literature of its rulers, but of its critics. The scribes and the prophets of Jerusalem refused to accept the world as it was. They invented the literature of political dissent and, with it, the literature of hope." (Elon, 1995)

"The Bible is...an incendiary device: who knows what we'd make of it, if we ever got our hands on it?" (Atwood, 1998)

Unearthing Forgotten Memories

The dreadful plight of the Palestinian nation since the 1948 and 1967 armed victories, military occupation, and territorial expansions of the newly created state of Israel (Said, 1980; Pappe, 2006) should be of prime consideration for any theology with emancipatory horizons that truly cares about the sufferings and aspirations of subjugated peoples and victimized communities (Rivera-Pagán, 2010). As the eminent African American author, Alice Walker, has recently noted after visiting Gaza: "whatever has happened to humanity, whatever is currently happening to humanity, it is happening to all of us. No matter how hidden the cruelty, no matter how far off the screams of pain and terror, we live in one world. We are one people" (Walker, 2009:35-36).

The Palestinian situation brings to the fore several crucial theological and hermeneutical issues. The search for justice, liberation and peace is essential to any authentic religious piety. The laureate Jewish-American writer, Isaac Bashevis Singer, at the end of his novella, *The Penitent*, avers: "There is a great element of protest in all religion. Those who dedicate their lives to serving God have often dared to question His justice, and to rebel against His seeming neutrality in humanity's struggle between good and evil. I feel therefore that there is no basic difference between rebellion and prayer" (Singer, 1983:169).

My purpose in this essay is to discuss briefly six hermeneutical dilemmas foregrounded by the project of reading the Hebrew sacred scriptures in the context of the actual conflict between Israel and the Palestinian people. They have to do with the following topics: Exodus and conquest; captivity, displacement, and exile; the Promised Land; the chosen people of God; the city of Jerusalem; and, finally, peace and reconciliation.

These conflictive issues are unavoidable if we are to engage genuinely in the hermeneutical circle of looking simultaneously and dialectically to both the biblical Hebrew testimonies of faith and the plight of the peoples that presently inhabit Palestine (Segundo, 1976). In the confrontation between Israel and Palestine, this circular and emancipatory hermeneutical perspective is vital due to the frequent reference to the Bible by Israeli intellectuals and political leaders in their quest to devise a transcendentally endowed national ethos (Masalha, 2007). According to Anita Shapira, a well-known Israeli scholar, "Zionism...took the Bible to its heart as the story of the formation of a nation...The Bible accorded the tender Jewish nationalism the mythic-historical foundation for conceiving the consciousness of the nation's singularity in its bond to the land of the forefathers. In an almost obvious way it [the Bible] served as proof of the 'naturalness' of the Zionist solution for the Jewish problem" (Shapira, 2006:3).

In the interpretative perspective we are adopting, the essential imperative is to remember and radicalize the prophetic words written by the imprisoned Dietrich Bonhöffer, in a note surreptitiously preserved by his friend Eberhard Bethge: "We have for once learnt to see the great events of world history from below, from the perspective of the outcast, the suspects, the maltreated, the powerless, the oppressed, the reviled – in short, from the perspective of those who suffer" (Bonhoeffer, 2000:16). This hermeneutical horizon, in constant critical and creative dialogue with contemporary liberation theologies and postcolonial theories (Moore & Segovia, 2005:23-78), is strikingly analogous to Edward Said's representation of the intellectual as a person who unearths "the memory of forgotten voices...of the poor, the disadvantaged, the voiceless, the unrepresented, the powerless" (Said, 1996:35,113). Its original source is an admonition on countless occasions reiterated by the Hebrew Bible, or *Tanakh*, itself: "Speak out for those who cannot speak, for the rights of all the destitute...defend the rights of the poor and needy" (Prov. 31:8-9).

Exodus and Conquest

Liberation theologies all over the world have focused on the biblical Exodus story as a key emancipatory hermeneutical paradigm (Croatto, 1981; Pixley, 1987). Yet, they have usually evaded the sinister dimensions of its accompanying story: the conquest of Canaan and its concomitant destruction of the Canaanite communities (Prior, 2000:1-12). Edward Said noticed this omission ("the injunction laid on the Jews by God to exterminate their opponents") in a critical review of Michael Walzer's much-read book, *Exodus and Revolution*, which he indicts as "so undialectical, so simplifying, so ahistorical and reductive." The exalting view of the Exodus biblical as a process of redemption of the Hebrew slaves oftentimes eludes the ethnic cleansing and genocide of the indigenous Canaanites and "minimizes, if it does not completely obliterate, a sense of responsibility for what a people undergoing Redemption does to other less fortunate people, unredeemed, strange, displaced and outside moral concern" (Walzer, 1985; cf. Said, 1986). This critical perspective might lead to read the Exodus/conquest biblical narratives "with the eyes of the Canaanites" (Prior, 2006).

Palestinian theological hermeneutics is able to foreground this usually silenced ominous dimension of the Exodus story, both in its biblical context – the atrocious rules of warfare that prescribed forced servitude or annihilation for the population encountered in Israel's route to the "promised land" (Deut. 20:10-17) – and in the present historical circumstances wherein the Palestinian people are harshly mistreated by the state of Israel. The narration of the massacre of the inhabitants of Jericho (Josh. 6:21) is chilling and dreadful: "Then they devoted to destruction by the edge of the sword all in the city, both men and women, young and old...". From a Palestinian perspective, the Exodus story can be read contrapuntally, the way that Edward Said, for example, analyses Albert Camus's occlusion of Algeria and the Algerians in several of his most important literary texts (*La Peste*, *L'Étranger*), though they take place in that specific Maghreb nation (Said, 1993:66-67).

In the biblical narrative of the Israelite invasion and conquest of Canaan, the indigenous communities were perceived as potential sources of ethnic, religious, and ethical contamination. The Hebrew tribes thus claimed divine right to displace, expel, and exterminate them: "As for the towns of these peoples that the Lord your God is giving you as an inheritance, you must not let anything that breathes remain alive. You shall annihilate them...just as the Lord your God has commanded" (Deut. 20:16f). A similar commandment is given to King Saul regarding the complete extermination of Amalek: "Now go and attack Amalek, and utterly destroy all that they have; do not spare them, but kill both man and woman, child and infant, ox and sheep, camel and donkey" (I Sam. 15:3). The divine mandate is to destroy even the historical remembrance of its existence: "You must blot out the memory of Amalek under heaven. Do not forget" (Deut. 25:19). Saul provokes God's wrath by not fulfilling completely this genocidal decree. Regarding the Midian kingdom, the divine order is to kill all its male inhabitants, including "the little ones," and all the women who have "known a man by sleeping with him" (Num. 31:17). Only the "young girls who have not known a man by sleeping with him" are to be spared. The God of grace, blessing, and redemption mutates into the God of wrath, curse, and devastation.

Later writings will attempt to explain and justify the annihilation of those peoples adducing their intertwined vices of idolatry and moral aberration. "For the idea of making idols was the beginning of fornication, and the invention of them was the corruption of life" (Wisd. of Sol. 14:12; see also 12:3-7 and 14:27). The purpose of these vindictive texts and genocidal commandments is to protect Israel from possible contamination by the collusion of religious impurity and moral perversion prevailing in the Canaanite nations. It constitutes a divine declaration of anathema (*herem*) against peoples whose impurity might pollute God's elected nation. An analogous attitude can be found in the process of reconstructing Jerusalem and the temple, as narrated by Ezra 9-10 and Nehemiah 13:23-30, resulting in the merciless expulsion of the foreign wives and their children in service of the xenophobic principle of ethnic purity as an absolute prerequisite for moral integrity and religious fidelity (Steicke, 2011). These are truly, in Phyllis Trible's apt phrase, "texts of terror" (Trible, 1984).

Dreadful resonances of this lethal and discriminatory outlook are found in the writings of some Spanish theologians and jurists during the sixteenth-century Iberian conquest of the Americas (Rivera-Pagán, 1992), in several admonitions of British theologians regarding the Native Americans of North America (Bosch, 2002) in the way certain South African Boers preachers looked at Black Africans, as well as in the proclamations of many contemporary Zionists who quote those biblical texts to legitimate their aspiration for a Greater Israel (*Eretz Israel*) sanitized from any possible "contamination" by Palestinians (Akenson, 1992; Prior, 1997).

The Hebrew Bible is thus transformed into a sacred vindicating source for the conquest of *Eretz Israel*, as a divinely awarded patrimony exclusively for the Jewish people, which also legitimates the dispossession of the new Canaanites, the Palestinians. The *Tanakh*, in this interpretative scheme, plays a twin role: it serves to construe the unity of the nation of Israel across millennia, from Abraham to David Ben-Gurion, and it gives to that national community exclusive proprietary rights over the land of Canaan/Palestine. The ultimate goal of this specific hermeneutics might just be to masquerade ethnic cleansing and displacement with a prestigious Biblical justification. As Nur Masalha, a distinguished Palestinian scholar and writer, has affirmed: "Inspired by a fundamentalist interpretation of the Old Testament, especially the books of Exodus, Deuteronomy and Joshua, their discourse [the Zionists'] presents ethnic cleansing as not only legitimate, but as required by the divinity" (Masalha, 2007:157). The Bible defeats, in this perspective, the second part of the 1917 Balfour Declaration that committed the British government to "the establishment in Palestine of a national home for the Jewish people...it being clearly understood that nothing shall be done which may prejudice the civil and religious rights of existing non-Jewish communities..." (Prior, 1999:13).

We are, thus, obliged to consider carefully and critically the ominous dimensions of the Exodus biblical narratives if we are to be faithful to the divine covenant of doing righteousness and pursuing justice. Otherwise, one might be complicit in evading the nefarious narrative proximity of the Exodus story and the tragic fate of the indigenous population inhabiting "the promised land that flows with milk and honey."

Captivity, Displacement, and Exile

From the painful memory of the *al-nakba* (the "great catastrophe"), Palestinian theology is able to highlight the biblical topos of exile, displacement, dispersion, and captivity, the crucial historical matrices of the biblical scriptures, as meaningful loci of theological enunciation and reflection. The heart-breaking experience of devastation, dispersion, and dislocation are at the core of the Hebrew sacred scriptures.

> How lonely sits the city that once was full of people! How like a widow she has become, she that was great among the nations!... Judah has gone into exile with suffering and hard servitude; she lives now among the nations, and finds no resting place. (Lam. 1:1,3)

The Hebrew Bible seems to have been composed, edited and reconfigured, after the traumatic experience of the Babylonian exile. It is from the sufferings entailed by national defeat, devastation, the destruction of the holy places, and exile (*galut*) that the biblical sacred scriptures emerge, fueled by the need and desire to remember, to preserve the memory of God as the ultimate source of liberation and of the desperate but obstinate hope for a peaceful return to the lost homeland (Smith-Christopher, 2002). Contrary to other ancient Middle East sacred scriptures, written by courtly scribes and characterized by their laudatory paeans to the national authorities, the Bible arises from the tragic experience of exile and captivity and evokes the flaws and misdeeds of the Israelite and Judean monarchs. They are sacred scriptures precisely because they surge and arise from a displaced people, who recall with profound sadness the devastation of their homes and places of worship and their forceful uprooting, but that do not abdicate their divinely inspired hopes for restitution. Exile, deportation, and captivity become the subterranean sources of liberative theological meditation and creativity of the remembrance of God as the Liberator (Steiner, 1996; de Wit, 2002; Boff, 1975).

In the Gospel According to Luke, the destruction of Jerusalem and the painful displacement and dispossession of its inhabitants, after the defeat of the Jewish rebellion against the Romans (66 – 70 CE), are constantly alluded to as a reason for Jesus's profound sadness, who mourns with heart-breaking lamentations the tragic fate of the people: "As he [Jesus] came near and saw the city [Jerusalem], he wept over it...the days will come upon you, when your enemies will set up ramparts around you and surround you, and hem you on every side. They will crush you to the ground, you and your children within you, and they will not leave within you one stone upon another..." (Lk. 19:41-44). Defeat, exile, and dispersion constitute the historical matrices also for the New Testament, the Christian sacred scriptures.

It has been an expatriate Palestinian, Edward Said, who with his typical literary eloquence, has described, like perhaps nobody else since the biblical psalmist, the plight and grief of exile, the painful dilemma of displacement: "Exile is strangely compelling to think about but terrible to experience. It is the unhealable rift forced between a human being and a native place, between the self and its true home: its essential sadness can never be surmounted" (Said, 2002:173). It situates the exiled person in a strange situation of being perennially "out of place," to refer to the title of Said's personal memoir (Said, 1999).

Israeli policy on Palestine has been neatly encapsulated in the formula "maximum land and minimum Arabs." The deportation and removal of the Palestinians has been a tragic but almost historically unavoidable consequence of the ideological structure of Jewish Zionism as a theological colonial nationalism. Those who for almost two millennia suffered the plight of exclusion and disdain, in their national resurgence and quest for a homeland have become, paradoxically and ironically, the perpetrators of new acts of dispersion and exile. And they do it in the name of their sacred traditions and their heritage of perseverance in the difficult predicament of diasporic displacement.

The Zionists' various strategies of dispossession and expulsion (usually sweet-termed as "transfer") have been radical: their goal has been not only to reclaim what they consider Israel's ancestral homeland, not only to dislodge the Arab indigenes, but something deeper: to erase the memory of the former presence of the ousted communities, to eliminate all the vestiges of a non-Israeli Palestine. The Palestinian indigenous inhabitants were expelled, their houses looted, destroyed or appropriated, their agricultural fields confiscated, their holy places desecrated. A cartographic discourse of Hebraization and Judaization was systematically put into place to obliterate traces and remnants from the Palestinian birthplace and to establish a new hegemonic experience of the land, intimately associated with Hebrew biblical resonances (Benenisti, 2000). Its intended objective was to eradicate the Palestinian people's historical ties with its homeland, truly an ideologically motivated memoricide. As Ilan Pappe, the dissident Israeli historian, has asserted: "The human geography of Palestine as a whole was forceably transformed...This transformation was driven by the desire to wipe out one nation's history and culture" (Pappe, 2006:216). Palestine is a palimpsest of memories wherein Israeli leaders pretend to inscribe an exclusive Jewish narrative, wistfully reconnected to the biblical geography and history, while simultaneously trying to occlude all the remnants and vestiges of the centuries' old former Arab communities. That project of erasure, however, is not always totally successful, as Hanna Musleh's fine documentary film, *Memory of the Cactus – A Story of Three Palestinian Villages* (2008), so graphically demonstrates.

Exile, an important feature of human historical experience and a vital source of the biblical sacred scriptures, becomes in Palestine a crucial philosophical and theological concern. Exile is, in the poetic words of Mahmoud Darwish, a "journal of an ordinary grief" (Darwish, 2010). In many Palestinian hearts and souls the nostalgic sadness inscribed in Darwish's verses from "I See What I Want to See" resonates with uncanny familiarity:

> There is no place on earth where we haven't pitched our tent of exile...
>
> Longing is the place of exile. Our love is a place of exile.
>
> Our wine is a place of exile
>
> and a place of exile is the history of this heart.

How many times have we told the trees

of the place to wipe off the invader's mask

so we might find a place? ...

Poetry is a place of exile.

The Promised Land

The geographical territory that Christians traditionally call Holy Land, Muslims name Palestine, and Jews designate as Israel, has been during many centuries a source of passionate and violent conflicts, truly a land of blood and tears (Brueggemann, 2002; Marchadour & Neuhaus, 2007). In the name of Yahweh, Allah, or Christ, ferocious warriors have bitterly clashed and fought for its possession and dominion.

God's promise of the land of Canaan to Abraham, according to the Hebrew sacred scriptures, is a basic tenet of the Zionist claim that the entire land of Palestine belongs by divine right to the Jewish people, more precisely to Israel as the Jewish state (Piterberg, 2008; Sizer, 2005; Smith, 2011). Genesis 12:1-7 ("To your offspring I will give this land"), 15:18-21 ("To your descendants I give this land"), and 17:1-8 ("I will give to you, and to your offspring, the land where your are now an alien, all the land of Canaan, for a perpetual holding...") reproduce several versions of God's promise to Abraham that Canaan will be the everlasting possession of his progeny. This is the biblical mythical/historical basis for Israel's claim of proprietary rights over the land of Palestine. As Hanan Porat, one of the founders of Gush Emunim ("Bloc of the Faithful") movement and a conservative Israeli politician, once asserted: "For us the Land of Israel is a Land of destiny, a chosen Land...It is the Land from which the voice of God has called to us ever since that first call to the first Hebrew: 'Come and go forth from your Land where you were born and from your father's house to the Land that I will show you'" (Masalha, 2007:138).

There is, however, an inner paradoxical tension in this biblical divine promise. Supposedly, in its fulfillment "all the families of the earth shall be blessed" (Gen. 12:3); yet many communities and nations already inhabit the land where Abraham is "now an alien". What, then, might be the destiny of the peoples and nations that are supposed to be blessed by the conquest and perpetual occupation of their land by Abraham's descendants?

The dispossession of the Palestinians has been defended by attributing to them the alleged decadence and defilement of the land before its redeeming Jewish colonization. The Promised Land has been transmogrified, according to this argument, into a Wasted Land. Mark Twain's pejorative description of Palestine, included in his book, *The Innocents Abroad* (1869), has been quoted by several Israeli leaders to justify the displacement of the indigenous population.

> Palestine sits in sackcloth and ashes. Over it broods the spell of a curse that has withered its fields and fettered its energies... Bethlehem and Bethany, in their poverty and their humiliation, have nothing about them now to remind one that they once knew the high honor of the Savior's presence...Renowned Jerusalem itself, the stateliest name in history, has lost all its ancient grandeur, and is become a pauper village; the riches of Solomon are no longer there to compel the admiration of visiting Oriental queens; the wonderful temple which was the pride and the glory of Israel, is gone...Palestine is desolate and unlovely. And why should it be otherwise? Can the curse of the Deity beautify a land? (Twain, 1869).

When Theodor Herlz, one of the main founders of political Zionism, wrote, in *The Jewish State*, "Palestine is our unforgettable historic homeland" (Marchadour & Neuhaus, 2007:127), two conflicting perspectives were brought to a horizon of violent confrontation. On one side, the Jewish people, scattered, ghettoed, and disdained in the melancholy of exile, forever preserving in their Diaspora (*Golah*) the memory of Zion as its birthright homeland by divine concession and liturgically proclaiming annually that they will gather again "next year in Jerusalem." On the other, the indigenous Arab inhabitants of Palestine, perpetual victims of successive foreign empires, upholding their profound sense of ancestral belonging and who could also claim, "Palestine is our unforgettable historic homeland." Whose, then, is the Promised Land? As it happens so many times in human history, that question has received contradictory answers, supported simultaneously by deeply rooted religious convictions and aggressive military strategies.

Palestinian theologians have been able to respond critically to the employment of the Hebrew Bible to justify Israel's policies of appropriation and exclusion, under the theological pretext that Palestine is supposedly the land promised by God to its biblical ancestors. After all, it is impossible to evade or sideline the prophetic core of the Hebrew sacred scriptures, with their indissoluble linkage of the knowledge of God and the deeds of justice (Jer. 22:16) and its emphasis on solidarity and compassion with the most vulnerable sectors of society – the poor, the widows, the orphans, the strangers (Jer. 7:4-7) – as the main expression of faithful obedience to God's will. According to the Hebrew prophets, the possession of the land is indissolubly connected with a covenant between its inhabitants and God: a pact of justice, mercifulness and solidarity. The violation of that covenant forfeits the right to posses the land. All the biblical narratives, be they juridical, historical, or prophetic, strongly express God's disavowal of Israel's endemic structures of social injustice and, therefore, call their hearers/readers to engage in resistance against them.

How can the *Tanakh* be quoted to justify the aggressive military actions of the actual state of Israel when those same sacred scriptures constantly rebuke and condemn the authorities of biblical Israel due to its unjust policies and oppressive actions? (Pixley, 2009:24). Compare the condemnation of king Jehoiakim in 2 Chronicles 36:5 ("He did what was evil in the sight of the LORD his God") with Jeremiah's invective against the same monarch's social policies: "your eyes and heart are only...for practicing oppression and violence" (Jer. 22:17). Both critical assessments take place under the shadow of the ominous Chaldean threat, perceived by the scribes in charge of narrating the history of Israel as a divine punishment against that nation's oppressive social structures (2 Chr. 36:14-17). As Walter J. Houston has noted, "This is the point on which the logic of the prophetic rhetoric pivots. YHWH destroys oppressors; the oppressors denounced in the oracles of judgment were representative of the Israelite kingdoms; this accounts, in the structure of the prophetic books as wholes, for the downfall of those kingdoms" (Houston, 2006:94).

There is a dialectical relationship between the biblical promise of land and the communal commitment to justice. As Alain Marchadour and David Neuhaus have appropriately written: "*mishpat* [justice] and *tsedaka* [doing righteousness]... summarize the requirements for living out God's will on the Land and they bear witness against and denounce the violations that are too often committed by Israel" (Marchadour & Neuhaus, 2007:19). They are probably right when they emphasize that the issues at stake in the prophetic denunciations of Israel's conduct "have less to do with offenses committed against God...than with injustices inflicted on the poor..." (Marchadour & Neuhaus, 2007:76).

The Chosen People of God

The theme of the "chosen people of God" has been a classic theological quandary. The first biblical confession of faith begins thus: "A wandering Aramean was my ancestor; he went down into Egypt and lived there as an alien...When the Egyptians treated us harshly and afflicted us, by imposing hard labor on us, we cried to the Lord, the God of our ancestors; the Lord heard our voice and saw our affliction, our toil, and our oppression" (Deut. 26:5-7). This is evidently an etiological narrative; it is an account of the origin of a special people, the people of God. But the question arises: Who are the authentic descendants of that wandering Aramean, ancestor of a divinely "chosen people"?

In Palestine, two conflicting views regarding this matter clash. Many Zionists allege that the Jews, wherever they are, and whatever their ethnic, cultural or linguistic heritage (Ashkenazi or Sephardic; Yiddish, Russian, or Arabic speakers), constitute the elected nation endowed with the divinely decreed legal obligations (the *Halakhah*) and privileges (mainly the possession of Palestine as *Eretz Israel*). They constitute a privileged genealogy of the biblical patriarchs. Israel's laws of return and nationality are based upon this premise of an ethnological distinction (Said, 1986:103). The term ethnocracy has been coined to describe this perspective (Yiftachel, 2006). This is, in the words of Shlomo Sand, "the active myth of an eternal nation [Israel] that must ultimately forgather in its ancestral land" (Sand, 2010:22). God's promises to Abraham, Isaac and Jacob are perceived as a divine legitimizing source for Israel's charter of exclusive national privilege for the Jewish people, but also as the transcendental justification for the displacement and opprobrium suffered by the Palestinians. Ironically, the theological nexus of a divinely elected people and an ancestral homeland, so intensely insisted upon by several Israeli advocates, seems uncomfortably evocative of the German Nazi *Blut und Boden* ideology, so fateful during the twentieth century for the European Jewish communities.

The history of Israel from this perspective is transfigured in a series of constructed narratives devoid of the disturbing presence of the Palestinian indigenous communities. The Palestinian indigenes are occluded, for they do not to belong to God's "elected" nation. They are not only displaced from their homeland; they are dislodged also from true history, or at least from the historical drama that occurs between God, the divinely chosen people, and the Promised Land, as construed by so many Israeli scholars and politicians.

A new people of God, the *Sabras*, the New Jews, are conceived as the only genuine historical agents in the "redeemed" land of Ancient Israel. The history of the "Others," of the Palestinian communities is marginalized, silenced (Trouillot, 1995; Whitelam, 1996). Not only their land is confiscated, their bodies expelled and their civic rights curtailed; their historical memory is also expunged, excised. The dominant collective narrator tries to impede or expunge other alternate and subaltern narratives (Said, 1993:xiii). Or, at least, that seems to be the prevailing project of identity politics in mainstream Israel, especially after the decline of the old socialist and leftist ideological dimensions of Zionism.

There is, however, a different perspective. The already-quoted biblical first statement of faith does not necessarily emphasize an alleged biological ancestry. Its crucial point is that there was an enslaved, subjugated, and exploited people and that God, after paying compassionate attention to their sorrowful cries, liberates them. It is not the flesh, but the socio-historical fate of Abraham's seed that defines the belongingness to God's elected people. The concept of "chosen people of God," therefore, does not allude to an absurd DNA genetic analysis, or ethno-racial lineage (Sand, 2010:256-280). It rather evokes a hermeneutic of oppression and liberation. The people of God are those who oppressed, in a seemingly hopeless situation, pray, hope, and struggle for liberation and redemption (Ellis, 2004; Ateek, 1989; Dabashi, 2008; Prior, 1995). What happens in Palestine is a reenactment of the traditional confrontation between two different perspectives: the consciousness of the victors and the consciousness of the victims. In a complex historical irony, "the classic victims of years of anti-Semitic persecution and the Holocaust have in their new nation become the victimizers of another people, who have become, therefore, the victims of the victims" (Said, 1980:xxi). But the Bible, let us not forget, tells the story of a God who stands with the victims against their victimizers.

Shlomo Sand, the Israeli dissident scholar, has asked a pertinent question: "To what extent is Jewish Israeli society willing to discard the deeply embedded image of the 'chosen people' and to cease...excluding the 'other' from its midst?" (Sand, 2010:312f). This change might be required not only to strengthen the democratic character of Israeli society, which is Sand's objective, but also and mainly to deepen its ethical texture. Reinhold Niebuhr contrasted, in a North American theological classic text, "moral man" with "immoral society" (Niebuhr, 1932), but God's Torah, according to the Hebrew prophets, requires a social life according to the strict norms of *mishpat* and *tsedaka*, justice and righteousness (Marchadour & Neuhaus, 2007:49). It prescribes a "moral society," a society where solidarity and compassion constitute the main rules for judging the conduct of the authority and power. Belonging to God's "chosen people," therefore, is not a privilege or a badge of honor, but rather a difficult to satisfy and formidable challenge, as the prophet Amos hinted when he told Israel: "You only I have known of all the families of the earth; therefore I will punish you for all your iniquities." (Amos 3:2)

The sacred scriptures have always proved to be a perilous minefield for all those who attempt to use it to legitimize or justify acts of conquest, domination, or exploitation (Horsley, 2008; Gottwald, 1983). As the Israeli writer Amos Elon has eloquently emphasized: "The Bible...unlike the books of other ancient peoples, was...the literature of a minor, remote people – and not the literature of its rulers, but of its critics. The scribes and the prophets of Jerusalem refused to accept the world as it was. They invented the literature of political dissent and, with it, the literature of hope" (Elon, 1995:19).

Decades ago, the German Marxist philosopher Ernst Bloch asserted provocatively that reading the Bible should be an imperative for every one whose life is devoted to the quest of liberty and justice for the oppressed (Bloch, 1968). To the astonishment of many Marxists, he insisted upon the basic prophetic and subversive character of the Bible. Bloch's heterodox assessment of the revolutionary potentialities of the Bible was written before the books usually considered as originators of liberation theology, authored by James Cone, Gustavo Gutiérrez or Hugo Assmann, were published. This is the hermeneutical key to recognize the authentic people of God. For, as Gutiérrez has affirmed: "The entire Bible, beginning with the story of Cain and Abel, mirrors God's predilection for the weak and abused of human history" (Gutiérrez, 1988:xxvii). God's truly chosen people, therefore, is defined not by genetic inheritance, but by obedience of the divine command: "Give justice to the weak and the orphan; maintain the right of the lowly and the destitute. Rescue the weak and the needy; deliver them from the hand of the wicked." (Ps. 82:3-4)

Israel's Zionists reiterate emphatically the restorative promise of Amos 9:14f:

> I will restore the fortunes of my people Israel, and they shall rebuild the ruined cities and inhabit them; they shall plant vineyards and drink their wine, and they shall make gardens and eat their fruit. I will plant them upon their land, and they shall never again be plucked up out of their land that I have given them, says the Lord your God.

But they tend to silence and occlude the severe critiques that same prophet Amos utters against Israel for her deeds of wickedness and injustice, actions that nullify its self-designation as "God's chosen people."

Jerusalem, Sacred and Sanguinary

As Naim Ateek has underscored, "the history of Jerusalem has been written with blood" (Ateek, 2009:140). In its long and tempestuous history, Jerusalem has been both blessed and cursed due to its recognition as sacred by the three Abrahamic monotheistic religions (Judaism, Islam and Christianity). For centuries they have considered it a "holy city," sanctified by the divine presence. Medieval cosmography and cartography situated Jerusalem as both the geographical and spiritual center of the world. It was perceived as the navel (*omphalos*) of the world, the *axis mundi*. This tradition arose from a literal reading of Ezekiel 5:5 – "Thus says the Lord God: This is Jerusalem; I have set her in the center of the nations, with countries all around her." The following verse, however, indicates the conflictive character of the history of this most holy city: "But she has rebelled against my ordinances and my statutes, becoming more wicked than the nations and the countries all around her, rejecting my ordinances and not following my statutes" (Ezek. 5:6). The blessed sacred city of God has become, so is the prophetic judgment, a cursed city of sin, where corruption and injustice prevails: "How the faithful city has become a whore!... Your princes are rebels and companions of thieves. Everyone loves a bribe and runs after gifts. They do not defend the orphan, and the widow's cause does not come before them" (Isa. 1:21, 23).

Jeremiah's admonitory words regarding the mystification of the Temple are, in this context, unforgettable: "Hear the word of the Lord, all you people of Judah, you that enter these gates to worship the Lord. Thus says the Lord of hosts, the God of Israel: Amend your ways and your doings, and let me dwell with you in this place. Do not trust in these deceptive words: 'This is the temple of the Lord, the temple of the Lord, the temple of the Lord'" (Jer. 7:2-4). If the religious rituals and liturgical ceremonies performed in the sacred sites displace obedience to the Torah and its norms of justice and righteousness, then the worship of God transmogrify into veneration of a Satanic idol and a source of dreadful strife.

The constant destruction and devastation of Jerusalem, by the Babylonian or the Roman armies, its nostalgic remembrance, and the expectation of its restitution, is the religious and historical matrix of the Bible. The Israeli author Amos Elon has magnificently described how the intense religious feelings evoked by Jerusalem (where the Church of the Holy Sepulcher [or Church of the Resurrection as called by Eastern Christians], the Wailing Wall, the Dome of the Rock, and the Al-Aqsa mosque are located) has transfigured it, in the active imagination of countless believers, pilgrims, holy warriors, and crusaders, into a dangerous, cruel, and bloody land, like perhaps no other city in human history (Elon, 1995; Armstrong, 1996; Montefiore, 2011). Jews, Muslims and Christians have claimed that it was there, in old sacred Jerusalem, where Adam and Eve were fashioned at the beginning of biblical times, where the stone for the unfulfilled sacrifice of Isaac by Abraham was located, and where Muhammad ascended to heaven. In his typical provocative style, James Carroll avers that for "Jews and Christians both, *the destruction of Jerusalem is what...defines the heart of our religion*" (Carroll, 2011:110f).

Many Jews, Christians, and Muslims have invoked the famous sorrowful words of the nostalgic biblical hymn to the lost city: "How could we sing the Lord's song in a foreign land? If I forget you, O Jerusalem, let my right hand wither! Let my tongue cling to the roof of my mouth, if I do not remember you, if I do not set Jerusalem above my highest joy" (Ps. 137:4-6). A magnificent lament, indeed! But let us not forget the revengeful last verses of that paean to the sacred city, when the lament is transmuted into vindictive and cruel hatred: "O daughter Babylon, you devastator! Happy shall they be who pay you back what you have done to us! Happy shall they be who take your little ones and dash them against the rock" (Ps. 137:8-9).

Paradoxically, the sacred nature attributed to Jerusalem has been for centuries a reason for extremely violent and sanguinary confrontations. Its sacred sites – the Wailing Wall, remnant of the destroyed second Temple of Yahweh, the Church of the Holy Sepulcher, the Al-Haram Al-Sharif (Noble Sanctuary), enclosing the Dome of the Rock and the Al-Aqsa mosque – places of worship to the divine Spirit, creator and redeemer, have frequently mutated into zones of hatred and warfare. Pilgrims, crusaders and jihadists have arrived at its famous gates "with love in their hearts, the end of the world in their minds, and weapons in their hands" (Carroll, 2011:1). Naomi Shemer's song, "Jerusalem of Gold," composed in the context of the 1967 conquest of East Jerusalem and the old city and which has become sort of a second Israeli national anthem, expresses the outburst of the contemporary nationalistic aspiration of Jerusalem as exclusively a Jewish sacred city.

> Jerusalem of gold, and of light and of bronze,
>
> I am the lute for all your songs.
>
> The wells are filled again with water,
>
> The square with joyous crowd,
>
> On the Temple Mount within the City,
>
> The shofar rings out loud.

Pope Urban II's famous and fateful speech at the Council of Clermont (27 November 1095) is a classic expression of the heinous mixture of the sacred and the sanguinary whenever the mater of contention happens to be Jerusalem. The Pope calls the Frankish knights, so proud of their warring traditions, to rescue Jerusalem, the city honored by the death and resurrection of Christ, from the impure hands of "an accursed race, a race utterly alienated from God."

Oh, most valiant soldiers...Enter upon the road to the Holy Sepulchre; wrest that land from the wicked race...Jerusalem is the navel of the world...This the Redeemer of the human race has made illustrious by His advent, has beautified by residence, has consecrated by suffering, has redeemed by death, has glorified by burial. This royal city, therefore, situated at the centre of the world, is now held captive by His enemies, and is in subjection to those who do not know God...She seeks therefore and desires to be liberated, and does not cease to implore you to come to her aid... Accordingly undertake this journey for the remission of your sins, with the assurance of the imperishable glory of the kingdom of heaven...It is the will of God!

Do we have the spiritual and intellectual resources to reconfigure the debate in such a way that the concepts of "holy city" and "holy land" might become a basis for dialogue, reciprocal respect, understanding and solidarity among the three great Abrahamic monotheistic religions? In the book of Revelation, the main core of the eschatological "new heaven and new earth," is a "new Jerusalem, coming down out of heaven from God, prepared as a bride adorned for her husband" (Rev. 21:2). This "new Jerusalem" will become a "home of God among mortals" (Rev. 21:3; cf. Isa. 65:17-19). Jerusalem, in the biblical apocalyptic perspective, will be the sacred city where the nations, at the end of times, will gather to praise and worship God in peace. (Zech. 8:20: "Many peoples and strong nations shall come to seek the Lord of hosts in Jerusalem, and to entreat the favor of the Lord." Isa. 56:7: "These I will bring to my holy mountain...for my house shall be called a house of prayer for all peoples.")

As the Palestinian *Kairos*, so movingly affirms: "Jerusalem is the heart of our reality. It is, at the same time, symbol of peace and sign of conflict...Jerusalem, city of reconciliation, has become a city of discrimination and exclusion, a source of struggle rather than peace" (*Kairos*, 2009:1.1.8). The fate of the diverse peoples inhabiting and sharing Palestine depend, in large part, upon the success or failure of the endeavor to allow peace to prevail upon conflict and strife in Jerusalem. Yehuda Amichai's poem, "If I Forget Thee, Jerusalem," faithfully mirrors the nostalgia that too many Jews, Muslims, and Christians deeply feel for their beloved holy city:

> If I forget thee, Jerusalem,
> Let my blood be forgotten.
> I shall touch your forehead,

Forget my own,
My voice change
For the second and last time
To the most terrible of voices –
Or silence.

Peace and Reconciliation

Palestinian theology, maybe more emphatically than other liberation theologies, emphasizes the intertwining of justice and reconciliation, truth-telling and forgiveness, prophetic denunciation and peacemaking annunciation, severe critique and hopeful aspiration. The ultimate purpose of the prophetic denunciation is neither the destruction nor the humiliation of the enemy, but the fulfillment of Isaiah's forecast of a new creation, a world free of bellicose violence and devastation, where the conflicting communities, Palestinian and Israeli, Jewish, Christian, and Muslim: "shall build houses and inhabit them; they shall plant vineyards and eat their fruit. They shall not build and another inhabit; they shall not plant and another eat...They shall not labor in vain, or bear children for calamity; for they shall be offspring blessed by the Lord – and their descendants as well..." (Isa. 65:21-23). And war will be no more: "they shall beat their swords into plowshares, and their spears into pruning hooks; nation shall not lift up sword against nation, neither shall they learn war any more" (Isa. 2:4).

This a dream shared by many Israelis and Palestinians, be they Jews, Muslims, Christians or non-believers. A dream of peace and reconciliation. It is the aspiration of two peoples with severely wounded memories: the memory of the *Shoah* and the memory of the *Al-nakba* (Longerich, 2010; Khalidi, 2006; Pappe, 2006; Masalha, 1992). Rightly has Judith Butler highlighted: "Exile may be in fact be a point of departure for thinking about cohabitation..." Butler, 2011:3). The traumatic and heartrending experience of devastation, persecution, and exile, suffered by both Jews and Palestinians can and should be construed as historical reasons for dialogue rather than conflict. This hopeful aspiration promises to become a main tenet of creative Palestinian theologies (Ateek, 1989:163-175; Raheb,1995:112-116; Ateek, 2009:153-187). As the Palestinian *Kairos* concludes: "We say that love is possible and mutual trust is possible. Thus, peace is possible and definitive reconciliation also. Thus, justice and security will be attained for all" (*Kairos*, 2009:9.1).

Whenever Christians recall Jesus's first public exposition of who he was and what his mission was, according to the Gospel of Luke (4:14-21), with its easy to recognize reference to Isaiah 61:1-2, attention should be paid not only to the concordances between both texts, but also to a significant and crucial omission. Jesus concludes his elocution with the proclamation, in his being and deeds, of "the year of the Lord's favor" (Lk. 4:19), a time of liberation of the oppressed and captives, an obvious quotation of Isaiah 61:2a. But he leaves out the prophet's ominous ending – "and the day of vengeance of our God" (61:2b). Jesus's being and mission is therefore liberation *and* reconciliation, not liberation and violent retribution or vengeance (Bosch, 2011:108-113).

Certainly, one can find, in many religious canonical scriptures, ominous and sinister images of divine exclusion and sacred violence against those who allegedly contaminate the integrity and purity of religious, national, or ethnic identity. Israeli punitive wars, Christian Crusades, Islamic Jihad, oppressive servitudes, despotic hierarchies, and intolerances of all kinds and types have claimed legitimacy by alluding to sacred texts. They have, too easily, "found justification for savagery in sanctified appeals to the will of God" (Carroll, 2011:164f). The idolatry of the "Word of God" has been used to devastate solidarities, consciences, hopes, and human lives (Schwartz, 1997; Armstrong, 2000; Juergensmeyer, 2000; Ali, 2002). But, those "texts of terror" are neither the decisive nor the predominant ones in most religious myths and symbols. Genuine religious thought, reflecting on the destiny of human history, does not emphasize the sinister symbols of Armageddon and their horsemen of terror, but the hopes for human liberation and universal reconciliation.

In the delicate and sensitive process of dialogue and reconciliation taking place between Israel and Palestine, Christians should be aware of the suffering and pain caused by the not-too- subtle anti-Semitism ensconced in the way some of the New Testament writings, like the Gospel of John (Pagels, 1995), construe Jesus' fate, intensified by the way those texts have been read and applied during two millennia, in which the Jews were accused of "deicide" (Chrysostrom, 1979). However, this deplorable history of Christian Judeophobia should not be a pretext for ignoring the human rights violations of the Palestinian people by the modern state of Israel. Sadly, the West has gone from one kind of anti-Semitism to another, from Judeophobia to Islamophobia. The dreaded "other" is not any more the Jew, but the Muslim. Either kind of anti-Semitic depreciation is a nefarious obstacle in the project of achieving peace with justice (Majid, 2000, 2004, 2007).

That project of reconciliation and righteousness has been complex and, to say the least, tortuous. It requires, today more than ever before, intellectual understanding and ethical empathy regarding the wave of anti-Judaism that between the Dreyfus affair and the *Shoah* rendered unsuccessful the sophisticate attempts by the Diaspora Jews to achieve emancipation and assimilation into

European culture; but, also and simultaneously, of the sufferings of the Palestinian people caused by the *Yishuv* (Heb. term for Jewish community in Palestine prior to 1948), its Zionist nationalistic ideology, and its military actions that led to a merciless ethnic cleansing. The first were victims of the infamous "final solution," the genocidal culmination of centuries of exclusion and persecution, perpetrated by heirs of the Christian Western civilization, memorialized in the sad and sober elegance of Yad Vashem. The second are the sufferers of the wrath and vindictiveness of the children of Yahweh, their return to Zion and their reliance in the kind of strong-armed attitude once expressed in the hard to read words by Moshe Dayan, the renowned Israeli military strategist, "our life's choice – to be prepared and armed, strong and tough, lest our fist would lose grip of the sword and our life would cease" (Piterberg, 2008:193).

As Miroslav Volf, with his characteristic lucidity, has emphasized, in a telling and critical conversation with Elie Wiesel, wounded memories do not necessarily lead to exclusion. They may, contrariwise, become a shared source for the humanly dignifying act of reciprocal recognition and embrace (Volf, 1996). What Sigmund Freud, in *Moses and Monotheism*, claims as a distinctive peculiarity of the Jewish people, namely that "they defy oppression, that even the most cruel persecutions have not succeeded in exterminating them" (Freud, 139:146), can be similarly predicated of the Palestinian people (Said, 2003). Both national communities have faced oppression and persecution; both carry a painful fissure at the heart of their collective identity; both face the sometimes attractive temptation to indulge in a rigid path of coercive and coercing exclusionary identity; both also resolutely hope and pray for peace and reconciliation.

Edward Said, in an article published less than a year before his demise, emphasized the requirement to avoid exclusionary attitudes vis-à-vis the "others": "Purifying the land of 'aliens', whether it is spoken of by Muslims, Christians or Jews, is a defilement of human life as it is lived by billions of people who are mixed by race, history, ethnic identity, religion or nationality" (Said, 2002). Jonathan Sacks, Chief Rabbi of the United Hebrew Congregations in the United Kingdom, who as a Jew confesses that he carries deep within himself "the tears and sufferings of my grandparents and theirs through the generations," and that "the story of my people is a narrative of centuries of exiles and expulsions, persecutions and pogroms," admonishes Israelis not to convert that history into a justifying narrative of violence and injustice against the Palestinians. "Until Israelis and Palestinians are able to listen to one another, hear each other's anguish and anger and make cognitive space for one another's hopes, there is no way forward" (Sacks, 2002:189f; Lerner, 2012).

The sacred vision of liberation *and* reconciliation, foreseen in the hallowed scriptures of the three great monotheistic Semitic religions, requires from Israeli and Palestinian civic and religious leaders rigorous critical consciousness and the disposition to pay the price that such an attribute frequently entails (Pappe, 2010). This dream of deliverance and peace, so meaningful for Israeli and Palestinian Christians, Muslims, and Jews, is also shared by many of us, *goyim* who in Gentile lands hope and pray that the time might come when in Palestine "justice and peace kiss each other" (Ps. 85:10; Rivera-Pagán, 2010:6-9).

> Stripped of my name and identity?
> On a soil I nourished with my own hands?
> Today Job cried out
> Filling the sky:
> Don't make an example of me again!
> Oh, gentlemen, Prophets,
> Don't ask the trees for their names
> Don't ask the valleys who their mother is
> From my forehead bursts the sword of light
> And from my hand springs the water of the river
> All the hearts of the people are my identity
> So take away my passport!
>
> — *Mahmoud Darwish, Passport*

Bibliography

Akenson, Donald Harman. *God's Peoples: Covenant and Land in South Africa, Israel, and Ulster*. Cornell. 1992.

Ali, Tariq. *The Clash of Fundamentalisms: Crusades, Jihads and Modernity*. Verso. 2002.

Armstrong, Karen. *Jerusalem: One City, Three Faiths*. Ballentine. 1996.

_____. *The Battle for God*. Knopf. 2000.

Ateek, Naim Stifan. *A Palestinian Christian Cry for Reconciliation*. Orbis. 2009.

_____. *Justice and Only Justice: A Palestinian Theology of Liberation*. Orbis. 1989.

Benenisti, Meron. *Sacred Landscpe: The Buried History of the Holy Land Since 1948*. University of California. 2000.

Bloch, Ernst. *Atheismus im Christentum*. Suhrkamp. 1968.

Boff, Leonardo. *Teología desde el cautiverio*. Indo-American Press Service. 1975.

Bonhoeffer, Dietrich. *Letters and Papers from Prison*. Eberhard Bethge, ed. Folio Society. 2000.

Bosch, David. *Transforming Mission: Paradigm Shifts in Theology of Mission*. Orbis. 2002.

Brueggemann, Walter. *The Land: Place as Gift, Promise, and Challenge in Biblical Faith*. Fortress. 2002.

Butler, Judith. "Who Owns Kafka?" *The London Review of Books*. Vol. 33, No. 5. 3/3/2011.

Carroll, James. *Jerusalem, Jerusalem: How the Ancient City Ignited Our Modern World*. Houghton Mifflin Harcourt. 2011.

Chrysostom, John. *Discourses against Judaizing Christians*. Catholic University of America. 1979.

Croatto, José Severino. *Exodus, A Hermeneutics of Freedom*. Orbis. 1981.

Dabashi, Hamid. *Islamic Liberation Theology: Resisting the Empire*. Routledge. 2008.

Darwish, Mahmoud. *Journal of an Ordinary Grief*. Archipelago. 2010.

de Wit, Hans. *En la dispersion el texto es patria: Introducción a la hermeanéutica clásica, moderna y posmoderna*. Universidad Biblica Latinoamericana. 2002.

Ellis, Mark H. *Toward a Jewish Theology of Liberation*. Baylor. 2004.

Elon, Amos. *Jerusalem: Battlegrounds of Memory*. Kodansha International. 1995.

Finkelstein, Israel and Neil Asher Silberman. *The Bible Unearthed: Archaeology's New Vision of Ancient Israel and the Origin of its Sacred Texts*. Free Press. 2002.

Freud, Sigmund. *Moses and Monotheism*. Hogarth. 1939.

Goldstein, Slavko. "A Turning Point for Croatia." *The New York Review of Books*. Vol. LVIII, No. 11. 23/6/2011.

Gottwald, Norman, ed. *The Bible and Liberation: Political and Social Hermeneutics*. Orbis. 1983.

Gutiérrez, Gustavo. *A Theology of Liberation*. Orbis. 1988.

Horsley, Richard, ed. *In the Shadow of Empire: Reclaiming the Bible as a History of Faithful Resistance*. Westminster John Knox. 2008.

Houston, Walter J. *Contending for Justice: Ideologies and Theologies of Social Justice in the Old Testament*. T & T Clark. 2006.

Juergensmeyer, Mark. *Terror in the Mind of God: The Global Rise of Religious Violence*. University of California. 2000.

Kairos Palestine. *A Moment of Truth: A Word of Faith, Hope and Love from the Heart of Palestinian Suffering*. 2009. http://www.kairospalestine.ps.

Khalidi, Walid, ed. *All That remains: The Palestinian Villages Occupied and Depopulated by Israel in 1948*. Institute for Palestinian Studies. 2006.

Lerner, Michael. *Embracing Israel/Palestine: A Strategy to Heal and Transform the Middle East*. North Atlantic. 2012.

Longerich, Peter. *Holocaust: The Nazi Persecution and Murder of the Jews*. Oxford. 2010.

Majid, Anouar. *A Call for Heresy: Why Dissent Is Vital to Islam and America*. University of Minnesota. 2007.

_____. *Freedom and Orthodoxy: Islam and Difference in the Post-Andalusian Age*. Stanford University. 2004.

_____. *Unveiling Traditions: Postcolonial Islam in a Polycentric World*. Duke University. 2000.

Marchadour, Alain and David Neuhaus. *The Land, the Bible, and History: Toward the Land That I Will Show You*. Fordham. 2007.

Masalha, Nur. *Expulsion of the Palestinians: The Concept of "Transfer" in Zionist Political Thought, 1882-1948*. Institute for Palestinian Studies. 1992.

_____. *The Bible and Zionism: Invented Traditions, Archaeology, and Post-Colonialism in Palestine-Israel*. Zed. 2007.

Montefiore, Simon Sebag. *Jerusalem: The Biography*. Weidenfeld & Nicolson. 2011.

Moore, Stephen D. and Fernando Segovia. *Postcolonial Biblical Criticism: Interdisciplinary Intersections*. T & T Clark. 2005.

Niebuhr, Reinhold. *Moral Man and Immoral Society: A Study in Ethics and Politics*. Scribner's. 1932.

Oren, Michael B. *Six Days of War: June 1967 and the Making of the Modern Middle East*. Oxford. 2002.

Pagels, Elaine. *The Origin of Satan*. Random House. 1995.

Pappe, Ilan. *Out of Frame: The Struggle for Academic Freedom in Israel*. PlutoPress. 2010.

_____. *The Ethnic Cleansing of Palestine*. Oneworld. 2006.

Piterberg, Gabriel. *The Returns of Zionism: Myths, Politics and Scholarship in Israel*. Verso. 2008.

Pixley, George. *Biblia teología de la liberación y filosofía procesual: el Dios liberador en la Biblia*. Editorial Abya Yala. 2009.

_____. *On Exodus: A Liberation Perspective*. Orbis. 1987.

Prior, Michael. "Confronting the Bible's Ethnic Cleansing in Palestine." *The Link*. Vol. 33, Issue 5. Dec. 2000.

_____. *Jesus the Liberator: Nazareth Liberation Theology (Luke 4:16-30)*. Sheffield Academic. 1995.

_____. "Reading the Bible with the Eyes of the Canaanites: In Homage to Edward Said." *A Living Stone: Selected Essays & Addresses.* Duncan Macpherson, ed. Living Stones of the Holy Land Trust and Melisende. 2006.

_____. *The Bible and Colonialism: A Moral Critique.* Sheffield Academic. 1997.

_____. *Zionism and the State of Israel: A Moral Inquiry.* Routledge. 1999.

Raheb, Mitri. *I Am a Palestinian Christian.* Fortress. 1995.

Rivera-Pagán, Luis. *A Violent Evangelism: The Political and Religious Conquest of the Americas.* Westminster-John Knox. 1992.

_____. "Desafíos teológicos del conflicto palestino-israelí." *Signos de Vida.* No. 55. March, 2010.

_____. "God the Liberator: Theology, History, and Politics." *In Our Own Voices: Latino/a Renditions of Theology.* Benjamin Valentin, ed. Orbis. 2010.

Sacks, Jonathan. *The Dignity of Difference: How to Avoid the Clash of Civilizations.* Continuum. 2002.

Said, Edward W. *Culture and Imperialism.* Knopf. 1993.

_____. *Freud and the Non-European.* Verso. 2003.

_____. *Out of Place: A Memoir.* Vintage. 1999.

_____. "Real Change Means People Must Change: Immediate Imperatives." *CounterPunch.* 21/12/2002.

_____. *Reflections on Exile and Other Essays.* Harvard. 2002.

_____. *Representations of the Intellectuals.* Vintage. 1996.

_____. *The Question of Palestine.* Routledge. 1980.

Sand, Shlomo. *The Invention of the Jewish People.* Verso. 2009.

Schwartz, Regina. *The Curse of Cain: The Violent Legacy of Monotheism.* University of Chicago. 1997.

Segundo, Juan Luis. *The Liberation of Theology.* Orbis. 1976.

Shapira, Anita. *The Bible and Israeli Identity.* Magnes. 2006.

Singer, Isaac Bashevis. *Collected Stories: Gimpel the Fool to the Letter Writer.* The Library of America. 2004.

_____. *The Penitent.* Farrar, Straus, Giroux. 1983.

Smith, Robert O. *"More Desired Than Our Owne Salvation": The Roots of American Christian Affinity for the State of Israel.* Ph.D. dissertation. Baylor. 2011.

Smith-Christopher, Daniel L. *A Biblical Theology of Exile.* Fortress. 2002.

Steicke, Elisabeth Cook. *La mujer como extranjera en Israel: Estudio exegético de Esdras 9-10.* Editorial SEBILA. 2011.

Steiner, George. "Our Homeland, the Text." *No Passion Spent: Essays 1978-1996*. Faber. 1996.

Trible, Phyllis. *Texts of Terror*. Fortress. 1984.

Trouillot, Michel-Rolph. *Silencing the Past: Power and the Production of History*. Beacon. 1995.

Twain, Mark. *The Innocents Abroad* [1869]. Wordsworth edition. 2010.

Volf, Miroslav. *Exclusion and Embrace: A Theological Exploration of Identity, Otherness, and Reconciliation*. Abingdon. 1996.

Walker, Alice. "Overcoming Speechlessness." *Tikkun*. Sept/Oct 2009.

Walzer, Michael. *Exodus and Revolution*. Basic. 1985.

Whitelam, Keith W. *The Invention of Ancient Israel: The Silencing of Palestinian History*. Routledge. 1996.

Yiftachel, Oren. *Ethnocracy: Land and Identity in Israel/Palestine*. University of Pennsylvania. 2006.

12 | Human Trafficking and Prostitution: Is there Hope?

Lauran Bethell

This is a rather personal presentation because what I share is what I've experienced and observed. Some 25 years ago, when I first arrived in Thailand, the words "human trafficking" were simply not used. I was hearing unbelievable stories of kidnap and abuse and exploitation and at the time I felt like no one knew or even cared. Even though human trafficking has been happening since the beginning of time, few people acknowledged its existence. The good news is that human trafficking now has been identified for what it is. And even though it's where evil has been viciously destroying lives—there is hope. Yes, there is hope! I've been witness to God's Spirit being poured out on this world during this past 25 years, calling people into creative ministries in Jesus' name. I've been witness to God's Spirit being poured out on this world shining light into these darkest of corners and exposing the evil for what it is. I've been witness to God's Spirit being poured out on this world, using media, governments and the public sector to expose and prosecute perpetrators and offer help and hope to victims. But even though during these last two decades we've been able to witness a massive movement of awareness and action, there is still much to be done.

First: some definitions. Human beings are trafficked for both labor exploitation as well as sexual exploitation in the prostitution and pornography industries. It includes both cross-border AND domestic situations and can also include involuntary servitude, slavery, debt bondage, and forced labor. Women, men and children are victims of human trafficking--but the majority of victims are women and children—and the vast majority of women and children are trafficked into the sex industry. Hence, I will focus of this report on the trafficking and prostitution of women and children.

And about statistics with regard to human trafficking: due to the covert nature of the crime, the invisibility of victims and high levels of under-reporting, actual statistics are often unavailable, and very often are contradictory. For example, the

United Nations estimates are between 700,000 to four million women and children who are trafficked around the world for purposes of forced prostitution, labor and other forms of exploitation every year. That's a huge range. And human trafficking is estimated to generate between $7 billion and $31 billion dollars annually. Those are enormous statistical gaps that simply cannot be verified. What we know for sure is that human trafficking is big business—and is second only to drugs in the world of illegal activity in this world. And what I know for sure, is that once your eyes have been opened to the reality of human trafficking in your midst, you will find it all around you.

My definition of human trafficking is "the exploitation of vulnerability." Human trafficking equals the exploitation of vulnerability. The aim of this paper is to look at the major vulnerability issues and then discuss ways that we as believers in Jesus and in Jesus' teachings can prevent victimization and also bring hope and healing to victims.

So why are people vulnerable to the victimization of human trafficking? My own experience and research points to three major broad categories. They all overlap in some ways, but I believe that these three categories illustrate the majority of reasons for vulnerability and victimization.

The first is the most obvious: economic hardship. Poverty. But not all impoverished women and girls work in prostitution. Twenty-five years ago, when I was first meeting Thai women and girls in prostitution in Bangkok, they told me that they were working in prostitution in order to send money home to their mothers and fathers and to support their brothers and sisters. They were providing food and new houses and vehicles and school fees for their families. They would tell me that they were "sacrificing" themselves for their families. They were raised from birth to believe that the value of their life was dependent on how much money they could make for their families. Their families' economic difficulty combined with the cultural value of familial obligation creates vulnerability that is exploited. In many community-based cultures around the world, the girl child is raised with this value—that she is economically responsible for her family. And if she has little or no education, and sees prostitution as the way to make the most money possible for her family, then she will sacrifice herself in this way.

One time I asked the father of a young woman why he had sold his daughter into prostitution not once, but twice. His answer: "whatever my daughter can do to make my life better is what she should do." At the Center where I served, we were able to help this young woman receive an education and get a good job. But every month up until the day he died, this young woman sent fully half of everything she earned back to her father—even though she knew that most of the money was going to support his opium addiction. Though we begged and pleaded and tried to help her in every possible way to do otherwise, it was deeply engrained that she had an obligation to support parents—no matter what. This familial commitment, especially in community-based cultures, is exploited by traffickers and perpetrators alike. How often I heard men justify their use of women and children in prostitution in Thailand, saying that by paying for sex, they were helping the girl's family because she was sending the money home. Poverty and culture interplay and create vulnerability that is exploited.

If poverty and culture are exploited in developing countries, then why are there so many women and young girls who are victims of human trafficking and prostitution in developed countries? The second vulnerability factor is the incidence of childhood sexual abuse. In my own country, the USA, as many as 70-95% of those working in prostitution have been sexually abused as children in their families or communities. Sexual abuse does inestimable harm to the soul of young person. Children who have been abused live with immense sexual confusion which can lead to their identities being defined by sexual expression. One young woman I know was abused at a young age by her stepfather. She told me that when she came into adolescence, the only way she could relate to boys was through sex. By the time she was 18, she said "I had given away sex so many times that I decided I should at least make money from it." A pimp, poised as her "boyfriend" encouraged her, took a cut of her money, acted as her "protector" and exploited her vulnerability. She descended into addictions to drugs and alcohol and continues to struggle with multiple mental health issues.

In the USA, Canada and the UK, substance abuse and prostitution very often go hand in hand. People often say, "They're working to support drug habits." That may be true. Often, drugs are used to numb the emotional pain of an abusive childhood— and result in the downward spiral of addiction to both the drugs and to the prostitution that supports the habit. In some cases, the pimps have forced the drug abuse in order to keep the girls and women dependent and in an endless cycle of working for drugs—and providing money for him.

In the USA the vast majority of women who are working in prostitution began when they were 12-14 years old. Often, they were running away from dysfunctional family and community situations, most often, as noted, victims of childhood sexual abuse. In their confusion they were met in bus stations and on the street by people who offered them shelter and food—and who exploited their immediate need and their vulnerability. After accepting the perceived "generosity" of their benefactors, they were raped and sometimes beaten and threatened into submission. Their "benefactors" turned into pimps posing as "protectors." What they do, should not be labeled "prostitution." It is child abuse. It has only been in this decade that this form of domestic human trafficking has finally been more widely identified for what it is: the trafficking of minor children. Human trafficking does not necessarily mean that geographic borders have been crossed—although more often than not, the girls and women they become are moved from one city to another, one step ahead of the law, and precluding them from developing any significant relationships which might enable them to seek alternatives for their lives.

For a number of years, I only used the two broad categories of poverty/culture and childhood sexual abuse that I have just named to describe vulnerability factors. And then I was confronted by a dear Christian woman in a wealthy country who chastised me: "My daughter is also a victim of human trafficking and prostitution" she told me. "And she is neither poor—nor was she abused. Rather she was "groomed" into prostitution by a man who developed a relationship with her with the goal that he would become her pimp and have her working in prostitution." I learned from this broken-hearted woman that I must include the category of "grooming" to describe a 3rd major vulnerability factor.

In The Netherlands, those who "groom" teenage girls into prostitution are called "lover-boys" by those girls. However, there's no true "love" involved—only exploitation. "Lover-boys" hang around places where teen-age girls would be: on the edge of high school grounds or shopping malls, at discotheques or beaches. They compliment the girls as they walk past: "oh you're so beautiful." If the girl has a strong sense of self-esteem, she will just say "thanks" and keep walking. But a girl who doesn't hear many compliments, whose self-esteem isn't so strong, will stop, the compliments will continue, dates will be made—and the "lover-boy" knows that he has her hooked. She'll first be given a cell phone that he calls multiple times a day, developing a co-dependent relationship. He will do everything to convince her that he is her only love—that her family and friends don't love her as much as he does, and in this way, he attempts to isolate her from her primary relationships. A sexual relationship develops, and thereafter, he convinces her that she should have sex with his friends. There may be gang rape. And then comes the moment as she approaches her 18th birthday, which is the legal age in The Netherlands for working in prostitution, when all of the sudden he has no money. And, he continues, since she's had sex with so many men already, working in prostitution will not be any different and will solve all their financial problems. She comes to believe that the more money she makes for him, the more he will love her—or love her again. By this time, she's found out that he has three or four or five other women working for him—but she's sure that she's the one he loves the most.

"Grooming" girls into prostitution as a form of human trafficking was previously an invisible phenomenon—and certainly wasn't identified as trafficking. The public preferred to wear blinders and believe that since the women were not chained to the brothels and could walk away at any time, they had obviously "chosen" to work there. And yes, there is an element of "choice." But I always say that "choice" has a very thin veneer. Scratch the thin surface of "choice" and you find the story behind the story behind the story of woundedness and helplessness and hopelessness. I know what little self-esteem I had at 15 or 16, and am thankful that, by the grace of God, no one set out to groom me into prostitution.

Up to this point in this paper, I've been focusing primarily on the victims of human trafficking and prostitution. But there would be no victims if there were not a demand. Simply put: demand fuels human trafficking and prostitution. It's economics at its simplest: Take away demand, you don't need supply.

Fortunately, we have an example of governmental legislation that has done just that. In 1999 in Sweden, the society recognized that prostitution promotes violence against women by normalizing the sexual exploitation involved in prostitution. The prevailing attitude in Sweden is that all people in prostitution are victims and therefore should not be criminalized. Rather, they should be offered social assistance. However, those who use people in prostitution—who buy sex— *are* criminals and are fined. At the same time, they, too, are offered social services, including individual and group counseling. Sweden is one of the only countries in the world where human trafficking has declined in the past decade—it's simply not a "friendly environment" for traffickers. Norway adopted a similar law in 2009. I'm thankful the Swedish officials are using their example and the research they have generated over the past 12 years and, with missionary zeal, are presenting programs all over the world, to try to convince governments to consider adapting forms of their law as a way of preventing human trafficking and exploitation.

To recap: Human Trafficking equals the exploitation of vulnerability which is fueled by demand. The three major vulnerability factors are:

- Poverty exacerbated by cultural attitudes towards girls
- Childhood sexual abuse
- "Grooming"

Where is the Hope?

When I started my little research project on the streets of Bangkok in 1986, I could only find one small Christian project that offered shelter to 8 young girls who had been rescued from brothels. Since then, God's Spirit has been pouring out on this earth, and the numbers of people being called to minister into these very dark corners of the earth is increasing exponentially! There is much reason to hope! At the same time, the sophistication of the traffickers, the ease of travel, the use of the internet and the fall of borders and boundaries has meant that we must use all of our God-given resources, ingenuity, wisdom and creativity in confronting this evil. I have the privilege of witnessing just such a global outpouring of God-infused energy and talent. Here are just few examples:

The first example is directed at poverty: most all of you know about Freeset Bags. Founded by New Zealand Baptist missionaries, Kerry and Annie Hilton, Freeset was started in one of the largest red-light districts in the world, located in Kolkata, India. It's a factory which produces jute bags and cotton t-shirts and the employees are women who have left prostitution. Working full-time in the factory, they are able to have the economic alternatives they need to support themselves and their children.

They are also learning about the dignity and self-worth that Jesus wants us all known as His children. Kerry has told me that the factory and most of the employees will continue to stay in residence in the red-light district because the vision is that one day this area will be transformed economically and spiritually from the inside outwards. We call this kind of endeavor "Business As Mission"—a "for-profit", self- sustaining company which offers hope and freedom through business *and* spiritual transformation.

Another endeavor, located in Thailand was founded by American Baptist missionary Annie Dieselberg. "NightLight Jewelry" factory is in the Nana red-light district in Bangkok and employs women who have worked in prostitution, most of whom have come from the rural, impoverished Northeast of Thailand and are supporting their parents, siblings and their own children. It's gratifying to see growing numbers of creative businesses that God is calling into existence to offer economic alternatives—and Jesus' Hope and Healing to the most abused and exploited people in our world. One great way for Christians to get in involved in anti-trafficking ministries is to market products from these organizations.

In The Netherlands, it was because Christians felt called to simply offer unconditional love to the women in prostitution that the myth of prostitution as life "choice" for many of the women was dispelled—and the victimization of "lover-boys" was uncovered. Twenty-five years ago, when many Christians were avoiding this "dirty part of town", these brave Jesus-followers started developing relationships with the women in prostitution by offering simple gifts of flowers and hot drinks and an unconditionally listening ear. By consistently "showing up", they began winning the trust of the women, and the story behind the story behind the story began to emerge. One after another of the women in prostitution shared their pain and their shame—and a pattern emerged of their vulnerability exploited by "lover-boys." Eventually, some of the women came to know Jesus, and to trust Him for their future. They courageously began to tell their stories, and the phenomenon of "lover-boys" has been unmasked. "The Scarlet Cord" is one of the stellar organizations that was established as a result of God's call in the hearts of a few individuals who just kept returning to the women and listening to their stories. The Scarlet Cord now is staffed with social workers, job placement professionals and trained volunteers. They have developed a prevention curriculum that is used throughout the country to warn teens and parents alike about the phenomenon of lover-boys. And they are often invited into high-level governmental offices and asked to influence public policy. And this is *not* because they ran anti-prostitution campaigns or railed against the fact that prostitution is legal in The Netherlands. But it IS because they were faithful and accountable in serving "the least of these"—and enabling the voices of women in and out of prostitution to speak the truth about their exploitation and abuse.

I cannot emphasize enough the importance of consistently "showing up" in the midst of this evil that we'd rather not see or acknowledge. It's a "showing up" that offers unconditional love and acceptance. It's a "showing up" that doesn't carry in preconceived notions about what we should DO about the situation—but rather listens carefully for the answer to the unspoken question "what is the greatest immediate need"? Often what WE feel that they need has nothing to do with the reality of their true need. Is the immediate need simply a listening ear? A smile? A warm drink? Once we have met the first immediate need, we move to the next and then the next: A safe place to gather? Shelter? Counseling? Mental health services? Substance abuse services? Employment? Child-care? Until we've truly listened and heard, we should not think we know.

"Showing up" in the midst can sometimes mean offering prevention. In northern Thailand, the girls needed to become literate. They needed further education, vocational training and a safe, community environment to live while going to school, and we were able to provide that at the New Life Center.

For four years (2008-2011), the Rev. Lindsay Comstock led an important ministry in rural Indonesia, developing human trafficking prevention materials and trainings. Living in the midst of communities where recruiters are actively seeking out the vulnerable, where children have been kidnapped and have some have reappeared in brothels, Lindsay has heard the needs of these communities. She's actively worked with village leaders to help them raise awareness among families about the risks of trusting those who promise "good jobs" in the city. She's helped families to report their missing children to the appropriate authorities so that they can be found. She's created "Child Safety Packets" for school teachers and trained them to educate children and their parents about children's rights and risk factors. And I'd like to read a part of her report which illustrates her perception and creativity.

> Throughout my travels in in Southwest Asia I often run into large groups of men and women who have been "hired" to agencies that specialize in overseas domestic help and/or manual labor. Unfortunately, many illegitimate agencies (traffickers) blend into the backdrop and make it difficult to advocate for victims. After only a short time serving in Southeast Asia, I found that the women's airport restroom serves as a safe place for many women to discuss their situation with travel colleagues without fear of being heard by "Johns," pimps, and/or oppressive employers. As a result, I have been traveling with brochures that discuss and explain the signs of trafficking to a possible trafficking victim, tips for safe travel abroad, safety tips for arrival in a new country, etc. In addition, if I am able to communicate, I often introduce myself and over my card, explain that I can connect the women with non-governmental organizations in their country of origin if they desire to return home.

God is at work, calling women and men to creatively enter into places where many Christians would rather pretend didn't exist. God is at work, and brings hope where some would simply feel overwhelmed. God is at work, desiring that all—abused and abusing, those prostituting as well as pimping—come to know God's help, healing and hope for an eternal future!

A Concluding Word from Henri Nouwen

Hope frees us from the need to predict the future and allows us to live in the present with the deep trust that God will never leave us alone but will fulfill the deepest desire of our heart.

When I trust deeply that today God is truly with me and holds me safe in a divine embrace, guiding every one of my steps, I can let go of my anxious need to know how tomorrow will look, or what will happen next month or next year. I can be fully where I am and pay attention to the many signs of God's love within and around me. (Nouwen, 1994:33)

Bibliography

Websites

European Baptist Federation (EBF) Anti-Trafficking Working Group—resource books http://www.ebf.org/resources.

International Christian Alliance on Prostitution (ICAP). http://www.icapglobal.org.

National Christian Alliance on Prostitution (NCAP). http://www.beyondthestreets.org.uk.

FreeSet Bags. http://www.freesetglobal.com.

NightLight. http://www.nighlightinternational.com.

U.S. Government's Trafficking in Persons Report. http://www.state.gov/g/tip/rls/tiprpt/2011.

Books

Allender, Dan. *Bold Love*. NavPress. 1992.

_____. *Healing Path*. NavPress. 2008.

_____. *Wounded Heart*. Waterbrook. 1999.

Batstone, David. *Not for Sale*. HarperOne. 2007.

Belles, Nita. *In Our Backyard*. Xulon. 2011.

Carson, Marion and Ruth Robb. *Working the Streets*. New Wine. 2003.

Dust, Harmony. *From Scars to Stilettos*. Monarch. 2009.

Farley, Melissa. *Prostitution, Trafficking and Post-Traumatic Stress*. Routledge. 2004.

Gately, Edwina. *I Hear a Seed Growing. 20th Anniversary* ed. Orbis. 2011.

CHAPTER 12

Jewell, Dawn Herzog. *Escaping the Devil's Bedroom.* Monarch. 2008.

Malarek, Victor. *The Johns: Sex for Sale and the Men Who Buy It.* Arcade. 2011.

Malarek, Victor. *The Natashas: Inside the New Global Sex Trade.* Arcade. 2011.

Manning, Brennan. *Ruthless Trust.* HarperCollins rep. 2009.

Nouwen, Henri. *Here and Now: Living in the Spirit.* Crossroads. 1994.

_____. *The Inner Voice of Love.* Doubleday/Image. 1994.

_____. *The Return of the Prodigal Son.* Doubleday/Image. 1994.

_____. *The Wounded Healer.* Doubleday. 1972.

_____. *Turn My Mourning Into Dancing.* Thomas Nelson. 2001.

Rivers, Francine. *Redeeming Love.* Multnomah. 1997.

Sanford, John. *Deliverance and Inner Healing.* Chosen. 2008.

Storkey, Elaine. *The Search for Intimacy.* Eerdmans. 1996.

13 | KAREN BAPTISTS AND RELIGIOUS FREEDOM

Saw Wado

In 1833 he [Ko Tha Byu] left for Rangoon to share the Gospel with his countrymen there… A great revival started among the Karens. But not long thereafter, the Burmese government forbade the church to meet. Pastors faced torture and imprisonment, or were killed if they refused to stop their activities. The persecution of the Christian Church in Burma was severe back then and the persecution continues today. Despite all this, the Church in Burma survives and is still growing. Forty percent of the Karen people are Christians in spite of fifty years of war with the current military regime (PW).

Who are the Karens? What role do they play in Baptist history? The Karens, in foreigner's eyes, often "are not intelligent people. They are nothing like as quick-witted as the Burmese or the Chinese. They are often extremely stupid" (Morrison, 1946:19). Ever since history begins to mention them they appears to be a god-forsaken race and people under the shadow of the cross as soon as they were taking up the Christian faith. The following definition of the Karen by *New Oxford American Dictionary* shows a fragile position of the Karen people and it also shows some people have a fragile grip on the reality and nature of the Karen as a nation.

Karen |kəˈren|. noun (pl. same or -rens) 1. a member of an indigenous people of eastern Myanmar (Burma) and western Thailand. 2. the language of this people, probably Sino-Tibetan.

Adjective: of or relating to this people or their language.

Origin from Burmese, *ka-reng*, "wild unclean man."

136

Who, therefore, are the Karens? The Karens are one of the people on earth of whom the Burmese are another. Many centuries ago they migrated southward from Tibet and south China, probably around 739 BCE in search of a warmer climate. 2011 marks the 2750 years of Karen settlement in the land called Burma or Myanmar. Ian Morrison acknowledged that, "Ever since they fist arrived in Burma, the Karens appear to have been a subject race, oppressed by their stronger neighbors and frequently used as slaves... they were a subject and despised race," (Morrison, 1946:16) and for centuries the Burman "bullied the Karen and regarded him as slave" (Morrison, 21) and bullies and oppression still continue today.

As I see it, the Karens are victims of: genocidal war, colonialism (not by British but by the Mons and later by Burmese), divide and rule policy, racial discrimination, religious persecution, ethnic cleansing policy, slavery, etc. To address the issues above will take more space and time than this paper permits. The issue I would like to emphasize, however, is how God, in spite of severe persecutions and zero tolerance, used the so-called "orphans," "stupid," "oppressed... subject and despised" race to ignite the Gospel movement in Burma. In fact, the Karens were pioneers in "one of the most remarkable Christian movements of modern times," (Morrison, 1946:27) to be precise, in Burma. Baptist mission in Burma was groundbreaking, it appears, though the Romans Catholic missionaries had been there as early as 1581. A few missionaries were martyred by 1693: "... it happened that during 1581 the Gospel of Christ carried by the Roman Catholic Mission arrived into Burma firstly at Than Hling (syrium)." Two French missionaries were martyred by AD 1693 for the sake of the Gospel. Saw Aung Hla recorded that Father Jean Genoud and Father Jean Joret were "... stripped naked so that mosquitoes would bite them. Finally 12.2.1693 the king's men put the priests into cotton bags, stitched closed and threw those martyrs into the Pegu River" (Saw Aung Hla, 297). Christianity was not welcome by the Burmese people partly because of Buddhism and partly because, the Burmese believe, Christianity being the religion of the western colonizers would be propaganda in promoting colonialism or that the missionaries share the same agenda as British officials. Saw Aung Hla writes,

> The American missionary couple Dr. and Mrs. Judson left America and arrived in Rangoon in the 13th July 1813 to form a Baptist mission church among the Burmese people. This was not welcome by the Burmese government due to the fact that Christianity, according to their thoughts are at loggerheads with Buddhism. So the effort given by Dr. Judson was not welcome by the Burmese people. Before the arrival of Dr. Judson into Burma

there also came two Anglican missionaries in the years AD 1807. They were Rev. Carter and Rev. Madoh who also came to work primarily for the Burmese people. After the few months, another missionary by the name of Rev. Felix Cary came to fill up the place of Rev. Madoh who left his ministry. These three Anglican missionaries came six years before Dr. Judson. The Burmese people did not accept their work to spread the holy Gospel. Rev. Carter left Burma to continue his ministry in Ceylon. When Dr. Judson arrived, he took up the work that Rev. Cary abandoned. At that time the fact that Karens live and exist in Burma was not known to those of the foreign land (Saw Aung Hla, 300).

But the conversion of Ko Tha Byu in 1828—an ex-bandit turned "the Apostle to the Karens," and "the freed slave…an illiterate, surly man who spoke almost no Burmese and was reputed to be not only a thief but also a murderer, who admitted killing at least thirty men, but could not remember exactly how many more" (KBC)—marked the beginning of successful Baptist mission in Burma.

Now, it is interesting how the Karens came to readily embrace Christianity. The Karen "lost golden book" legend (Morrison, 1946:26) played substantial role in what made Christianity fit into the worldview, ethical code and cultural values of the Karens. According to this legend, once upon a time God had three sons, the first and beloved son was Karen, the second was Burman and the third was "white." When they became adults God was going back to his country far away. They youngest brother happened to accompany his father when the first and second sons excused themselves for being busy. Upon returning God gave three books—the golden book assigned to the so-called beloved Karen, to his second son, the Burman, a palm-leaf book; to the youngest son, a book of leather.

The white brother read the three books on his journey home and found out that the golden book was filled with the word of God, various theories of commerce, and a wide range of knowledge written in it. The youngest son decided the golden book was the most valuable among the three books. As it was told the youngest son swapped the book and presented the leather book to the Karen. The Karen was busy toiling his farm and asked his youngest brother to leave it on the tree trunk. He forgot the book days after days. A bush fire came and destroyed the book. The Karen later went to the location and found out the book was burned along with the tree trunk. He found only the footprints of wild chicken. For this reason the original Karen alphabets resembled the chicken footprints (Htoo Hla E., 1955:80-83).

Be that as it may, the Karen believed their "golden book" was lost and that his youngest brother will return it to him one day. So when the American Baptist missionaries, Adoniram Judson, Francis Mason and Jonathan Wade, came with the Bible, it brought a large stir among the Karens. The story is told that in 1831 on his first trip into Karen territory, an old man confronted Jonathan Wade with this question: "Where is our book?" he asked, referring to the Karen legend mentioned before. "If you bring us our lost book, we will welcome you." Wade was quick to respond. It is said that he transposed the Karen language to writing even before he could speak it, and Dr. Mason took Wade's adaptation of the Burmese alphabet to Karen sounds and threw himself into the arduous task of translating the Bible into Sgaw Karen. Thus did the Karens receive "their Lost Book"—their written language and Bible in their own language. The first printed portion was the Sermon on the Mount in 1837; the New Testament appeared in successive printing stages from 1843 to 1861, and the Old Testament in 1863 (KBC).

San C. Poe, a Karen intellectual who lived and served during the British occupation of Burma narrated the turbulent incident as thus:

> The Karen God-tradition, so firmly believed in and strongly adhered to, was: "Our younger white brother to whom God temporarily entrusted the Book of Silver and the Book of Gold is coming back to return them to the elder Karen brother." So when news was received that the white brother had arrived in Burma, there was no little stir in Karendom. Adoniram Judson gained the first convert to Christianity in Ko Tha Byu (1828) who lost no time in spreading the gospel among his people, declaring that the long-lost "Book of God" had been brought back by the white brother and that the Karen God-tradition was fulfilled. Consequently, a number of young men from different parts of the country went over to Arakan, and later to Moulmein, to find the Missionaries who had brought the gospel of Christ and to learn more about the truth, which it was their intention to preach among their own people (Poe, 1928:2).

Rev. T. Thanbyah, a Karen historian recorded that after the British annexation of lower Burma (Tanasarim Division and Arakan in 1824 and 1826) written history of Karens began to appear significantly when Ko Tha Byu became the disciple of Jesus Christ. There was almost nothing prior to this. The fact that the Karens had been living in Burma were known to the Burmese and the Talaing or Mons but they were not known to foreigners until the conversion of Ko Tha Byu by 1828.

The Gospel was not in the first place intended for the Karen but it came to them as coincidence and as the gift of heaven. From here on, the name "Karen" and the story about the Karens began to make the written history books (Thankbyah, 1904:6).

The conversion of a slave people inaugurated a new order of life for Karen and, concretely, the dawn of a new era to them. The resurrection of this nation rested on no human merit but solely rested upon divine grace. It was neither human plan nor cosmic chance that these most humbled slaves became heirs to the Gospel but by the gift of heaven.

What were the implications of the encounter with Gospel of Jesus Christ for the socio-political development of the Karens? Htoo Hla E. said that multitudes of Karens came together and formed themselves into churches and associations and later eventually formed their churches' Convention (Htoo Hla E., 1955:129), what is now called Karen Baptist Convention in Burma, established in 1913 as a result of the encounter. (Subsequently, "Karen Baptists from Burma first sent missionaries to the Karens in Thailand in 1880, and soon two churches were established. The Karen work grew to twenty churches with 800 members by 1954," (Wardin, 164) and Thailand Karen Baptist Convention was formed in 1955.)

This came naturally, I think, as a response to the saving act of the Great God in their history. Because Christianity came firstly as "civilizing process" and secondly, Christianity was identified with "education" in the mind of the people:

> Christianity made such rapid strides because it was accompanied by, was indeed mainly responsible for, two other processes— the gradual civilizing of a hitherto rude and unlettered people, and the growth of Karen unity and prestige. Christianity was identified in the mind of the people with education. Education raised their standard of living, gave them confidence and pride, and aroused what has been called heir "federative capacity" (Morrison, 1946:28).

Moreover, sadly so, from here on began yet another form of suppression along with long existing political and racial ill-treatments, namely, religious persecution. San C. Poe documented some of the fracases as below:

> The lot of the Karens under Burmese rule had been hard enough, but when declared between Burma and Great Britain, heard that the Karens were taking up the Christian religion they proceeded to make life unbearable for the new converts to Christianity.

Persecution, religious and political, began in earnest. Karens were caught and thrown into prison, suffering untold agonies, and a few were crucified. One man, by the name of Klaw Meh was nailed to a cross, the abdomen ripped open with intestines hanging down, which the crows were picking while the poor man writhed in agony in an impossible attempt to drive away the crows. His voice gradually grew weaker until at last he died a martyr on the cross like his Master, Jesus Christ, whom he had lately embraced (Poe, 1928:2).

American Baptist International Ministries "Resolution Against Slavery" documented that in Burma in the 1830s American Baptist missionaries worked with the Karen minority who were virtually serfs, forbidden to own books and learn to read. The missionaries persisted in petitioning the Burmese King on religious and civil liberty,

In Burma in the 1830s, American Baptist missionaries reached out to the ethnic Karen minority, dominated as virtual serfs by the majority Burmese who forbid them to possess books or learn to read. Enslavement, beheading and crucifixion were punishments for those who violated the restrictions. Because they were found with books, several early Karen Baptist converts were shackled in heavy irons and forced to work as slaves on the grounds of Shway Dagon pagoda in Rangoon. The American Baptist missionaries persistently petitioned the Burmese king regarding religious and civil liberty (IM).

Burma shows no sign of improvement in this regard. Human rights violation tied along with religious persecution prevails. In its article "Burma's Almost Forgotten," *Christianity Today* writes, "Christians find themselves battered by the world's longest civil war and a brutally repressive regime" (CT, 2004), and that, "The U.S. State Department has ranked Burma as one of the six worst violators of religious freedom," as in 2011.

In an effort to terrorize the ethnic groups into submission, the Burma Army uses religion as a weapon of war. When it is convenient to do so, the army cloaks itself in Buddhism and stirs up anti-Christian sentiment. Churches are often the first targets in attacks on ethnic villages, while more often than not Buddhist temples are left untouched (CT, 2004).

In spite of intense challenges and formidable repression (e.g., widespread religious persecution, churches burned to the ground, Christians forced to convert to the state religion (Buddhism) and their children discriminated in schools), the foundation of Christianity in Burma never wavers. The Karen Baptists Convention in Burma has made remarkable growth.

The Formation of the Kawthoolei Karen Baptist Churches

The Karen people were hit hard by the so-called "four cut operation" of the regime in the 70s. The 'four cut operation' is the regime's policy intended to deprive the ethnic resistance movement of their food, money, intelligence and recruits. Along with the "four cut operation" came widespread displacement and the crisis of refugees. Thousands of refugees flowed into Thailand and thousands more became displaced and re-displaced. Thus the Karen churches in the Eastern Burma were cut off from mainstream Karen Baptist Convention headquartered in Insein, Rangoon. Ministers, pastors and members of churches in the Kawthoolei area were unable to attend meetings/conference conveyed. Relationships were cut off; Karen churches were divided-and-ruled. Today, the need for strengthening, nurturing of churches along Thai-Burma border has become both a matter of urgency and priority.

> Thus the Kawthoolei Karen Baptist Organization was organized and formed on 1st October 1983 having its office located in Wallei in the Karen side. In the same year the Bible School was moved to Wallei due to the Burmese troops' invasion and occupation of places (Karens' strongholds) near and around Tea Ka Haw where the Bible School was first located. Then, on the 31st of January 1984 the KKBO annual meeting was held at Wallei. We are so grateful to God for sending us Rev. Edwin I. Lopez, then the General Secretary of ABF and Rev. Hespid to be with us during this meeting. We felt so blessed, encouraged and strengthened. It was during this meeting that the name Kawthoolei Karen Baptist Organization (KKBO) was officially changed to Kawthoolei Karen Baptist Churches (KKBC) as suggested by them (KKBC).

The KKBC as a convention, for want of liberty, shuffled its Churches Association, from north to south, ranging along the Thai-Burma border. The KKBC consists of seven areas of Churches associations:

1. Tavoy Mergui Area (Tamhin and Ban Donyang Karen Refugee Camps);

CHAPTER 13

2. East Daw Na Area (Umpium and Noh Poe Refugee Camps);

3. Thoo Mwei Area (1) (Maela Camp Karen Refugee Camp);

4. Mae Ra Moe Area (Mae Rah Moe Camp Karen Refugee Camp);

5. Cholodraw Area (Mae La Oo Camp Karen Refugee Camp);

6. Has Mu Ber Area (Internally Displaced Persons Area);

7. Shwe Gyin Area (Internally Displaced Persons Area).

The KKBC serves an independent body alongside TKBC of Thailand and the KBC of Burma. The Karen Baptist churches suffered again severely from 1995-2000 when the Democratic Karen Buddhist Army, (now BGF, Border Guard Force) split from the mainline Karen National Union, backed by the Burma military regime. They began to gnaw on their own brothers and sisters who are Christians. They launched a series of attacks upon Christian churches in the Karen State and churches in the refugee camps. One possible reason for this conflict is,

> …though the majority of Karens are Buddhist, the Karen political leadership and leadership of the Karen insurgency have always been overwhelming Christian, a legacy of American missionary influence over the 19th and early 20th centuries. The DKBA breakaway was rooted in the perceived discrimination by the Christian leadership against local Buddhist Karen communities and the Buddhist Karen rank-and-file of the Karen insurgency KNLA (DKBA).

Thus the DKBA turned against the Christian Karens because they felt marginalized and not properly represented in the leadership affairs. They joined the Burmese military regime and become an irritant for the KNU and a source of fear for the refugee camps. The regime knew how to strike the iron when it was hot and as a result of that there were a series of massive attacks on several refugee camps in Thailand side. At present, things have improved as Karen Baptist churches in the refugee camps enjoy favorable freedom, though travel outside of the camps is restricted.

Suffice to say, today Burma is still controlled by military dictatorship. Perhaps Burma remains one of the most repressed countries on earth. Rosalie Hall Hunt recognizes that, "Among those hardest hit by the nation's woes is the community of faith. Often Christians are deliberately targeted, especially the ethnic minorities, where the percentage of Christians is impressively high" (Hunt, 2005:353). But there is hope: "along with thousands of pagodas, the spires of churches dot the landscape." And hence, in Judson's own words, "the future is as bright as the promises of God."

If asked, "Lord, is it how you build your Church?" The answer will be invariably "yes!" It is how he builds his Church—among the weak and the oppressed; amidst severe persecution and zero tolerance. Yes, he will continue to build his Church among the refugees and the displaced—the gates of hell will not overcome it. Religious freedom for the Karens is fragile and Walter Shurden (*Four Fragile Freedoms*) is right. But the fragile freedom can be a solid ground upon which Christ will build his Church. In this I am a witness, a cheerleader and a player.

Bibliography

Democratic Karen Buddhist Army (DKBA), en.wikipedia.org.

Hla, Saw Aung. *The Karen History*.

Htoo, Hla E. *The Golden Book*. Go Forward Press. 1955.

Hunt, Rosalie Hall. *Bless God and Take Courage: The Judson History and Legacy*. Judson. 2005.

International Ministries (IM). "Resolution Against Slavery." ABC-USA.org.

Karen Baptist Convention (KBC). en.wikipedia.org.

Kawthoolei Karen Baptist School and College (KKBC). www.sites.google.com/site/kkbbsc/about-k-k-b-c.

Morrison, Ian. *Grandfather Longlegs: Gallant Death of Major H.P. Seagrim*. Faber and Faber LTD, 1946.

Poe, San C. *Burma and the Karens*. Elliot Stock, 1928.

Rogers, Benedict. "Burma's Almost Forgotten." *Christianity Today*. Vol. 48, Issue 3. March 2004.

Thanbyah, T. *The Karens and Their Persecution*. 1904.

"The Rise of Christianity Among the Karens." www.partnersworld.org (PW).

Wardin, Albert W. *Baptists Around the World*.

14 | Working for Peace and Justice in Latin America

Francisco Rodés González

In order to understand the work for peace and justice in Latin America, it is necessary to have, above all, an understanding of the historical context of the continent in the last decades. Allow me to offer a brief summary. Perhaps for some, this is already very well known.

This continent is the cradle of Liberation Theology. It is a land that is alive with the intense dream of a society built upon justice and freedom. While being one of the continents in the world with the most inequality and economic poverty, it is also predominately Christian.

The historical impact of the Cuban revolution decisively affirmed the idea that it was possible to create a different society, one not based on capitalism, free from foreign control of natural resources and that celebrates indigenous cultural values. It was a marking point in the wave of revolutionary fervor that washed over the continent.

One of the fruits of this movement occurred here in Chile with the democratic election of a socialist president. During this time, the Catholic Church also witnessed the flourishing of base communities where simple people from rural and poor areas gathered themselves around the Bible with the question of "what does the Word of God tell us about our situation of poverty and marginalization?"

In Brazil, Paulo Freire was teaching a method that invited the humble to become protagonists of their own liberation, empowering them to create their own agendas, converting themselves into co-creators of a new present and future. This method is known as Popular Education.

But the reaction of the great economic interests did not wait to see what would happen. The establishment of National Security forces, that is to say governance by the military with atrocious repression, shook the continent. This produced thousands of disappearances, tortures and relentless persecution. Many religious leaders were killed. A bishop was even immolated.

Pastors and lay people suffered the same fate. In some places, simply finding a Bible was the justification for such repression. The Bible came to be considered a subversive text. Severe condemnation of Liberation Theology also came from the Vatican. Steps were taken to replace the progressive leadership with a conservative one through a slow but irreversible process. Even still the Catholic Church was recognized, in those darkest moments, as a defender of the human rights of the persecuted.

In the middle of the 80s, democracy began to return. Along with it came a neo-liberal economic model and its growing belief in the privatization of services that had previously been provided by the state. The role of the state was reduced to guaranteeing the function of the free market.

But the current of history cannot be stopped. The liberating energy of the continent was able to be halted, but only temporarily, in order to reappear with a different face but with the same aspiration for justice and liberty. As a result, in a few decades the majority of Latin American governments are progressive and politically leftist. They defend the national interests with nuanced shifts in the prevailing models but with the goal of eliminating poverty and disparity.

These progressive governments have created new forms of continental solidarity like UNASUR, which brings countries together without the presence and influence of Northern powers; like EL ALBA, which is a regional organization with clear objectives to build a form of socialism of its own making that practices solidarity in ways that are very practical and creative (e.g., the exchange of petroleum for healthcare services).

This is the moment that we are living, a very hopeful time. But perhaps the most interesting and significant part is the role that "civil society" is taking. That is to say all those that feel that political parties alone cannot express nor carry out their aspirations and that it is necessary to include the energy and dreams found in organizations that rise up to provide the grass-roots its own way to express itself.

This is where a range of social, indigenous, landless farmer, marginalized poor, student, ecological and other movements take place. They are represented publicly in the World Social Forum, where diverse theological and religious prospects come together. There is a change of mentality even though political action is not lessened. The priority becomes social mobilization and consciousness.

Challenges

There is some agreement on the major obstacles that the movement for peace and justice in Latin American must face.

- The global hegemony of the rich. That is to say that globalization is not a neutral phenomenon which is open to equal possibilities for all. It is important to understand that globalization is a model built on consumerism and individualism that is trying to impose a competitive, violent and egotistical culture which threatens native cultures and the values that they represent;

- The neo-liberal model that still persists and which insists on a secondary role for the state with diminished public services. Also, it makes the national economy subordinate to foreign capital which generates privileged minorities that represent this capital, islands of prosperity in the middle of a broad and pervasive poverty;

- From the religious perspective, there exists a massive influence of churches working internationally with their canned programs of evangelization and Christian education. There are mega-churches that act like grand centers of religious entertainment and promote the "prosperity gospel" with no sense of solidarity;

- Drug trafficking, with its war that is creating thousands of deaths in Mexican communities. Corruption, another widespread wrong in our countries, erodes our moral and social fabric.

Opportunities

What does that all mean for the life and mission of the church in Latin America? We are conscience that a portion of believers are victims of a globalized vision which does not permit them to participate in a new present and future on earth and leaves them only with personal salvation. However, other Christian sectors are participating in the work of building peace and justice. Given this context, here are a few ideas that speak to opportunities for Christian witness.

- See ourselves as a part of civil society, like a sphere of activity at the heart of the social movement web offering support to the struggles that demand social and human rights. Churches can raise their voices, participating and offering their spaces in order to achieve common goals without pretentiousness or the need to be in charge;

- The shared reading of the Bible that represents a major turn in the traditional reading, which is done from on high with a banking educational model (the teacher knows all and deposits knowledge), to a participatory approach where all have something essential to contribute to biblical and contextual interpretation from their life experiences. In reality, there is already a growing movement of biblical reinterpretation in the continent that promotes this method;

- The churches assuming their role as deacons, serving those who are impoverished, old, young, drug addicted, alcoholic, unemployed, incarcerated, etc. Thousands of churches in Latin America develop social programs and become signs of a practical and militant solidarity. These services must see themselves as leaving less of a proselytizing mark than a witness of love for those in need;

- Evangelical churches and among them the Baptist churches, unifying their forces and their witness through ecumenical organizations like The Latin American Council of Churches, CLAI, that has a holistic vision for being a witness for peace and justice in Latin America;

- The promotion of contextualized liturgies that uphold the cultural roots of the continent, that values Latin American identity and that honor the mix of its ancient cultures.

These are, briefly, some of the paths for peace in Latin America. I don't pretend that this is exhaustive but if we affirm our confidence in the way of justice and peace, there will come a day when the sun shines on all of our communities, on all of God's people.

RECOVERY
OF
SIGHT TO THE BLIND

15 | Gender Equality: Incorporating a Christian Perspective

Elsa Leo-Rhynie

Abstract

This paper defines and examines gender equality in the context of biblical teaching and the reality of a patriarchal society. Manifestations of such a society are explored through an examination of socialization and the formation of gender identities, the sex roles adopted in the society and the associated issues of gender stereotyping and the sexual division of labour; the factors which influence these and result in continued expressions of gender inequality. Initiatives taken to address gender inequality since the 1970s are briefly traced and Christian teaching in relation to cultural and traditional gender roles is examined. The importance of continued action to address gender inequality is highlighted by reference to the Millennium Development Goals, and the special role which the Church and Christians have to play in achieving these goals is underscored.

Introduction

The issue of gender equality continues to be controversial in most societies, and is even more so among Christians.

Gender equality can be defined as the recognition of the equal value of men and women in all spheres of societal functioning. While acknowledging that the sexes differ in many ways, their human rights demand that they receive equal treatment. It is important to note that "equal" does not necessarily mean "same."

Definition and expansion of this definition is vital in order to fully appreciate the necessity for and the difficulties involved in achieving equality. Gender refers to the social and cultural differences between the sexes established during the socialization process and reinforced throughout life. It differs from sex, which is determined before birth and is not normally modifiable. Gender therefore, incorporates a broad range of behaviours, roles and positions that are cultural norms for women and men and which determine the contexts and ways of life and work of individuals. Inequality arises because of the power differential which exists between the two groups in terms of access to resources and resource allocation. Most societies are patriarchal, with men enjoying greater power, privilege and status derived from their greater access to those opportunities, benefits and resources which allow them to gain and sustain power.

The pursuit of gender equality is justifiable, not only because of the fact that women and men are equally represented within the population, but also because traditionally the power differential has resulted in women continuing to be disadvantaged and discriminated against. Although the church has been acknowledged as a major influence in societal change, within the patriarchal system of the traditional church itself, gender equality has taken a long time in coming, and the church has been frequently described as the "last bastion of male hegemony."

Many Christians are uncertain how to treat with gender equality. The church's attitudes towards sex, sexual relationships, and gender have been largely based on the biblical guidelines set out by Paul in his letters to the Ephesians and Corinthians – those best known are:

> Wives, submit to your own husbands, as to the Lord. For the husband is head of the wife, as also Christ is head of the church; and He is the Savior of the body. Therefore, just as the church is subject to Christ, so let the wives be to their own husbands in everything (Eph. 5:22-24).

> Now I want you to realize that the head of every man is Christ, and the head of the woman is man, and the head of Christ is God... For man did not come from woman, but woman from man; neither was man created for woman, but woman for man ... (1 Cor. 1: 3, 8-9 NIV).

And in Timothy chapter 2:

> A woman should learn in quietness and full submission. I do not permit a woman to teach or to have authority over a man; she

must be silent. For Adam was formed first, then Eve. And Adam was not the one deceived; it was the woman who was deceived and became a sinner (1Tim. 2:11-14 NIV).

These guidelines set out very definite roles for women and men, and traditionally these have been accepted as "gospel truth." This has led to the strong religious and cultural support for a patriarchal society. Manifestations of this type of society are reflected in many cultural forms and practices, which have been established over time and transmitted across generations during the process of socialization.

Socialization and Gender Identity

A comprehensive research project on socialization in the Caribbean was undertaken 20 years ago between 1993 and 1995, funded by UNICEF and designed, directed and administered by Janet Brown of the Caribbean Child Development Centre and the late Professor Barry Chevannes of the Faculty of Social Sciences of the University of the West Indies. It was mainly concerned with understanding the social behaviour of men in Caribbean societies, and exploring the processes relating to the origins and expressions of gender-related behaviour. The study focussed on children and youth in the working classes of three Caribbean countries - Dominica, Guyana, and Jamaica.

A review of the study (Leo-Rhynie, 1998) revealed many interesting findings - the gender distinctions in socialization and labour in the Caribbean and the extent to which these are clearly rooted in strong beliefs about masculinity and femininity, manhood and womanhood; based to some extent on religious teachings as well as on traditional cultural values. Assertion of male supremacy and dominance is clear: a man is tough, he is the provider, the head of the house. Chevannes (2001) notes that: "a man minds but a woman cares." "Minding" refers to protection and financial support whereas "caring" refers to the domestic and caregiving roles expected of the mother. The following statements from male participants vividly reflect their opinions.

"God made us to control the world, animals, women, everybody;"

"[N]o woman can brilliant like a man, because once you is a man you is a king. A woman is only a queen;"

"[A] woman no suppose to be the head a nutten as long as man involve in a it - a so the earth set up."

Stereotypes of dominant, public, male; and accommodating, private, female persist. Gender polarization is also strongly displayed in attitudes to sexual behaviour. Men are expected to take the initiative in sexual approaches, and women are still treated as victims and/or property - subject to rape, abuse, violence, and abandonment. Brown and Chevannes reported that both men and women consider that man/woman violence is deserved when a woman does not adequately fulfill her expected role in terms of domestic duties and sexual fidelity. There is the assertion, strongly supported, that "uman fi get lik" (women are to be beaten).

In the socialization of children many parents follow a public/ private; street/ yard; male/female divide described in Guyana as **"tie the heifer, loose the bull." Girls are confined to the yard and closely guarded, while boys have greater freedom to roam and experiment.** Using the term "male privileging" Figueroa (2004) draws attention to the "historical privileging of males which has provided them with a wider social space," i.e. an extension of the domestic "space" accorded the girls, to include the street and the community. The girls are expected to be confined to the domestic sphere and involved in activities such as cleaning, cooking and laundry.

Brown and Chevannes report that it is assumed that if girls are allowed too much freedom they will "get into trouble." They will be exposed to sexual abuse and assault, sexual involvement and the possibility of pregnancy; boys are also exposed but the danger for them is crime, including drugs. The street, however, is expected to toughen and prepare boys for survival, but the street has nothing to offer girls besides danger and disgrace.

Gender identities are also influenced by the media and popular music - male/ female roles in society are very often reflected in the lyrics of popular songs - calypso , soca, reggae and dance hall in Jamaica - and many of these reveal a contempt for women on the one hand, and admiration on the other. Lake (1998) comments that:

> Even in instances where female artists write and record their own lyrics, they often add to the sexist ideas and negative imagery which only serve to further denigrate women and undermine their integrity.

Cable TV, films and other media depict scenes of male/female violence and inappropriate representations of male/female relationships. Social media have captured the minds of our youth and Marcia Forbes (2012) in her excellent book

Streaming: Social Media, Mobile Lifestyles based on research among youth, points to the ways in which the new digital communication technology is changing the life styles of our young men and young women yet maintaining the patriarchal ideology. Such influences are powerful in the shaping of the attitudes of men towards women, of women to men, and the attitudes of both men and women to themselves.

Gender Roles in the Society

Socialization prepares girls and boys to assume certain expected gender roles as adults. These roles are therefore socially constructed from established social patterns and determine to a large extent the relationships which exist between adult men and women. The roles are enforced because of accepted social norms, and are not static; they can and do change over time as a result of power shifts and new norms within the society.

In 2010, Leo-Rhynie reported on research to determine the contemporary views of young people about gender; a wide ranging study in the Anglophone Caribbean conducted by the UWI Institute for Gender and Development Studies. Most of the young people responding felt that gender equality was a desirable objective and that in terms of school subjects, occupations and work tasks, there should be little distinction between men and women. There were, however, some notable differences which indicate that some traditional attitudes persist. I include a few of the results from the Jamaican sample to illustrate:

> A majority of students felt that the following occupations are more suited to men than women: Airline pilot, bus driver, construction worker, engineer farmer and car mechanic, while hairdresser and nurse were seen as "female" occupations.

> Washing the car and protecting the family were seen as men's chores while washing clothes and cleaning the house should be women's chores.

> The majority of male students felt that women should not take action on any important matter before first seeking the permission of their male partners/ husbands/ boyfriends, while the majority of girls disagreed.

A majority of both boys and girls felt that:

- final decisions about important domestic matters should always be made by men;

- men need to have better jobs than women in order to provide for their families.

Boys felt that it was alright for girls to make the first move in boy-girl relationships; while boys agreed and girls disagreed that men need to give gifts to their girlfriends /partners in order to sustain the relationship.

The roles which women and men traditionally play in society differ. In 1989, Caroline Moser wrote of women's triple roles in society: reproductive, productive and community based. Women are expected to assume primary responsibility for the reproductive work of the family – household duties as well the bearing of children, their rearing and care as well as the care of the elderly and the sick. In many instances, they also have to be involved in productive work to maintain the family and very often, despite the limited time available for such involvement, they also participate in community activities – usually church based.

Men, whose major role is expected to be productive and who, in most instances, bear little or no responsibility for reproductive work, have the time to devote to the community activities and they use this to leverage themselves into leadership positions and so gain the power and status which help to maintain the patriarchal structures of society. Women traditionally have little opportunity to demonstrate their leadership capabilities and skills and so these are undervalued and underused.

This sexual division of labour creates norms, identities and institutions that stereotype and discriminate against women. Linnette Vassell in 2006 presented figures to show that in 2002, the percentage of women who were parliamentarians in Jamaica was 12.3 percent. This was well below the Caribbean average of 20.8 per cent and significantly lower than the 50 percent which feminist activists the world over have been proposing. The appointment of a woman as Prime Minister of Jamaica in 2006 and again in 2011 was hailed as a victory for women but this merely masked the lack of gender parity and under representation of women at the level of national policy determination.

It is not only at the level of parliament and policy determination that women are underrepresented. Despite the fact that in the Anglophone Caribbean including Jamaica, more girls than boys attend school; more girls than boys progress to the second cycle of secondary schooling; more girls than boys sit CXC CSEC and CAPE examinations; more girls than boys are successful in these examinations; more women than men enter university, and more women than men gain degrees; several barriers exist to women achieving their productive potential (Miller, 2000). The following comments from a range of sources highlight the problem:

> Against the background of higher educational qualifications of females, it is interesting to find that translation to the labour market is not as expected. Females are still heavily represented among the unemployed group, and are particularly vulnerable to the shocks that affect the economy. Females require higher education to break the pattern that exists in the labour market whereby males with lower levels of education can attract relatively good quality employment. For females, the labour market is not as generous.   (Ricketts & Benfield, 2000)

> Although females were, in a number of instances, more qualified than their male counterparts, this was not always proportionately reflected in pay packages. (Jamaica Employers Federation Survey of Salaries, 2000)

> The presence of women in decision-making is not commensurate with their contribution to society. … [This] can be demonstrated by objective data. It is a fact that women have been steadily leaving the domestic sphere and entering the labour market and different areas of public life. Nonetheless, their new participatory role is a subordinate one and does not extend to the political and social spheres where power is exercised. (ECLAC Report, 1999).

> Women applying for loans will need more documentation than men and are often viewed as credit risks by bank officials even when they are as qualified as men who are granted loans. (Paulin, 2003).

Barriers to women who seek independence through business ownership are many, including:

- Lack of access to capital and credit;

- Discriminatory attitudes on the part of creditors and clients, and stereotypes about women in business; many women complain that they are treated as though they are involved in a hobby rather than in a serious enterprise;

- Exclusion from the business information "network;"

- Women's self-perceptions and lack of socialization to entrepreneurship at home, school or in the society. This results in a lack of self-confidence and concerns about issues such as competition and profit.

Despite this, women are increasingly identifying and exploiting the advantages of being their own bosses: ownership allows them to exercise levels of influence that are often denied them as employees in large organisations. These include

- Access to, as well as responsibility for, decision making;

- Authority to plan for and bring about change;

- Opportunities for leadership;

- Opportunities to re-evaluate one's self worth, and to assess one's achievement value.

Business ownership also provides women with status and recognition and allows them to escape the blatant harassment as well as subtle messages of hostility and repression which are often communicated in large organisations, and which erode their self-confidence and self-esteem.

Women, therefore, have been using their education and earnings as tools of resistance and empowerment; they allow women to have options, and their increased self-esteem and self-confidence allow them to challenge the authority of their mates. This is not appreciated by the men, who often resort to violence to keep the women "in line" and also bemoan the fact that women are refusing to "know their place", and will try to fight back in the face of abuse and violence.

Caribbean women have always been feminists, even before the word was coined. They have always exercised the power they have to bring about change; and the active role which women have played in determining their life experiences has been documented by a number of writers. Challenges to the patriarchal society have taken place slowly over the years and in the twentieth century a wave of feminist activism led to increased awareness of the inhumane ways in which women all over the world were kept as second class citizens. Women agitated for the right to vote, and for many other rights which young people today take for granted.

About seven years ago, a group of students doing a project for their sociology course asked if they could interview me about gender issues. I agreed, and the session with six of them, two male and four female students, lasted for about an hour. That interview brought me sharply into contemporary perspective as these students, who were all born between 1985 and 1987, and were just touching twenty, were looking to me to share my experience of what was for them history. It was very possible that their parents had been teenagers or in their early twenties when the first United Nations International Conference on Women was held in Mexico in 1976, the oldest of them was born in the final year of the United Nations Decade for Women 1976 – 1985 when the wave for change in the oppression and subordination of women worldwide was international in scope, and when women gradually began to appreciate the objectives and driving force behind the worldwide Women's Movement. My interviewers were babies when the world was waking up to the reality of life for women all over the world, and the plight they faced as they were treated as second or no class citizens with no access to resources, no rights, no hope for an independent existence without the sponsorship of or partnership with a man. They were shocked when I told them that when I had my children there was no legal provision for Maternity Leave, and that women working in the commercial sector at that time had to resign once they became pregnant, whether or not they were married. Use of the term 'illegitimate' to describe a child born out of wedlock prior to the Status of Children Legislation in Jamaica in the 1970s was new to them.

They had grown up in a Jamaica and a Caribbean which had responded to the global call to examine the status of women and to take deliberate steps to improve this status; a world where the words "feminism" and "feminist" may still have been debated, but these words were in their dictionaries and did not generate the strong political and emotional reactions which they did in the 1970s and 1980s. I referred them to the second Lucille Mathurin Mair lecture given by Dr Peggy Antrobus in 2000, in which she recounted the legislative, social and political change which women's activism, fuelled by the world women's movement, was able to bring about in the Caribbean since the early 1970s.

These young people have entered adulthood in an altered landscape, and today, gender issues do not raise emotional temperatures to the extent that they did 35 years ago; indeed, there are many people who feel that there are no more issues for women, especially Caribbean women, to address in the promotion of women and women's rights. Several individuals express the view that the Movement has been too successful; and they point to the larger numbers of women than men attending universities in the USA, the UK, Australia and other parts of the world to support their viewpoint. At our local and regional universities the enrolment is predominantly female, and the 'male marginalisation' and 'men at risk' theses, regarded with some suspicion in the 1980s, are now strongly supported.

The Christian Response to Gender (in)Equality

Despite the gains, however, gender equality is still an issue for concern: issues such as sexual discrimination in all its forms, equal work for equal pay, sexual harassment, domestic violence, gender violence including rape, are all compelling contemporary indicators of gender inequality which need to be tackled in today's world.

Achieving gender equality is a highly relevant concern for Christians who commit to following the commandment of Christ to "love one another, even as I have loved you", and who died on the Cross for both women and men.

At the start of this presentation I quoted a number of verses which are often used to justify the gender inequality, sex role stereotyping and sexual discrimination frequently observed in the church and by Christians. It is interesting that the verses of scripture which follow these assertions are not as firmly etched in the consciousness and memory of practising Christians. These verses seem to concede to a complementary and equal valuing of roles rather than the dominance /submissiveness earlier implied.

> Husbands, love your wives, just as Christ loved the church and gave himself up for her to make her holy... without stain or wrinkle or any other blemish, but holy and blameless ... In this same way, husbands ought to love their wives as their own bodies. He who loves his wife loves himself. ...However, each one of you also must love his wife as he loves himself, and the wife must respect her husband (Eph. 5: 25-26, 28, 33).

This follow up verse which indicates that husbands must love their wives and wives must respect their husbands suggests instead that the man and woman have equal power and say in decision-making. I cannot believe that God expects women to submit to their husbands "in everything", and allow their lives to be completely taken over by another individual. What if the decisions of the husband are cruel and criminal? Dishonest and immoral? Harmful to others? Discussion and agreement on the best possible decision gives equal value to both in the decision making process. My mother – a good Christian woman – once conceded that my father, her husband, was the head of the house....but, she added: I am the neck!

Paul also acknowledges the complementarity of the male and female roles when he continues his letter to the Corinthians:

> Nevertheless, in the Lord woman is not independent of man, nor is man independent of woman. For as woman came from man, so also man is born of woman. But everything comes from God (1 Cor. 11: 11-12 NIV).

Women's unique reproductive role is highlighted in Paul's letter to Timothy:

> But women will be saved through childbearing—if they continue in faith, love and holiness with propriety (1Tim. 2:15 NIV).

The theologian, Antony Webb comments:

> … we can glean that even if the creation account is to be taken literally, and that God did indeed create man first and then womyn from man, it all becomes inconsequential in the end since God is the Creator of all things. Thus, we find equality here amidst an unequal statement of how the world is ordered. (Webb, 2001:275).

Monnica Terwilliger (1998) points to a number of instances in which as she puts it, "Jesus was an advocate for women's freedom and equality." She highlights the mercy he showed for the woman caught in adultery, and his recognition of the injustice of punishment for the woman while the man or men involved remained unpunished; the woman at the well was not ignored because of her race, but Jesus gave her hope by sharing the scriptures with her; and he raised from the dead a widow's only son. His appearance after His death was to women first, and it became their task to "tell the disciples." As a result, Terwilliger asserts that "women were central in the early church; the Bible depicts women co-ministering as leaders, teachers, benefactors, and even apostles." She uses this as a strong and cogent argument against the decision of some churches to deny women leadership roles/positions in their congregations.

Hannah Mudge (2013) is part of a collective of five women in the United Kingdom who have established a Christian Feminist network. Their agenda "reflects the interests and expertise of all members – from theology and relationships to race and violence against women." The network is growing as they base their work on the recognition that "gender inequality wasn't part of the message of Jesus and it's time to get the word out." This was recognized earlier by Terwilliger (1998) who asserted that:

> Contrary to the beliefs of some, being a Christian and a feminist is not a contradiction. It simply means that, as women, we are empowered to be whom God calls us to be - homemakers, grandmothers, pastors, engineers, or all of the above at different times in our lives. God's plan for women and men is spelled out in the Bible. There He provides an outline for how the family should function, how to love each other, and, by example, the central role of women in society. By applying these truths, we can experience both true feminism and true Christianity.

The Future

Goal 3 of the Millennium Development Goals seeks to "Promote Gender Equality And Empower Women." Highlighted are the facts that:

- Globally, women occupy only 25 per cent of senior management positions and, in 2008/2009, were on average paid 23 per cent less than men;
- Business ownership is concentrated in men's hands throughout the developing world;
- Women are largely relegated to more vulnerable forms of employment.

Over the past 40 years significant change has taken place but the power structures have remained highly resistant to the demand for transformation. Not only is there a reluctance on the part of the "power groups" to surrender this power, but women lack the political, socio-cultural, physical and personal autonomy which would allow them to exercise the power which is needed. Men are usually regarded as possessing the attributes required for political participation and leadership, and women's self-worth and self-esteem are often eroded by repeated instances of psychological, sexual and physical hostility, abuse and violence.

The church can play a major part in ensuring that the gender equality being sought is achieved. The Rev. Dr. Hyacinth Boothe (2000) Jamaican theologian, in her book, *Breaking the Silence – a Woman's Voice,* highlights the fact that women's voices, though vociferously heard in a wide range of areas have been largely silent in the traditional churches except in the choir, in Sunday School and in women's organizations. She notes that women seeking to have a voice have had to counter the many theological arguments – based on Biblical interpretation - which have been advanced to deny women access to church leadership. These arguments have been so accepted by men and women alike, that women who strive to break with tradition find themselves in many instances without the support of their own gender in their struggle.

Paul, writing to Timothy, advised:

> Do not rebuke an older man harshly, but exhort him as if he were your father. Treat younger men as brothers, older women as mothers, and younger women as sisters, with absolute purity (1 Tim. 5:1-2 NIV).

In his letter to the Galatians Paul also says:

> So in Christ Jesus you are all children of God through faith, for all of you who were baptized into Christ have clothed yourselves with Christ. There is neither Jew nor Gentile, neither slave nor free, nor is there male and female, for you are all one in Christ Jesus (Gal. 3:26-29 NIV).

Paul makes it clear that we are all children of God through our shared faith. And that we ought not to identify ourselves by gender, race, or class.

The church is one of the major societal socializing agents and so must assume responsibility for transmission of gender messages, directly from the pulpit and indirectly through its governance and auxiliaries, its organization, systems and practices. It is critical that Church leaders understand the influences which socialize and create the gendered identities which our young people develop as they grow, so that programmes designed by the church to reach the youth can incorporate interventions which can address these influences and promote change leading to greater gender equality.

I close using the words of the Rev. Dr. Boothe who urged:

> We need to say 'no' to the historical and cultural stereotypes attributed to women....we are human beings made in the image of God...we are called upon to promote a new day – of decency, morality and dignity and this we must teach our sons and daughters. ...Women before us have struggled, marched, borne ridicule, been imprisoned, so that we might enjoy the fruits of their pain and tears. Let us make sure that we do not fail them.

Bibliography

Allen, C. "Researching STD's in the Caribbean." *Gender: A Caribbean Multidisciplinary Perspective.* E. Leo-Rhynie, B. Bailey & C. Barrow eds. Ian Randle Publishers. 1997.

Antrobus, P. *The Rise and Fall of Feminist Politics in the Caribbean Women's Movement 1975 – 1995.* Lucille Mathurin Mair Lecture. CGDSMona Unit UWI. 2000.

Bailey, B. "Sexist Patterns of Formal and Non-formal Education Programmes: The Case of Jamaica." *Gender: A Caribbean Multidisciplinary Perspective.* E. Leo-Rhynie, B. Bailey & C. Barrow, eds. Ian Randle Publishers. 1997.

Brown, J. *"Why Man Stay So, Why Woman Stay So": Findings of the Gender Socialization Project.* St, Michael, Barbados: Women and Development Unit, UWI. May 1995.

Brown, J. and Chevannes, B. *Why Man Stay So: Tie the Hiefer, Loose the Bull. An Examination of Gender Socialisation in the Caribbean.* The UWI, UNICEF. 1998.

Chevannes, B. *Learning to be a Man: Culture, Socialization and Gender Identity in Five Caribbean Communities.* UWI Press: Kingston, Jamaica. 2001.

Drayton, K.. "White man's knowledge: Sex, race and class in Caribbean English language textbooks.", *Gender: A Caribbean multidisciplinary perspective.* E. Leo-Rhynie, B. Bailey & C. Barrow, eds. Ian Randle Publishers. 1997

Economic Commission on Latin America and the Caribbean (ECLAC). *Participation and Leadership in Latin America and the Caribbean: Gender Indicators.* Santiago, Chile. 1999.

Ffolkes, S. "Violence against women: Some legal issues." *Gender: A Caribbean Multidisciplinary Perspective.* E. Leo-Rhynie, B. Bailey & C. Barrow, eds. Ian Randle Publishers. 1997.

Figueroa, M. "Male privileging and male 'academic underperformance' in Jamaica." *Interrogating Caribbean Masculinities: theoretical and empirical analyses.* R. Reddock, ed. UWI Press. 2004.

Forbes, M. *Streaming; Social Media, Mobile Lifestyles.* Phase 3 Productions:Kingston, Jamaica. 2012.

Hodge, M. "The shadow of a whip: A comment on male-female relations in the Caribbean." *Is Massa Day Dead? Black Doods in the Caribbean.* O. Coombs, ed. Anchor Books. 1974.

Jamaica Employers Federation Survey of Salaries. Jamaica Employers Federation. 2000.

Lake, O. *Subordination in the Midst of Liberation Theology.* Carolina Academic Press. 1998.

Lal, E. *Gender Equality in Christianity: A Psychological Analysis of Religious Tradition.* Azusa Pacific University. 2011.

Leo-Rhynie, E. "Girls' toys, boys' toys: forming gender identity." *Caribbean Journal of Education*. Vol. 17 No. 2. 1995.

_____. "Class, Race, and Gender Issues in Child Rearing in the Caribbean." *Caribbean Families: Diversity Among Ethnic Groups*. J. Roopnarine and J. Brown, eds. Ablex. 1997.

_____. "Socialization and the Development of Gender Identity: Theoretical Formulations and Caribbean Research." *Caribbean Portraits: Essays on Gender Ideologies and Identities*. C. Barrow, ed. Ian Randle Publishers. 1998.

_____. "Gender Ideology." *Gender Differentials at the Secondary and Tertiary Levels of the Educational System in the Anglophone Caribbean*. Regional Coordinating Unit of the Institute of Gender and Development Studies (IGDS) of the University of the West Indies. 2010.

Miller, E. *Education for all in the Caribbean in the 1900s: Retrospect and Prospect*. UNESCO. 2000.

Moser, C. *Gender planning and development: theory, practice, and training*. Routledge. 1993.

Mudge, H. "Christian feminists aim to spread the word on gender equality." *The Guardian*. 28 February 2013.

Paulin, D. "Female entrepreneurs battle discrimination." *Jamaica Observer*. July 29, 2003.

Ricketts, H. & Benfield, W. "Gender and the Jamaican Labour Market: the decade of the 90s." *The Construction of Gender Development Indicators for Jamaica*. P. Mohammed, ed. Kingston: Jamaica PIOJ/UNDP/ CIDA. 2000.

Taylor, E. "Women in school administration." *Gender: A Caribbean Multidisciplinary Perspective*. E. Leo-Rhynie, B. Bailey & C. Barrow, eds. Ian Randle Publishers. 1997.

Taylor, P. Nation *Dance: Religion, Identity and Culture Differences in the Caribbean*. Indiana University Press. 2001.

Terwilliger, M. *Christianity requires Gender Equality and Respect for Life* www.fnsa.org/fall98/terwilliger.html. 1998.

United States Agency for International Development. *A gender analysis of the educational achievement of boys and girls in the Jamaican educational system*. 2005.

Vassell, Linnett. "Bringing the broader context home: gender, human rights and governance in the Caribbean." *Caribbean Quarterly: Unraveling Gender, Development and Civil Society in the Caribbean*. Taitu Heron and Hilary Nicholson, eds. Vol.52, Nos. 2 & 3 June – Sept. 2006.

Webb, W. J. *Slaves, Women and Homosexuals: Exploring the Hermeneutics of CulturalAnalysis*. InterVarsity Press. 2001.

16 | The Challenges of a Changing Environment in the Asia Pacific Region

Les Fussell

Praise be to the God and Father of our Lord Jesus Christ, the Father of compassion and the God of all comfort, who comforts us in all our troubles, so that we can comfort those in any trouble with the comfort we ourselves have received from God. 2 Cor. 1:17

The challenges of a changing environment in the Asia Pacific Region are closely linked to the phenomena of climate change and the factors linked to it. Climate change, also known as global warming, is being monitored across the globe and much scientific research has gone into determining what is contributing to it. While there is some conjecture around the extent that climate change is a natural occurrence versus that caused by human-induced changes to the environment, the global community is well aware it must address the issue. The parties to the United Nations Framework Convention on Climate Change have met annually from 1995 in Conferences of the Parties (COP) meetings to assess progress in dealing with climate change. In 1997, the Kyoto Protocol was produced at the COP meeting, establishing legally binding obligations until 2012 for developed countries to reduce their greenhouse gas (GHG) emissions. The COP meeting in Copenhagen in 2009 was an attempt to develop binding obligations for both developed and developing countries for later than 2012. The Copenhagen Accord, a non-binding agreement, was not formally adopted as part of the UN Framework Convention on Climate Change at that meeting, but was signed by 139 countries. The political will at the policy level in many of the world governments lacked the fortitude in Copenhagen to adequately address the issue and the man-made causes of this environmental issue.

The COP meeting Cancun December 2010 was seen by many as an opportunity to progress the Copenhagen Accord with firmer commitments in the areas of reducing emissions, verification, climate change aid, sharing clean technology, forests, and adaption. The incremental, non-legally binding Cancun Accord, signed by more than 190 countries, included arrangements for protecting rainforests, a planned $US100 billion green climate fund to help the most vulnerable nations cope with the effects of climate change, while also providing assistance in adaptation strategies for the most vulnerable countries. The Cancun Accord includes steps to ensure transparency in emissions measurement and reporting - a key sticking point for China and the USA in the Copenhagen Accord. But while representatives from more than 190 countries agreed to seek "deep cuts" in emissions, the Accord does not include targets big enough to meet the goal of limiting the global temperature rise since industrialisation to two degrees. It is estimated that the emissions pledges in the Cancun Accord would set the world on course for 3.2 degrees warming - enough, scientists say, to cause droughts, crop failure, species extinction and increased damage from floods and storms.

This paper seeks to outline some of the features of the global climate change phenomena and looks broadly at environmental difficulties that have been observed in the Asia Pacific in the last couple of decades. It summarizes what are the broad implications for the region and what will it mean, particularly for the vulnerable poor, if nothing is done to address underlying fundamental cause of these environmental difficulties.

General Observations on Climate Change Globally

"The scientific evidence is overwhelming: climate change is a serious global threat, and it demands a global response," Sir Nicholas Stern warned in a report compiled for the UK government in 2006. Stern's report assessed a wide range of impacts of climate change, particularly economic costs as well as other risks (Stern, 2006). Global climate change poses a threat to the well-being of human and non-human environments through impacts on human health, lifestyles, biodiversity, productivity, and ecosystem functioning. It is not the intent of this paper to put the argument for the veracity of climate change. Nor is it the intent of the paper to argue the case of the extent that climate change is linked to human factors and/or natural climatic variations.

Nonetheless, national academies such as the Australian Academy of Science, the Royal Society in Britain, the U.S. National Academy of Sciences and the French Academy of Sciences, and the Geological Society of London, to name a few, have all in recent times produced statements detailing the extent of consensus about climate change science. The independent messages are consistent and urgent. They include that the role of greenhouse gases in the atmosphere is well understood, and that increasing the atmospheric concentration of the principal anthropogenic greenhouse gas, CO2, leads to higher mean global surface temperatures. It is accepted that CO2 has increased substantially during the past century, to the highest levels seen in 800,000 years, and that this increase is primarily from human activity as a result of burning fossil fuels, with a lesser contribution from other activities such as the manufacture of cement and deforestation. The global warming observed over the past 150 years of about 0.7oC is due primarily to human-induced emissions of heat-trapping gases. This evidence links climate change to an increase in atmospheric CO2 levels, which are linked to rising levels of pollution (U.S. Global Change Research Program, 2009).

Since the beginning of the industrial revolution, atmospheric concentrations of carbon dioxide (CO_2), the chief heat-trapping GHG, have risen 35%, from about 280 to 377 parts per million. Atmospheric concentrations of methane, the second leading GHG, have more than doubled over the past two centuries. These and other GHG increases have led to a 0.6°C increase in the global average surface temperature since 1900. Eleven of the last twelve years (1995-2006) rank among the warmest years since record keeping of global surface temperatures began in 1850. Furthermore, the UN's World Meteorological Organisation (WMO) and the US National Climate Change Centre have observed that 2010 was in the top three warmest years on record: tying with 2005, with only 1998 being warmer since records began, and only marginally so. The decade from 2001 to 2010 has set a new record as the warmest decade ever since temperatures were recorded.

If current emissions trends are not altered, global temperatures are expected to rise up to 5.8°C by 2100, according to the Intergovernmental Panel on Climate Change (IPCC) (2007). To keep the global average temperature from rising more than 2°C above pre-industrial levels, worldwide emissions would need to peak around 2015 and subsequently decline by 40 to 45% by 2050 compared to 1990 levels (Baumert *et al.*, 2005). That would mean reducing annual carbon dioxide emissions to the equivalent of 22 billion tonnes by 2050 -- compared with 56 billion tonnes emitted now.

General Global Impact of Climate Change

Climate change through rising air temperatures has contributed to a loss of biodiversity, arctic ice, glacial and snowfields disappearance, rising sea levels, reduced food yields, increased climatic variability and increased economic challenges (Simiyu, 2009). Climate change has been shown to impact ecosystems by modification in species distributions and in population sizes; changes in the timing of reproduction or migration events; increase in the frequency of pest and disease outbreaks; destruction coral reefs through bleaching episodes when local sea surface temperatures have increased (Simiyu, 2009).

It is estimated that every year climate change leaves over 300,000 people dead (roughly equivalent to the 2004 Asian tsunami annually). These deaths are from weather-related disasters and gradual environmental degradation (Climate Change Human Impact Report, 2009). Over 90% of this death toll relates to gradual onset of climate change from deterioration in environmental quality, such as reduction in arable land, desertification and sea level rise. Furthermore, the Climate Change Human Impact Report (CCHI) states that "every year climate change leaves 325 million people seriously affected, and economic losses of US$125 billion. Four billion people are vulnerable to the effects of climate change, and 500 million people are at extreme risk."

The CCHI Report (2009) reported the findings of IPCC in its Fourth Assessment Report that found world weather patterns to have become more extreme, with more intense heat waves, prolonged droughts, frequent and intense rainfall events. The changes in timing and location of rainfall have been linked to the more unpredictable weather rhythms. Moreover, the number of weather-related disasters (storms, hurricanes, floods, heat waves, droughts) has doubled in the last 20 years. There are 400 weather-related disasters per year, resulting in almost 90 million people requiring immediate assistance.

Notwithstanding such immediate impacts of extreme weather, climate change is gradual. The CCHI Report (2009) summarizes these gradual changes as "rising earth surface temperatures, rising sea levels, desertification, changes in local rainfall and river run-off patterns with increased precipitation in high latitudes and decreased precipitation in sub-tropical latitudes, salinisation of river deltas, accelerated species extinction rates, loss of biodiversity and a weakening of ecosystems." The impacts of these gradual changes are substantive:

- Reduction in access to fresh and safe drinking water, negatively affects health;

- Threats to food security due to limiting crop choices and decreasing yields resulting in famines;

- Forced migration, possibly leading to conflict, due to poverty, famine, desertification, land degradation and rising sea levels (leading to permanent displace on small island Pacific nations such as Kiribati and Tuvalu);

- Increased insect-borne diseases such as malaria, other health problems such as diarrhea and respiratory illnesses (CCHI Report 2009).

Global Impact of Climate Change on the Poor

While the threat of climate change is global, the prospects are worst for the poorer developing countries. The Stern report concluded that if temperatures rise by 5°C, up to 10% of global output could be lost (Stern, 2006). This means the poorest countries would lose at least 10% of their output. However, poverty increases vulnerability to climate change, resulting in a disproportionate burden on the poorest countries. Margareta Wahlstrom, the United Nations Assistant Secretary General stated that "the countries least responsible for global warming – the poorest developing nations – will be the most affected by its consequences. In the cruel calculus of disasters, the poorer the community, the greater its vulnerability to natural hazards and the more difficult its recovery" (quoted in CCHI Report, 2009).

This is grossly unjust given the largest consumers and thus polluters are not the poor, but the rich. The poorest 20% of the world consume only 1.6% of the world's resources, where as the richest 20% of the world consume 76% of the world's resources (World Bank Development Indicators 2008). "It is a grave global justice concern that those who suffer most from climate change have done the least to cause it. Developing countries bear over nine-tenths of the climate change burden: 98% of the seriously affected and 99% of all deaths from weather-related disasters, along with over 90% of the total economic losses. The 50 Least Developed Countries contribute less than 1% of global carbon emissions" (CCHI Report, 2009).

Those most vulnerable to the human impact of climate change, the poor, are exposed to both the physical changes and the socio-economic implications. The CCHI Report (2009) estimates that 2.8 billion poor people are most vulnerable to physical changes "such as weather-related disasters and gradual environmental degradation, which are already occurring faster and more intensely in developing countries than in developed countries because of warmer starting temperatures and increased proximity to the Equator, where many of the poorer countries are geographically located."

On the other hand, 60% of the world's population or 4 billion people (those living on less than US$10 a day) are subject to socio-economic vulnerability (a measure of how well individuals and communities respond and adapt to climate change) due to climate change (CCHI Report 2009). The poor are vulnerable and less able to adapt in socio-economic terms as they live without access to basic social development and infrastructure (affordable health care, water, electricity and paved roads).

Environmental Difficulties in the Asia Pacific

There are a range of environmental difficulties in the Asia Pacific region, of which some may be linked to climate change, while others appear to have no linkage.

Earthquakes/tsunamis

In the past two decades, the Asia Pacific region has seen the impact of devastating earthquakes, with some followed by equally devastating tsunamis. Some of these earthquakes have flattened whole cities and regions (e.g. Gujarat, 2001; Pakistan, 2005, 2008; multiple locations in Indonesia - Nias, 2005; Aceh, 2004; Yogyakarta, 2006; Padang, 2009), causing significant loss of life. Indonesia is the most disaster-prone country in the world, according to the UN Office for the Coordination of Humanitarian Affairs. In 2009 alone, it experienced 469 earthquakes with a magnitude of five or higher – more than any other nation.

Earthquakes, when they have occurred in the ocean floor, can cause large tsunamis that once they reach land, wash all before them. The earthquake off the coast of Indonesia on 26 December 2004 produced a tsunami that caused a huge loss of life (more than 300,000) across multiple countries (Indonesia, Thailand, Malaysia, Burma, Sri Lanka and India). In the last decade or so, small though devastating tsunamis have also occurred along the coasts of Papua New Guinea (1998), the Solomon Islands (2007 & 2010) and the Samoan islands (2009).

More recently, the Mentawais islands of Indonesia were pummeled by a 3m-high tsunami triggered by a 7.7 magnitude earthquake off the coast of western Sumatra on 25 October 2010. More than 500 people lost their lives. Some 27 villages in coastal areas were destroyed and almost 15,000 people were left living in emergency shelters.

Volcanoes

While volcanic eruptions have been much less prolific than earthquakes in the Asia Pacific region, the recent volcanic eruptions of Mt. Merapi are an indication of the presence of active volcanoes in the region, particularly in Indonesia and the Philippines. Mt. Merapi's recent eruptions began on 26 October in Indonesia's central Java displacing at least 278,000 from their homes and claimed more than 240 lives, while injuring 453 people.

A devastating mud volcano in Indonesia has been linked to drilling at a gas exploration well. The hot mud started spewing from the East Java drilling site in 2006 and has now displaced nearly 60,000 people.

Floods

A near daily reading of the newspapers of the Asia Pacific region records floods in one country or other of the region. In the last decade, flooding has been reported in the Philippines, China, Cambodia, Vietnam, Nepal, Indonesia, India, Bangladesh, Australia, Pakistan, to name just a few countries. Some of these floods are very large, such as the floods in Pakistan at the end of 2010, which affected the lives of 20 million people who lost their homes and livelihoods, including more than 1760 who lost their lives. They also found it difficult to protect themselves against either malaria or dengue - both potentially deadly diseases of flood-hit areas. In August 2010, floods in China saw 1470 lives lost. In late 2010 and this month, Australia has experienced floods across five of its seven states. The Bureau of Meteorology's annual Australian climate statement released showed 2010 year was Australia's wettest year since 2000 and the third-wettest since records began to be kept in 1900. The three weeks from Christmas 2010 in Queensland has seen one of the wettest periods on record. Flooding in Queensland has affected an area the size of Germany and Belgium combined. The flooding of Brisbane and surrounding towns on 11-12 January 2011 saw more than 30,000 homes and businesses inundated by flood waters.

Some floods in the Asia Pacific region have been much smaller, such as in the highlands of the provenance of West Papua of Indonesia in February 2009. While loss of life was small, the devastation to the subsistence agriculture of the area caused famine and health related diseases. Some localised flooding and landslide are linked to deforestation in those areas.

Other flooding occurs annually in some countries situated on flood plains, like Bangladesh and parts of Myanmar and India. However, this flooding has been intensified by unusually severe monsoonal rains. Compounded flooding is caused when these monsoonal floods are combined with extended and greater flows from rapidly melting glaciers of the Himalayas, caused by higher air temperatures. These flows come down the Ganges and into the river systems of Bangladesh and India. In fact, the Himalayas feeds into six major rivers (Ganges, Brahmaputra, Indus, Mekong, Yellow and Yangtze) that run through China, India, Pakistan,

Bangladesh, Tibet, Nepal, Burma, Thailand, Laos, Cambodia and Vietnam. The changed glacial flows alter rain patterns and will eventually reduce water in rivers as well as food supply to nearby communities.

Jerome Robles from Malaysia witnesses to changing rainfall patterns resulting in flooding and landslides, destroying homes, lives and livelihoods:

> There does not seem to be a distinct monsoon season anymore. The rain is more frequently, random and certainly more intense. I wonder whether the more intense rains could be a result of global warming. Long gone are the days when children are able to play in the rain like I used to. Now we are afraid of flash floods and strong winds which normally accompany the intense rains (CCHI Report, 2009).

Cyclones/Typhoons

Cyclones and typhoons are a regular feature of the yearly weather patterns of the Asia Pacific region, causing devastation in countries such as the Philippines, Vietnam, Cambodia, China, Taiwan, Myanmar, Bangladesh, India and Australia, to name just a few countries. However, it would appear from occurrences in the last few decades that their number and severity have been increasing. Their impact on impoverished and vulnerable communities has been devastating. Their frequencies are such that only a couple of examples are given below.

A particular example of the severity of the impact of a single cyclone in the region was the impact of Cyclone Nargis which devastated Myanmar's Ayeyarwady Delta in May 2008, leaving more than 140,000 dead and affecting two million people. The storm and the tidal surge that occurred in the delta not only caused many deaths but overwhelming devastation to housing and subsistence agriculture in the low lying communities. Rice fields and drinking wells were flooded with salty water. More recently, Cyclone Giri swamped the western coast of Myanmar on 22 October 2010 affecting an estimated 200,000 people, destroying more than 75,000 homes and 320 schools. Thankfully, the loss of life was much, much lower than Nargis (only 45 deaths).

Bangladesh is the most vulnerable country in the world to tropical cyclones and the sixth most vulnerable to floods. It is a nation on the frontline of the climate change crisis. For example, Cyclone Sidr struck Bangladesh in 2007 resulting in a death toll of 3,400, and economic damages of US$1.6 billion. The CCHI Report (2009) shows how this country is on the frontline of the climate change crisis:

More than 68 million people in Bangladesh have been directly affected over the last eight years, and millions of lives and livelihoods are threatened by frequent weather-related disasters. With low-lying lands, coastline areas and floodplains occupying 80% of the country, Bangladesh is highly exposed to weather related disasters and the sea level rising. Of its 155 million inhabitants, half live below the poverty line and over a third suffers from malnutrition and hunger. Since 2000 the country has experienced more than 70 major disasters. Tropical cyclones, local storms, floods and droughts, have killed 9,000 people and caused damages of more than $5 billion. One-fifth of the country is flooded every year, and in extreme years, two-thirds of the country has been inundated. To demonstrate the magnitude of the problem, agricultural production losses due to flooding in 2007 were estimated at 1.3 million tons. Although agriculture accounts for only 20% of GDP, over 60% of the country's people depend on its products. Losses of both food and cash crops are common occurrences, which seriously disrupt the economy. In addition to food security, weather-related disasters due to climate change cause outbreak of disease such as diarrhea and dengue fever. Poverty and environmental degradation have caused migration from rural to urban areas (migration into urban areas is increasing by over 2 million people each year).

Nonetheless, it must be noted that Bangladesh has taken steps over the past few years to be better prepared, and less vulnerable to the vagaries of the weather. The CCHI Report (2009) suggests "these steps helped reduce mortality in Bangladesh during Cyclone Sidr in 2007 which killed approximately forty times fewer people than a similar scale cyclone in same country in 1991 (3,400 deaths versus 143,000)," and much less than the similar scale cyclone Nargis, which hit Myanmar in 2008, resulting in more than 140,000 deaths.

Drought/Famines

While droughts and famines have been a common occurrence globally since biblical times (e.g., the story of Joseph and the famine in Egypt), it is the occurrence of drought in areas that have not known drought before that is particularly worrying. For example, in recent times rice crops have not been able to be planted in parts of Nepal because of late monsoons, or in some areas rice crops have failed due to drought, as in the example given for Indonesia below.

Often it is difficult to determine if a drought is just a normal part of the cyclic weather patterns that occur in some countries. Australia has just gone through a devastating ten year drought. Lengthy droughts have occurred in the past in this continent, but it appears this drought was intensified by climate change. Even rich countries like Australia are not immune to the human and environmental impact of heat waves, floods, storms and forest fires. The CCHI Report (2009) states that "Australia is perhaps the developed nation most vulnerable to the direct impacts of climate change and also to the indirect impact from neighboring countries that are stressed by climate change."

Famine can follow the devastation caused by cyclone and flooding, particularly where subsistence crops have been wiped out and cannot be replanted in time to get a yield. This appears to be becoming a common occurrence in a country such as Cambodia. As already mentioned, floods in the West Papuan highlands meant that food supplies had to be flown or trucked in. In 1997, Papua New Guinea, normally regarded as a high rainfall country, went through an unexpected drought period where the staple food crop, sweet potato, was unable to sustain many of the subsistence farmers and their families. This affected more than 40% of the population. In the high hills of Assam, India, minimum temperatures have risen by a degree and rainfall fallen over the last 60 years, resulting in lower and poorer quality tea yields.

Indonesia is used by the CCHI Report (2009) as a case study of the impact of seasonal variation in rainfall resulting in widespread hunger:

> It reported that food insecurity is nothing new to the 4 million residents of the Indonesian province of East Nusa Tengarra, but climate change and rising food prices are making the situation even worse. Climate experts have linked the recent effects of El Niño Southern Oscillation to increased seasonal variation in rainfall, which leads to increased drought frequency and reduced rice yields. More than 115 million poor Indonesians rely predominantly on rice production for their food and income. An estimated 13 million children suffered from malnutrition in Indonesia in 2009 as many residents faced failed crops due to drought and were unable to afford to buy food. While climate change is predicted to lead to a 2-3% increase in annual rainfall, the additional rains come at the least favourable times. In fact, there are drier conditions and delayed monsoon rainfall for most of the year, followed by a condensed and even wetter three month

rainy season in all of Indonesia. In 2008, severe drought reduced food supply and food prices increased by as much as half. In East Nusa Tengarra, the number of deaths from malnutrition doubled compared to 2007 and more than half of all children under five years of age showed signs of stunted growth, a 15% increase from 2007.

Deforestation

Deforestation also plays a major role in CO_2 emissions, accounting for over 25% of global emissions in the 1990s with the CCHI Report (2009) estimating that "a majority of deforestation is carried out by slashing and burning (54%) and the remainder by cattle raising (5%), heavy-logging (19%) and the growing palm oil industry (22%), an industry projected to grow due to its use in biofuel production." The deforestation rate of primary forests (2000-2005) reported by the FAO (Food and Agricultural Organization 2005) showed Vietnam second (54.5%), Cambodia third (29.4%), Sri Lanka fourth (15.2%), Indonesia sixth (12.9%) and Nepal eighth (9.1%).

In the Asia Pacific region the majority of remaining forests are located in high growth nations such as Indonesia and China. Deforestation depletes natural resources permanently and leaves the land exposed to environmental disasters, including those associated with climate change (e.g. erosion, mudslides etc.). Without doubt, the abounding deforestation in many of the Asia Pacific countries is contributing to the factors bringing about climate change. Forests are rapidly disappearing (often, though not always, through illegal logging) in countries like Indonesia, the Solomon Islands, Myanmar and Papua New Guinea. This combined with deforestation in earlier centuries in countries like Australia, Malaysia and India means that important sinks for CO_2 capture are being lost, as well as from contributing to CO_2 emissions.

Pollution

Developed nations bear the most responsibility for climate change, through their human activities and contribution to pollution, as well as past exploitation of natural resources such as forests. However, there are an increasing number of cases where low- and middle-income countries also contribute significantly to climate change (CCHI Report, 2009). The top ten emitting countries by total fossil-fuel CO_2 emissions for 2007 included, first China (22.3%), third India (5.5%), fifth Japan (5.4%) and ninth South Korea (1.7%) (cf. second USA (19.91%) (Carbon Dioxide

Information and Analysis Center, 2007). Some of these countries have rich natural resources and are experiencing fast economic growth. Many of these rapidly industrializing nations rely on coal to drive their power-hungry economies. Fossil fuel usage is the largest single contributor to global carbon emissions producing climate change (coal alone accounts for roughly 20% of global emissions). It should also be noted Australia is one of the largest coal exporters in the world, thereby contributing to the CO_2 problem through the mining of this resource.

China emits more GHG emissions than any other country, due in large part to its reliance on coal to fuel its expanding economy. In 2009, China derived 70% of its primary energy from coal, and this heavy dependence is expected to double again by 2030, with major implications for emissions of GHGs. On a per capita basis, however, China emits much less per person than the United States or other developed countries (e.g. Americans emit 7.5 times more CO_2 than the average Chinese on a per capita basis (Seligsohn, 2010)).

The CCHI Report (2009) points out that poverty can drive practices that contribute to climate change, and gives the release of black carbon (soot) released from under-ventilated fireplaces and primitive cooking stoves, of which many are found in the Asia Pacific region amongst poor communities. Black carbon from soot contributes as much as 18% of global warming, compared to 40% by carbon dioxide. As soot only remains in the atmosphere for a few weeks providing affordable alternatives for cooking would by an easy, fast way to curb global warming.

Rising Sea Levels

Jyotsna Giri, of India, provides a human face to the impact of sea level rises caused by climate change. Jyotsna had a small farm on Lohachara Island in West Bengal. Fifteen years ago she had to move to a refugee colony on a neighboring island when the sea claimed her home and farm:

> I still remember that fateful day when I lost everything. When we approached Lohachara Island, I suddenly noticed that my sheep were all drifting in the river. I found that half of my house was washed away by the river. Slowly, the entire island got submerged (CCHI Report, 2009).

Small islands are especially vulnerable to sea-level rise and storm surge, particularly islands such as Tuvalu, Kiribati and the Maldives. Tuvalu, in the South Pacific Ocean, is less than 4.5 meters above sea level. Frequent saltwater flooding, accelerated coastal erosion and increasing difficulty growing vegetables and plants are everyday challenges. The people of Tuvalu started to relocate to New Zealand, under the terms of a negotiated migration scheme. Similarly, evacuations have occurred from Papua New Guinea's low-lying Carteret Islands, due to climate change.

What is Going On?

It may well be asked what is going on, when this list of environmental difficulties are considered from the Asia Pacific region. While earthquakes, tsunamis and volcanic eruptions cannot be attributed to the changing climate, most of the other environmental difficulties listed are in some way linked. Certainly, those directly being impact by climate change and the vagaries of the environment are asking what is going on. For example, hear the voice of Tulsi Khara, from India, who has lived all her 70 years in the world's largest delta, where the Brahmaputra and Ganges rivers meet and flow into the Bay of Bengal:

> We are not educated people, but I can sense something grave is happening around us. I couldn't believe my eyes — the land that I had tilled for years, that fed me and my family for generations, has vanished. We have lost our livelihood. All our belongings and cattle were swept away by cyclones. We have moved to Sagar Island and are trying to rebuild our lives from scratch. It wasn't like this when I was young. Storms have become more intense than ever. Displacement and death are everywhere here. The land is shrinking and salty water gets into our fields, making them useless. We feel very insecure now (CCHI Report, 2009).

Scientists indicate that if climate change is not effectively and urgently addressed, by keeping the temperature rise to less than 2°C, then not only will sea levels rise and threaten tens of millions of people and their homes, but tropical diseases like malaria and dengue fever will also continue to spread. Floods like those recently experienced in Pakistan will become more frequent, and storms and cyclones, like those experienced last year in the Philippines or in Myanmar with Cyclone Nargis and Giri, will become more frequent and more intense. Devastation in coastal areas will become more common with these more extreme weather patterns, particularly when combined with increased sea levels. Moreover, hundreds of thousands of species of plants and animals will be pushed to extinction. Droughts will increase and rainfall will become less predictable which will see an increase in crop failure.

The impacts of climate change globally are apparent in what can be seen happening in the Asia Pacific region. Climate change is impacting human health, livelihoods, safety and society in the Asia Pacific region in a similar way it is impacting the rest of the globe. Generalized, CCHI Report (2009) summarizes this by stating that

> ... climate changes impacts people in the following ways:

- Food security: More poor people, especially children, suffer from hunger due to reduced agricultural yield, livestock and fish supply as a result of environmental degradation;

- Health: Health threats like diarrhea, malaria, asthma and stroke affect more people as temperatures rise;

- Poverty: Livelihoods are destroyed when income from agriculture, livestock, tourism and fishing is lost due to weather-related disasters and desertification;

- Water: Increased water scarcity results from a decline in the overall supply of clean water and more frequent and severe floods and droughts;

- Displacement: More climate-displaced people are expected due to sea level rise, desertification and floods (60 million expected in Bangladesh alone);

- Security: More people live under the continuous threat of potential conflict and institutional break down due to migration, weather-related disaster and water scarcity.

What has God Given to Us?

In Genesis, God created the universe through purposeful and careful labor. He filled His creation with beauty and abundance, stopping at each stage of its development to declare it was good. He appointed humankind as vice-regents over creation; granting dominion over all that He had created. In this act, God made humankind stewards of His earth, with the power to be its protectors.

Nonetheless, it is easy to encounter skepticism among Christians who doubt that humans could have any substantive impact on the Earth's environment. "How can we be causing the earth's climate to change?" they wonder, and "how can we do anything to stop it changing? After all, is it not God's sovereignty alone that regulates the rains, the oceans, the winds, and the sun? Does not the Bible say that, 'The earth is the Lord's and everything in it' (Psalm 24:1)?"

It is not hard to find instances in the Asia Pacific region to see where humankind has moved from being protectors of God's creation to its destroyers. Each attendee at this colloquium could recount localised instances from the communities and countries we come from. For example, in Australia, the over-allocation of available water from the Murray-Darling basin rivers system for irrigation for food and cotton production has destroyed the river system and changed its ecology to the detriment of the wildlife, plants and people. Similarly, China is now discovering, just as the developed world did, that the pollution caused by unregulated coal-fired power stations is devastating for the local environment. Sulphur-dioxide creates acid rain which affects waterways and crops, nitrogen oxide contributes to carcinogenic smog and mercury causes neurological damage in children. In contrast to these localised issues, the global nature of climate change combined with the relatively long time-lag between action and consequence has meant that climate change remains a problem too large and too distant for many to claim any responsibility of being the perpetrators or destroyers.

What is Likely to Happen if We Do Nothing or Change What We Do?

Even when acknowledged that God has given humankind power over His earth, it is understandably hard to conceptualize how our actions could fundamentally reshape the entire planet. However, consider that since 1750 there has been a tenfold increase in the world's population and an equivalent per person increase in consumption: humankind is effectively drawing upon 100 times more of the earth's resources than prior to industrialization. The Nobel Prize winning atmospheric chemist, Paul Crutzen, argues that this has been enough to throw every life sustaining system on the planet off kilter, including the climate (Sachs, 2008).

Stern (2006) suggests that the effects of global warming could shrink the global economy by 20 percent. Whatever be the scale, climate change is a reality. The non-binding pledges made in Copenhagen and Cancun put the world on track for a catastrophic temperature rise of 3-4° Centigrade. If nothing is done, air temperature will continue to rise, sea levels will continue to go up, more extreme climate conditions will happen and become more frequent, the most vulnerable and least able to cope and adapt, the poor, will suffer and loss of life due to climate change will increase.

It is argued that what is needed is aggressive and immediate policy action to stabilize and reduce total emissions in the coming decades and hold global warming to below 2° Centigrade. To lower carbon emissions the world community must cut back the use of fossil fuels and steps taken for substituting other energy sources. However, there is common but differential responsibility in the action to be taken. When the United Nations Framework Convention on Climate Change was formulated and then signed and ratified at the Rio Earth Summit (1992) by most of the world's countries (including the United States), the principle of common but differentiated responsibilities was acknowledged. In short, this principle recognized that:

- The largest share of historical and current global emissions of GHGs has originated in developed countries;

- Per capita emissions in developing countries are still relatively low;

- The share of global emissions originating in developing countries will grow to meet their social and development needs.
(United Nations Framework Convention on Climate Change, 1992)

Similarly, the World Resources Institute highlights that the industrialized countries are the biggest polluters (Baumert, 2005). In terms of historical emissions over the last 100 years, industrialized countries account for 65% of the carbon dioxide build-up in the atmosphere to date. In same period, China and India's cumulative shares were 7.6% and 2.2%, respectively. The environmental consequences of the policies of industrialized nations have had a large, detrimental and costly effect on developing countries - especially the poor in those countries that are already burdened with debt and poverty.

Stern, in his report (2006), argues that the richer countries should take responsibility for between 60% and 80% of reductions in emissions from 1990 levels by 2050. However, rapid development in the Asia Pacific region is bringing hundreds of millions of people out of poverty but the very same issues of pollution attributed to the richer nations go unchecked. Along with this economic expansion there has been a rise in environmental pollution including GHG emissions. The developing countries of Asia now account for one-third of global emissions brought about by energy consumption, deforestation and land use (Gnanakan, 2009).

While annual emissions of carbon dioxide (CO_2) from the burning of oil, gas and coal fell by 1.3 per cent in 2009 compared with 2008, a record year, the picture for the Asia Pacific was mixed. Emissions fell by 11.8% in Japan, compared to 6.9% in the United States, by 8.6% in Britain, by 7% in Germany and by 8.4% in Russia. In contrast, emissions rose by 8% in China, by 6.2% in India and 1.4% in South Korea. As a result, China strengthened its unenvied position as the world's No 1 emitter of fossil fuel CO_2, accounting for a whopping 24% of the total. The United States remained second, with 17% (Global Carbon Project, 2009).

Climate change threatens sustainable development and achievement of all eight Millennium Development Goals. The international community agreed at the beginning of the new millennium to eradicate extreme hunger and poverty by 2015. Yet, today, climate change is already responsible for forcing some 50 million additional people to go hungry and driving over 10 million additional people into extreme poverty (CCHI Report 2009). If nothing is done to slow down and ameliorate the effects of climate change, this can only be expected to get worse. Many of the countries that are most vulnerable to climate change are in Asia and the Pacific. They are vulnerable to the effects of the melting Himalayan ice sheets, droughts, floods and storms. The most affected countries include India, Pakistan, Bangladesh, southern and eastern China, Myanmar, Vietnam, Philippines and Indonesia. In addition, a number of the small island developing states at risk to sea-level rise and cyclones are in the region (Comoros islands, Kiribati, Tuvalu, and the Maldives).

If nothing is done in the next twenty years the CCHI Report (2009) postulates that:

- Those seriously affected by climate change are expected to more than double to 310 million within 20 years, and lives lost every year are expected to increase by at least two-thirds;

- Economic losses due to climate change are expected to more than double to US$340 billion in the next 20 years;

- By 2030, the number of hungry people because of climate change is expected to grow by more than two-thirds to 75 million;

- Climate change threatens to slow, halt or reverse progress towards reducing the spread of diseases and aggravates already enormous health problems, especially in the poorest parts of the world;

- By 2030, climate change is expected to increase the number of people suffering from the health consequence climate change by more than one-third and lives lost by more than one-half;

- Climate change is expected to increase poverty, doubling the number by 2030 already pushed into poverty by the changing environment (in 2009 this was 12 million), many who are in India and South East Asia;

- Climate change will exacerbate already shrinking fresh water availability, where 1.3 billion people world-wide are water stressed;

- Continued climate change will increase the number of people displaced due to rising sea levels, desertification and loss of livelihoods. Currently there are 26 million climate displaced persons and this is projected triple within 20 years, with many coming from China, India, Bangladesh, and the delta areas, coastal zones and islands of a number of countries.

However, to assume nothing is being done is incorrect. Carbon dioxide emissions from deforestation fell sharply in 2009, thanks to slowing forest loss in tropical countries and to a pickup in reforestation in Europe, temperate zones of Asia and North America. In the 1990s, emissions from deforestation were more than 25% of the global total. In 2009, though, they were only 12% (Global Carbon Project, 2009). Some countries like China are actively pursuing the CO_2 emissions target it reported in Copenhagen. For example, China has ordered the shutdown of inefficient and high-emitting coal-fired power stations and their replacement with high efficiency coal-fired generators. This is just one of a range of measures being undertaken by one country.

Nonetheless, to do nothing or even a little to address climate change and the factors contributing to global warming will have devastating consequences for future generations, and particularly for the poor.

Conclusion

The challenges of a changing environment globally, and therefore in the Asia Pacific region are many. Climate change is a reality. As God's vice-regents given the task of being good stewards of His creation, and particularly as dedicated followers of Christ Jesus, we need to take an active role in both mitigating the effects of climate change and helping communities, particularly the vulnerable and poorer, to adapt to the changes in the environment. In a similar way, help is needed for those affected by earthquakes, tsunamis, volcanoes and what might be considered other environmental disasters. Disaster risk reduction and climate change mitigation and adaptation share a common space of concern: reducing the vulnerability to adapt to the new environmental conditions that they are facing. This is a task for all the members of the global community, and particularly Christians (2 Cor. 1:17).

Christians need to work to uncover a substantive and compelling theology that leaves in no doubt that God's people are to be at the forefront of the global society as it works together to overcome the challenge of a climate in flux and an environment that leaves the vulnerable particularly exposed. God's heart for the poor runs deep throughout his revelation – the Bible – as it must also run deep through our theology.

Presented at the 2011 Asia Pacific Baptist Federation Theological Educators Colloquium in Daejon, South Korea. Originally published in Torch Trinity Journal. Reprinted with permission.

Bibliography

Baumert, Kevin A., Herzog, Timothy, & Pershing, Jonathan. *Navigating the numbers greenhouse gas data and international climate policy.* World Resources Institute. 2005.

Carbon Dioxide Information and Analysis Center. http://cdiac.ornl.gov/trends/ emis/ tre_tp20.html. 2007.

Climate Change Human Impact Report. *The anatomy of a silent crisis.* Global Humanitarian Forum. 2009.

Food and Agricultural Organization. *The global forest resources assessment 2005.* Food and Agriculture Organization of the United Nations. 2005.

United Nations Framework Convention on Climate Change. http://unfccc.int/resource/ docs/convkp/conveng.pdf. 1992.

Gnanakan, Ken. "Climate change and global economics." Paper presented at the Micah Network 4th Triennial Global Consultation on Creation, Stewardship and Climate Change, Nairobi, Kenya. July, 2009.

Sachs, Jeffrey. *Common wealth: Economics for a crowded planet.* Penguin Press. 2008.

Simiyu, Stella. *The 21st century challenge: Climate change & biodiversity depletion.* Paper presented at the Micah Network 4th Triennial Global Consultation on Creation, Stewardship and Climate Change, Nairobi, Kenya. July, 2009.

Stern, Nicholas. *Stern review on the economics of climate change.* Cambridge. 2006.

Seligsohn, Deborah, Liu, Yue, Forbes, Sarah, Dongjie, Zhang, & Wes, Logan. *CCS in China: Toward an environmental, health, and safety regulatory framework.* World Resources Institute. 2010.

Pachauri, R.K., & Reisinger, A., eds. *The fourth assessment report of the intergovernmental panel on climate change.* IPCC. 2007.

U.S. Global Change Research Program. *Global climate change impacts in the United States.* 2009.

Global Carbon Project. http://www.globalcarbonproject.org/carbonbudget. 2009.

17 | Beyond Rio: The Releational Character of God as Trinity as a Basis for Ecological Renewal

Helle Liht

Introduction

This short theological reflection is an attempt to shape the understanding of integration, one of the main concepts of Rio +20 outcome document, "The Future We Want" that aims to secure sustainable development for the future. I will use Jürgen Moltmann's theological insights about God's relational character and apply it to the concept of integration, hoping that this will help to reveal some aspects, which are important for the ecological renewal of the Earth.

The Challenge for Earth Summits

The United Nations inter-governmental conference on sustainable development Rio +20 has recently taken place in Rio de Janeiro from 20-22 June 2012. The outcome document entitled "The Future We Want" was adopted by 193 member states of the United Nations, renewing the commitment "to sustainable development and to ensuring the promotion of an economically, socially and environmentally sustainable future for our planet and for present and future generations" (UN, FW:1).

"The Future We Want" is developed on the same lines as the outcome document of the United Nations Conference on Environment and Development in 1992 called "Rio Declaration on Environment and Development" and is reaffirming its principles and past action plans (UN, DED). The 1992 Declaration was adopted by 172 governments and received by some 2.400 non-governmental organisations (UN, GI). The 1992 Declaration, in turn, was a reaffirmation and development of the Declaration of the United Nations Conference in the Human Environment, adopted in Stockholm in 1972 by 113 governments and received by a number of inter-governmental and non-governmental organisations (UN, EP). Forty years – one generation – has passed since the first major UN's conference on international environmental issues took place and urged governments to take action for sustaining and protecting the natural environment, an integral part of people's well-being.

When we look at the global environmental situation today, some things have changed for the better since the first UN inter-governmental meeting in Stockholm – different environmental policies in many countries are in place and being implemented at least to a certain extent, environmental awareness among people has increased and is shaping their attitudes, governmental and non-governmental initiatives are committed to assisting developing countries, etc. However, the Rio +20 zero draft of the outcome document acknowledges,

> that there have also been setbacks. […] Food insecurity, climate change and biodiversity loss have adversely affected development gains. New scientific evidence points to the gravity of the threats we face. New and emerging challenges include the further intensification of earlier problems calling for more urgent responses. We are deeply concerned that around 1.4 billion people still live in extreme poverty and one sixth of the world's population is undernourished, pandemics and epidemics are omnipresent threats. Unsustainable development has increased the stress on the earth's limited natural resources and on the carrying capacity of ecosystems. […] [Despite efforts by Governments and non-State actors in all countries, sustainable development remains a distant goal and there remain major barriers and systemic gaps in the implementation of internationally agreed commitments (UN, ZD).

The *Co*NGO Committee on Sustainable Development in its paper prepared for the Earth Summit Rio +20, among others supported also by the Baptist World Alliance, pictures the current situation even more drastically stating that "[t]he 1992 Summit's promise to make 'environmental protection … an integral part of the development process' has not been fulfilled, and its call to action document … is largely forgotten.…Clearly, there is reluctance to critique present economic and social systems, as well as a lack of political will for action based on such critiques" (*Co*NGO, CSD). A similar criticism has been raised about the Rio +20 outcome document by many observers and commentators.

For one generation I believe genuine attempts have been made by different groups to introduce, encourage and implement the principles of sustainable development. Yet the crisis and disappointment are growing, and more and more people are becoming the victims of unjust economic structures and environmental degradation. Is there at all a way forward? Is there anything Christian communities can offer in this struggle against exploitation, destruction, poverty and injustice?

The Challenge for Christian Communities

A year ago after my lecture on the church's role in ecological renewal, a participant made a claim that the church has lost its prophetic voice (or rather has never had it) as much as the ecological crisis is concerned. As much as I wanted to, it was difficult to give a positive response. Although evangelical theological discussion on creation care has intensified in recent years enormously, much of it has been a reflection of Christianity's ambiguous message developed especially since the Enlightenment and throughout the Modern Area. It has been an attempt to reshape its rather individualistic and anthropocentric focus. Often these theological claims have been made in an apologetic context as a response to accusations, which view Christian theology and history as a major reason for current ecological crisis, however, these ideas have not yet become an essential part of the grass-root Christian communities.

So it has been an internal struggle of returning to the Scriptures from the perspective of the Creator's central role in the whole of universe, and to the Biblical story from creation to eschatology, God's future for the whole creation. In this struggle, Christian thought and tradition has been revisited again and much of its ecological thought that has rested in dusty books for hundreds of years has been dug out again. This struggle has revealed, and is continuously revealing, the immense potential of Christian tradition to respond to the current ecological crisis and to participate in God's redeeming work for the whole of creation.

For this paper I have chosen to enter into theological conversation with Jürgen Moltmann and to discuss one of the key convictions of Christian faith – the faith in the Triune God and some of its essential characteristics–which, I believe, might lead the Christian communities to taking the Rio +20 outcome beyond its formal decisions and embody God's redeeming presence in this troubled world.

Understanding "Integration"

One of the key concepts of Rio +20 outcome document is integration. It calls "for holistic and integrated approaches to sustainable development that will guide humanity to live in harmony with nature and lead to efforts to restore the health and integrity of the Earth's ecosystem" (UN, FW:3). In the context of Rio +20 outcome document, integration is characterised by the common efforts of many different people groups in many different areas such as food security, water, energy, green economy, social inclusion, forests and biodiversity, etc. Integration is an assumption for sustainable development that is wished, hoped and encouraged. Although the document establishes a framework for integrated action to achieve the goals, it does not expound the concept of integration as such. Yet the question how integration is understood is crucial for moving towards ecological renewal of the earth and just civil societies.

The English word 'integration' comes from the Latin *integrātus* which means "having been made whole" (Latin *integer* means "whole"). It can also be translated as "renewed", "restored", "re-created", "refreshed." The original meaning of the word indicates that "integration" is an answer to the question as to how different characters co-exist together in order to form the whole, which is satisfactory and pleasing for all involved characters.

Looking at the 40-year history of different Earth Summits, the commitments of their parties to sustainable development and the current ecological crisis, integration as such has certainly been a challenge until now, and its importance for the future is rightly emphasised in the Rio +20 outcome document. But how can such reciprocally satisfactory and pleasing co-existence be achieved? What does it require from the characters involved? I believe here insights from Christian theology can lead the way and help to establish an understanding of integration that is based on life-style (the way of being) rather than (or in addition to) the programmes to be implemented.

In his recent book, *Sun of Righteousness, Arise: God's Future for Humanity and the Earth*, Jürgen Moltmann draws together insights from different theologians and Christian traditions into what he calls "the new trinitarian thinking" (Moltmann, 2010:149). I propose that discovering more fully the nature of the Triune God and its defining character for Christian life as envisioned by Moltmann leads also to a fuller understanding of integration, and when embodied by Christian communities, can become a prophetic act in the suffering world.

Triune God – God of Relationships

The history of Christian theology is very rich in its attempts to describe and explain the essence and the nature of the triune God. Different Christian traditions have emphasised different aspects of the Trinity and developed their own approaches. The way God has been described and understood in these traditions has also shaped their understanding of human beings and their place and role in the world. In contrast to the theological understanding of the modern western church where "God remains the subject of himself," Jürgen Moltmann takes the journey through the Old Testament, New Testament, the theology of Greek fathers and several contemporary theologians to develop an understanding of the triune God who "is a God in sociality, rich in inner and outward relationships" (Moltmann, 2010:149-152).

Shekinah

One of the sources of Moltmann's understanding is the Biblical approach of Shekinah (Hebrew: הגירכש) – the Hebrew word, which is used to describe God's majestic "indwelling" in the midst of Israelites through the desert journey, in the exile and in the Temple in Jerusalem. The same vision of God being present in the world continues to echo in the New Testament: "The Word became flesh and dwelt among us" (Jn. 1:1), in Christ "dwells the fullness of God bodily" (Col. 2:9), the Holy Spirit "dwells" in Christians (1 Cor. 6:19) and in the Christian community (Moltmann, 2010:152). These different ways of God's indwelling within God's created order reveal God's inward and outward relationships to the extent of "emptying himself" (Phil. 2:6-8) for the benefit of the others and God's commitment to the world, which is corrupted by sin.

Perichoresis

The concept of Shekinah (indwelling) is further explored and strengthened in the theology of Greek fathers who use it to describe the nature of Triune God and the relationships between different persons within the Trinity, expressed with a Greek word *perichoresis*, meaning "interpenetration," "reciprocal indwelling." In the framework of this paper I will only describe the main idea of *perichoresis* and draw attention to some aspects of it that contribute to our discussion about integration as one of the keys for ecological renewal.

Semantically, the word *perichoresis* conveys the meaning of a dynamic movement between and among different persons, including "surrounding, embracing, enclosing." It is a term, which enables us to understand each person in his or her unique wholeness and at the same time to see the unity that they form together. In the theology of Greek fathers this concept is used in two ways. Firstly, it describes the relationships between different natures, the divine and the human, as they become together in Christ. John 14:9 and 11 express the oneness as well as the diversity of Jesus the Son and God the Father "in their reciprocal indwelling." And secondly, *perichoresis* also describes the relationships between the persons of the same nature – Father, Son and Holy Spirit (Moltmann, 2010:152-153). In this way the concept of *perichoresis* respects the different characters of each person, yet it emphasises the unity that is formed by reciprocal indwelling in the two other persons. This way the Trinity forms a "non-hierarchical community" of a shared co-existence where the other person is respected, adored, served, supported, nurtured, glorified (Moltmann, 2010:152).

The concept of perichoresis as a defining motive for integration

Following this description of the "perichoretic" understanding of the Triune God, I would like to draw attention to some of its aspects, which I believe, are important for understanding the heart of integration.

The concept of *perichoresis* envisions the Triune God as a fully relational God where the whole is not a result of different persons complementing each other with their characters, or a metaphysical divine substance commonly shared by each person, but a relationship where "the power of perfect love … allows each person to go out of itself to such an extent that it is wholly present in the others" (Moltmann, 2010:155). Therefore, the "perichoretic" approach understands each person of the Triune God not only as a person related to the two others but also as an open space because each person offers a dwelling place for the other two (Moltmann, 2010:155). It is a relationship in which each trinitarian person in its wholeness limits itself to prepare space for the other two to represent the whole and one God.

As spiritual and physical beings, the space we have available (or we are) is spiritual (or mental) as well as physical. As Baptists, I assume we understand the importance of the spiritual space quite well when we describe our relationship with God, when we talk about "Christ living in us" and also in terms of worship and prayer. However, I am afraid that we too often undermine the physical space, which is also defined by various relationships.

In the increasingly globalised world, the physical space as a source of someone's wellbeing is becoming more and more crucial. For example, in recent years a new term – environmental migrants – has emerged. These are people who have fled their homes because of extreme weather conditions, triggered by environmental degradation and climate change caused mainly by human exploitation of the Earth's resources. At home the lives of these people have become endangered by the rising sea level, droughts and natural catastrophes. According to the

International Organisation for Migration (IMO), "in 2008, 20 million people have been displaced because of extreme weather events compared to 4.6 million internally displaced by conflict and violence over the same period." The estimation is that by 2050 the number of international environmental migrants will increase to approximately 200 million (IOM). To these numbers characterising human suffering, we need to add animal and plant species, which have become extinct because of the destruction of their habitats.

And so the space, which current environmental migrants as well as animal and plant species have shared with each other and which has been a source of life, has been taken over by others whose main desire is to increase their wealth. Too often a consumerist life style has turned a space of life-affirming relationships into a graveyard.

Everyday examples like this, reveal the fundamental interdependence between the different human and non-human members of the Earth's ecosystem, which binds together the consumerist lifestyle of one group and the pain and suffering of the other; greenhouse gas emissions produced in one part of the world, and drought, hunger and death in others; irresponsible clearing of forests to increase the business of home-and-office ware, and the floods which force people to leave their homes and close down their offices. These are just a few examples of the interdependence between the world-wide human communities and the natural environment, which is a shared physical space for the entire creation.

Therefore the question everyone needs to ask is whether the space I shape and create with my consumption habits, daily work, social and political involvement, worship – the space I ultimately am – is a private comfort zone, which I enlarge for myself, or whether it is an open and safe space embracing others in their joy and suffering, and inviting others to dwell in there.

A "perichoretic" understanding envisions the Triune God as an "open, inviting and integrating unity" – "the open Trinity" as Moltmann calls it (Moltmann, 2010:157). It embraces unity and diversity in a proper relationship, creating space for others to enter. In the Johannine theology it is expressed for example in Jesus' prayer for the disciples: "As you, Father, are in me and I am in you, may they also be in us, so that the world may believe that you have sent me." (Jn. 17:21). And Paul's eschatological vision of God being "all in all" (1 Cor. 15:28) somehow includes in the divine relational community the entire renewed created order (Moltmann, 2010:157).

Therefore, created in the image of God, our privilege and challenge is to image the Triune God, in whom each trinitarian "person" in its relationships and perfect love in a sense limits itself to prepare space for the other two and ultimately for the entire redeemed created order (Hall, 2004:98-108). It is only by limiting our own space and offering space for others that we can more fully participate in the redeeming and integrating work of God who is embracing the entire creation, renewing it and bringing it to its wholeness.

Understanding the open relational character of the Triune God unfolds a new perspective for the concept of integration as a process of renewing and making things whole. At the heart of integration as laid out in the Rio +20 outcome document, is the concern for the world's poor and most vulnerable people groups and a desire to bring the worldwide human societies into a harmonious co-existence with a healthy and sustainable Earth's ecosystem. For this, I believe we need the understanding of integration that is based on an open and relational life-style (the way of being) rather than (or in addition to) the programmes to be implemented.

Conclusion

If we understand the Triune God "perichoretically" as God who is rich in inner and outward relationships, as God who for the sake of renewing and redeeming the relationships with and within the entire created order has "emptied himself," as God who is continuously at work to make the broken whole by inviting others into the divine relational community, then we ought to reflect continuously on our faith and its practical expressions in the light of who God is, and in the context of our contemporary society. I have suggested that we might make a start by basing such a reflection on the two aspects of God's relational character described above – in the fruitful and creative dynamics between person and space; and in the open nature of the Triune God, finding that perfect balance between unity and the embracing of diversity which is fundamental to any concept of integration. I believe that this is one contribution that we can offer into the on-going concern and debate about our human stewardship of the Earth's resources.

Bibliography

CoNGO Committee on Sustainable Development. *Earth Summit Rio + 20.*

Hall, Douglas J. *Imaging God: Dominion as Stewardship.* Wipf & Stock. 2004.

International Organisation for Migration (IOM). *Migration, Climate Change and the Environment.* www.iom.int.

Moltmann, Jürgen. *Sun of Righteousness, Arise: God's Future for Humanity and the Earth.* SCM Press. 2010.

"Rio Declaration on Environment and Development" (UN, DED).   United Nations. www.un.org/esa/dsd/agenda21.

United Nations Conference in the Human Environment (UN, EP). www.unep.org/Documents.Multilingual/Default.asp?documentid=78&articleid=1163.

United Nations General Information (UN, GI).   www.un.org/geninfo/bp/enviro.html.

The Future We Want (FW).   United Nations.   www.uncsd2012.org.

Zero Draft of the Outcome Document (ZD).   United Nations.   www.uncsd2012.org.

18 | Islam in Turkey as Shaped by the State, its Founder and its History: Insight through Baptist Eyes and Three Key Muslim Figures

Paul Weller

Introduction

The origins of this paper are in a presentation made to the Muslim-Christian Relations Commission at the 2014 Baptist World Alliance Gathering in Izmir, Turkey. Turkey is, of course, the modern day country which covers the geography of what was known as Asia Minor and which the early Christian Church had a strong presence, but where the contemporary Christian (and even more so the Baptist Christian) minority is very small. Because of both the factors it is important to understand something of the country's religious and socio-political history and contemporary context.

In this chapter, I therefore seek to provide some insight into key aspects of Turkish history and society and to do so by reference to the founder of the modern Turkish state, Mustafa Kemal Atatürk (1881-1938) as well as to three significant Muslim figures who have contributed to the religious inheritance of Turkey and beyond – namely Jalāl ad-Dīn Muḥammad Rūmī; Said Nursi (1877-1960); and Muhammad Fethullah Gülen (1941-). In doing so, as one who stands within the Baptist tradition of Christianity I will inevitably (but also in this context in a consciously engaged way) do so through Baptist Christian eyes. In the process, I will highlight some aspects of Baptist Christian tradition that I would like to argue resonate with aspects of this Turkish inheritance in ways that might be of constructive help to contemporary Baptist Christian understandings of Turkey, of Muslims of Turkish heritage, and of Muslims and Islam more generally.

"Turks"/Muslims in Early English Baptist Christian Perspective

One of the early and distinctive aspects of Baptist theological perspectives in relation to the plurality of religious traditions and their adherents was the standpoint articulated by Thomas Helwys when, in relation to matters of religious freedom, he made the oft-quoted pronouncement, "Let them be heretics, Turks, Jews, or whatsoever, it appertains not to the earthly power to punish them in the least measure" (Groves, 1998:53). In the context of the Europe of his time, of course, "Turks" stood not only for those who were related to a particular ethnic group or lived in a particular geographical area, but also more generally for Muslims. This is because, following the ending of Islamic Spain (which had existed from the times of the Umayyad Caliphate in 8th century until the early 17th century expulsion of the remaining so-called Moriscos - former Muslims who had been forced to convert to Catholic Christianity on pain of death or expulsion), the main European Christian experience and/or image of Muslims had become that of the Muslim Turks of the Ottoman empire.

The Ottoman Empire was founded in 1299 by Oghuz Turks under Osman I in the north-west of Anatolia. In 1453, under Mehmet II, it had conquered the eastern Christendom capital of Constantinople and was a military and economic power that was still on the rise to its zenith. Although both Helwys' home country of England and the territories of the Netherlands from which he wrote his famous tract 1612 tract, *A Short Declaration of the Mistery of Iniquity*, were not as geographically close to the borders of the Ottoman Empire as some parts of Europe, his affirmation of religious freedom for Turks/ Muslims was nevertheless a remarkable a position to take in the context of a Christendom Europe which, following the Ottoman conquest of many southeast European territories and its (albeit unsuccessful 1529) siege of Vienna, very often identified Turks/Muslims with the threat of military conquest.

What is clear from Helwys' writings and from those of other early Baptists, is that their positions were not the expression of a modern approach to "toleration," but rather were rooted in particular theological and ecclesiological understandings of the nature of Christian (and other) believing and belonging. These, it was argued, should be voluntary matters between the believer(s) and God rather than being determined either by geographical accident of birth or the military violence or legal force of those holding earthly power (Weller, 1990a, 1990b, 2014). At the same time, it is interesting to note that when some other 17th century English Baptists made reference to what one might call "really existing Islam" in the Constantinople of their time, they did also cite historical evidence concerning the practice of Ottoman Turks as one that was relatively generous in relation to religious plurality and freedom. Thus, Leonard Busher (Underhill, 1846:24) wrote that:

> I read that a bishop of Rome would have constrained a Turkish emperor to the Christian faith, unto whom the emperor answered, 'I believe that Christ was an excellent prophet, but he did never, so far as I understand, command that men should, with the power of weapons be constrained to believe his law: and verily I also do force no man to Mahomet's law.' And I read that Jews, Christians, and Turks are tolerated in Constantinople, and yet are peaceable, though so contrary the one to the other.

In citing this example, Busher was not merely giving recognition to the practice of a majority Muslim state that had some resonance what the early Baptist Christians were arguing for on theological grounds. Rather he cited it in order to press home his other points concerning religious liberty in a way intended to shame other European Christians of his time, through arguing that this was a practical example from which Christians could and should learn by contrast with what had been the practice in much of Christendom:

If this be so, how much more ought Christians not to force on another to religion. AND HOW MUCH MORE OUGHT CHRISTIANS TO TOLERATE CHRISTIANS, WHEN THE TURKS DO TOLERATE THEM? SHALL WE BE LESS MERCIFUL THAN THE TURKS? OR SHALL WE LEARN THE TURKS TO PERSECUTE CHRISTIANS? IT IS NOT ONLY UNMERCIFUL, BUT UNNATURAL AND ABOMINABLE. YEA, MONSTROUS FOR ONE CHRISTIAN TO VEX AND DESTROY ANOTHER FOR DIFFERENCE AND QUESTIONS OF RELIGION [sic] (Underhill, 1846: 24).

A Distinctive "Flavour" of "Anatolian Islam"?

Despite the approach cited by Busher, the Ottoman Empire and Turkish Muslims were, of course, also not without the ambiguities and dark sides that impinge on the actualisation of all religious traditions and communities within human history. But in picking up on this example, Busher might at least in part be reflecting the idea that a distinctive "flavour" of Islam and of Muslim tradition -

often referred to as "Anatolian Islam" - was developed among those who adopted and lived Islam in the geographical area of what is modern Turkey and in which, especially, the Sufi Muslim traditions of openness and spirituality are argued to have had a profound influence.

This Anatolian and Sufi Muslim tradition is often cited in connection with the famous Muslim historical figure of Jalāl ad-Dīn Muḥammad Rūmī, also known by the title of "Mevlana" (meaning "our guide"). In the contemporary wider world, knowledge of Rūmī's poems has spread beyond Turkey and is often taken as inspirational by those who advocate a broad spirituality of a kind that they believe goes beyond specific religious traditions and origins. Why this might be so can be seen in the following poetic works which exhibit a spirit of openness to all:

Come, Come, Whoever You Are

Wonderer, worshipper, lover of leaving.
It doesn't matter.
Ours is not a caravan of despair.
Come, even if you have broken your vow
a thousand times
Come, yet again, come, come.

There Is A Candle In Your Heart

There is a candle in your heart,
ready to be kindled.
There is a void in your soul,
ready to be filled.
You feel it, don't you?
You feel the separation
from the Beloved.
Invite Him to fill you up,
embrace the fire.
Remind those who tell you otherwise that
Love
comes to you of its own accord,
and the yearning for it
cannot be learned in any school.

However it is important to understand that, although his works do exhibit a universality of spirit, Rūmī was himself also very much rooted in Anatolian Sunni Muslim tradition as a trained theologian. He thus had a theological integrity as a Muslim that is generally recognised by other Muslims, while his writing and person has also achieved resonance with people of other traditions. The relationship between these factors is reflected in his famous saying that "one of my feet is in the center and the other is in 72 realms [i.e., in the realm of all nations] like a compass." Rūmī is often cited by Fethullah Gülen, the third of the Muslim figures who will be engaged with later in this chapter, and who in relation to Rūmī's image of the compass said of Rūmī that, "he drew a broad circle that encompassed all believers" (Gülen, 2004: 199).

From Multi-Ethnic Ottoman Empire Diversity to Modern Nationalist Turkey

The development of the flavour of "Anatolian Islam" exemplified by such figures as Rūmī took place in the context of what, while it was ruled by the Muslim Ottoman Turks who were clearly Muslims, was also a multi-ethnic and multi-religious environment. That there is no straight line between that environment that the contemporary Muslim majority state of Turkey is clear from the fact that, today, Turkey's religious profile is considered by various sources to be between 96-99% Muslim, with the Jewish, Christian and other religious communities now being only a very small remnant of their historical presence which, especially in the case of cities such as Izmir and Istanbul, had been numerically quite substantial. This difference between contemporary Turkey and the earlier historical period comes about because the geographical, political and religious space of the territory concerned has undergone extensive upheavals and transformations. This was especially so during the course of latter part of the 19th century, and particularly the first part of the 20th. During the 19th century the Ottoman Empire increasingly came to be referred to (in a phrase often attributed to Tsar Nicholas I of Russia, but the origins of which or what was precisely said by him are not entirely clear) as "the sick man" and/or the "sick man of Europe."

Faced with the Empire's relative economic, political and military decline, and seeing the apparent interrelationship between industrialisation, modernisation and the development of the new European colonial powers, groups of people within the Ottoman Empire began to "look west" for inspiration. Among these were the so-called "Young Turks" (later officially known as the Committee for Union and Progress, or CUP). This group favoured replacement of the inherited absolutist imperial rule with a form of what might now be described as "constitutional monarchy" and their agitation eventually led to the so-called "Young Turk Revolution" of 1908 in which a form of multi-party democracy was established. But the most far-reaching upheavals and revolutionary changes came about following the First World War (1914-1918) in which the Ottoman Empire became engaged on the basis of its involvement with the ultimately losing side of the Quadruple Alliance along with Germany, Austro-Hungary, and Bulgaria.

These changes were intimately connected with the towering life and influence of Mustafa Kemal Atatürk (1881-1938). Having been an officer during the First World War, he led the Turkish National Movement and in the successful Turkish War of Independence (1919-1922) during the period during which the victorious allied powers threatened to colonise what was left of the Ottoman Empire, establishing the provisional Government of the Grand Assembly in Ankara and eventually issuing in the 24th July 1923 Treaty of Lausanne and the 29th October 1923 founding of the modern Republic of Turkey. His importance in the national narrative of modern Turkey is reflected in the title ascribed to him of "Atatürk" - which means "Father of the Turks" - and to this day his image remains almost omnipresent in public buildings in Turkey.

One of the early and significant consequences of the foundation of the modern state of Turkey was the 1924 abolition of the Caliphate that had most recently been associated with the Ottoman Muslim rulers. The term "Caliphate" conceptually represents the political unity of the global community of Muslims (the *ummah*), ruled by a single Caliph, while historically it has been seen as the ruling institution of the Islamic state in which the Caliph was the chief Muslim civil and religious ruler and was regarded as the successor of Muhammad. The Caliphate therefore began with the death of Muhammad and the appointment of the first Caliph, Abu Bakr Siddiqui. But even when Islamic unity was fractured with the emergence of the Shi'a Muslims and other groups, the term also continued to be applied to the rulers of various historical Sunni Muslim empires including, eventually, the Ottoman Empire.

The abolition of the Caliphate therefore represented a major social, political, and religious rupture with the previous order, not only for Muslims in Turkey at the time it occurred, but also having an impact on Islam and Muslims worldwide which echoes down to today. Thus a range of contemporary Muslim groups have seen the attempt to restore the Caliphate as an Islamic duty - whether by political agitation (as in the case of the modern Muslim movement, Hizb ut-Tahrir, or Liberation Party) or by force of violence as in the recent emergence of ISIL (Islamic State of Iraq and the Levant) or ISIS (Islamic State of Iraq and Syria).

By contrast with the inheritance of the Caliphate, the form of government that developed in the new state of Turkey, and the ideological perspectives that informed it (often called "Kemalism") emerged in a historical period where other forms of secular and statist ideology were ascending, such as the Bolshevism which following the Bolshevik and Russian Revolutions of 1917 eventually led to the formation, in 1922, of the Soviet Union. In the case of "Kemalism," its key principles can be summarised in what were known as its "Six Arrows". These were: Republicanism (*cumhuriyetçilik*); Populism (*halkçılık*); Nationalism (*milliyetçilik*); Secularism (*laiklik*); Statism (*devletçilik*); and Reformism (*devrimcilik*). In the shaping of modern Turkey these principles operated on multiple levels in the context of a society in which traditional Islam met revolutionary modernity. As the British historian Arnold Toynbee put it in a mid-20th century essay on "Islam, the West and the Future":

> Here, in Turkey, is a revolution which, instead of confining itself to a single plane, like our successive economic and political and aesthetic and religious revolutions in the West, has taken place on all these planes simultaneously and has thereby convulsed the whole life of the Turkish people from the heights to the depths of social experience and activity (Toynbee, 1948: 196).

At the same time, in the case of Turkey, the degree to which these changes became embedded in (at least significant parts of) society and also the nature of particular complications arising from the changes, came about through what was ultimately the internal (albeit externally influenced) revolutionary movement of Kemalism. In this, the history and inheritance of Turkey is, in many ways, different from the kind of disruption between Islamic traditionalism and secular modernity experienced by most other countries of Muslim majority populations and Muslim former rulers and which was the product of a more purely external and colonial imposition. The kind of broad social and cultural changes that occurred in connection with Kemalism in Turkey were both given effect by, and symbolised in, among other things, the "Hat Law" of 1925. This outlawed the wearing of the traditional fez and turban and determined that head coverings for men should in future be in the western style of hats, which were promoted as an expression of modern civilization.

In 1928, the Arabic script was abolished and replaced with Turkish script. The Turkish language had historically developed in a way that was rich with various sources including many words of Arabic and Persian origin. But its "Turkification" was an aspect of the nationalist project of the modern Turkish state, within which the declared need for a common language became politically significant. Arising from this the Kurdish language (the historical language of the many people in southeast Turkey and of a significant minority throughout the country) was not recognised by Turkish governments for use in the public sphere. This issue has continued to be contentious, although there have been recent openings around it linked to the ongoing peace process that has been developing between the Turkish Government and the PKK (the Kurdish acronym for the *Partiya Karkerên Kurdistanê*, or Kurdish Workers' Party) following the 2013 suspension of armed conflict.

The shift from relative Ottoman traditionalism and plurality to a Turkish nationalist approach built around notions of "oneness" and of modernity has taken place not only in relation to cultural and linguistic matters, but also in relation to religion. A radical change from the previously more diverse religious composition of the population came about because both during the First World War and following it, concerns had grown among Turks about the potential and actual use of the empire's ethnic and religious minorities by the allied powers. It was in such a context that the massacres of very large numbers of Armenians (which most Armenians describe as "genocide," but which Turkey does not recognise as such) took place, and in which it is estimated that a million to a million and a half Armenian Christians lost their lives. In addition, following the Greek-Turkish War of 1919-1922, and establishment of the Republic of Turkey, under the 1923 *Convention Concerning the Exchange of Greek and Turkish Populations*, there was a compulsory mutual transfer between Turkey and Greece. This included the transfer of around 350,000 Greek Muslims to Turkey which formalised the fact that around a million Greek Orthodox Christians had already fled to Greece from Turkey.

At the same time, following this change in population profile to Turkey to that of an almost completely Muslim country in terms of its religious population profile, following the abolition of the Caliphate, and despite the generally secularist approach of the Kemalists, a complete separation of religion and the state was not established in relation to the Muslim religious traditions, networks, organisations and institutions. Rather, after a period in which there was a Government Ministry of Religious Affairs and Charitable Foundations (1920-1924), under 1924 Law 429, a Presidency of Religious Affairs (*Diyanet İşleri Başkanlığı*) was established. Its remit was to carry out and oversee work concerning the beliefs, worship, and ethics of Islam, to enlighten the public about their religion, and to administer places of worship.

Then, in 1925, what had been the previously very important and extensive network of Sufi Orders in Turkey was abolished and its lodges were turned into museums, the Orders having been by Kemalists as both corrupt and as hindering the modernisation project of the new Turkish Republic. One of the by-products of these developments is that the Sunni Muslim orientation of Diyanet and, indeed, of Turkish nationalism in general, in many ways disguises the degree of religious diversity that actually exists among Turkish Muslims, since according to some estimates perhaps up to as many as 25% of the population are, in fact, Alevis or Bekhtashis – traditions which connect Sufi influences with Shi'a Muslim traditions.

With regard to the relations between believers and non-believers in Turkey, it is important to understand that the form of secularism espoused by Kemalism was not that of the Anglo-Saxon tradition of the secular understood primarily as a pragmatic separation of religion and state. Rather, it was a more ideological and radical version of French Revolutionary Laicism, which Yavuz and Esposito (2003:xvi) call a "radical Jacobin laïcism" in which secularism is treated "as above and outside politics" and in which, therefore, "secularism draws the boundaries of public reasoning." One of the consequences of this approach was a series of moves to exclude religious identities and identity markers from public life and institutions. Particularly symbolic of this was the 1982 ban brought in on women civil servants wearing headscarves and which, in 1997, was though a further interpretation of the law, extended to the wearing of headscarves in universities. The issue has continued to be a contentious one following (what were ultimately unsuccessful) moves in recent years from within the socially and religiously conservative AKP (*Adalet ve Kalkınma Partisi*, or Justice and Development Party) government to remove the ban.

Key Figures: Said Nursi (1877-1960)

The distinctively Turkish encounter of traditional Islam, revolutionary modernity and Kemalist secularism which Daniel Lerner's book on Turkey, *The Passing of Traditional Society*, encapsulated in a vivid phrase as posing the alternatives of "Mecca or mechanization" (Lerner, 1958: 405), resulted in also in the emergence of distinctive Islamic responses from Muslims within the new state. One particularly important and influential example of this was Said Nursi (1877-1960). Coming from a Kurdish background, Nursi was known to those inspired by him by the title of "Bediuzzaman", meaning "The most unique and superior person of the time". His influence has endured through the development of an identifiable Nurcu cemaat (or community).

In his major influential work, the *Risale-i-Nur* (or *Treatise of Light*), Nursi identified the three key enemies of Islam and Muslims as being ignorance, poverty, and disunity. Because of this, in his engagement with the new social order in Turkey and beyond, Nursi sought to distinguish science (which he saw as in principle compatible with religion) from the philosophy of atheistic materialism. In so doing, Nursi was attempting to chart a pathway between what, in his previously mentioned mid-20th century reflection on the encounter between Islam and modernity, the historian Arnold Toynbee (1948) called (by typological analogy with two key groups in Jewish history), on the one hand the "Zealots," and on the other hand, the "Herodians." By "Zealot," Toynbee (1948:188) was typologically identifying a group that, as he puts it "takes refuge from the unknown in the familiar," in contrast with the "Herodian" who "acts on the principle that the most effective way to guard against the danger of the unknown is to master its secret" (Toynbee, 1948:193).

In many ways, in terms of Toynbee's typology, in Turkey one could see Muslim traditionalists as "Zealots," while in its adoption of a particular form of secularising modernisation, Toynbee himself identified the Kemalist state as the epitome of the typologically "Herodian" approach. Indeed, in terms that find echoes in Muslim critiques of Kemalism, Toynbee argued that such an approach "can bring salvation – even mere salvation in this world – only to a small minority of any community" (Toynbee, 1948: 199) and that this because, fundamentally, such an approach can only be "mimetic and not creative" (Toynbee, 1948: 198).

Cleavages and Fractures of Left and Right, and Issues of Human Rights

Alongside the tensions between traditionalist Islam and revolutionary modernity, Turkish society has also experienced some cleavages and fractures in terms of the political Left and Right. This came about partly because of its strategic geopolitical position in the Cold War between the capitalist "West" and the Communist "East" in which, despite its ruling party having historically been quite "statist" in domestic politics and economics, Turkey had been a member of NATO (the North Atlantic Treaty Organisation) since 1952.

Especially in the later 1970s, both external Cold War tensions and internal Turkish conflicts were played out on the streets of Turkish cities in violent confrontations between leftist and rightist forces leading to several thousand deaths, until the military intervened (as it had also previously done in 1960 and 1971) in a coup. In some ways these coups could be seen as a response to civil disorder of a kind that at times was verging on civil war by the armed forces in their role as historical guarantors of Turkish independence and stability. But the coup resulted in around 50 executions; the imprisonment of around a half million people; and the death of several hundred of these while in prison.

In 1997, there was a different kind of coup – often described as a "postmodern coup" – in which the government of Necmettin Erbakan of the RP (*Refah Partisi*, or Welfare Party) was forced out of office without the suspension of Parliament or the constitution. This intervention was in many ways framed by a concern among Kemalist secularists about the development and coming to power of religio-political movements and political parties that in today's language might be perceived as being "Islamist," and thus seen as being a threat to secular basis on which the modern Turkish state was founded.

The historical occurrence of these military coups and the long history of concern about external interference exploiting internal conflict is, in many ways, linked with the almost omnipresent sense within Turkish politics and society of perceived conspiracy thinking, as well as the reality of actual conspiracies, and the difficulty for all involved of being able to tell the difference between these. And it is within such an overall context that the significance of the third major Turkish Islamic figure to be highlighted in this chapter can be seen.

Muhammad Fethullah Gülen (known to those inspired by his teaching by the title of *Hojaefendi*, or "Respected Teacher") was born in 1938, was a traditionally formed Sunni Islamic scholar who became an official preacher in 1953, taking up a teaching position in Edirne mosque, in 1959. In 1966-69, the so-called "Izmir Community" emerged around his teaching, inspiration and example. He retired from formal duties in 1981, but from 1988-91 he was a preacher emeritus. In 1994 he founded the Journalists and Writers Foundation which, among other things, through its so-called Abant Platform, has played an important role in facilitating constructive dialogue around sensitive topics in Turkish society, including that between secularists and believers in relation to the development of what could be a more shared understanding of, and approach to, secularism.

Reflecting some of the already noted wider tensions and cleavages in Turkey society, Fethullah Gülen is a figure around whom there has been considerable controversy and divided opinions. Thus an early Wikipedia article summary about him carried the following neutrality dispute note: "His supporters hail him as an important Islamic scholar with liberal ideas, while detractors accuse him for illegal activities aimed at undermining the secular republic and replacing it with an Islamic state." In fact, at one or another time, Gülen's detractors have seen him as either a secret Cardinal of the Roman Catholic Church; an agent of Mossad;

an agent of the CIA; a follower of Sun Myung Moon; or as someone planning for a Khomeini-like return from exile to Turkey, a combination of which would perhaps be unlikely!

After the military coup of 12 March 1971, Gülen was arrested under suspicion of "changing the social, political, and economic basis of the regime in Turkey; founding an association and secret community for this purpose and thereby taking advantage of the people's religious feelings for this purpose." More recently, he faced another legal process, based on what he was alleged to have said in a number of tape recordings in terms of encouraging his followers to infiltrate key positions in the police and the military, in order one day to take over. This started in absentia in 2000, after he had in 1998 left Turkey to live in the USA - where he now lives in Saylorsburg, Pennsylvania, and from where he continues to teach and write. Following a long process with many twists and turns he was formally acquitted in 2008 (Harrington, 2011).

Against the background recounted above of the history of a strongly secularist Kemalism and of military coups, the coming to power of the AKP Government in 2002, and perhaps even more so its managing to remain in power without a coup taking place and with increased majorities in 2007 and 2011 was, in many ways, a remarkable achievement. In the early days of the AKP government, the movement associated with Fethullah Gülen's teaching (more usually known to "insiders" in Turkish as *Hizmet*, or "Service") was sometimes seen by some as being almost the religious face of the government. But during Recep Tayyip Erdoğan's long period in power as Prime Minister, and since 2014 as President, tensions have grown between the AKP and Hizmet, becoming particularly strong in the context of the 2013 corruption scandal involving members of Erdoğan's family, and in the light of the government's declared intention to close some of the Hizmet inspired schools.

Positive evaluations of Fethullah Gülen and of his work see it as a Muslim-Turkish Sufi synthesis that has emerged out the Turkish Muslim engagement with modernity. As Ahmet Kuru (Yavuz & Esposito, 2003: 130) argues:

> Gülen does not try to create an eclectic or hybrid synthesis of modernity and Islam or to accommodate the hegemony of modernity by changing Islamic principles. What he does is reveal a dynamic interpretation of Islam that is both compatible with and critical of modernity and Muslim tradition.

Following the collapse of the Soviet Union, the influence of this tradition spread outside of Turkey especially into the Turkic states of the former Soviet Union, but also beyond, and especially in connection with its commitment to education. But it was with the events of 11 September 2001 that Fethullah Gulen became more globally well known. In relation to this, he first of all was clear in his condemnation of the claimed Islamic inspiration for that attack. But he (Gülen, 2004: 462) also issued a prescient warning about what might be the response of the government of the USA:

> Before America's leaders and people respond to this heinous assault out of their justified anger and pain, please let me express that they must understand why such a terrible event occurred and let us look to how similar tragedies can be avoided in the future. They must also be aware of the fact that injuring innocent masses in order to punish a few guilty people is to no one's benefit; rather, such actions will only strengthen the terrorists by feeding any existing resentment and by giving birth to more terrorists and more violence.

But as with his general approach to the relationship between Islam and modernity, Gulen's intervention in relation to terror conducted in the name of Islam was also not a merely reactive matter in the face of the horror of September 11th. Rather, as noted above, Gülen's work and thought had already been formed in engagement with a context that had already experienced violent cleavages, including in the name of Islam and reflecting on this Gülen explained that:

> Everybody was a terrorist. The people on that side were terrorists; the people on this side were terrorists. But, everybody was labelling the same action differently. One person would say, "I am doing this in the name of Islam." Another would say "I am doing it for my land and people." A third would say, "I am fighting against capitalism and exploitation." These were all just words. The Qur'an talks about such 'labels'. They are things of no value. But people just kept on killing. Everyone was killing in the name of an ideal. (Gülen, 2004: 7)

Against "Islamism" and Resonant with a "Baptistic" Vision

One of the key slogans of the form of political Islam that has come to be known as "Islamism" is that "Islam is the solution." The advocates of such an approach have argued that such an Islamic solution can be brought about through capturing the organs of the state (either through a democratic process, as originally during the Arab Spring with the Muslim Brotherhood in Egypt, or on the basis of more direct action such as that advocated by Salafists) on the basis of which then to bring about a transformation of the whole of the society in a way consistent with Islamic ideals. Fethullah Gülen clearly understands the historical and psychological origins of such approaches in his explanation that:

> Islamic societies entered the twentieth century as a world of the oppressed, the wronged, and the colonized; the first half of the century was occupied with wars of liberation and independence, wars that carried over from the nineteenth century. In all these wars, Islam assumed the role of an important factor uniting people and spurring them to action. As these wars were waged against what were seen as invaders, Islam, national independence and liberation came to mean the same thing (Gülen, 2004:239).

But in contrast to the charge that he is, like Khomeini, waiting to return to Turkey to initiate a theocratic system, in his teaching and writing Fethullah Gülen very clearly challenges the instrumentalization of the state and of politics in the service of religion, and of religion in the service of politics and the state.

> Politicizing religion would be more dangerous for religion than for the regime, for such people want to make politics a means for all their ends. Religion would grow dark within them, and they would say: "We are the representatives   of   religion." This is a dangerous matter. Religion is the name of the relationship between humanity and God, which everyone can respect (Ünal, 2000:166).

In this and other things, as a believing and pious Muslim, Fethullah Gülen is taking an approach that the author of this chapter has elsewhere argued is resonant also with the theologically grounded position of "Baptistic" traditions with regard to the integrity of religion in its relationship with society, politics, and the state (Weller, 2008). As a consequence of his general position, while noting that "[s]upposedly there are Islamic regimes in Iran and Saudi Arabia," Gülen argues that these claimed Islamic states are "state-determined and limited to sectarian approval" (Ünal, 2000:151). And in a 2000 interview with Hakan Yavuz he went even further to advocate the argument that "Islam does not need the state to survive, but rather needs educated and financially rich communities to flourish.

In a way, not the state but rather community is needed under a full democratic system" (Yavuz, 2003: 45).

Gülen and Dialogue in Practice

One of the key themes of organisations and initiatives that trace their inspiration to the teaching and example of Fethullah Gülen (alongside a strong commitment to education) is their engagement in dialogue. Speaking at the start of the present millennium, Fethullah Gülen declared that:

> I believe and hope that the world of the new millennium will be a happier, more just and more compassionate place, contrary to the fears of some people. Islam, Christianity and Judaism all come from the same root, have almost the same essentials and are nourished from the same source. Although they have lived as rival religions for centuries, the common points between them and their shared responsibility to build a happy world for all of the creatures of God, make interfaith dialogue among them necessary. This dialogue has now expanded to include the religions of Asia and other areas. The results have been positive. As mentioned above, this dialogue will develop as a necessary process, and the followers of all religion will find ways to become closer and assist each other (Ünal, 2000: 231).

Such a vision is one in which those in the Baptist Christian tradition, and indeed Christians and people more widely ought, with integrity within their own traditions, also be able to share. As Father Thomas Michel (from 1988-1994 Head of the Office for Islam of the Vatican's Pontifical Council for Interreligious Dialogue, and since 1996 Director of the Jesuit Secretariat for Interreligious Dialogue) has put it: "Non-Muslim believers will agree that these are people with whom we can live and co-operate for the benefit of all" (Gülen, 2004:iii). The outworking of such a vision now also has international influence due to the presence and activities of Hizmet throughout the world. Nevertheless it began in Turkey itself, and precisely in the historical, social, political and religious contexts explained in this chapter, and in relation to which Bekim Agai has pointed out that:

> Although many Islamic leaders may talk of tolerance in Islam, it may be problematic to put it into practice. Gülen himself has shown that he has no fears of meeting leaders of other religions, including the Pope and the representative of the Jewish

community in Istanbul. He also crossed the borders of Islamic discourse to meet with important people in Turkish society who are atheists. These activities were not easy from a religious perspective because Islamic discourse in Turkey has definite boundaries that do not appreciate close ties to the leaders of other religions and nonreligious persons. Also, his support for the Alevis was not very popular among most Sunni-Islamic groups (Yavuz & Esposito, 2003:65).

It is an important evaluative criterion of the Christian tradition that "by their fruits you will know them". Emerging from the crucible of Turkish history and society, an evaluation of the fruits of Hizmet (Weller & Yilmaz, 2013; Weller, Yilmaz & Barton, 2013) might therefore make an important contribution to an assessment of whether or not, in the continuing encounter between Islam and modernity, a "third way" might in practice be possible between Toynbee's typologically dead end responses of "Zealotry" and "Herodianism."

Bibliography

Groves, R. ed. *Thomas Helwys: A Short Declaration of the Mystery of Iniquity*. Mercer. 1998.

Gülen, M. F. "At the Threshold of a New Millennium." *Advocate of Dialogue*. Ünal, A and Williams, A., eds. Farrfax, Virginia: The Fountain. 2000.

_____. *Towards a Global Civilization of Love and Tolerance*. New York: The Light. 2004.

Harrington, J. *Wrestling with Free Speech, Religious Freedom and Democracy in Turkey: The Political Trials and Times of Fethullah Gülen*. University Press of America. 2011.

Lerner, D. *The Passing of Traditional Society*. The Free Press. 1958.

Toynbee, Arnold. *Civilization on Trial*. Oxford University Press. 1948.

Ünal, A. and Williams, A., eds. *Advocate of Dialogue*. The Fountain. 2000.

Underhill, E., ed. *Tracts on the Liberty of Conscience and Persecution, 1614-1667*. Hanserd Knollys Society. 1846.

Yavuz, Haken and John Esposito, eds. *Turkish Islam and the Secular State: The Gülen Movement*. Syracuse University Press. 2003.

Weller, Paul. "Freedom and witness in a multi religious society: A Baptist perspective, Part I." *The Baptist Quarterly*.Volume 33, April 1990.

_____. "Freedom and witness in a multi religious society: A Baptist perspective. Part II." *The Baptist Quarterly*. Volume 33, July 1990.

_____. "Religious Freedom in the Baptist Vision and in Fethullah Gülen", *Islam in the Age of Global Challenges: Alternative Perspectives of the Gülen Movement*. Georgetown. 2008.

_____. "Theological Ethics and Interreligious Relations: A Baptist Christian Perspective." *Internationale Kirchliche Zeitschrift/Bern Interreligious Oecumenical Studies*. Volume 1. 2014.

Weller, P. and Yilmaz, I., eds. *European Muslims, Civility and Public Life: Perspectives on and From the Gülen Movement*. Continuum. 2012.

Weller, P., Yilmaz, I. and Barton, G., eds. *The Muslim World and Politics in Transition: Creative Contributions of the Gülen Movement*. Bloomsbury. 2013.

To Let

THE

Opressed Go Free

19 | Causes and Effects of Migration and the Role of the Church

Edgar Palacios

Introduction

It is remarkable that we are gathered together to discuss and reflect upon the phenomenon of migration, assembled with the purpose of adopting a position that acknowledges the presence of the resurrected Jesus in migrant families. As Baptists, we believe that human beings reflect God's image, possessing dignity and inalienable rights, and the right to life, liberty, and happiness. According to the Gospel of Luke, Jesus Christ delivers his plan of action in Nazareth. The text says,

> The Spirit of the Lord is upon me, because he has anointed me to bring good news to the poor. He has sent me to proclaim release to the captives and recovery of sight to the blind, to let the oppressed go free, to proclaim the year of the Lord's favor (Lk. 4:18-19).

As Jesus' disciples, we identify with his ministry and are called to continue his teachings and practices. The Bible is not alien to the phenomenon of migration. The liberation experienced by the Egyptian slaves would mark Israel's faith; from this event, strangers and immigrants should see themselves as part of our family and should love themselves as we love our own selves. Leviticus 19:33-34 says,

> When an alien resides with you in your land, you shall not oppress the alien. The alien who resides with you shall be to you as the citizen among you; you shall love the alien as yourself, for you were aliens in the land of Egypt: I am the Lord your God.

Jesus Christ taught that those who practiced hospitality with strangers or immigrants would inherit his Kingdom. He said, "...I was a stranger and you welcomed me" (Mt. 25:35c).

The fact that we have gathered to share our interest and concern for global population's mobility signals God's presence with us. Jesus travels ahead of us to Galilee, a town belonging to the poor people of the world, to preach the Gospel message of love, justice, and life with dignity, and travels with immigrant families to destination countries to share in their struggles and anguish, their hopes and dreams. If we yearn to see the resurrected Jesus, we need to travel to Galilee and accompany immigrant families as they seek out the realization of their hope. We are only able to see and feel Jesus when we practice love and justice.

The Global Migratory Movement

In order for us to understand the global migratory movement, I present some data from the International Organization for Migration's "2010 World Migration Report" (IOM, 2010:115-116):

- In 2010, the estimated total number of global international migrants was 214 million persons;

- The United States of America has the highest number of migrants;

- 57% of all migrants live in high-income countries and may make up 10% of the population in these countries;

- Most of the main destination countries consider their current level of immigration to be "satisfactory," as do 152 governments worldwide;

- There are more that 20 cities in the world with over 1 million foreign-born inhabitants;

- In 2009, remittances made up USD 414 billion.

Causes of Migration

Economic

The neoliberal economic system sustains itself on the premise that profits are most important and that human beings are a means to this goal and not an end. This system aims to reduce the role of the state to an administrative one and guarantor of social stability, necessary for the functioning of capital. This system does not want rules or control, but wants freedom for its monopolies, oligarchies, and transnational corporations. It promotes free-trade treaties that are disadvantageous to poor countries. It aims to privatize state assets and also to reduce social services in order to ensure payment of external debt. This situation consolidates and deepens structural social injustice generating poverty. The neoliberal development model widens the gap between wealthy and poor families. As a consequence, in countries rich in natural resources, families are forced to emigrate to other countries due to their poor living conditions, for lack of opportunities, abuse, and violence.

Political

Democracy was not born with an inherent system of economic liberalism. These are two realities that do not complement each other nor do they form a harmonic unit. Democracy is an ideal and *sui generis* reality for each country that adopts it. It is government by the people and for the people. This problem is documented in history when many countries do not fulfill the rule of law and respect for human rights. Increasingly, democracy is a political system devoid of real substance. Now, the government works for a minority. Individual liberty is increasingly restricted and threatened. Democracy as a political system has subordinated itself to economic powers and in doing so has distorted itself. In many countries, governments are militaristic, dictatorial, imperialist, warring, and function on behalf of powerful economic interests. In this way, these governments serve special interests, lending themselves to irresponsible exploitation of their country's energy and natural resources. The population in these countries, assaulted by these forces, suffers the scourge of war and violence. These situations lead them to emigrate to save their lives, to survive, to find conditions that allow them to live with safety and dignity.

Social

Poverty is the evil of all evils, a product of structural injustice. In theoretical terms, governments are elected to manage resources through citizens' taxes, with the goal of returning those resources to citizens in the form of health, education, and housing services. It is an entity by all for all. The government should also regulate everything that affects the life of its citizens, especially the economy. The economy should always be in function of the common good. But as stated earlier, states and governments have been experiencing a denaturation. Stemming from the emergence of the republics, and in a more profound and accelerated way since the emergence of economic neoliberalism, social problems have increased, adding to this the economic crisis that Europe and the United States have with their negative effects on peripheral economies. Regarding poor countries, they cannot carry out minimal social services for their population. Privileged sectors of the population live in first-world luxury. There are also efforts by some countries to overcome their limitations in providing social services, and they are creating new models of sustainable development, affirming their sovereignty and their population's human rights. The historical accumulation of poverty has nonetheless caused a perpetual current of migrants.

Effects of Migration

Briefly, we can see the effects of migration on migrant families, on countries of origin, and on destination countries.

Effects of migration on the irregular migrant family

Negative Effects

The family that emigrates for economic, political, or social reasons, does so as a means of survival and achieving a worthy life. However, many times fathers are the people who emigrate, leaving their children and wives in their countries of origin. Because of this, families are divided. And when a reunion does not occur in the destination country, families are destroyed. Migrant families also carry significant debt because economic resources are needed to move to the destination country. It is also well documented that the migratory journey is not safe. Migrants are vulnerable, and are easy prey for migrant smugglers, drug smugglers, human traffickers, and organized crime.

The *via crucis* of many migrants continues when they arrive at their destination country. Social groups adhering to "nationalistic," fundamentalist, and xenophobic ideologies attack immigrants with anti-immigrant laws. Due to language barriers, their undocumented status, and economic situation, they are very vulnerable and are not able to defend themselves. They end up becoming an invisible population, living in the shadows, and maintain a forced silence in order to prevent deportation.

Immigrants are considered cheap manual labor and while they are taxpayers, they do not enjoy the privileges of health and education services like citizens.

Positive Effects

Some of the positive effects of family migration are:

- With the help of remittances, they are able to improve their family's living conditions;

- They can reunite their family by bringing them to the destination country;
- Children born in destination countries can usually become citizens and can enjoy educational and health services;
- They can learn the language of the destination country;
- They can attain migratory documentation status and are able to better integrate themselves into society by sharing their culture and values.

Effects of migration on countries of origin

Negative Effects

Among the negative effects of migration, it can be pointed out:

- Work force is lost;
- There is skilled labor or brain drain;
- Divided families can become dysfunctional for children, who might fall into the clutches of drugs or youth gang violence;
- Some individuals who are deported are criminals and may cause social disruption in their countries of origin;
- Countries that do not have migrant reintegration policies are not productively managing their returning migrants for the purposes of economic development;
- Many who depend on remittances use these for consumption, and this squanders an opportunity to take advantage of remittances for productive investment.

Positive Effects

Some of the positive effects of migration are:

- Remittances help with maintaining and reactivating the economy;
- Remittances can help with economic development. Remittances can be invested in small or medium-sized businesses. They can be invested in private and public mixed capital projects;
- Migrants can contribute to the tourism economy and the culture of their country of origin;

- Migrants are consumers of "sentimental products" from their countries of origin;

- Migrants might encourage future sister-city collaborations;

- Governments in countries of origin can promote laws to educate migrants on their rights in transit countries, in order to present the social and cultural context and for a smoother reentry in case of return;

- Governments can plan to use migrants' professional and technical skills acquired in their destination countries and use these for development.

Effects of Migration on Receiving or Destination Countries

In reality, immigrants themselves bear the heaviest burden of the negative effects of migration. Citizens often do not understand the causes of migration and refuse to recognize the contributions immigrants offer their countries. Some of the negative effects have been pointed out earlier in this article. Throughout the process of integration, immigrants continue to overcome the problems and difficulties presented to them.

Positive effects

Among the positive effects, we can list:

- Using immigrants as inexpensive labor;

- Immigrants are consumers, and help to activate the economy;

- Immigrants can contribute to economic development by creating production or service companies;

- Immigrants are taxpayers;

- Immigrants contribute to multiculturalism by way of their presence in a community;

- Destination countries benefit from migrants' skilled labor without incurring the preliminary costs of their training;

- In countries with a demographic deficit, immigrants help overcome the problem of a small workforce by supplying the workforce that the economy needs.

Contribution of Latin American Immigration to the United States

Because the United States has the highest percent of immigration in the world, I present some data on the contributions that Latin Americans offer this country, despite the fact that U.S. immigration policies are dysfunctional and the situation generates injustice for millions of immigrants.

Alejandro Canales, an expert on the migratory phenomenon from the Economic Commission for Latin America and the Caribbean (ECLAC), believes that the relationship between development and migration should be studied and investigated within the context of globalization. Remittances are not only valued for their role in development but other aspects of this relationship are considered important. In particular, Canales identifies three levels and processes in which Latin American immigration is contributing to social reproduction in the United States. These levels are: demographic transfers, economic transfers, and migration as a social reproduction (Canales, 2011:325).

With respect to demographic transfers, Latin American immigration has allowed the United States to maintain demographic growth. Between the years 2000 and 2008, immigrants contributed more than 20% of the population's growth. They have also filled a void left by an economically active but aging population. They have even contributed their own offspring. In 2011, Latin American population contributed 25% of all births; in other words, one in four new Americans was of Hispanic descent (Canales, 2011:325).

Latin American immigration (men and women) to the United States contributes one third of the growth of the work force in this country, demonstrating the effects of economic transfer in migration. Men, as a group, have contributed a greater percentage. Again, between 2000 and 2008, men contributed over 40%. The native non-Latin American population is aging and the growth of the population capable of working is slowing, so they are not able to fill all of the jobs that the new economic dynamic is producing. Between 2000 and 2008 the United States generated 1.3 million new jobs, of which native non-Latin American work force only covered one-third of this number (Canales, 2011:326). Also, Latin American immigration has contributed to economic growth in the United States. "Between 2000 and 2007, Latin American immigrants contributed almost 17% of the GDP" (Canales, 2011:326).

Latin American immigration has also offered social reproduction to United States citizens through the type of work they perform. From one perspective, the work might be considered unskilled, but from the perspective of producing life satisfaction, these jobs are very important. I refer to jobs in construction, food preparation, cleaning, and domestic services. Latin American immigrants make up 23% of the cleaning and maintenance labor force, represent 20% in food preparation, and 12% of domestic service workers are Latin American women immigrants (Canales, 2011:327).

It can be said that in our globalized reality, the migratory phenomenon demonstrates interrelatedness between people, helping shape them socially, economically, and culturally. Societies receptive to immigrants are multicultural. In the case of the United States, Latin American immigration contributes to social, economic, and cultural reproduction. What would happen if this immigration flow were disrupted? The country simply could not reproduce itself with the current dynamics. From a realistic and ethical standpoint, the United States should approve just, humane, and comprehensive immigration reform.

The Role of Churches

The global migratory movement is an extraordinary phenomenon facing the world stage. This movement underscores the fact that globalization is not only about capital but covers other areas of human existence. This movement expresses the fact that we are all human beings and live in this shared space called Earth. With the global migratory movement, we are necessarily multicultural, and economically interdependent. This reality cannot be denied or deleted. It's possible to distort one's reading and interpretation of scripture and view migration as an evil, or one can humanize it and view it as an opportunity for human realization. Some churches have already discovered this and have channeled their scarce resources to supporting this movement, humanizing and Christianizing it. These churches are growing in membership. Other churches have yet to be moved by mercy. We want to better understand this topic and reflect upon our faith in Jesus Christ to make decisions leading us to a planned and organized practice of love and service.

The church is a community of love, solidarity, and service. Its message is to live out, proclaim, and teach the kingdom of God. We are tasked to listen to the cries of the children, to be touched by their reality, and to participate in God's transforming mission in the world. It's a matter of choice. Taking up the challenge implies a willingness to act, acting by making another's situation one's own, accompanying them through their liberation and contributing by following Jesus in creating a new world where structural injustice is defeated, human rights are respected, and everyone experiences God's shalom.

In the following, I signal some things that can be done in the face of the international migratory movement.

- Persuade media outlets to convey an objective picture of the migratory phenomenon, especially focusing on the contributions that immigrants offer destination countries;

- Denounce and work to transform institutional injustice in countries of origin;

- Advocate for unity and the reunification of migrant families;

- Educate immigrants in opportunities for service and training available in destination countries;

- Promote intergovernmental accords to protect migrants from threats and abuses on routes leading to destination countries;

- Provide economic conditions between governments and the private sector to facilitate investment of migrants in their countries of origin;

- Support immigrants' political participation in their countries of origin through absentee voting abroad;

- Stand united, denominationally and ecumenically, to promote just and humane immigration reform in destination countries if they do not have it;

- Elevate local churches and temples as sanctuaries for immigrants where they might encounter Christian compassion, friends, and family;

- Share the way of Jesus Christ with immigrants so they might freely choose the kingdom of God.

Conclusion

Faith in Jesus Christ and the presence of the Holy Spirit from within us are the tools that incarnate Baptists' participation in the international migratory movement. Faith moves us to practice and transformation. The Spirit unites us, gives us power, and life to move forward. We move forward not as individuals but as a united people of goodwill. We move forward with sister churches and with governments that obey God's design of working for the common good of humanity. As Baptists, we have a role to play: to love the immigrant, the stranger, and the foreigner. This is our reality; will we accept the challenge?

Bibliography

Alejandro Canales. "The Profound Contributions of Latin American Immigrants in the United States."

International Migration in Latin America and in the Caribbean: A Summary of Trends and Patterns, Economic Commission for Latin America and the Caribbean (ECLAC), 2011.

World Migration Report 2010, International Organization for Migration, 2010.

20 | Xenophilia or Xenophobia: Towards a Theology of Migration

Luis N. Rivera-Pagán

"I have Dutch, nigger, and English in me, and either I'm nobody, or I'm a nation." (Walcott, 1986:346)

"To survive the Borderlands, you must live *sin fronteras*. Be a crossroads." (Anzaldúa, 1999:217)

A Homeless Migrant Aramean

The Bible's first confession of faith begins with a story of pilgrimage and migration: "A wandering Aramean was my ancestor; he went down into Egypt and lived there as an alien..." (Deut. 26:5). We might ask, did that "wandering Aramean" and his children have the proper documents to reside in Egypt? Were they "illegal aliens?" Did he and his children have the proper Egyptian social security credentials? Did they speak properly the Egyptian language?

We know at least that he and his children were strangers in the midst of a powerful empire, and that as such they were both exploited and feared. This is the fate of many immigrants. In their reduced circumstances they are usually compelled to perform the least prestigious and most strenuous kinds of menial work. But at the same time they awaken the schizophrenic paranoia typical of empires, powerful and yet fearful of the stranger, of the "other," especially if that stranger resides within its frontiers and becomes populous. "Paranoia," Elias Canetti reminds us, "is the disease of power" (Míguez, 2009:45). More than half a century ago, Franz Fanon brilliantly described the peculiar gaze of so many white French people at the growing presence of Black Africans and Caribbeans in their national midst (Fanon, 1952). Scorn and fear are entwined in that stare.

The biblical creedal story continues: "When the Egyptians treated us harshly and afflicted us, by imposing hard labor on us, we cried to the … God of our ancestors; the Lord heard our voice and saw our affliction … and our oppression" (26: 6). So important was this story of migration, slavery and liberation for biblical people of Israel that it became the core of an annual liturgy of remembrance and gratitude. The already quoted statement of faith was to be solemnly recited every year in the thanksgiving liturgy of the harvest festival. It reenacted the wounded memory of the afflictions and humiliations suffered by an immigrant people, strangers in the midst of an empire; the recollection of their hard and arduous labor, of the contempt and scorn that is so frequently the fate of the stranger and foreigner who possesses a different skin pigmentation, language, religion, or culture. But it was also the memory of the events of liberation, when God heard the dolorous cries of the suffering immigrants. And the remembrance of another kind of migration, in search of a land where they might live in freedom, peace, and righteousness, a land they might call theirs.

We might ask: who might be today the wandering Arameans and what nation might represent Egypt these days, a strong but fearful empire?

Dilemmas and Challenges of Migration

The United States undergoes a significant increase of its Latino/Hispanic population. In 1975, little more than 11 million Hispanics made up just over 5 percent of the US inhabitants. Today they number approximately nearly 47 million, around 15 percent of the nation, its largest minority group. Recent projections estimate that by 2050 the Latino/Hispanic share of the US population might be between 26 to 32 percent. This demographic growth has become a complex political and social debate for it highlights sensitive and crucial issues, like national identity and compliance with the law. It also threatens to unleash a new phase in the sad and long history of American racism and xenophobia (Pyong, 2005). Two concerns have become important topics of public discourse:

1. What to do regarding the growth of unauthorized migration? Possibly about a quarter of the Hispanic/Latino adults are unauthorized immigrants. For a society that prides itself of its law and order tradition that represents a serious breach of its juridical structure;

2. What does this dramatic increase in the Latino/Hispanic population might convey for the cultural and linguistic traditions of the United States, its mores and styles of collective self-identification?

Unfortunately, the conversation about these difficult issues takes place in an environment clouded by the gradual development of xenophobic attitudes. There are signs of an increasing hostile reaction to what the Mexican American writer Richard Rodríguez has termed "the browning of America" (Rodriguez, 2002). One can clearly recognize this mind-set in the frequent use of the derogatory term "illegal alien." As if the illegality would define not a specific delinquency, but the entire being of the migrant. We all know the dire and sinister connotations that "alien" has in popular American culture, thanks in part to the sequence of four "Alien" [1979, 1986, 1992, and 1997] films with Sigourney Weaver fighting back atrocious creatures (cf. Buchanan, 2008).

Let me briefly mention some key elements of this emerging xenophobia:

1. There is what one might call the Lou Dobbs syndrome: The spread of fear regarding the so-called "broken borders," the possible proliferation of Third World epidemic diseases, and the alleged increase of criminal activities by undocumented immigrants (Leonhardt, 2007). A shadowy sinister specter is created in the minds of the public: the image of the intruder and threatening "other."

2. The xenophobic stance intensifies the post 9/11 attitudes of fear and phobia regarding the strangers, those people who are here but who do not seem to belong here. Surveillance of immigration is now located under the Department of Homeland Security. This administrative merger links two basically unrelated problems: threat of terrorist activities and unauthorized migration.

3. Though U.S. racism and xenophobia have had traditionally different targets – people with African ancestry the first (be they slaves or free citizens), marked by their dark skin pigmentation, foreign-born immigrants the second, distinguished by their particular language, religiosity, and collective memory - in the case of Latin American immigrants both nefarious prejudices converge and coalesce (Fredrickson, 2006); as was also the case with the nineteenth century Chinese indentured servants, which led to the infamous 1882 Chinese Exclusion Act (Miller, 1969).

4. There has been a significant increase of anti-immigrants aggressive groups. According to a recent report by the Southern Poverty Law Center, "'nativist extremist groups' –organizations that go beyond mere advocacy of restrictive immigration policy to actually confront or harass suspected immigrants – jumped from 173 groups in 2008 to 309 last year [2009]. Virtually all of these vigilante groups have appeared since the spring of 2005" (Potok, 2010).

5. Proposals coming from the White House, Congress, states, and counties have tended to be excessively punitive. Some examples are:

- A projected wall along the Mexican border (compare it to Eph. 2:14, "Christ ... has broken down the dividing wall");

- The criminalization as felony not only of illegal immigration but also of any action by legal residents that might provide assistance to undocumented immigrants. This was one of the most controversial sections of the "Border Protection, Anti-terrorism, and Illegal Control Act of 2005" (H.R. 4437), a bill approved by the House but not the Senate;

- Draconian legislation prescribing mandatory detention and deportation of non-citizens, even for alleged minor violations of law. Arizona's notorious and contentious Senate Bill 1070 is a prime example of this infamous trend. It has been followed by Alabama's even harsher anti-immigrants legislation (House Bill 56), soon to be cloned by other states;

- Proposed legislation to curtail access to public services (health, education, police protection, legal services, drivers' licenses) by undocumented migrants;

- Some prominent right-wing politicians have suggested the possibility of revising the first section of the fourteenth amendment of the US constitution, which begins with, "All persons born or naturalized in the United States, ... are citizens of the United States and of the State wherein they reside." Their purpose, apparently, is to deprive the children of immigrants of their constitutional right of citizenship. A campaign against the so-called "anchor babies" has been part and parcel of the most strident xenophobic campaign in years;

- A significant intensification of raids, detentions, and deportations. This is transforming several migrant communities into a clandestine underclass of fear and dissimulation. It brings to mind the infamous Mexican deportation program, authorized in 1929 by President Herbert Hoover. That program led, according to some scholars, to the forceful deportation of approximately one million people of Mexican descent, many of which were, in fact, American citizens (Hoffman, 2006);

- Congress has been unable to approve the Development, Relief and Education for Alien Minors Act (DREAM Act), that would provide conditional permanent residency to certain deportable foreign-born students who graduate from U.S. high schools, are of good moral character, were brought to the U.S. illegally as minors, and have been in the country continuously for at least five years prior to the bill's enactment, if they complete two years in the military or at an academic institution of higher learning.

The xenophobia and scapegoating of the "stranger in our midst" has resulted in the chaotic condition that now plagues the immigration system in the United States, judicially, politically, and socially. All recent attempts to enact a comprehensive immigration reform have floundered thanks to the resistance of influential sectors that have been able to propagate efficaciously the fear of the "alien" (Soerens, 2009:138-158). The increasing support that such phobic anxiety against the "outsiders" within the frontiers of the nation seems to enjoy among substantial sectors of the American public brings to mind Alexis de Tocqueville's astute critical observation: "I know no country in which there is so little true independence of mind and freedom of discussion as in America… In America, the majority raises very formidable barriers to the liberty of opinion" (Tocqueville, 1959:192).

From a Clash of Civilizations to a Clash of Cultures

In this social context tending towards xenophobia and racism, the late Professor Samuel P. Huntington wrote some important texts about what he perceived as a Hispanic/Latino threat to the cultural and political integrity of the United States. Huntington was chairman of Harvard's Academy for International and Area Studies, and cofounder of the journal *Foreign Policy*. He was also the intellectual father of the theory of the "clash of civilizations" (Huntington, 1993), with disastrous consequences for the foreign policies of George W. Bush presidency.

In 2004, Huntington published an extended article in *Foreign Policy*, titled "The Hispanic Challenge" (Huntington, FP, 2004), followed by a lengthy book, *Who are We? The Challenges to America's National Identity* (Huntington, 2004). The former prophet of an unavoidable civilizational abyss and conflict between the West and the Rest (specially the Islamic nations) now became the proclaiming apostle of an emerging nefarious cultural conflict inside the United States. Immersed in a dangerous clash of civilizations *ad extra*, this messenger of doom prognosticated that the United States is also entering into a grievous clash of cultures *ad intra*.

American national identity seems a very complex issue for it deals with an extremely intricate and highly diverse history. But Huntington has, surprisingly, a simple answer: The United States is mainly identified by its "Anglo-Protestant culture" and not only by its liberal republican democratic political creed. It has been a nation of settlers rather than immigrants. The first British pioneers transported not only their bodies, but also their fundamental cultural and religious viewpoints, what Huntington designates as "Anglo-Protestant culture." In the formation of this collective identity Christian devotion – the Congregational pilgrims, the Protestantism of dissent, the Evangelical Awakenings - has been meaningful and crucial. This national identity has also been forged by a long history of war against a succession of enemies (from the Native Americans to the Islamic jihadists). There is a certain romantic nostalgia in Huntington's thesis, an emphasis on the foundations of American culture and identity, in their continuities rather than its evolutions and transformations.

But the main objective of Huntington is to underline the uncertainties of the present trends regarding this nation's collective self-understanding. After the dissolution of the Soviet threat, he perceives a significant neglect of the American national identity. National identity seems to require the image of a dangerous adversary, what he terms the "perfect enemy." The prevailing trend is supposedly one of a notable decline and loss of intensity and salience of US awareness of national identity and loyalty.

But then emerges the sinister challenge of the Latin American migratory invasion. It is not similar to previous migratory waves. Its contiguity, intensity, lack of education, territorial memory, constant return to the homeland, preservation of language, retention of homeland culture, national allegiance and citizenship, its distance to Anglo-Protestant culture, its alleged absence of a Puritan work ethic, makes it unique and unprecedented. This immigration constitutes, according to Huntington, "a major potential threat to the cultural and political integrity of the United States" (Huntington, FP, 2004:33). This Harvard professor has discovered and named America's newest "perfect enemy"—the Latin American migrant!

Huntington's discomfiture is intense regarding the encroachment of Spanish in the American public life. He calls attention that now in some states more children are ominously christened José rather than Michael. This increasing public bilingualism threatens to fragment the US linguistic integrity. Linguistic bifurcation becomes a veritable menacing Godzilla. He neglects altogether the economic causes for the Latin American migration - its financial and social benefits both for the sending (remittances; Ratha, 2009) and the receiving nations (lower wages for manual jobs; Ruiz, 2003:86, 93). He does not seem to have any concern regarding the process whereby they become our new *douloi* and *μέτοικοι*, servants at the margins of our society, in a kind of social Apartheid, cleaning our stores, cooking our meals, doing our dishes, cutting our grass, picking our tomatoes and oranges, painting our buildings, washing our cars, staying out of our way.

Obfuscated by Huntington are the consequences of the present trend among metropolitan Third World diasporas towards holding dual citizenship. An increasing number of Latin American nations now recognize and promote double citizenship, a process that leads to multiple national and cultural loyalties and to what Huntington classifies, with a disdainful and pejorative tone, "ampersand peoples." Dual citizenship, Huntington rightly recognizes, leads to dual national loyalties and identities. Huntington perceives this trend towards dual citizenship and national fidelity as a violation and disruption of the Oath of Allegiance and the Pledge of Allegiance, essential components of the secular liturgy in the acquisition of the United States citizenship.

He seems to suggest stricter policies regarding illegal migration, stronger measures to enforce cultural assimilation of the legal immigrants, and the rejection of dual citizenship. This perspective would not only be utterly archaic; it might also become the theoretical underground for a new wave of xenophobic white nativism (Portes, 2006). The train has already left that outdated station. What is now required is a wider acceptance and enjoyment of multiple identities and loyalties and, if religious compassion truly matters, a deeper concern regarding the burdens and woes of displaced peoples. The time has come to prevail over the phobia of diversity and to learn how to appreciate and enjoy the dignity of difference (Sacks, 2003). For, as Dale Irvin has recently asserted, "the actual world that we are living in … is one of transnational migrations, hyphenated and hybrid identities, cultural conjunctions and disjunctions" (Irvin, 2009:181).

Do the Latino/Hispanics truly represent "a major potential threat to the cultural and political integrity of the United States," as Huntington has argued? Whether that is something to lament, denounce, or celebrate depends on the eyes of the beholder. Maybe, just maybe, it would not be that negative a historical outcome if the Latino immigrants prove in fact to be that dramatic and decisive "major potential threat to the cultural and political integrity of the United States."

To expand on this, at least Huntington recognizes the critical urgency of the substantial Latin American immigration for the cultural and political integrity of the United States. Cornel West, in another key text published in 2004, remains cloistered in the traditional White/Black American racial dichotomy and is unable to perceive the salience and perils of xenophobia and nativism as a chauvinistic reply to immigration (West, 2004). Is there any possible conceptual manner of bridging the concerns of the African-American ghettoes, struggling against color-coded racism, and the growing Latino/Hispanic barrios, facing an insidious cultural disdain? Both communities suffer a lack of recognition of their genuine human dignity, which should imply more than mere tolerance for their distinctive cultural traits, of socio-economic deprivation and political powerlessness. An always complex and difficult to achieve dialectics between cultural recognition and social-economic redistribution might be the key clue for solving this dilemma (cf. Fraser, 2003). Ernesto Laclau and Chantal Mouffe emphasize this dialectics in the preface to the new edition of their famed text, *Hegemony and Socialist Strategy: Toward a Radical Democratic Politics*: "One of the central tenets of *Hegemony and Socialist Strategy* is the need to create a chain of equivalence among the various democratic struggles against subordination ... to tackle issues of both 'redistribution' and 'recognition'" (Laclau, 2001:xviii).

Xenophilia: Towards an Ecumenical Ethical Theology of Migration

Migration and xenophobia are serious social quandaries. But they also convey urgent challenges to the ethical sensitivity of religious people and persons of good will. The first step we need to take is to perceive this issue from the perspective of the immigrants, to pay cordial (that is, deep from our hearts) attention to their stories of suffering, hope, courage, resistance, ingenuity, and, as so frequently happens in the wildernesses of the American Southwest, death (Harding, 2011). Many of the unauthorized migrants have become *nobodies* (Bowes, 2007), *disposable people* (Bales, 2004), or *wasted lives* (Bauman, 2004). They are the Empire's new μέτοικοι, *douloi*, i.e., modern servants. Their dire existential situation cannot be grasped without taking into consideration the upsurge in global inequalities in these times of unregulated international financial hegemony. For many human beings the excruciating alternative is between misery in their third world homeland and marginalization in the rich West/North, both fateful destinies intimately linked together (Milanovic, 2009; Stalker, 2000).

Will the Latino/Hispanics, during these early decades of the twenty-first century, become the new national scapegoats? Do they truly represent "a major potential threat to the cultural and political integrity of the United States?" This is a vital dilemma that the United States has up to now been unable to face and solve. We are not called, here and now, to solve it. But allow me, from my perspective as a Hispanic and Latin American Christian theologian, to offer some critical observations that might illuminate our way in this bewildering labyrinth.

We began this essay with the annual creedal and liturgical memory of a time when the people of Israel were aliens in the midst of an empire, a vulnerable community, socially exploited and culturally scorned. It was the worst of times. It became also the best of times: the times of liberation and redemption from servitude. That memory shaped the sensitivity of the Hebrew nation regarding the strangers, the aliens, within Israel. Their vulnerability was a reminder of their own past helplessness as immigrants in Egypt, but also an ethical challenge to care for the foreigners inside Israel (Kidd, 1999).

Caring for the stranger became a key element of the Torah, the covenant of justice and righteousness between Yahweh and Israel.

> When an alien resides with you in your land, you shall not oppress the alien. The alien who resides with you shall be to you as the citizen among you; you shall love the alien as yourself, for you were aliens in the land of Egypt: I am the Lord your God (Lev. 19:33f);

> You shall not oppress a resident alien; you know the heart of an alien, for you were aliens in the land of Egypt (Ex. 23:9);

> The Lord your God is God of gods ... who executes justice to the orphan and the widow, and who loves the strangers, providing them food and clothing. You shall also love the stranger, for you were strangers in the land of Egypt (Deut. 10:17ff);

> You shall not withhold the wages of poor and needy laborers, whether other Israelites or aliens who reside in your land in one of your towns ... You shall not deprive a resident alien ... Remember that you were a slave in Egypt and the Lord redeemed you from there (Deut. 24:14, 17-18).

The twelve curses that, according to Deuteronomy 27, Moses instructs the Israelites to liturgically proclaim at their entrance to the promised land, include the trilogy of orphans, widows and strangers as privileged recipients of collective solidarity and compassion: "Cursed be anyone who deprives the alien, the orphan, and the widow of justice" (Deut. 27:19).

The prophets constantly chastised the ruling elites of Israel and Judah for their social injustice and their oppression of the vulnerable people. Who were those vulnerable persons? The poor, the widows, the fatherless children, and the foreigners. "The princes of Israel ... have been bent on shedding blood ... the alien residing within you suffers extortion; the orphan and the widow are wronged in you" (Ezek. 22:6f). After condemning with the harshest words possible the apathy and inertia of temple religiosity in Jerusalem, the prophet Jeremiah, in the name of God, commands the alternative: "Thus says the Lord: Act with justice and righteousness ... And do no wrong or violence to the alien, the orphan, and the widow" (Jer. 7: 6). He went on to reprove the king of Judah with harsh admonishing words:

> Thus says the Lord: Act with justice and righteousness, and deliver from the hand of the oppressor anyone who has been robbed. And do no wrong or violence to the alien, the orphan, and the widow ... If you do not heed these words, I swear by myself, says the Lord, that this house shall become a desolation" (Jer. 22:3, 5).

The prophet paid a costly price for those daring admonitions.

The divine command to care for the stranger was the matrix of an ethics of hospitality. As evidence of his righteousness, Job witness that "the stranger has not lodged in the street" for he always "opened the doors of my house" to board the foreigner (Job 31:32). In Genesis 19, it was the violation of the divinely sanctioned code of hospitality that led to the dreadful destruction of Sodom (cf. Jordan, 1997). The perennial temptation is xenophobia. The divine command, enshrined in the Torah is xenophilia - the love for those whom we usually find very difficult to love: the strangers, the aliens, the foreign sojourners.

The command to love the sojourners and resident foreigners in the land of Israel emerges from two foundations (Cervantes Gabarrón, 2003:262). One has already been mentioned; the Israelites had also been sojourners and resident foreigners in a land not of theirs ("for you were strangers in the land of Egypt") and should, therefore, be sensitive to the complex existential stress of communities living in the midst of a nation whose dominant inhabitants speak a different language, venerate dissimilar deities, share distinct traditions, and commemorate different historical founding events. Love and respect towards the stranger and the foreigner is thus, in these biblical texts, construed as an essential dimension of Israel's national identity. It belongs to the essence and nature of the people of God.

A second source for the command of care towards the immigrant foreigner is that it corresponds to God's way of being and acting in history: "The Lord watches over the strangers" (Ps. 146:9ᵃ); "God ... executes justice for the orphan and the widow and loves the strangers ..." (Deut. 10:18). God takes sides in history, favoring the most vulnerable: the poor, the widows, the orphans and the strangers. "I will be swift to bear witness ... against those who oppress the hired workers in their wages, the widow, and the orphan, against those who thrust aside the alien, and do not fear me, says the Lord of hosts" (Mal. 3:5). Solidarity with the marginalized and excluded corresponds to God's being and acting in history.

How comforting would be to stop right here, with these fine biblical texts of xenophilia, of love for the stranger. But the Bible happens to be a disconcerting book. It contains a disturbing multiplicity of voices, a perplexing polyphony that frequently complicates our theological hermeneutics. Regarding many key ethical dilemmas, we find in the Bible often times not only different, but also conflictive, even contradictory perspectives. Too frequently we jump from our contemporary labyrinths into a darker and sinister scriptural maze.

In the Hebrew Bible we also discover statements with a distinct and distasteful flavor of nationalist xenophobia. Leviticus 25 is usually read as the classic text for the liberation of the Israelites who have fallen into indebted servitude. Indeed it is, as its famed tenth verse so eloquently manifests: "Proclaim liberty throughout all the land unto all the inhabitants thereof." But it also contains a nefarious distinction: "As for the male and female slaves whom you may have, it is from the nations around you that you may acquire male and female slaves. You may also acquire them from among the aliens residing with you, and from their families ... and they may be your property ... These you may treat as slaves ..." (Lev. 25:44-46). And what about the terrifying fate imposed upon the foreign wives (and their children), in the epilogues of Ezra and Nehemiah? They are thrown away—exiled, as sources of impurity and contamination of the faith and culture of the people of God (Steicke, 2011). In the process of reconstructing Jerusalem, "Ezra and Nehemiah demonstrate the growing presence of xenophobia," as the Palestinian theologian Naim Ateek has appropriately highlighted. He immediately adds: "Ezra and Nehemiah demonstrate the beginning of the establishment of a religious tradition that leaned toward traditionalism, conservatism, exclusivity, and xenophobia" (Ateek, 2009, 132). Let us also not forget the atrocious rules of warfare that prescribes forced servitude or annihilation of the peoples encountered in Israel's route to the "promised land" (Deut. 20:10-17). These all are, in Phyllis Trible's apt expression, "texts of terror" (Trible, 1984).

The problem with some evangelically oriented books like Matthew Soerens & Jenny Hwang's *Welcoming the Stranger* and M. Daniel Carroll R., *Christians at the Border: Immigration, the Church, and the Bible* (Carroll, 2008) is that their hermeneutical strategy evades completely and intentionally those biblical texts that might have xenophobic connotations. Both books, for example, narrate the postexilic project of rebuilding Jerusalem under Nehemiah (Soerens, 2009:85,98; Carroll, 2008:83-84), but fail to address the expulsion of the foreign wives—an important part of that project (Ezra 9-10, Neh. 13:23-31). The rejection of foreign wives in the biblical texts of Ezra and Nehemiah does not seem too different from several modern anti-immigrants xenophobia: those foreign wives have a different linguistic, cultural, and religious legacy - "half of their children ... could not speak the language of Judah, but spoke the language of various peoples. And I contended with them and cursed them and beat some of them and pulled out their hair" (Neh. 13:24-25).

This conundrum is a constant irritating *modus operandi* of the Bible. We go to it searching for simple and clear solutions to our ethical enigmas, but it strikes back exacerbating our perplexity. Who said that the Word of God is supposed to make things easier? But have I not forgotten something? A distinction of the Protestant tradition is its Christological emphasis; *Solus Christus* is the main tenet of the Reformation. What, then, about Christ and the stranger?

Clues to address Jesus' perspective regarding the socially despised other or stranger can be found in his attitude towards the Samaritans and in his dramatic and surprising eschatological parable on genuine discipleship and fidelity (Mt. 25:31-46). Orthodox Jews despised Samaritans as possible sources of contamination and impurity. Yet Jesus did not have any inhibitions in conversing amiably with a Samaritan woman of doubtful reputation, breaking down the exclusion barrier between Judeans and Samaritans (Jn. 4:7-30). Of ten lepers once cleansed by Jesus, only one came to express his gratitude and reverence, and the Gospel narrative emphasizes that "he was a Samaritan" (Lk. 17:11-19). Finally, in the famous parable to illustrate the meaning of the command "love your neighbor as yourself" (Lk. 10:29-37), Jesus contrasts the righteousness and solidarity of a Samaritan with the neglect and indifference of a priest and a Levite. The action of a traditionally despised Samaritan is thus exalted as a paradigm of love and solidarity to emulate.

The parable of the judgment of the nations, in the Gospel of Matthew (25:31-46), is pure vintage Jesus. It is a text whose connotations I refuse to reduce to a common and constraining ecclesiastical confinement. Jesus disrupts, as he loved to do, the familiar criteria of ethical value and religious worthiness by distinguishing between human actions that sacramentally bespeak divine love for the powerless and vulnerable from those that do not. Who are, according to Jesus, to be divinely blessed and inherit God's kingdom? Those who in their actions care for the hungry, thirsty, naked, sick, and incarcerated, in short, for the marginalized and vulnerable human beings. But also those who welcome the strangers, who provide them with hospitality; those who are able to overcome nationalistic exclusions, racism, and xenophobia and are daring enough to welcome and embrace the alien, the people in our midst who happen to be different in skin pigmentation, culture, language, and national origins. They belong to the powerless of the powerless, the poorest of the poor, in Franz Fanon's famous terms, "the wretched of the earth," or, in Jesus' poetic language, "the least of these."

Why? Here comes the shocking statement: because they are, in their powerlessness and vulnerability, the sacramental presence of Christ. "For I was hungry and you gave me food, I was thirsty and you gave me something to drink, I was a stranger [xénos] and you welcomed me, I was naked and you gave me clothing, I was sick and you took care of me ..." (Mt. 25:35). The vulnerable human beings become, in a mysterious way, the sacramental presence of Christ in our midst (Cervantes Gabarrón, 2003:273-275; cf. Carroll, 2008:122-123). This sacramental presence of Christ becomes, for the first generations of Christian communities, the corner stone of hospitality, *philoxenia*, towards those needy people who do not have a place to rest, a virtue insisted upon by the Apostle Paul (Rom. 12:13; Phan, 2008). When, in this powerful and imperial nation, the United States of America, its citizens welcome and embrace the immigrant, who reside and work here with or without some documents required by the powers that be, they are blessed, for they are welcoming and embracing Jesus Christ.

The discriminatory distinction between citizens and aliens is therefore broken down. The author of the Epistle to the Ephesians is thus able to proclaim to human communities religiously scorned and socially marginalized: "So then you are no longer strangers and aliens, but you are citizens" (Eph. 2:19). The author of that missive probably had in mind the peculiar vision of post-exilic Israel developed by the prophet Ezekiel. Ezekiel emphasizes two differences between the post-exilic and the old Israel: the eradication of social injustice and oppression ("And my princes shall no longer oppress my people" – Ezek. 45:8) and the elimination of the legal distinctions between citizens and aliens ("You shall allot it [the land] as an inheritance for yourselves and for the aliens who reside among you and have begotten children among you. They shall be to you as citizens of Israel; with you they shall be allotted an inheritance among the tribes of Israel. In whatever tribe aliens reside, there you shall assign them their inheritance, says the Lord God" – Ezek. 47:21-23).

There is a tendency among many public scholars and leaders to weave a discourse that deals with immigrants mainly or even exclusively as workers, whose labor might contribute or not to the economic welfare of the American citizens. This kind of public discourse tends to objectify and dehumanize the immigrants. Those immigrants are human beings, conceived and designed, according to the Christian tradition, in the image of God. They deserve to be fully recognized as such, both in the letter of the law and in the spirit of social praxis. Whatever the importance of the economical factors for the receiving nation (which usually, as in the case of the United States, happens to be an extremely rich country), from an ethical theological perspective the main concern should be the existential well-being of the "least of these," of the most vulnerable and marginalized members of God's humanity, among them those who sojourn far away from their homeland, constantly scrutinized by the demeaning gaze of many native citizens.

One of the main concerns energizing and spreading the distrust against resident foreigners is fear of their possible consequences on national identity, understood as an already historically fixed essence. We have seen that anxiety in Samuel P. Huntington's assessment of the Latin American immigration as "a major potential threat to the cultural integrity of the United States." It is an apprehension that has spread all over the Western world, disseminating hostile attitudes towards already marginalized and disenfranchised communities of sojourners and strangers. These as perceived as sources of "cultural contamination." What is therein forgotten is, first, that national identities are historical constructs diachronically constituted by exchanges with peoples bearing different cultural heritages and, second, that cultural alterity, the social exchange with the "other," can and should be a source of renewal and enrichment of our own distinct national self-awareness. History has shown the sad consequences of xenophobic ethnocentrism. There have been too intimate links between xenophobia and genocide (Maloof, 2000). As Zygmunt Bauman has so aptly written, "Great crimes often starts from great ideas… Among this class of ideas, pride of place belongs to the vision of purity" (Baumann, 1997:5).

We need to countervail the xenophobia that contaminates public discourse in the United States and other Western nations with an embracing, exclusion-rejecting, perspective of the stranger, the alien, the "other" (Volf, 1996), one which I have named *xenophilia*—a concept that comprises hospitality, love, and care for the stranger. In times of increasing economic and political globalization, when in a megalopolis like New York, many different cultures, languages, memories, and legacies converge (Schweiker, 2004), *xenophilia* should be our duty and vocation as a faith affirmation not only of our common humanity, but also of the ethical priority in the eyes of God of those vulnerable beings living in the shadows and margins of our societies.

The United States has a tendency to play the role of the Lone Ranger. Yet, migration and xenophobia are international problems, affecting most of the world community, and have thus to be understood and faced from a worldwide context. The deportation of Roma people (Gypsies) in France and other European nations is an unfortunate sign of the times. Roma communities are expelled from nations where they are objects of scorn, contempt and fear, to other nations where they have traditionally been mistreated, disdained, and marginalized. They are perennial national scapegoats, whose unfortunate fate has for too long been silenced (cf., SEC, 2010). It would also do good to compare the American situation with that prevailing in several European nations where in the difficult and sometimes tense coexistence of citizens and immigrants resonate the historically complex conflicts between the Cross and the Crescent, for many of the foreigners happen to be Muslims, venerators of Allah, and thus subject to insidious kinds of xenophobia and discrimination (cf. Sartori, 2000).

Migration is an international problem, a salient dimension of modern globalization. Globalization implies not only the transfer of financials resources, products, and trade, but also the worldwide relocation of peoples, a transnationalization of labor migration, of human beings who take the difficult and frequently painful decision to leave their kin and kith searching for a better future. Borders have become bridges, not only barriers. For, as Edward Said has written in the context of another very complex issue, "in time, who cannot suppose that the borders themselves will mean far less than the human contact taking place between people for whom differences animate more exchange rather than more hostility?" (Said, 1992:176).

The intensification of global inequalities has made the issue of human migration a crucial one (Ehrenreich, 2010:15-18). It is a situation that requires rigorous analysis from: 1) a worldwide ecumenical horizon; 2) a deep understanding of the tensions and misunderstandings arising from the proximity of peoples with different traditions and cultural memories; 3) an ethical perspective that privileges the plight and afflictions of the most vulnerable; and 4) for the Christian communities and churches, a solid theological matrix ecumenically conceived and designed.

The churches and Christian communities, therefore, need to address this issue from an international ecumenical and intercultural perspective (Fornet-Betancourt, 2004; Castillo Guerra, 2008:243-270). The main concern is not and should not be exclusively our national society, but the entire fractured global order, for as Soerens and Hwang have neatly written: "Ultimately, the church must be a place of reconciliation in a broken world" (Soerens, 2009:174). In an age where globalization prevails, there are social issues, migration one of them, whose transnational complexities call for an international ecumenical dialogue and debate. One goal of that discursive process is the disruption of the increasing tendency of developed and wealth countries to emphasize the protection of civil rights, understood exclusively as the rights of *citizens*, vis-à-vis the diminishment of the recognition of the human rights of resident non-citizens (Oliván, 1998).

Pope Benedict XVI rightly reminded the global community, in his 2009 social encyclical *Caritas in Veritate*, of the urgent necessity to develop that kind of international and ecumenical perspective of migration:

> [M]igration … is a striking phenomenon because of the sheer numbers of people involved, the social, economic, political, cultural and religious problems it raises . . . [We] are facing a social phenomenon of epoch-making proportions that requires bold, forward-looking policies of international cooperation … We are all witnesses of the burden of suffering, the dislocation and the aspirations that accompany the flow of migrants … [T]hese laborers cannot be considered as a commodity or a mere workforce. They must not, therefore, be treated like any other factor of production. Every migrant is a human person who, as such, possesses fundamental, inalienable rights that must be respected by everyone and in every circumstance" (2009:62).

Allow me to conclude, disrupting the English-only character of this essay, with some verses of the song *Extranjeros*, written by the Spanish songwriter Pedro Guerra, in the language of most undocumented immigrants of this nation, the United States.

> Por ser como el aire su patria es el viento
>
> Por ser de la arena su patria es el sol
>
> Por ser extranjero su patria es el mundo
>
> Por ser como todos su patria es tu amor
>
> Recuerda una vez que fuimos así
>
> los barcos y el mar, la fe y el adiós
>
> llegar a un lugar pidiendo vivir
>
> huir de un lugar salvando el dolor.

Bibliography

Anzaldúa, Gloria. *Borderlands/La Frontera: The New Mestiza*. Aunt Lute Book. 1999.

Ateek, Naim Stifan. *A Palestinian Christian Cry for Reconciliation*. Orbis. 2009.

Balderrama, Francisco, & Raymond Rodriguez. *Decade of Betrayal: Mexican Repatriation in the 1930s*. University of New Mexico. 2006.

Bales, Kevin. *Disposable People: New Slavery in the Global Economy*. University of Califonia. 2004.

Bauman, Zygmunt. *Wasted Lives: Modernity and Its Outcasts*. Polity. 2004.

Bowe, John. *Nobodies: Modern American Slave Labor and the Dark Side of the New Global Economy*. Random House. 2007.

Buchanan. Patrick. *State of Emergency: The Third World Invasion and Conquest of America*. Thomas Dunne/St. Martin's. 2008.

Carroll R., M. Daniel. *Christians at the Border: Immigration, the Church, and the Bible*. Baker. 2008.

Cervantes Gabarrón, José. "El immigrante en las tradiciones bíblicas." *Ciudadanía, multiculturalidad e immigración*. Jose A. Zamora, ed. Editorial Verbo Divino. 2003.

Ehrenreich, Ben. "A Lucrative War." *The New York Review of Books*. Vol. 32, No. 20. 21 October 2010.

Fanon, Franz. *Peau Noir, Masques Blancs*. Éditions du Seuil. 1952.

Fornet-Betancourt, Raúl, ed. *Migration and Interculturality: Theological and Philosophical Challenges*. Missionswissenschaftliches Institut Missio. 2004.

Fraser, Nancy, & Axel Honneth. *Redistribution or Recognition? A Political-Philosophical Exchange*. Verso. 2003.

Fredrickson, George. *Diverse Nations: Explorations in the History of Racial & Ethnic Pluralism*. Paradigm. 2006.

Harding, Jeremy. "The Deaths Map." *London Review of Books*. Vol. 33, No. 20. 20 October 2011.

Higham, John. *Strangers in the Land: Patterns of American Nativism, 1860-1925*. Atheneum. 1968.

Hoffman, Abraham. *Unwanted Mexican Americans in the Great Depression: Repatriation Pressures, 1929-1939*. University of Arizona. 1974.

Huntington, Samuel. "The Clash of Civilizations?" *Foreign Affairs*. Summer 1993. Vol. 72, Issue 3.

_____. *The Clash of Civilizations and the Remaking of World Order*. Simon & Schuster. 1996.

_____. "The Hispanic Challenge." *Foreign Policy*. March/April 2004.

_____. *Who Are We? The Challenges to America's National Identity*. Simon & Schuster. 2004.

Irvin, Dale. "The Church, the Urban and the Global: Mission in an Age of Global Cities." *International Bulletin of Missionary Research*. Vol. 33, No. 4. October 2009.

Jordan, Mark. *The Invention of Sodomy in Christian Theology.* University of Chicago. 1997.

Kidd, José E. Ramírez. *Alterity and Identity in Israel: The "ger" in the Old Testament.* De Gruyter. 1999.

Laclau, Ernesto, & Chantal Mouffe. *Hegemony and Socialist Strategy: Toward a Radical Democratic Politics.* Second ed. Verso. 2001.

Leonhardt, David. "Truth, Fiction and Lou Dobbs." *The New York Times.* 30 May 2007.

Maalouf, Amin. I*n the Name of Identity: Violence and the Need to Belong.* Arcade. 2000.

Míguez, Néstor, Joerg Rieger, & Jung Mo Sung. *Beyond the Spirit of Empire.* SCM. 2009.

Milanovic, Branko. *Global Inequality and the Global Inequality Extraction Ratio: The Story of the Past Two Centuries.* The World Bank, Development Research Group & Poverty and Inequality Group. September 2009.

Miller, Stuart Creighton. *The Unwelcome Immigrant: The American Image of the Chinese, 1775-1882.* University of California. 1969.

Oliván, Fernando. *El extranjero y su sombra. Crítica del nacionalismo desde el derecho de extranjería.* San Pablo. 1998.

Phan, Peter. "Migration in the Patristic Age." *A Promised Land, A Perilous Journey: Theological Perspectives on Migration.* Daniel G. Groody & Gioacchino Campese, eds. Notre Dame. 2008.

Portes, Alejandro, & Rubén Rumbaut. *Immigrant America: A Portrait.* Third ed. University of California. 2006.

Potok, Mark. "Rage in the Right." *Intelligence Report.* Southern Poverty Law Center. Spring 2010.

Pyong, Gap Min, ed. *Encyclopedia of Racism in the United States* (3 vols.). Greenwood. 2005.

Ratha, Dilip. "Dollars Without Borders: Can the Global Flow of Remittances Survive the Crisis?" *Foreign Affairs.* 16 October 2009.

Rodriguez, Richard. *Brown: The Last Discovery of America.* Viking. 2002.

Ruiz, Javier Blázquez. "Derechos humanos, inmigración, integración." *Ciudadanía, multiculturalidad e immigración.* José A. Zamora, ed. Editorial Verbo Divino. 2003.

Sacks, Jonathan. *The Dignity of Difference: How to Avoid the Clash of Civilizations.* Continuum. 2003.

Said, Edward. *The Questions of Palestine.* Vintage. 1992.

Sartori, Giovanni. *Pluralism, multiculturalismo e estranei: saggio sulla società multietnica.* Ruzzoli. 2000.

Schweiker, William. *Theological Ethics and Global Dynamics In the Time of Many Worlds.* Blackwell. 2004.

Secretariat-General European Commission (SEC). *Roma in Europe: The Implementation of European Union Instruments and Policies for Roma Inclusion.* Progress Report 2008-2010. 7 April 2010.

Soerens, Matthew, & Jenny Hwang. *Welcoming the Stranger: Justice, Compassion & Truth in the Immigration Debate.* InterVarsity. 2009.

Stalker, Peter. *Workers Without Frontiers: The Impact of Globalization on International Migration.* International Labor Organization. 2000.

Steicke, Elisabeth Cook. *La mujer como extranjera en Israel: Estudio exegético de Esdras 9-10.* Editorial SEBILA. 2011.

Tocqueville, Alexis de. *Democracy in America.* Oxford. 1959.

Trible, Phyllis. *Texts of Terror: Literary-Feminist Readings of Biblical Narratives.* Fortress. 1984.

Volf, Miroslav. *Exclusion and Embrace: A Theological Exploration of Identity, Otherness, and Reconciliation.* Abingdon. 1996.

Walcott, Derek. "The Schooner Flight." *Collected Poems, 1948-1984.* Farrar, Straus and Giroux. 1986.

West, Cornel. *Democracy Matters: Winning the Fight Against Imperialism.* Penguin. 2004.

21 | HUMAN RIGHTS CHALLENGES IN CONTEMPORARY NIGERIA AND NIGERIA 2012: PROBLEMS POSED IN SANTIAGO

B. Uche Enyioha

Introduction: A Profile of Nigeria

Nigeria, with a land mass of 356,669 square miles, has a population of over 160 million people, making it the most populous country in Africa. Located by the west coast of Sub-Saharan Africa, Nigeria has gradually gained ascendancy as a regional power, not only because of her large population, but due also to her economic resources.

Nigeria currently runs a presidential system of democratic government organized in three tiers of federal, state and local governments. The Federal Government is constituted by three arms – an Executive Presidency, a Bicameral Legislature (the Senate and the House of Representatives), and the Judiciary. The current President, Dr. Goodluck Ebele Jonathan, assumed office last year following a general election.

Nigeria's economy has remained strong, with crude oil sales contributing about ninety percent of her annual income. Export of other items such as cocoa beans, palm oil, groundnut, rubber and cotton also contribute to the economy. The goal of the government now, which has become encapsulated in the economic development slogan of "vision 20, 2020," is for the nation to emerge as one of the first 20 developed economies of the world by the year, 2020. With all her resources and economic potentials, however, Nigeria remains one of the poorest countries in the world, with a per capita income of US$1,160.00. (*Time Almanac 2011*, 2010:383).

About 250 ethnic groups, with their various languages, make up the Federal Republic of Nigeria, with the Hausa, Igbo and Yoruba being the major ones. English remains the official language of the nation, a carry-over from the colonial era. Nigeria gained independence from Great Britain on 1 October 1960.

With adherents numbering about 45 percent of the population each, Christianity and Islam have a claim as the major religions of Nigeria. The remaining ten percent belong to various forms of African traditional religion. Although adherents of the two major religions can be found all over the nation, a predominance of Christians are in the south while Muslims predominate the northern half of the country. The Southwest appears divided between Christians and Moslems. Mistrust, antagonism, competition for political power, and frequent outbreaks of violence have remained the bane of Christian – Muslim relationship, particularly in the north of the country.

Nigeria and Human Rights: Traditional Culture

Nigerian peoples have a long history of human rights considerations. The traditional cultures usually place premium on equity and fairness. Emphasis is also laid on responsibility for the care of family and neighbours. This explains the important role the extended family system plays in the African culture. Among the Igbo, for instance, instruments of justice and equity such as *Omenala* (custom) and *Ofo-na-ogu* (staff of justice and sense of equity) are given a very high regard in social interaction and contracts. Violation of the norms and ethics of human relations (which usually included the case of the less privileged) and the terms of social contracts draws the ire and condemnation of the entire society, many times with severe penalties. The consequence of any form of Nmeru-ala (desecration of the land) serves as a deterrent to those who might be tempted to act against the norms and expectations of the society. This kind of common understanding promoted and enhanced communal equilibrium and harmony. Any breakdown of this social order was known for what it is and handled accordingly. This kind of social ordering, which generally takes care of human rights concerns can be found in different forms in many African sub-cultures.

The Role of Christianity

The coming of Christianity to the area known today as Nigeria (Nigeria was constituted as a nation in 1914; there was Christian work in the area much earlier) brought a new dimension to the people's understanding of human relations. With the Old Testament emphasis on the need for justice and equity, the care of the poor, widows, and orphans no one is left in doubt as to what God expects of all who acknowledge and worship Him (Lev. 19:10; Isa. 11:4; Deut. 14:29; Isa. 1:17; Amos 5:24). This, of course, is complemented by the premium the New Testament places on grace, love, forgiveness, mercy, and care of the indigent (Mt. 25:31-36; Eph. 4:32; I Cor.13). The Christian message of good news of salvation in Jesus Christ and freedom for every child of God added a major impetus to the modern understanding of human rights. For many in Nigeria, therefore, the thinking and practice of human rights is rooted in the Christian message.

Endorsement of Human Rights Declarations

In addition to the norms of the traditional culture and the teachings of the Christian faith that have prepared her people for modern human rights considerations, Nigeria has also formally endorsed a number of human rights declarations or documents. She is a signatory to the United Nation's "Universal Declaration of the Rights of Man" (10 Dec. 1948), the "Declaration on the Elimination of all Forms of Intolerance and Discrimination Based on Religion or Conviction" (25 Nov. 1981), and the Organization of African Unity's "African charter on Human and People's Rights" (27 June 1981). Nigeria has also endorsed the U.N.'s "Convention on the Elimination of All Forms of Discrimination Against Women" (18 Dec. 1979), and the "African Union Charter on the Rights and Welfare of the Child" (African Union – all 2003). In addition to all of these and many others not mentioned here the current constitution of the Federal Republic of Nigeria (1999) makes extensive provision on human rights concerns (e.g., chapter IV, section 33-44). Given this scenario, a firm basis exists for an assessment of the human rights situation in Nigeria (Constitution of the Federal Republic of Nigeria, 1999; Alemika, 2004; National Human Rights Commission, 2007).

Human Rights Challenges

In spite of all of the above, however, human rights abuses have remained the bane of the Nigerian nation. Abuses of people's rights have continued despite the efforts of the governments and society at large to stem the tide.

Testimonies of human rights abuses abound from the daily experiences of citizens. The mass media – electronic and printed – are also awash with reports of human rights abuses in the country, almost on a daily basis. Whether it has to do with the assassination of individuals by hired assassins, armed robbery attack on defenseless people, or terrorist bombing of places of worship and public buildings, the story is the same. Human lives are wasted and people's rights are denied them.

Incidents of rape, discrimination on the basis of gender, ethnicity, and religion also abound.

Unfortunately, although the law enforcement apparatus of the nation (especially the police) have been making efforts, they appear to be overwhelmed. In many instances there have been allegations of long detention without trial, extortion of money, and extra-judicial killings on the part of the law enforcement officers. The situation gets so bad sometimes that one hardly knows where to begin to tell the story.

Summaries of the human rights situation in Nigeria can be presented by way of the formal reports of some of those who monitor and assess the setting.

The Human Rights Watch World Report, published 2 January 2012, has the following on Nigeria: "Endemic corruption, poverty, poor governance, and unchecked police abuses have created an environment where militant groups thrive and find ready recruits in the vast cadre of Nigeria's unemployed youth . . ."

A series of bombings and targeted killings by the Boko Haram militant Islamist group in Northern Nigeria has at this writing left more than 425 people dead in 2011.

According to The Source magazine (The Source, 2012:18), the Nigerian Police have been accused of carrying out unauthorized executions of members of the public, sometimes for bribery, sometimes the result of political rivalries. Incidences of extra-judicial killings have assumed a near daily occurrence with the perpetrators often left unpunished after some charade investigations.

Insecurity and violent death have, however, not excluded the security operatives themselves. A *Newswatch* magazine report provides an insight into this in its report on Kano, the largest city in northern Nigeria.

> Residents of the once peaceful town still live in fear. The fear was heightened again following the recent killing of about 20 security operatives, mostly policemen, in some parts of the metropolis barely one month after the January 20 massacre; and only a few days ago, gunmen on a motorcycle, shot dead a soldier outside the home of senior military officer he was guarding at Hotoro district. The killing of the soldier came after three police officers attached to the Kano residence of Mohammed Abubakar, inspector general of police, were murdered by the sect; two others were killed at a check point in the city same day (*Newswatch*, 2012:25).

The *Newswatch* report goes on to quote a 67-year-old Imam, Sanusi Danladi, as lamenting that "the insecurity arising from the activities of the Boko Haram sect has increased tension among Muslims and Christians in the State."

Incidences of killings, kidnapping, assault, persecution on ethnic and religious grounds, and other forms of human rights abuses abound in contemporary Nigeria. Just this past Sunday, 17 June 2012, suicide bombers attacked three churches engaged in their morning worship services. Although casualty figures have varied, conservative reports are that over 20 people died.

The state of insecurity in the country currently makes Nigeria look like a nation under siege: from kidnappings in the South to killings of Christians and burning of church buildings in the North. Apprehension and fear pervade the land.

Areas of Human Rights Violation in Nigeria: Focus on Particular Groups

Children

- Almajiri problems;
- Child labour;
- Street trading and hawking;
- Children out of school;
- Ritual killing of children;
- Children accused of being witches, wizards, or being possessed of demons.

Women

- Female circumcision (Female Genital Mutilation);
- Wild widowhood practices;
- Inheritance problems;
- Rape;
- Women trafficking.

Churches

- Killing of believers (shooting, machete attacks, fire bombing, suicide bombing, etc.);

- Burning of church buildings and other property;
- Intimidation of believers;
- Denial of property ownership rights (e.g., not being granted right to purchase land for building places of worship);
- Prohibition of open preaching in some areas of the country.

General

- High unemployment rate;
- Armed robbery;
- Assassination;
- Arson – to cover up fraud and corruption;
- Kidnapping – for ransom;
- Suicide bombing;
- Corruption;
- Devastation of land of communities where crude oil is explored (e.g., through oil spillage, gas flaring, etc., especially in the Niger Delta).

Specific Examples of Human Rights Abuses

Corruption

1. A federal legislator, Farouk Lawan, who served as chairman of the House of Representatives Committee, investigated for fraud in the oil subsidy regime, ended up being accused of receiving a $620,000.00 bribe (part of an alleged three million USD deal) in order to exonerate one of the oil merchants. The case is currently under police investigation, and the legislator has been suspended by his colleagues (*The Source*, 2/7/2012:5, 36-37).

2. Seven Non-Governmental Organizations (NGOs) in Nigeria were recently said to be indicted by the Global Fund (GF), an agency of the United Nations, "for alleged mismanagement of money which they received as grant in aid of the global fight against HIV/AIDS, tuberculosis and malaria in Nigeria." The GF is demanding "a refund of about $7.3 million from them" (*Newswatch*, 26/3/2012:12-13).

Kidnapping

1. Last May (2012) a retired school teacher, Mr. Eugene Orlu-Orlu of Ubima in Rivers State, was kidnapped from his residence. Although he eventually died in the custody of the kidnappers, they still insisted that the family should pay them the sum of two million naira [Nigerian monetary unit] for them to release his corpse. The State Security Service was eventually able to apprehend one of the culprits who then showed the family the lifeless body of the retired teacher (*The Source*, 2/7/2012:35).

2. On Sunday 11 March 2012, four Baptist pastors (Revs. J.C. Amadi, S.A. Ajoku, S.A. Iwuchukwu, and A.G. Emukah), who are lecturers at the Baptist College of Theology, Obinze, Imo State, were kidnapped while on their way to preaching engagements in churches in Rivers State. They had boarded a taxi together at Elele going to Omoku that morning. The kidnappers held them for four days during which time they subjected the pastors to all forms of indignity and brutality, including beatings. They were released after much pleading and negotiation. This incident was not reported to the media and thus was not widely publicized.

Killings

1. *The Source* magazine reported that three people were killed when armed robbers attacked their bus traveling on the East-West road. The dead included the driver of the vehicle. According to the report, the victims "were attacked 10 minutes before arriving at their destination" (*The Source*, 2/7/2012:14).

2. On 10 March 2012, people of Ajilari, a suburb of Maiduguri in Jere Local Government area, awoke to a gory sight. *Newswatch* magazine reported the dastardly act as follows:

> Suspected Boko Haram members attacked the residence of one Mallam Tijani, an electrician, burning him and his pregnant wife alive. A neighbor of the deceased told reporters in the State that when the assailants arrived the area, they had combed a nearby house before finding their way into Tijanis house. As at press time, last week, neither the state police command nor the joint task force, was able to explain why Tijani and his wife were subjected to such brutal death (*Newswatch*, 26/3/2012:19-20).

Persecution–attacks on places of worship

1. On Sunday, 17 June 2012, two churches in Zaria (Christ the King Catholic Church and Evangelical Church of West Africa, ECWA) and one in Kaduna city (Sharon Pentecostal International Church), all in Kaduna State, were attacked by suicide bombers when they were at worship. Casualty figures have varied, but generally said to be over 25 dead. Many of the worshippers were celebrating Fathers Day Services (*The Source*, 2/7/2012:38-39).

2. The 18 June 2012 issue of *Newswatch* magazine reported that:

> On Sunday, 3 June, members of the Living Faith Church, otherwise known as Winners Chapel, who had just concluded the days first services were about to leave for their various homes when suddenly, a loud explosion rent the air. It turned out to be a bomb attack. Eyewitness accounts said a car owner, on a suicide mission, had accelerated towards the Winners Chapel despite attempts to halt it by the security operatives stationed within the area. Even though the driver failed to hit his intended target as the speeding car finally rammed into the iron barricade leading to the church, he did achieve his aim. The resulting loud explosion left many people dead. Apart from the human casualty which included injuries to scores of people and cars that got engulfed by the inferno, part of the Harvestfield Church of Christ, which is located close to the Winners Chapel, caved in. Boko Haram, the Islamic fundamentalist [sic], claimed responsibility for the attack. The report indicated also that the bombing "claimed the lives of at least 17 Christian worshipers in Yelwa, Bauchi State" (*Newswatch*, 18/6/2012:23-24).

Rape

1. It was reported that a commercial bus was flagged down by robbers who then "drove the bus to a nearby bush where they molested their victims. It was alleged that all the female passengers in the bus, except a medical student of the University of Port Harcourt, UNIPORT, were raped" (*The Source*, 2/7/2012:14).

2. According to *The Source* magazine, "cases of reported rape are becoming rampant and frightening of recent. Early last month (April 2012), a 65 year old man was remanded in prison in Ilorin for raping two fellow church members" (*The Source*, 14/5/2012:15).

Steps Toward Resolution

In spite of the challenges and uncertain nature of the situation, however, all hope is not lost. The government, religious groups, and non-governmental organizations are all making efforts towards resolution of the human rights challenges of the nation.

Many citizens, of course, are concerned and are crying out for amelioration of the situation. Christians have intensified their prayers for the peace and security of the nation. Many denominations and faith groups have organized periods of fasting and prayer vigils. Everyone is showing concern.

The federal government's security agencies have also been active in trying to stem the tide of insecurity and human rights abuses in the country. A state of emergency has been declared over some of the areas that have been prone to violence. In other cases periods of curfew have been imposed to reestablish stability and control of the situation. The government has also deployed security agencies in many of the troubled areas. With every indication, however, it appears that the battle for human rights, and for a stable and peaceful society in Nigeria, will be a long drawn out one. The hope is that with the concerns being expressed by everyone, the efforts of the government, and the commitment of Christians to prayer and peace, the battle will be won. As it is often said in Nigeria, all hands must be on deck for this to be achieved.

Fundamental human rights

- Right to life;
- Right to liberty (freedom);
- Right to freedom of speech;
- Right to freedom of religion or worship;
- Right to shelter;
- Right to food;
- Right to freedom of conscience;
- Right to freedom from want;
- Right to freedom from fear;
- Right to freedom of association;
- Right to work – in a safe and secure environment;

- Right to own property;
- Right to the pursuit of happiness;
- Right of citizenship;
- Right from arbitrary arrest and confinement.

Civil rights

- Right to education;
- Right to participation in the governance of a persons nation;
- Right to vote and be voted for;
- Right of citizenship;
- Freedom from arbitrary arrest and confinement;
- Right to healthcare.

Major types of rights

- Natural rights;
- Human rights;
- Civil rights;
- Religious rights;
- Legal rights;
- Economic rights;
- National rights;
- Social rights.

Laws that govern humankind

- Natural laws;
- Divine laws (Eternal, Religious);
- Customary laws;
- National / Civic laws;
- Economic laws;
- Metaphysical laws;

- International laws;
- Constitutional laws.

Declarations and Writings In Pursuit of Human Rights, Freedom, and Well-being

- African cultural traditions of human rights (Oral) (e.g., *Omenala, Nmeru-ala, Ofo na Ogu, Oha na Eze*, etc.);
- The Old Testament;
- The New Testament;
- The English Magna Carta (1215);
- English "Petition of Rights" (1628);
- English "Bill of Rights" (1989);
- The French "Declaration of the Rights of Man and of the Citizen" (26 August 1789) – passed by the French National Assembly;
- The American Declaration of Independence – 4 July 1776;
- American Bill of Rights – 15 Dec. 1791 (Amendments to the Constitution of the USA in favour of Human Rights and Freedom);
- American Emancipation Proclamation – 1 January 1863 (Proclamation by President Abraham Lincoln to free the slaves);
- Universal Declaration of the Rights of Man – 10 December 1948 (made by the United Nations Organization);
- Declaration on the Elimination of all forms of Intolerance and Discrimination based on Religion or Conviction – 25 November 1981. (Adopted by the 26th General Assembly of the UNO);
- The Canadian Charter on Rights and Freedoms – 17 April 1982;
- "African Charter on Human and People's Rights" (adopted 27 June 1981; also known as the "Banjul Charter" – Articles 2, 4-6, 9, 11-12, 15-16, 26, 28, 70;
- "Convention on the Elimination of All Forms of Discrimination Against Women" (CEDAW; adopted 18 Dec. 1979), Article 2;
- The Constitution of the Federal Republic of Nigeria (1999) – (sections 15-17, 33-36, 39, 40-42, 46);
- International Covenant on Civil and Political Rights – (articles 6 (1), 9, 19, 20, 21);

- Convention Against Torture and other Cruel Inhuman or Degrading Treatment or Punishment – (Article 2);
- United Nations Standard Minimum Rules for the Treatment of Prisoners (Article 8, 10);
- United Nations Rules for the Protection of Juveniles Deprived of their Liberty (Articles 1 & 2);
- International Convention on the Rights of the Child – Article 3;
- African Union Charter on the Rights and Welfare of the Child (AUCRWC);
- Child's Rights Act, 2003 (Nigeria) – Section I;
- International Covenant on Economic, Social and Cultural Rights – Articles 7, 11.

Bibliography

Alemika, E.E.O., et al. *Rights of the Child in Nigeria.* Geneva. 2004.

"Countries of the World." Time Almanac 2011. *Encyclopedia Britannica.* 2010, 383.

"Multimillion – Dollar Mess in NGOs." *Newswatch.* 26 March 2012. 12-13

Newswatch. 26 March 2012. 25.

"Quit, Lawan Quit." *The Source.* 2 July 2012. 5, 36-37.

"Rape: Women's Nemesis." *The Source.* 14 May 2012. 15.

"Red Card." *The Source.* 2 July 2012. 35.

State of Human Rights in Nigeria, 2005-2006. National Human Rights Commission, UNDP, and NORAD. 2007.

The Source. 12 March 2012. 18.

"Undeterred by Emergency Rule." *Newswatch.* 26 March 2012. 19-20.

"Unholy Attack." *The Source.* 2 July 2012. 38-39.

"Yet, Another Boko Haram Massacre." *Newswatch.* 18 June 2012. 23-24.

22 | Martin Luther King Jr.'s Legacy for United States-Based Peacemakers

Paul C. Hayes

When Martin Luther King, Jr. delivered his monumental address, "Beyond Vietnam: A Time to Break Silence," at The Riverside Church on 4 April 1967—a year to the day before his assassination—it was widely perceived to be his first public venture into the national debate over the Vietnam War. Though he was lauded by those within the anti-war movement for his articulate and timely commentary, King was excoriated by the mainstream press and much of the public, including some of his closest allies in the Johnson administration.

The *Washington Post* editorialized: "Many who listened to him with respect will never again accord him the same confidence. ... He has diminished his usefulness to his cause, to his country, and to his people" (Branch, 2006:597).

The *New York Times*, normally friendly to King and a noted critic of the war, commented that King's address was "a fusing of two public problems that are distinct and separate... [forecasting that his effort] "could very well be disastrous for both causes" (Branch, 2006:597).

The two causes, of course, were civil rights for racial minorities (mainly African- Americans) and the anti-war movement. For most, they were separate issues; for King, they were inextricably linked—outgrowths, one from the other.

King was the acknowledged leader of the Civil Rights movement in America, having successfully led the campaign for the Civil Rights Act of 1964 and the Voting Rights Act of 1965—both of which were landmark legislation that helped to reverse almost two centuries of racial discrimination in the U.S. Though he was the most prominent African-American figure in the mainstream of the Civil Rights movement, he was surrounded, supported, and sometimes challenged by a large cast of characters, including the more militant Black Power movement (e.g., Stokely Carmichael; Tommie Smith and John Carlos at the Mexico City Olympic Games in 1968; cf. Malcolm X) and the Black Panthers (e.g., Bobby Seale, Huey Newton, Eldridge Cleaver, et al.)—both of which frequently used hostile rhetoric and violent measures to address systemic injustice. As evidenced by the media attention and political response, Dr. King was the preferred spokesperson for African-Americans within the circles of governmental power and, with his colleagues, was invited to Washington to bear witness to the moment when each of the civil rights laws was passed.

However, the immediate and enduring reaction to King's speech at Riverside changed all of this. In sharply eloquent fashion, King attacked the heart of the American myth in Vietnam—that the United States was a liberating force, that the real enemy was communism, and that the American government was forthcoming and truthful regarding its execution of the war.

> I should make it clear that while I have tried…to give a voice to the voiceless on Vietnam and to understand the arguments of those who are called enemy, I am as deeply concerned about our troops there as anything else. … Before long they must know that their government has sent them into a struggle among Vietnamese, and the more sophisticated surely realize that we are on the side of the wealthy and the secure while we create a hell for the poor.

> Somehow this madness must cease. We must stop now. I speak as a child of God and brother to the suffering poor of Vietnam. I speak for those whose land is being laid waste, whose homes are being destroyed, whose culture is being subverted. I speak for the poor of America who are paying the double price of smashed hopes at home and death and corruption in Vietnam. I speak as a citizen of the world, for the world as it stands aghast at the path we have taken. I speak as an American to the leaders of my own nation. The great initiative in this war is ours. The initiative to stop it must be ours.

Then, in quoting one of the Buddhist leaders of Vietnam, King went on:

> Each day the war goes on the hatred increases in the heart of the Vietnamese and in the hearts of those of humanitarian instinct.

The Americans are forcing even their friends into becoming their enemies. It is curious that the Americans, who calculate so carefully on the possibilities of military victory, do not realize that in the process they are incurring deep psychological and political defeat. The image of America will never again be the image of revolution, freedom and democracy, but the image of violence and militarism (Washington, 1986:238).

Had he been alive, King would have made the same blistering commentary about Iraq or Afghanistan—the "Vietnams" of the past decade. Though King had spoken out against the war many times prior to the Riverside address, he had not expressed his opposition so directly and forcefully as that evening. From that point on, for the last year of his life, he became, in effect, an enemy of the state.

I share this background with you because I believe it illustrates why Martin Luther King Jr. both influences and challenges the thinking and actions of the current peace movement in the U.S., directly or indirectly, and particularly those within faith-based communities. On the surface, a half-century later, it appears King's influence is widespread, spanning from the halls of Congress to the playgrounds of our schools. Obvious to all is King's legacy as an American icon, even if an appreciation of what that means varies greatly among age groups, social classes, and political parties. The fact that there is a federal holiday in his honor and a monument on the National Mall in Washington is no small matter. Across the country there are public and private buildings, schools, agencies, streets, and parks honoring his name. His legacy graces the pantheon of American heroes even among those who would have opposed his values and politics. As it's been said, "a conservative is one who worships a dead radical." That is certainly true in the folk hero status of King. He is appreciated more today by the institutions and conventions of U.S. society than during his lifetime.

However, those who actually embrace his vision and goals number far less than his hero status might suggest, even among the African-American population. Though endless programs honor King's legacy, the impact of his mission for peace is muted by the economic and political realities of our time. With the collapse of the Soviet Union twenty years ago, U.S. imperialism has grown virtually unabated, with the American military taking on a global "policing" role compared to the more limited "freedom-fighting," anti-communist incentives fifty years ago. Likewise, the U.S. economy has improved the lot for many minorities (including many who benefited from the Civil Rights legacy), but the gap between the rich and the poor in this country has only widened.

Since 11 September 2001, the war on terrorism has become the current crusade against foreign "evil." Though Gandhian nonviolence practiced by King is admired as a personal ideal for many Americans, there is little sense that it is a reasonable tactic to stop militants who use suicide bombs against civilians to advance their agenda. Even among progressive peacemakers, there has been remarkable tolerance toward actions taken by the U.S. military against al-Qaeda (ubiquitous surveillance, drone attacks, harsh interrogation tactics, extra-judicial imprisonment, etc.), including the mission to deliberately assassinate Osama bin Laden. King, a likely critic of those actions, would have found himself as much an enemy of the state as he was in the last year of his life.

The question is, then, where does King's influence actually remain, particularly as a proponent of nonviolence? The most likely places are among groups that make relatively little impact on public policy. Faith-based and secular groups and organizations, such as the Fellowship of Reconciliation, the National Campaign for Nonviolent Resistance, Voices for Creative Nonviolence, Mennonites, Quakers, Christian Peacemaker Teams, and the various peace fellowships with denominational ties (e.g., Baptist Peace Fellowship of North America, Episcopal Peace Fellowship, etc.) will carry the ethical mantle in promoting principles of nonviolent direct action, but their influence is marginal at best on society, and certainly on national policy. As a whole, nonviolence is not a widely-embraced approach for addressing the evils of our time, especially those which are violent in nature.

Where King's influence is fruitful, though, is in the grassroots and educational efforts to humanize the enemy. As the U.S. has become more ethnically, racially, and religiously diverse, conventional stereotypes of "enemies" no longer go unchallenged. King's influence may have indirectly contributed to this rising social consciousness and the diminishing of "tribal" identities, evidenced by the common integration of schools and workplaces, the number of cross-cultural educational programs for students, and even the concerted efforts to better understand other religions (e.g., Islam) in the aftermath of 9/11. This is by no means universal across society (e.g., police profiling, right-wing rhetoric, the increase in militant hate groups, etc.), but a more sophisticated appreciation of religious, cultural, and social differences exists today in general society than in the past. The circles of power in the U.S. are no longer defined by white, Anglo-Saxon, Protestant males. King's humanizing approach toward relating to one's enemy has influenced a generation that no longer accepts the conventional racial and tribal biases that marked much of American history.

Another area where King's influence is evident is in progressive faith-based worldviews, mainly Christian, though not exclusively so. King has become a patron saint of progressive preachers, teachers, and causes, especially among religious communities. His vision of the "beloved community" is widely embraced as an ecclesial and social ideal for which to strive and his critique of the "-isms" that dominate the world (e.g., imperialism, militarism, materialism, racism, colonialism, etc.) is standard fare in most progressive faith-based social analyses. Though there are others who identified the root causes of conflict in the world, King's articulation of them and the heroic example he provided allow him to be easily referenced.

King often quoted Mohandas Gandhi in recognizing that peace is not just the absence of war, but the presence of justice. However, Gandhi's nonviolence was read through the realism of Reinhold Niebuhr, whose influence upon King was greater than Gandhi. The two in tension allowed King to interpret Jesus' call to love one's enemies. For King, the *telos* (or ultimate hope) was in seeking a peaceful security through right and just relationships with all people around the globe. This wasn't through an appeal to an idealistic morality, but through the transformation of society that would alter human structures and relations. That has become a unifying bridge between those who are focused on peacemaking and other elements of social justice.

In many respects, King validated the role of prophet in society better than virtually anyone else in modern times. He embodied what Walter Brueggemann called "the prophetic imagination" (*The Prophetic Imagination,* 1978, 2001) that rises up to challenge the "royal consciousness" of the imperial paradigm. This continues to justify a role for religious leaders today whose words and actions critique the prevailing views of government or culture, while offering a more inclusive, holistic, and affirming image of human relations in global community.

In a Christmas sermon delivered at Ebenezer Baptist Church, King recognized global interdependence that is substantiated even more in the 21st century world:

> It really boils down to this: that all life is interrelated. We are all caught in an inescapable network of mutuality, tied into a single garment of destiny. Whatever affects one directly, affects all indirectly. ... Did you ever stop to think that you can't leave for your job in the morning without being dependent on most of the world? [listing several examples of everyday products that were made in other countries]. ...We aren't going to have peace

on earth until we recognize this basic fact of the interrelated structure of all reality (Washington, 1986:254).

King's comprehensive understanding of what created human conflict through various forms and causes of injustice is instructive to peacemakers today as we discern the obstacles and challenges in resolving international conflicts and civil wars.

> I am convinced that if we are to get on the right side of the world revolution, we as a nation must undergo a radical revolution of values. We must rapidly begin the shift from a "thing-oriented" society to a "person-oriented" society. When machines and computers, profit motives and property rights are considered more important than people, the giant triplets of racism, materialism, and militarism are incapable of being conquered (Washington, 1986:240).

Fifty years later King's analysis is still pertinent, perhaps even more than when he lived. Thus, the challenge we face today is how to summon his courage and make his dream a reality.

Bibliography

Branch, Taylor. *At Canaan's Edge*. Simon & Schuster. 2006.

Washington, James, ed. *A Testament of Hope: The Essential Writings of Martin Luther King, Jr.* Harper & Row. 1986.

23 | Living with the Horror: Psychological Trauma in Victims of Domestic Violence

Liliana Da Valle

Introduction

In this paper I have addressed the psychological trauma experienced by victims of domestic violence (DV), especially women and children. In the beginning, I have presented the background of the problem, introducing statistics and facts. The problem was stated in relation to the life-long effects of DV in the emotional lives of women and children who were subject to it. After offering a conceptual framework for the problem, I have included a review of professional and academic literature on the issue. I have related my personal story as a testimony of the struggle to survive emotionally; and I have recommended possible pastoral responses to the problem. After suggesting opportunities for further study, I have offered concluding thoughts.

Background of the Problem

Suffering violence at the hands of close relatives or live-in partners is one of the greatest horrors a person can experience. In domestic violence, victims are hurt by a loved one, usually one whose life-long commitment is to seek their well-being and protection, such as a parent or a spouse. Issues of power and control are present in most cases, making that the number one reason for abusing, exploiting, humiliating, and destroying the lives of those more vulnerable. There are four kinds of domestic abuse: physical, emotional, sexual, and damage to property. All of them are forms of diminishing the personhood of the victim.

Many writings about DV refer to the *cycle of violence*. This is a representation of the reality that violence exists in families for generations; it is endlessly transmitted from parents to children. Typically, girls who grow up in abusive homes tend to become victims, and boys tend to become perpetrators. Both women and children are prone to believe what they have been told over and over. If they live with insults, humiliation, and pain, they assume that is their lot; if they are told once and again that they are *stupid,* they believe it and begin to act that way.

One of the recurrent questions in this topic is, why do women stay in abusive relationships? The answer is very complex and is part of the issues addressed in this work; women stay because they develop a *victim mentality*, and they do not think they can survive without the man who is controlling them. Another common question is, are not men also abused by women? The answer is yes, but the degree of incidence is so small compared with women abused by men, that the problem cannot be treated as pandemic.

Problem Statement

In order to establish the seriousness of the problem at hand, we can observe some global statistics (Facts About Violence, 2012):

> *Fact #1:* Globally, at least one in three women and girls is beaten or sexually abused in her lifetime (UN, 2000);

> *Fact #2:* A recent survey by the Kenyan Women Rights Awareness Program revealed that 70% of those interviewed said they knew neighbors who beat their wives. Nearly 60% said women were to blame for the beatings. Just 51% said the men should be punished (*NYT*, 1997);

> *Fact #3:* A 2005 World Health Organization study reported that nearly one-third of Ethiopian women had been physically forced by a partner to have sex against their will within the 12 months prior to the study (WHO, 2005);

> *Fact #4:* The most common act of violence against women is being slapped—an experience reported by 9% of women in Japan and 52% in provincial Peru. Rates of sexual abuse also varies greatly around the world—with partner rape being reported by 6% of women from Serbia and Montenegro, 46% of women from

provincial Bangladesh, and 59% of women in Ethiopia (WHO, 2005);

Fact #5: So-called "honor killings" take the lives of thousands of young women every year, mainly in North Africa, Western Asia and parts of South Asia (UNFPA);

Fact #6: The Human Rights Commission of Pakistan reported that 2002 saw a 25% increase in "honor killings" of women, with 461 women murdered by family members in 2002, in two provinces (Sindh and Punjab) alone (Pakistan HRC, 2002);

Fact #7: In eastern and southern Africa, 17 to 22% of girls aged 15 to 19 are HIV-positive, compared to 3 to 7% of boys of similar age. This pattern—seen in many other regions of the world—is evidence that a much older cohort of men is infecting girls with HIV (UNICEF/UNAIDS, 2007);

Fact #8: A 2005 study reported that 7% of partnered Canadian women experienced violence at the hands of a spouse between 1999 and 2004. Of these battered women, nearly one-quarter (23%) reported being beaten, choked, or threatened with a knife or gun (Family Violence in Canada, 2005);

Fact #9: In Zimbabwe, domestic violence accounts for more than 60% of murder cases that go through the high court in Harare (ZWREN);

Fact #10: A study in Zaria, Nigeria found that 16% of hospital patients treated for sexually-transmitted infections were younger than five (UNFPA).

All these victims deal with trauma for the rest of their lives. A clear link exists between domestic violence and mental health problems for women. Depression, trauma symptoms, and suicide attempts are issues that seriously undermine the emotional well-being of women who have been subjected to violence and abuse from their partner or ex-partner (Humphreys, 2009:186). The problem to be addressed in this paper is the long-term emotional trauma experienced by victims of DV.

Conceptual Framework

The conceptual framework of this paper is Post Traumatic Stress theory. Studies using the 100 item Trauma Symptom Inventory (TSI) have revealed that a history of interpersonal trauma is associated with elevations on all TSI scales. Post hoc multiple regression analyses showed that TSI scales varied according to victim's age, gender, child abuse, and adult sexual assault (Briere, 1995). According to *attachment theory,* adults develop attachments to their romantic partners similar to those children develop with their caretakers. Research showed two categories of people in intimate relationships; a *secure* group where relationships are positive and trusting, and an *insecure* group with two types of individuals. In the insecure group, the *avoidants* were characterized by fear of intimacy, and the *anxious-ambivalent* people were obsessed with the desire for reciprocation and union. The insecure group reported more negative experiences in their romantic relationships. In synch with these types, we find three attachment patterns: closeness, dependency, and anxiety (Scott, 2010). Chemtob, et al., stated that "Trauma exposure and PTSD are associated with hyper-vigilance for threat stimuli (that have a negative valence)" (Chemtob, 2011:110). Research shows that the storing of traumatic memories is neurologically different than the storing of ordinary, non-traumatic ones. Traumatic memories remain stored in the right side of the brain and don't cross over to the left side where reason and logic can be accessed. Therefore, traumatic memories stay emotionally charged, unable to be articulated and verbally described (Flemke, 2009:125).

Review of Professional and Academic Literature

Abby Stein, PhD, of the John Jay College of Criminal Justice, NY conducted research about the development of self-states; not just as a product of interpersonal trauma, but in the broader context of cultural demands for women to dissociate feelings that have been labeled antithetical to accepted gender norms for heterosexual behavior. The most prevailing self-states are dissociation, depersonalization, derealization, dissociative amnesia, identity confusion, and identity alteration (Stein, 2012:34).

Dissociation is a disconnection between things usually associated with each other. The result is discontinuity in conscious awareness, memory, identity, or perception. The most clear example is thinking about a very upsetting event and having no feelings about it. This is also known as *emotional numbness,* and is one of the hallmarks of post traumatic stress disorder.

Depersonalization is the feeling of not being attached to one's body. This is usually known as an *out-of-body* experience. Some people go to the extreme of not recognizing themselves in the mirror. *Derealization* is the feeling that the world is not real. Some people experience the world as a far place, foggy, or as watching a movie. *Dissociative amnesia* is the inability to recall important personal information. This is beyond regular forgetfulness. In most cases, these amnesias are important events that are forgotten, such as abuse incidents. *Identity confusion* is a sense of confusion about who the person is; the person may become confused about what they like or dislike. *Identity alteration* is the feeling of being different from another part of oneself; a person may develop an alternate personality (ISSTD).

Dawn Johnson, from the Summa-Kent State Center for the Treatment and Study of Traumatic Stress, and Caron Zlotnick, from Brown University, wrote about other emotional consequences of DV. They stated that battered women suffer a higher rate of mental health difficulties than non-victims; among them, the authors mentioned substance use disorders, anxiety disorders, and depression. These conditions bore further consequences that are devastating for women, e.g., employment dysfunction push women to go back to the abuser. Abused women experience a cycle of resource loss that propels them into a downward spiral that causes further trauma. It is virtually impossible to break this cycle without therapy (Johnson, 2009:234-235).

Simon Lapierre, of the School of Social Work, McGill University, Montreal, QC, Canada, has focused his work on how DV affect the *mothering* capability of battered women. He stated that women are central in providing welfare for their children; in the case of children exposed to DV, women's mothering has focused on providing protection. This focus on children has relegated women to the periphery in terms of caring for themselves and the effects of DV in their own lives. On top of that, women in this predicament are perceived as "failing" mothers because their children still exhibit problems commonly attributed to deficiencies in women's mothering (Lepierre, 2008:456).

Personal Experience

From 1986 to 1990, I was a battered women's counselor. First, I worked in California answering phones in Spanish and English. I also opened safe houses, trained volunteers, opened two new offices across the region, worked with batterers, and offered trainings to local police departments on how to respond to DV calls. Second, I worked in Illinois at a shelter for battered women. I had the graveyard shift, from Midnight to 8 am. There I processed emergency intakes during the night, answered the phones, and conducted support groups, even at that late hour. Working with victims of DV was part of my own healing journey. When I first applied for the job in California, the lady that interviewed me asked, "You don't have a degree in counseling, you don't have any experience, and you have not been a battered woman; so, why do you think you can do this?" My response was, "I have known abuse, and I have enough compassion." She said, "you are hired." Working with battered women helped my healing process. There were mornings when I went back home sick to my stomach from listening to stories that so resembled my own.

I grew up in a very dysfunctional home where both my parents were abusive. My mother was verbally, emotionally, and physically abusive; my father abused me sexually for five years, between the ages of 13 and 18. Prior to that, he had been my refuge. My parents did not get along, and DV was in the air. In this case, my mother was the aggressive one; my father was passive-aggressive. He never raised his voice, but he was a gambler and a womanizer. They both were very sick: my mother was narcissistic and my father a sexual psychopath.

I have spent most of my childhood trying to survive. I used to think, "they may break my body, but if I'm strong, they cannot touch my mind." I have also spent most of my adult life trying to figure out why they were like that. I begun by thinking my mother hated me because I was unwanted (I have no evidence of this). Then, I thought I was a disappointment to her because I was fat and uncool. Later, I came to believe that she was mentally ill. My mother was extremely violent. She tried to kill me three times; in turn, I tried to commit suicide twice. She would insult me, beat me, enslave me, and neglect me. My grandparents lived very close to us, and they knew what was happening, but they were very afraid of her.

Regarding my father, the story is a little different. He was not outwardly violent. Although he raped me, he did not use force, but persuasion. I was so afraid of my mother that I would do anything to avoid her wrath; he used that to convince me that if she found out about us, she would kill me. I had nobody to go to. I felt so lonely that I cried every night in bed; I remember waking up in the morning with crusts in my eyes from the tears. This went on for years!

When I was in High School, I was a very good student (I had to, or my mother would've killed me) and became very popular. I used dissociation as a survival mechanism from an early age. I had a double life: in school, I was happy, funny, popular, and loud; at home, I was in a very dark tunnel with no way out, very quiet, and depressed. Nobody cared. My parents had taught me that "what happens at home, stays at home," and I would've not dared to betray them. I started going with boys very early, when I was 12. I would use them to be popular, but I didn't care about them. I would be with them for a week and dump them. I never wanted to have sex with boys because sex was the dirty thing I did at home. I did not know how to love.

When I was 16 years old, I went steady with this boy who was a Baptist Christian. That changed my life forever. Although in the beginning I asked him to promise me not to talk to me about his God, nor to invite me to church (and he did that for two years) when I needed to confide in someone, he was the only one I could trust. When I was 18 years old, and we were celebrating our second dating anniversary, I told him about my father. He knew about the abuse I was getting from my mother; he had even witnessed it. But for a teenage girl it is very difficult to disclose sexual abuse. When I told him, he hugged me, he cried with me, and he led me to Christ. I was 18, and he was 20. We've been married for 37 years!

For one reason or another, my case is not typical. I did not marry an abusive person, I did not get into drugs or alcohol, I did not sleep around. But in a sense, I went through the same psychological trauma as every other abused woman. Being a mother was particularly challenging because I did not have a good role model. I did not want to be like my mother, but the violent tendencies were there. Also the self-doubt and lack of self-esteem were present all the time. Even today, after years of therapy, prayer, and success, I look back, and I feel I was an unfit mother.

Soon after leaving home behind (did not go back until 18 years later, when my father was already dead), I had a defiant attitude. I said to myself, "nobody will ever shout at you or abuse you anymore; nobody has a right to tell you what to do," and I tried to live that way. That engendered relational problems with many people; my response was, "this is who they made me to be." During therapy, one day, my therapist sat me down and told me, "you are 18 now, you can decide who you want to be." I decided there that I wanted to be nurturing and loving, that I wanted to be a follower of Christ, and a person of integrity. My healing had begun. It took years to even come close to be that person, and it is a constant struggle even until today. Some of the psychological consequences of the abuse I received were low self-esteem, nightmares, dissociation, depression, insecurity, and anger.

The *double life* I have mentioned above, came to bear in my quest for integrity. When living at home, lying was a survival tool. Now, free and out in the world, being a new Christian, abandoning that habit was difficult. It was almost like quitting an addiction. One of my highest values now is to be a *single-face* person.

At one point in my life, I was under the illusion that I was completely healed. I was able to share my testimony without feeling any emotion (dissociation again); I was even able to go back home, face my mother and her unchanging wickedness, and be happy that I had changed so much. Now, I'm 56 years old, both my parents and grandparents are gone, and I have no relationship with my siblings. Yet, I know that my journey toward wholeness is not over; the ghosts are still there. Now I know that recovery lasts a lifetime.

To Leave or Not to Leave

While working with battered women, I witnessed the devastating psychological effects of DV. A woman in her 60s suffered a terrible case of dry skin. She went to the doctor, and he said it was caused by depression. After several counseling sessions, she realized she had been abused as a child, but had "bottled up" her experiences; menopause did the rest.

As a pastor, I have found many cases of women and children that were damaged by someone they loved. I know from personal experience that God can heal, but I also know we must be intentional about seeking healing. The number of women murdered by their intimate partners is astonishing. In Argentina, 82 women were killed by their husbands or partners in the first half of 2009 (Middleton-Dentzer, 2009); in Massachusetts, a woman is killed by her partner every 22 days, and 50% of the women who die violently, do so at the hands of their intimate partners (Cole, 1992:5). Yet, survival is possible; however, the issue at hand is not survival, but quality of life afterwards.

Many women manage to leave their abuser, although this is a daunting task. Women have a hard time leaving the abusive situation, not because they enjoy it, but because they are not empowered to do so. The same man who beats them up is the one there when they need an aspirin, so women tend to believe they love them, but cannot control their temper; this is an illness, i.e., *would you leave your spouse because he or she had a heart condition?*

In many cases, women live imprisoned, enslaved, and without any outside resources. One of the abusers' favorite techniques is to cut their women off from any outside support system; they alienate them from family, friends, job, school, and any other kind of support. By the same token, women end up without financial resources. Sometimes, abuse is so pervasive that women are not even allowed to go to the bathroom alone. They learn to depend on the abusers; they believe their lies about how inept and unable they are to survive without them.

Women come to shelters every day saying they cannot get a job because they are useless. They are scared to death, they cannot sleep, they have no resources; finally, they decide to go back. A woman may go back many times before *really* leaving. It is important that counselors and churches build a firm support system for them, with patient people who can take them back every time they leave. If supporters express anger because they go back to the abusive relationship, women may not even try to leave again, importing deadly consequences.

A good technique to help women take enough distance from their abusers is to convince them to leave for an extended period of time to give the abuser time to think and change. Four months seems to be an acceptable period of time; women are to tell the abuser they will not go back unless they pursuit counseling. After four months, many women are strong enough to make the final decision if necessary.

A Pastoral Response

When I worked as a counselor at a shelter for battered women, I was a seminary student. The women knew that, and many of them came to me for spiritual advice, especially when they were Christian. There, I learned of the awful responses offered by clergy to women in this situation. The most common was, *he is your husband and you should try to be a better wife*. This is a reinforcement of the submissive role of women at home and in society. If the gospel of Jesus Christ is not used as a message of freedom and power, it is like the salt that looses its saltiness.

Churches should be part of the solution. Clergy need to be trained in issues of DV so they can respond appropriately. Pastoral counseling and pulpit opportunities should be used to empower women, and to spread the message that no one has the right to mistreat another human being. Churches need to teach about marriage, anger management, and addiction to love. As a pastor, I do not want to promote divorce, but I need to tell my congregation that divorce is the only way out when the sanctity of marriage is being adulterated by violence (Renzetti, 2010:310).

Suggestions for Further Research

DV is a global problem; it crosses all barriers: cultural, social, economic, educational, and more. Statistics, though, may only show certain portions of the population in different countries because women with resources do not need to resort to places like shelters; they may have the money to run away on their own, or the family support necessary to leave without a trace. Studies have shown that alcohol and drugs worsen the problem of domestic abuse, but are not the cause of the problem. Other studies have focused on the type of clinical services offered to survivors of DV, and their capacity to adapt to the medical model. Much research has been done globally about the psychological effects of DV in women and children.

Further research should focus on the psychological characteristics of survivors. Why is it that some women are able to break the cycle, and others cannot? There must be something these women have in common. A study of women who leave their abusers and move on to healthier relationships could be conducted to find out what are the most helpful tools women should pursuit in this endeavor. Statistics show that women who have grown up in homes without DV are prone to reject abuse in their own lives; but what about those who have seen it all their lives and yet are able to say "enough." There must be strong emotional, spiritual, or rational forces that compel such ability to move away from abuse.

Another topic for further research could be, what psychological, emotional, and spiritual characteristics should new partners have to attract women who were formerly abused, so they will not seek to go back to abuse? Most women who grew up with abuse end up in abusive relationships; one after the other, these women find abusers as life partners. Some, though, are able to move on and establish relationships with healthy, nurturing men. Who are these men, and what do they bring to the relationship?

Finally, an excellent topic for further study would be how family systems theory can help victims of DV to break the cycle and reach freedom and healing. This theory states that human systems have a tendency to repeat themselves from generation to generation (Friedman, 1985). This psychological theory has revolutionized the therapeutic community by changing the focus of healing, from the victim to the whole system. Through understanding *self-differentiation*, women could be able to break away from abuse much sooner, and with long-lasting results.

Conclusion

This work was not intended to be a scientific paper; I am not a scientist. Although I have researched what Psychology scholars and practitioners say about the pervasive psychological effects of DV in victims, I do not claim any authority in this field. Rather, my area of expertise springs from experience, both personal and professional.

Domestic violence marks persons in ways we cannot even imagine. Even years after becoming free from it, people carry the scars of having been humiliated, put down, ignored, beaten up, threatened, and endangered. There is an existential grief that constantly accompanies individuals who have lost their dignity, self-esteem, and trust.

Battered women are robbed of their confidence, their sense of love, and their roots. Many stay with their husbands because of their children, wrongly thinking that having a father is better than not, and offering a childhood full of fear and trauma. The cycle of violence perpetuates from generation to generation until someone breaks it. The victim cannot help fix the abuser, but she can break the cycle by saying "no;" this requires empowerment and determination that can only be present when there is a solid support system. The church should be a part of that system.

Bibliography

Briere, John, Diana M. Elliott, Kathryn Harris, and Ann Cottman. "Trauma Symptom Inventory: Psychometrics and Association With Childhood and Adult Victimization in Clinical Samples." *Journal of Interpersonal Violence*. Vol. 10, No. 4. 1995.

Chemtob, Claude M., Sascvha Griffing, Erika Tullberg, Elizabeth Roberts, and Peggy Ellis. "Screening for Trauma Exposure, and Posttraumatic Stress Disorder and Depression Symptoms among Mothers Receiving Child Welfare Preventive Services." *Child Welfare*. Vol. 90, No. 6. 2011.

Cole, Ellen, Esther D. Rothblum, and Constance Bean. *Women Murdered by the Men they Loved*. Taylor & Francis, Inc. 1992.

"Dissociative Disorders." International Society for the Study of Trauma and Dissociation (ISSTD). http://www.isst-d.org/education/faq-dissociation.htm.

"Facts about Violence." http://www.feminist.com/antiviolence/facts.html.

Family Violence in Canada: A Statistical Profile, 2005. http://www.statcan.gc.ca/pub/85-224-x/4064472-eng.htm.

Flemke, Kimberly. "Triggering Rage: Unresolved Trauma in Women's Lives." *Contemporary Family Therapy*. Vol. 31. 2009.

Friedman, Edwin H. *Generation to Generation: Family Process in Church and Synagogue*. Guilford Press. 1985.

Humphreys, Catherine. "Responding to the Individual Trauma of Domestic Violence: Challenges for Mental Health Professionals." *Social Work in Mental Health*. Vol. 7, No. 1-3. 2009.

Johnson, Dawn M., and Caron Zlotnick. "HOPE for Battered Women With PTSD in Domestic Violence Shelters." *Professional Psychology: Research and Practice*. Vol. 40, No. 3. 2009.

Lepierre, Simon. "Mothering in the context of domestic violence: the pervasiveness of a deficit model of mothering." *Child and Family Social Work*. Vol. 13. 2008.

Middleton-Dentzer, Althea. "At Least 82 Women were Killed by Gender-based Violence in the FirstHalf of this Year in Argentina." *The Advocacy Project*. http://www.advocacynet.org. 8/3/09.

Pakistan Human Rights Commission, 2002. http://www.hrcp-web.org/pdf/Archives%20Reports/AR2002.pdf.

Renzetti, Claire M., Jeffrey L. Edleson, and Raquel Kennedy Bergen. *Sourcebook on Violence Against Women*. SAGE. 2010.

Scott, Shelby, and Julia C. Babcock. "Attachment as a Moderator Between Intimate Partner Violence and PTSD Symptoms." *Journal of Family Violence*. Vol. 25. 2010.

Stein, Abby. "Dissociated Affect, Social Discourse, and the Forfeiture of Agency in Battered Women." *Psychoanalytic Psychology*. Vol. 29, no. 1. 2012.

The New York Times. 10/31/97.

UNICEF/UNAIDS 2007. http://www.unaids.org/en/aboutunaids/unaidscosponsors.

United Nations Commission on the Status of Women, 2/28/2000. http://www.un.org/womenwatch/daw/csw/e200027.pdf.

United Nations Population Fund (UNFPA). http://www.unfpa.org/public/

World Health Organization. Multi-country Study on Women's Health and Domestic Violence Against Women, 2005.

Zimbabwe Women's Resource Centre and Network. http://www.zwrcn.org.zw/Family Violence Prevention Fund.

To
Proclaim
the Year of
the Lord's Favor

24 | RELIGIOUS LIBERTY AND PEACE

Kenneth L. Sehested

A teacher in an urban school with a religious diverse student population asked the kids to bring something to class related to each family's faith tradition. One by one, the students came before the class for a show-and-tell:

> The first child said, "I am Muslim and this is my prayer rug."
>
> The second child said, "I am Jewish and this is my Star of David."
>
> The third child said, "I am Catholic and this is my rosary."
>
> The final child said, "I am Baptist and this is my casserole dish."

[*The English word "casserole" might not be familiar to all of you; maybe you'll get the humor if I paraphrased this way: "The final child said, 'I am a Baptist, this is my dinner plate. When do we eat?'"*]

It's a funny story. But maybe more significant than it first appears, since every war is ultimately a war over bread. In my opinion, the fact that Baptists are known for eating together is a hopeful sign—and maybe instructive, in regards to the implications of our passion for religious liberty.

My assignment is to comment on the intersection between the historic Baptist championing of religious liberty—sometimes called "soul freedom" or "soul competency"—together with the kinds of concerns that occupy the Peace Commission of the BWA Freedom and Justice Division, of which I am a grateful member.

Two recent statements by Baptist leaders frame the context for these comments. Rev. Suzan Johnson Cook, the first Baptist, and the first female, to be appointed by the President of the United States as Ambassador at Large for Religious Freedom. Speaking to the March meeting of the Baptist World Alliance executive committee, Rev. Johnson Cook pointed to research indicating that a "third of the global population live where there are government restrictions on religion, or where there are acts of social hostility targeting religious groups." She went on to say that "religious freedom is pivotal to peaceful, prosperous and secure societies," and that "many conflicts in the world today are fueled by religious intolerance" (Callam, 2012).

The second statement is by our esteemed BWA general secretary, Neville Callam, in comments about this special 400th anniversary of Thomas Helwys' historic defense of religious liberty. Dr. Callam wrote:

> Contrary to what some authors have said, Helwys was not the first person to issue a call for freedom of conscience to be respected by all. Therefore, we need not make exaggerated claims in order to show our appreciation of Helwys' outstanding contribution in the cause of religious liberty. What we may need to do, instead, is to ask ourselves if we have always maintained respect for the principle of religious liberty that Helwys promoted (Callam, internet posting, Jan. 2012).

That quote reminds me of another, from Thomas Jefferson, considered one of my country's founders—who was also accused of being an atheist by his political opponents because of his irregular theology. In one of the last letters of his life, Jefferson wrote:

> The general spread of the light of science has already laid open to every view the palpable truth that the mass of mankind has not been born with saddles on their backs, nor a favored few booted and spurred, ready to ride them legitimately, by the grace of God" (Meacham, 2006:7).

I'll leave it to the professional historians to sort out which had more influence in the promotion of religious liberty: the European Enlightenment or the early Baptist movement, with figures such as Helwys and Baptist pastors Roger Williams and John Leland in the U.S. I lift up Jefferson's quote simply because his image of the mass of humanity "being born with saddles on their backs" is so graphic. Every modern indicator reveals that the world's disparity is escalating to unprecedented levels. Even in my own country. And I wonder if our congregations possess enough soul freedom to stand up and name this as an abomination!

Even the briefest survey of religious liberty and peacemaking history would require a mention of Roger Williams, among the early dissenting Christian immigrants to Britain's colonies in the "new world." It didn't take long for Puritan religious establishment in the Massachusetts Bay Colony to censor and finally expel Williams in 1635, who fled to the wilderness of what is now the state of Rhode Island to found the first Baptist church in the American hemisphere. Religious liberty was his well-known passion. But of the four charges brought against him, the most damning was his claim "that we have not our land by patent from the king, but that the natives are the true owners of it, and that we ought to repent of such a receiving of it by patent" (TAB, 1986:18).

What is little known about Williams, even among Baptists, is his commitment to living with Native Americans, especially the Narragansetts, and his devotion to learning their language and religious worldview. On numerous occasions he successfully mediated conflicts between Native Americans and the new European immigrant communities. He wrote blistering commentary on the settlers forced baptism of indigenous peoples, "sometimes by wiles and subtle devices, sometimes by force compelling them to submit to that which they understood not" (Womack, 1991:12-13). What we most often fail to note in our celebrations of the legacy of religious liberty pioneers is that some of these very advocates were themselves the least willing to grant liberty to others. William Bradford, governor of the early Plymouth Colony, wrote of his Pilgrim community's battle with the Pequot Indians at Mystic River, beginning with the torching of the Pequot village:

> It was a fearful sight to see them thus frying in the fire and the streams of blood quenching the same, and horrible was the stink and scent thereof; but the victory seemed a sweet sacrifice, and [we] gave the praise thereof to God (Philbrick, 2006:7).

You would think that anyone promoting religious liberty to a group of Baptists would be a remarkably easy sell. This stuff is in our DNA, is it not?! But remember—it wasn't that many years ago when the pastor of what was then the largest Baptist church in the U.S. publicly denounced the separation of church and state as "the figment of some infidel's imagination" (Sanders, 2000:4). And also remember: It was the ruthless political philosopher Machiavelli who wrote in his *Discourses* that the Roman Empire "turned to religion as the instrument necessary above all others for the maintenance of a civilized state" (Meacham, 2006:25). It is no coincidence that the Gospel writers chose words like "Lord," "Savior," "Son of God" and "Prince of Peace" to describe Jesus. These exact same terms were also used of the great Caesar Augustus, ruler of the Roman Empire. At the time, no one needed to point this out. *Pax Christi,* the "peace of Rome," was described this way by a first century historian: "They rob, butcher, plunder ... and where they make a desolation, they call it 'peace'" (Horsley, 2003:15).

I have to confess that what concerns me the most is not explicit restrictions on religious liberty in numerous dictatorial regimes around the world. What concerns me most is the capacity of governments—particularly in the Western world—to bribe religious communities into turning their focus away from warmongering policies. It was the Nazi Minister of Propaganda Joseph Goebbels who warned: "Churchmen dabbling in politics should take note that their only task is to prepare for the world hereafter" (Barclay, 1983:18). You'll be interested to learn that the Official Report of the Fifth Baptist World Congress meeting in Berlin in 1934 noted: "It is reported that Chancellor Adolf Hitler gives to the temperance movement the prestige of his personal example. ..." (Allen, 1982). A German Baptist delegate spoke out, saying that vigorous races overcoming weaker ones by force is an expression of natural law, and that "we must face the facts" (Allen, 1982).

The state's more common form of repressing soul liberty is more subtle and more perceptively described as in 2 Timothy, of those "holding the form of religion but denying the power thereof" (I Tim. 3:5). In my country, only two classes of citizens are granted a special tax break related to housing costs: members of the military and ordained clergy.

One of the most egregious examples of state bribery of religious freedom comes from 1962. A group of 200 business executives and university presidents formed what was called the Committee for Economic Development. The report they issued from their deliberations is titled "An Adaptive Program for Agriculture." One of the recommendations from that report is this chilling statement: "Where there are religious obstacles to modern economic progress, the religion may have to be taken less seriously or its character altered" (Peacework, 1987:12).

I wish we could spend several days together telling stories about the struggle for religious freedom around the world. One of extraordinary reports coming out of the Arab Spring movement was a political reporter's photo and written account of Egyptian Christian youth surrounding and protecting Muslim youth during their prayers in Tahrir Square in Cairo. This past fall I wrote about the work of the Rev. Rusudan Gotsiridze, a Baptist pastor in the Republic of Georgia. A national figure in the human rights advocacy in her country, Rusudan played a pivotal role in her country's expanded protection of religious minorities. Last July the parliament passed an amendment to George's Civil Code giving legal recognition to five non-Orthodox groups, including Baptists. Rusudan initiated a meeting with leaders of the newly-recognized bodies and convinced them to remove all limiting language, effectively extending legal status to all faith communities (Sehested, 2012:5).

Without a doubt the people who have most influenced me over the past 25 years are our Baptist friends in Cuba. I can still vividly recall my first encounter with a Cuban Baptist pastor, who could quote from memory long passages from the writings of Dr. Martin Luther King Jr. I had no idea that Dr. King was known there. Before long, I came to realize I had no idea of just about anything related to Cuba, primarily because of the long-standing U.S. embargo. It is certainly true that in the early decades after the Cuban Revolution, religious liberty was severely restricted and penalized. But beginning in the mid-‘80s brought a slow thaw in church-state relations. To tell the story of that developing conversation would take too long to tell here. Suffice it to say, I believe the global church needs to learn from our Cuba friends—and other Christians in similarly restrictive lands. We in the West especially need these lessons, from communities of faith who have had to learn to live without being privileged by the state. Many of our Cuban friends have come to know the power of the Gospel in a profound new way, precisely because of the marginalized condition in which they found themselves.

"In the language of the Bible," Dietrich Bonhoeffer wrote, "freedom is not something you have for yourself but something you have for others" (Bonhoeffer, 1959:37). At its deepest level, freedom is not something someone gives you. Freedom is what you assume. Then, when someone comes to take it away, to paraphrase Utah Phillips, the amount of resistance you offer is the degree to which you are free.

Bibliography

Allen, William L. "How Baptists Assessed Hitler." *Christian Century*. September 1-8, 1992.

Barclay, William. *Barclay on Peace*. Fellowship Publications. 1983.

Bonhoeffer, Dietrich. *Creation and Fall/Temptation: Two Biblical Studies*. MacMillan. 1983.

Callam, Neville. "'Window on the World' Banquet report." *Baptist World*. April/June 2012.

Horsley, Richard. *Jesus and Empire: The Kingdom of God and the New World Disorder*. Augsburg/Fortress. 2006.

Meacham, Jon. *American Gospel: God, the Founding Fathers, and the Making of a Nation.* Random House. 2006.

Peacework. September/October. 1987.

Philbrick, Nathaniel. *Mayflower: A Story of Courage, Community, and War.* Penguin. 2006.

Sanders, Al. *Report from the Capital.* June 12, 2000.

Sehested, Kenneth L. "Listen to the Daisies: A Profile of Georgian Baptist Bishop Rusudan Gotsidridze." *Folio.* Winter 2012.

Womack, Paula. "Made of One Blood: The Story of Roger Williams and Native Americans." *Baptist Peacemaker.* Winter1991-Spring 1992.

25 | To know and to do the will of God: J. Deotis Roberts' Moral Epistemology as Foundational for his Theology of Reconciliation

Samuel K. Roberts

Reconciliation must be based upon a one-ness in nature and grace between all people upon the principle of equity.

– J. Deotis Roberts, *Liberation and Reconciliation: A Black Theology*

I am pleased to join my colleagues on this panel as we bear witness to the theological legacy of J. Deotis Roberts. For almost three generations Professor Roberts has been a mentor and friend to many, an inspiring teacher to still more, and for countless others, a productive scholar whose writings have enriched theological discourse within the church and the academy. We will be forever in his debt.

The Birth of Black Theology and Cone's thesis

Because all human thought is contextual, whenever anyone refers to J. Deotis Roberts as a "theologian of reconciliation," it is inevitable that references will be made to his classic rejoinder to James Cone's theological manifesto, *Black Theology and Black Power* (1969). Roberts' book, *Liberation and Reconciliation: A Black Theology* (1971) was a response to Cone's theological appropriation of the Black Power movement. By embracing this movement, Cone's book amounted to a Copernican revolution in the theological world. Employing a hermeneutic that unabashedly privileged the oppressed, particularly the black oppressed, Cone praised the Black Power movement as the "complete emancipation of black people from white oppression by whatever means black people deem necessary" (Cone, 1969:6). His hermeneutic (bolstered in good measure by the political theology of Jürgen Moltmann) led him to affirm that "Black Theology knows no authority more binding than the experience of oppression itself. This, alone, must be the ultimate authority in religious matters" (Cone, 1969:120). Cone's hermeneutical framework led him as well to reinterpret significant aspects of Christian theology in ways that supported the aspirations of the black oppressed. For him, "Jesus' work is essentially one of liberation" (Cone, 1969:35). Moreover, "in Christ, God enters human affairs and takes sides with the oppressed" (Cone, 1969:36). Cone's second book, *A Black Theology of Liberation* (1970), was a fuller elaboration on his vision for a black theology. Within that volume, Cone's political hermeneutic had become so vigorous that at one point he could declare that through the Incarnation, both God and Jesus shared in the existential condition of blackness (Cone, 1970:216).

Roberts' Response

With the publication of J. Deotis Roberts' book, *Liberation and Reconciliation: A Black Theology*, the framework for a significant debate within the burgeoning black theology was put in place. Although there were others who critiqued Cone's theology (Jones, 1973) including his own brother, Cecil Cone (Cone, 1974), it would be J. Deotis Roberts who would be recognized as his principal opponent. The very title of Roberts' book signaled that he would chart a path at variance with Cone's theology. Indeed, within the early pages of the preface that intent was made manifest with these words:

> We are aware of the gospel of freedom to which Christ as Liberator
> has called us. But, as Christians, black and white, we surely know
> that separation, however rewarding to set the record straight,
> cannot be an ultimate Christian goal. Separation must give way
> to reconciliation (Roberts, 1971:10).

Thus was set in place the groundwork for a major cleavage between these two theologians.

Yet, at the outset, it is important to realize how much Cone and Roberts agreed with each other on critical issues, including some aspects of reconciliation itself. Despite their generational differences, Roberts affirmed that both he and his younger interlocutor shared a "passion for social justice" (Roberts, 1971:xii). Both shared a disdain for a facile integration that would continue to foster disproportionate white power. Both affirmed that any eventual reconciliation between blacks and whites could occur only between equals. Roberts insisted emphatically that, "[r]econciliation, between blacks and whites, is a two-way street. It depends as much upon what whites will do to make conditions in race relations better as it does upon what blacks will not do" (Roberts, 1971:10).

How then, can we account for the great conflict between these two theologians, both committed to social justice, both suspicious of superficial racial integration, and both agreeing on the validity of reconciliation itself? To be sure, part of the difference may be attributed to the different generations to which each belonged. By 1968, Cone reflected many of his generation's growing disaffection with the movement led by King and he would ultimately become rather dismissive of the tactical and ideological rationale for non-violence (Cone, 1969:136). Roberts, by contrast, confessed that he "was influenced by the period of race relations impacted by the 1954 school decision, the Civil Rights Movement, and the nonviolent program of Dr. M. L. King, Jr." (Roberts, 1994:xii). In fact, it would be a moral justification of King's vision for social justice that in large measure inspired him to write *Liberation and Reconciliation*; his intent was, in truth, to "mediate between the position of King and Cone rather than a response to Cone" (Battle, 2005).

But the reason for the conflict between Cone and Roberts lay deeper even than the different generations to which they belonged; it had to do with a fundamental difference in how the world is known. As Roberts would reminisce in the 1994 edition of *Liberation and Reconciliation: A Black Theology* (Roberts, 1994:xiii):

> Not only my personal history, but my intellectual pilgrimage has been epistemological—a quest for a reasonable place for a stand. This had taken me into the history of ideas in the West. But it had also sent me on a global religious quest prior to my encounter with the issues presented by the black religious experience. My encounter with Euro-American religious thought had been deep on both sides of the Atlantic as well as in principal universities and divinity schools across this nation. It would not have been possible, therefore, to be in concert with Cone or merely react to what he had to say.

So, by the time Roberts responded to Cone in 1971, the methodological die, in a sense, had already been cast. A critical difference between the two men would lie in the moral epistemology with which J. Deotis Roberts began his vocation in theology. In marking out the distinct way in which he would differ from Cone on the nature of reconciliation between blacks and whites, Roberts wrote this trenchant statement: "Reconciliation must be based upon a one-ness in nature and grace between all people upon the principle of equity" (Roberts, 1994:10). With this statement, we have a clear indication that Roberts' early aim was to inquire into the nature of moral reality itself and the extent to which God undergirded that reality. Having made this connection he would be in a position to offer some pronouncements about the theological ethics of reconciliation.

For the balance of this essay, I want first to explore Roberts' moral epistemology and the extent to which it shaped –and was shaped—by his views of the nature of God. Second, I hope to show how this moral epistemology was foundational for his analysis of human cultural systems—the contexts in which theology is shaped and articulated. Finally, I will suggest how this moral epistemology was foundational to Roberts' vision of the role of the theologian, specifically, the black theologian in contemporary culture.

Roberts' Critique of Moral Epistemology

A moral epistemology will always describe one's attempt to understand the nature of moral reality. Attempts to know the essence of a reality will of necessity require a mode of thinking that comports with rational inquiry. J. Deotis Roberts was not unique in that such an inquiry would eventuate in a wrestling with the relationship between faith and reason. In his words, it would involve the search for a "reasonable place for a stand." His own search began with his work on the S.T.M. degree, which he completed at Hartford Theological Seminary in 1954.

It can be reasonably presumed that Roberts began his theological studies at Hartford with a faith in God formed in good measure by the evangelical piety of a Baptist upbringing. Such a faith was very much intact as he began these studies. By his biographical accounts, his goal was to secure a reasonable foundation for a faith that was never in doubt. Faith, for Roberts, was always seeking understanding. He understood that moral epistemology always presumes some prior normative structure against which one will be able to affirm truth and any moral reality. For the theologian who has an active faith, God will ultimately form the basis for this normative structure and this resultant moral reality. To be sure, critics of this position will always point out its inevitable circularity, but for Roberts this is a starting point in the search for a "reasonable place for a stand" on matters of faith. One dare not forsake one's faith, even as one seeks reason and clarity by which to understand that faith. As he would say later,

Theology includes epistemology but it is clearly more than that. It goes beyond a neat abstract edifice however neatly packaged. It is only a rational structure; it is dry bones for faith. It has most to do with a reasonable understanding of what happens when a human being puts ultimate trust in the living God" (Roberts, 1976:28).

To be sure, after years of theological reflection, Roberts' notion of God would reflect the careful and modulated nuances of the theologian, or in his own words, "somewhere between monotheism and panentheism." Yet, his understanding of God would always prove rather robust, grounded in the tenets of Christian faith. He confessed that he stood "in a theological circle based upon an affirmation of faith in the God of the Bible who is revealed supremely in the Incarnation" (Roberts, 1976:25). Moreover, God would be affirmed as benevolent and just. "If faith is to be both comforting and meaningful to the black man [sic] in the United States, he must be assured that the God of the Christian creed is a benevolent and provident God" (Roberts & Gardiner, 1971:69).

The central thrust of his thesis at Hartford was the search for thinkers who best articulated his thoughts on the reasonable foundation for faith. Three alternatives came to the fore: the pragmatist William James, the mystic Henri Bergson, and the French Enlightenment thinker, Blaise Pascal. After painstakingly assessing the strengths and weaknesses of these thinkers, he opted for Pascal in the end. On the last page of his thesis, published ten years later as *Faith and Reason: A Comparative Study of Pascal, Bergson and James*, he explains why:

>...we are only partially satisfied with what Bergson and James offer, but we feel that what they seek Pascal has found. Joy, peace, certainty are expressed in his affirmation of faith and this is the kind of faith we need. He communes with God to receive a saving knowledge which comes through revealed truth and by the illumination of Grace (Roberts, 1962:81).

Thus, following Pascal's vision, Roberts found the basis for a reasonable view of God. To be sure, Roberts, like Pascal, affirmed that this vision presumed that all human beings had access to God through these "reasons of the heart."

After Hartford, Roberts continued his search for the relationship between human reason and a faith posture, a quest would lead him to the University of Edinburgh. There he wrote a dissertation entitled, *From Puritanism to Platonism in Seventeenth Century England*. The principal subject for the dissertation was the Puritan theologian and preacher, Benjamin Whichcote (1609-1685), a leading thinker among a group of philosophically-oriented theologians gathered around the University of Cambridge. Grounded in classical philosophy, particularly Plato and Plotinus, they came to be known as the Cambridge Platonists. Yet, by embracing the scientific explorations of their own age these theologians came to be convinced of the compatibility of faith and reason.

But while Roberts admired much of Whichcote's posture with respect to reason, he ultimately judged that this rationalist theologian deferred to reason a bit too much as it confronted revelation. While Roberts instinctively sought a balance between the two, "this rationalism which Whichcote attempts to root securely in Scripture and to use as the receiver of revelation, loses its balance and separates itself from the source that gives it life" (Battle, 2005:37). Lifeless rationalism, taking its cues from cold universals, could not in Roberts' judgment adequately convey the will of a God of history. This epistemological inadequacy led in turn, for Roberts, to an ethical inadequacy in Whichcote's position. This Puritan academic divine was quite wealthy and was solidly ensconced in the ruling gentry of his era. He was, like many of his class, quite impervious to the conditions of the poor. His theological explanation for this state of affairs is telling. On one hand, the inequities in society are the result of inheritances, which are themselves a function of "nature rather than grace." But at other times, Whichcote affirms that the differences between human economic fortunes are a result of divine action. But, as Frederick Ferre has noted, Roberts indicts Whichcote for attempting to have it both ways: "either providence is involved in the distribution of wealth or it is not. It appears that in this latter assertion, Whichcote without meaning to do so, gives a religious cloak to the oppressor of the poor and at the same time deals a deadly blow to the disinherited" (Battle, 2005:38).

Roberts' inquiry into moral epistemology led him ultimately to affirm that a God of justice required the liberation of all humanity. Following Pascal, discernment of the will of such a God could be attained through the "reasons of the heart," but mindful of the negative example of Whichcote, reason ought always be tempered such that the liberation of all humanity might be accomplished.

Moral Epistemology, Hermeneutics and the Critique of Human Cultures

Roberts would certainly agree with the observation that all theological assertions are contextually grounded within human cultures. God speaks to all human beings through and within the medium of human culture. This observation was foundational for his critique of human culture.

Roberts' inquiry into the nature of moral reality and his assertion that a God of grace mediates universal access to God led him to affirm that a God of justice willed the liberation of all people who were oppressed. At the same time, he was well aware that all human cultures will give evidence of God's presence. Each culture will of necessity develop its own hermeneutic. At the same time, Roberts was always aware that theology must be "contextual": "This contextual approach to theological discourse, because it is 'live' and rooted in experience, may turn out to be the best thing that has happened to theology" (Roberts, *JRT*, 1971). Yet, Roberts was persuaded that a black hermeneutic would ultimately be in tension with other culturally-based hermeneutics. It was obvious to Roberts that all theological assertions must be articulated through the media of cultural expression. If this is true then it was equally true for him that no one culture could claim rights to a universal norm. Any hermeneutic that emerged from a truly liberationist theology should have this broader concern of humanity as a goal. As he would say, "The hermeneutics must be seen in the light of God's creation in all humans, of all cultures, and of all religions. A black hermeneutic cannot be hemmed in by a circle too small to include the entire human family" (Flinn, 1982:319).

Roberts' reluctance to give any one culture the sole prerogative to determine a universal norm, even black culture, informed his theological vision as well. His moral epistemology, in which a moral view of God was discovered—a God for all human beings—led to the way in which he viewed human cultures. And then, tellingly, he goes on to write, "The black man [sic] must place his trust in a gracious God who superintends *all* his creatures" (Roberts & Gardiner, 1971:69).

As J. Deotis Roberts developed his argument in *Liberation and Reconciliation*, he affirms that liberation and reconciliation are the two poles of black theology. He advises against a notion of "chosenness" in black religion. While he seems to affirm Black Power as a political ideology, his conception of this ideology is understood as a political movement, without any attending racialist overtones. For him the cry for "black power" is simply the rational goal of exerting "through all constructive means—through the exercise of Black Power, we should seek to improve the lot of Black people economically, politically, socially—in every way" (Roberts, *JRT*, 1971:12).

Both James Cone and J. Deotis Roberts would affirm that theology could be understood as reasoning about God in the context of the black experience. Yet, it is clear that Roberts feels a special burden to go beyond the limits of his cultural and ethnic heritage, an impulse that James Cone would probably not share. Presuming that every cultural or ethnic group has a perspective to share with the wider church, Roberts feels that Cone is much too limited. He charges that "the narrowness which Cone has sought to impose upon Black Theology must be rejected. This must be done for the sake of Black Theology itself" (Roberts,

1971:19). With a view toward articulating God's desire that all people be liberated, Black Theology cannot be victimized by the narrowness of cultural vision to which it is fundamentally opposed. In Roberts' view, "the liberating experience of reconciliation will be one in which black theology will speak redemptively to all sorts and conditions of men, women and children the world over" (Roberts, *JRT*, 1976:35). Further, Roberts warned, "if we unwisely mark off a little space for our operation as black scholars, most white scholars will gladly let us operate only within those bounds. There will be no need to admit the black theologian to the comprehensive field of theology (Roberts, 1971:19-20).

Moral Epistemology and the Tasks of the Black Theologian

Finally, Roberts' moral epistemology led him to affirm the unique tasks and burdens of the black theologians. Whereas Cone had framed his project of liberation in particular reference to the political ferment around him, Roberts struck a note of defiance by suggesting that the task of the theologian was not to be in service to any sole political ideology, even Black Power.

"A Christian theologian," he averred, "is not an interpreter of the religion of Black Power" (Roberts, 1971:21). He went on to say:

> His task is not popular. He runs the risk of being misunderstood by black militants and moderates as well as by white radicals and liberals. His only encouragement is the urgency and need arising from the new situation. The religious need is latent and even unconscious for many blacks, but the black theologian senses a clear mandate to engage in the challenge before him.

This rather lonely task is perhaps inevitable because, in Roberts' eyes, the black theologian is speaking to many and varied audiences—blacks, whites, liberals, conservatives. Indeed, the task of these theologians "is a type of ministry to blacks and whites" (Roberts, 1971:21). Yet, when one recalls the context of the epistemology with which Roberts began his quest for moral imperatives, what might have appeared to some as a naïve and sentimental wish was, in fact, the necessary implication of theological logic.

One sees, as well, a suggestion that the black theologian has a special burden, fraught with vocational challenges. In looking back over his professional life, Roberts was fearful of being pigeonholed as "only a black scholar." He was fearful of being compartmentalized—and possibly trivialized—by an overwhelmingly white academic establishment. In critiquing his younger colleague, James Cone, he forthrightly confessed that "…it is my impression that the main burden of his course load is directed to the Black religious experience. This may be due to his own choosing," or, sensing the racism that infected even liberal seminaries in the 1970s, Roberts believed it

> may be due to the blind spot in much liberalism which limits appointments of black scholars to Black subjects. At any rate, the exposure to perspectives and resources needed for theological construction and maturation will be found in the broad field of theology and not merely in reflection upon the Black religious experience (Roberts, *JRT*, 1971:15).

Concluding Observations

J. Deotis Roberts has been rightfully acknowledged as a "theologian of reconciliation." To be sure, he has come to be regarded as such because of his historic rejoinder to James Cone's theological position. Yet, as this paper has asserted, the roots of Roberts' position with respect to the moral norm of the reconciliation between blacks and whites, indeed, between all estranged human beings, can be traced to his moral epistemology. The roots of this epistemology predate his response to Cone by at least fifteen years. It is only through reference to his entire theological career, the fruits of which have given us at least thirteen books and a vast number of essays and articles, that we are able to surmise the full backdrop to his method and his vision for theology as a vocation. Thus, it would be a grave error to view his theological contribution only within the limited context of a response to James Cone. Such an error would suggest that were there no Cone, there would be no Roberts.

Yet, in a larger sense, the legacy of Roberts' work is that it points beyond the man himself in two important respects. One, J. Deotis Roberts' message of reconciliation, which he offered forty years ago, laid the foundation for the role theologians are called to play in an increasingly multicultural society. As he would write in the preface to the revised edition (1994) of *Liberation and Reconciliation*, "the balance between liberation and reconciliation remains essential in our pluralistic society. The multicultural emphasis now in vogue makes the urgency of genuine reconciliation more significant than before" (Roberts, 1994:xiii).

Second, Roberts' work points us to an evolving vision for Black Theology. His vision always exceeded the demands of the historical moment. His quest was always to understand the nature of moral reality and the human condition. Given this broad perspective, Black Theology was envisioned as a light unto the nations, in a very real sense. As he would write in *Quest for a Black Theology*,

> Our justification for a black theology is based upon the primary need of all enlightened Christians to think theologically about their affirmation of faith. The need to love God with all our minds as well as to feel God within our hearts, creates a demand for hard and sound theological thinking for all Christians (Roberts & Gardiner, 1971:67).

In an essay honoring Roberts, Frederick Ferre affirms that a careful perusal of Roberts' entire writings is essential to understanding this "theologian of reconciliation." In assessing Roberts' contributions to theology, Ferre (Battle, 2005:38-39) could write:

> Through this rewarding reading program, I came to see Roberts as exponent of passionate concern for justice and also as leading prophet of reconciliation. His mature passion for reconciliation between groups and individuals, within and between races, and even within and between religious traditions is a continuation of his youthful passion for reconciliation between faith and reason. He does not rest easy in either-or dilemmas. He presses to resolve them into *whole* solutions that offer *balance* and *inclusion.*

All theological visions, insofar as they attempt to convey God's will for a fractured humanity, seek to convey critical aspects of this "whole solution," to which Ferre alluded in his assessment of J. Deotis Roberts' work. In a broken world in which reconciliation is still too often a faint glimmer, we are grateful for any testimony that prods us toward that fulfillment.

Bibliography

Battle, Michael, ed. *The Quest for Liberation and Reconciliation: Essays in Honor of J. Deotis Roberts.* John Knox Westminster. 2005.

Cone, Cecil. *The Identity Crisis of Black Theology.* Emory. 1974.

Cone, James H. *Black Theology and Black Power.* Seabury. 1969.

Flinn, Frank K., ed. *Hermeneutics and Horizons: The Shape of the Future.* Rose of Sharon Press. 1982.

Jones, William. *Is God a White Racist?: A Preamble to Black Theology*. Beacon. 1973.

Roberts, J. Deotis. "Black Liberation Theism." *The Journal of Religious Thought*. 1976.

_____. "Black Theology and the Theological Revolution." *The Journal of Religious Thought*. 1971.

_____. *Faith and Reason: A Comparative Study of Pascal, Bergson and James*. Christopher. 1962.

_____. *Liberation and Reconciliation: A Black Theology*. Westminster. 1971.

Roberts, J. Deotis and James J. Gardiner, eds. *Quest for a Black Theology*. Pilgrim. 1971.

26 | Pax Vobis: Peace and Mission of God

Donald L. Berry

I began this paper on the day that the world was made aware of the death of Osama Bin Laden, the leader of al-Qaeda and the mastermind of the September 11 attacks. Many Americans celebrated the death of one they labeled as the symbol of terrorism. I noted alerts in the United States and other nations for protests and potential acts of retaliation. I realized how fragile peace can be in our ever-changing world.

This paper attempts to explore peace as an important part of the Mission of God and a challenge facing Christ's Church. Before we can explore peace as a component of the Mission of God, the concept of the Mission must be introduced in its historical context.

Historical Background

The term *missio Dei* can be traced to Augustine who recognized that evangelism was God's overture to human beings to offer them redemption through Jesus Christ (Bowen, 2007). Martin Luther proclaimed the mission of God as the coming of God's kingdom (Scherer, 1987:55). The modern use of the term *missio Dei* was promoted by Karl Barth, when he "articulate[d] mission as an activity of God himself" in a paper presented at the Brandenburg Missionary Conference in 1932 (Bosch, 1991:389). Another text, which appeared twenty-three years prior to Barth's declaration in Berlin, offered a similar message:

> The origin of mission is ultimately to be found in the heart of God. His are the redemptive purpose and plan. No thought of God is true to His revelation of Himself that does not rest on the fact that He "so loved the world that He gave His only begotten Son" that by believing in Him "the world should be saved through Him" (Carver, 1909:12-13).

The author of this watershed work was missiologist, W. O. Carver, who taught at the Southern Baptist Theological Seminary in Louisville, Kentucky. The basic premise was that mission begins with God who sent his Son, i.e., the Father sent the Son, the Son sent the church, and the Father and Son sent the Holy Spirit (Jn. 20:21; cf. 14:26).

Yet, human events also altered the theological landscape. The closing of China to Christian missions due to the growth of communism, as well as the Second World War, made many Christian scholars wary of the church holding the keys to the kingdom of God as the sole agent of missions in the world. Instead of viewing the church as the sender of missionaries, God was the one who sent the church into the world as part of a larger missionary effort. Although the term *missio Dei* was not widely used at the time, the International Missionary Council Conference held in Willigen, Germany in 1952 came to a consensus that the mission of God must be the focus of the missionary movement and that the church is part of God's ongoing mission:

> The missionary movement of which we are part has its source in the triune God Himself. Out of the depths of His love for us, the Father has sent forth His beloved Son to reconcile all things to Himself, that we and all men might, through the Spirit, be made one in Him with the Father, in that perfect love which is the very nature of God (Goodall, 1953:189).

The Council saw the need for redefining mission as emerging from the loving God who acts in human history to reconcile the world to Godself by establishing God's kingdom.

Disagreement, though, arose between members in their understanding of the kingdom of God. As Johannes Christian Hoekendijk argued, "Church-centric missionary thinking is bound to go astray because it revolves around an illegitimate centre" (Hoekendijk, 1952:332). He and others were concerned that some theologians referred to the kingdom of God as the reign of God over the whole of creation, which focuses on the political and social realm, with the church being a partner or an obstacle to the work of God (Engelsviken, 2003:483). The removal of the church from the mission of God was evident in the writings of several authors in the 1960s and 1970s. Specifically, the call for the church to embrace divine justice meant that the church must challenge all forms of injustice perpetrated by political and social institutions around the world. As God seeks to create solidarity with the world, therefore, the church's role is to express the same solidarity to establish peace and justice in the world (McIntosh, 2000:631-633). This understanding of the kingdom of God, expressed well in Liberation Theology, emphasized God's solidarity with the poor and the oppressed just as Jesus identified with them in the Gospels.

A contrasting view of the kingdom of God, held by many Evangelical missiologists, seeks to prepare humanity for an eschatological judgment under the assumption that God's kingdom will not fully come until Christ returns. The primary focus here remains the proclamation of the gospel to the world so that many may know the salvation made possible through Jesus Christ.

Georg Vicedom, in his book, *The Mission of God: An Introduction to a Theology of Mission* (1965), argued for a needed tension between these two contrasting views of the kingdom of God for a proper understanding of the *missio Dei*. He embraced both the need for recognizing the salvific history of God in preparation for the return of Christ and the mission of God to reconcile all of creation. David Bosch and Lesslie Newbigin as well clarified the *missio Dei* for today's missiologists. Both maintained the tension found in the biblical text between the dual foci of the kingdom of God in this world and the next. They argued for Evangelicals to engage more in the present world and its struggles, whereas arguing also for Conciliar Christians to remember the salvific act of God in the person of Jesus Christ.

This background provides an important debate that has shaped missiology for more than fifty years. When *missio Dei* became the focus, missiologists began to explore topics previously left to theologians, ethicists, historians, and biblical scholars. The remainder of the paper will address the theme of peace by exploring its biblical, theological and ethical meaning.

Peace in the Bible

The theme of peace (*shalom* in the Hebrew Bible and *eirene* in the Greek New Testament) provides perspective on the kingdom of God from both Jewish and Christian traditions. The word *shalom* provides such a rich tapestry of meaning that no single English word can fully capture its meaning. "Shalom has many dimensions of meaning: wholeness, completeness, well-being, peace, justice, salvation, and even prosperity" (Swartley, 2006:29).

The most common translation for shalom is "peace," meaning, for most English speakers, the absence of conflict or war. The Hebrew Bible offers several examples. The instructions given to the Israelites through God's revelations to Moses provide not only a promise of a land, but the necessary groundwork by which they can live in peace with God and with each other. The notion also insisted that peace should be sought with other nations if they, in turn, were so willing. "Living in peace" is a divine desire expressed in the Hebrew Bible. The same is echoed in the writings of Paul (e.g., 2 Cor. 13:11).

One word associated with peace is *righteousness*. Isaiah states "The fruit of righteousness will be peace; the effect of righteousness will be quietness and confidence forever" (Isa. 32:17). James insists, "peacemakers who sow in peace reap a harvest of righteousness" (Jas. 3:18). Shalom may come from God, but it also demands that a person live a righteous life. Why this inter-relation between peace and righteousness? When righteousness is pursued, the life God intended is fulfilled, whereas unrighteousness leads to conflict. In short, humans own the responsibility for peace as our actions either hinder or assist God's desire for peace. Jesus infers this in the Beatitudes: "Blessed are the peacemakers, for they will be called the children of God" (Mt. 5:9).

A second concept that relates to shalom is *covenant*. In Ezekiel, the LORD says, "I will make a covenant of peace with them; it will be an everlasting covenant. I will establish them and increase their numbers, and I will put my sanctuary among them forever" (Ezek. 37:26). This verse refers to God's covenant relationship with Israel. But, similar to righteousness, it implies the responsibility of the covenant community to help create the peace God desires. To pursue righteousness is to establish a bond or covenant with God. Jeremiah as well appropriates covenantal language, where the law would be engraved on the hearts and minds of God's people and God would offer them forgiveness (Jer. 31:31-34). In the New Testament, Jesus associates the Passover cup with his shed blood for the forgiveness of sin as the sign of the disciples' covenant with God. Covenant enables humanity to choose to be part of God's desire to bring peace to the earth.

A third concept related to shalom is *blessing*. Psalm 29:11 states, "The LORD gives strength to his people; the LORD blesses his people with peace." One could interpret this to say that God's people will never experience conflict or that in spite of conflict, peace remains the blessing to God's covenant people. Having a relationship with God enables His covenant people to live righteously. Peace is one of the blessings, or assurances, of covenant faithfulness.

The Bible also speaks of peace as a blessing of God for individuals and the community of faith. One of the more beautiful blessings in Scripture reflects this: "The LORD bless you and keep you; the LORD make his face to shine upon you and be gracious to you; the LORD turn his face toward you and give you peace" (Num. 6:24-26, NIV). Although this blessing may include the wellbeing of God's people, the blessing of peace carries the full range of meaning of shalom.

Jesus, likewise, promised peace to his disciples as his time to face the cross approached: "Peace I leave with you, my peace I give to you" (Jn. 14:27a). The peace that Jesus gave to his disciples can be perceived as a blessing that provides personal strength, comfort, calm in the midst of life's storms and so much more. Philippians records yet another beautiful blessing that features the peace of God: "And the peace of God, which transcends all understanding, will guard your hearts and your minds in Christ Jesus" (Phil. 4:7). The blessing of peace unites the body of Christ and that peace represents a calling of all Christians (Col. 3:15).

Salvation provides a fourth concept related to shalom. "How beautiful are the feet of those who bring good news, who proclaim peace, who bring good tidings, who proclaim salvation, who say to Zion, 'Your God reigns'" (Isa. 52:7)–a hopeful message to hear in a world filled with danger, conflict, and hate. In many ways, the good news Isaiah proclaimed foreshadows what is found in the life and teachings of the Messiah, Jesus Christ. In Luke's announcement of the birth of Jesus, he is called the Messiah and Savior who offers peace to those on whom his favor rests (Lk. 2:11-14). The identity of Jesus as God's messiah and the bringer of peace is found in Simeon's testimony, who thanks God for seeing God's source of salvation with his own eyes (Lk. 2:29-32). The testimony of the early church echoes their gratitude to God by recognizing the salvation made possible through Jesus (Acts 4:12).

The key element of the biblical concept of peace is that it emerges from God's basic nature and is not merely the absence of human conflict. More than half of the New Testament books point to peace as a gift from God through the Son. In the book of Romans Paul refers to peace as coming from the Holy Spirit (Rom. 8:6; 14:17; 15:13) and in Galatians lists peace as one of the fruits of the Spirit (Gal. 5:22). The Trinitarian basis for peace as a vital part of the Mission of God is furthered advanced with theological and ethical implications.

Theological and Ethical Implications of Peace in the *Missio Dei*

J. C. Hoekendijk, in his influential work, *Kirche und Volk in der deutschen Missionswissenschaft* (which appeared in English as *The Church Inside Out*), recognized the central role that peace played in the Mission of God (Hoekendijk, 1964:21).

> The Messiah is the prince of shalom (Isa. 9:6), he shall be the shalom (Micah 5:5), he shall speak shalom unto the heathen (Zech. 9:10); or, in the prophecy of Jeremiah (ch. 29:11), he will realize the plans of shalom, which the LORD has in mind for us, to give us a future and hope.

In the New Testament, God's shalom is the most elementary expression of what life in the aeon actually is. Jesus leaves shalom with his disciples—"Shalom I leave with you, my shalom I give unto you" (Jn. 14:27), and the preaching of the apostles is summarized as "preaching shalom through Jesus Christ" (Acts 10:36; cf. Isa. 52:7). "We are ambassadors therefore on behalf of Christ . . . working together with him" to proclaim "now is the day of shalom" (II Cor. 5:20; 6:1-2).

Influenced by the writings of Karl Barth, Hoekendijk pointed to the need to correct some misunderstandings regarding the realization of hope found in Jesus Christ, i.e., the need to focus on the kingdom of God rather than on church planting or propaganda (Hoekendijk, 1964:22-14). Coming out of Europe following the Second World War, he advocated for a rethinking of mission that emphasized the kingdom of God rather than the strengthening of Christendom. Instead of merely surviving in a turbulent world, he saw the church's future in dynamically and humbly sharing the good news of Christ as part of God's redemption of all of creation. Unfortunately, some misunderstood him, resulting in a position where the church no longer had a role to play in the kingdom of God.

The tension between human and salvific history should remain, as David Bosch and Lesslie Newbigin have argued. In salvific history, Jesus Christ is viewed as the Prince of Peace predicted by Isaiah, and the peace he brings begins with a covenant with God made possible through his shed blood, which empowers disciples to seek righteousness, receive the blessing of peace and, ultimately, the salvation that comes through Christ.

On the other hand, Jesus commands his disciples to be peacemakers and not merely lovers of peace. What does it mean to be a peacemaker? Through salvation history we see our role as peacemakers as being instruments of God's peace by our words and our deeds. We seek to be Christ's ambassadors to bear witness to the salvation made possible through Jesus Christ. Yet, we are also called to follow the example of Jesus, who stood up to the religious authorities of his day and identified with those who had been abandoned by the rest of society. The theological debate between Evangelicals and Conciliar Christians reflects the difficult dichotomy between the personal and social aspects of ministry.

Peace as Personal Transformation

The peace that Jesus offers inspires personal transformation. Individuals can be "born from above" and be guided by the Holy Spirit to lead a life of piety and purpose. As Paul describes, we are to walk in the newness of life as a Christian. The proclamation of the gospel through our words and lives can be used by God to help others know of the good news of salvation. However, is the fullness of the kingdom of God solely focused on personal transformation or does the kingdom also emphasize the transformation of the community gathered by God?

Peace as Communal Transformation

From our earliest beginnings, Baptists have believed the church should be composed of transformed lives that unite together in spite of their differences for the glory of God. The unity of the church bears witness to the world of the transforming power of God. Unfortunately, disunity bears witness to the weakness of human beings, with pride and self-gratification often creating friction and conflict. Seeking dialogue with Christians who do not share our convictions provides an opportunity to embrace them as brothers and sisters in the faith even if we do not agree with their theological perspective. Unity is not obtained by insisting on uniformity in theology, binding to all Christians around the world. The unity that Christ seeks for his church is that we might be unified *in our love for God* through our service to Jesus Christ in spite of our differences. We adjust to theological differences in our own churches. Why can we not learn to live with differences within the wider Church?

Peace as Global Imperative

One last term to be associated with peace is *love*. The love of God provides the context for God's offering personal and corporate transformation. To be loved by God means to receive God's peace, as that love gives birth to peace that passes all understanding. Yet, if this is limited to our sisters and brothers in the faith, we miss an important part of the ministry of Jesus. The love and peace of God is meant to be shared with the world around us. Most Christians agree that to "love one another" is applicable to those outside our churches, but what that means may be debated. Some insist on cultivating a "personal relationship" with Jesus Christ, while others suggest that we should address the social needs of others through the love of God and avoid tying spiritual expectations to the offering of a "cup of cold water" in the name of Jesus. However, as I have argued, the *mission Dei* compels us to help people in their search for the living God and to help people provide for their other basic necessities.

Peace and Partnerships

I have already addressed the need for Christians to work together cooperatively so that the world may see the transforming power of God through Jesus Christ.

The percentage of Christians that come from the Southern Hemisphere rises each year and they are continuing to shape the face of Christ's Church today. As I witnessed many years ago in both the World Council of Churches and Lausanne conferences, Christians from the Southern Hemisphere see no dichotomy between evangelism and social action. By the early 1990s, evangelism reappeared in the WCC documents and Lausanne participants dedicated themselves to the whole gospel for the entire world. Even moreso today, we cannot allow theological differences to pound a wedge in Christ's Church or, through finances, force rivals to compromise their integrity in order to meet urgent needs through partnerships. Nor can we allow racial or cultural differences to keep us apart from worshipping and serving God together.

One of my fondest memories is recalling the General Secretaries of the Croatian Baptist Union and the Serbian Baptist Union embrace at a European Baptist Federation Meeting while their countries were engaged in war. Partnership demands that we first partner with God to engage in ministry with God's guidance and leadership. Partnership also demands that we engage other members of the body of Christ for the sake of Christ's kingdom. Lastly, partnership presumes parties consider each other equal in the eyes of God. Paternalism and Partnership are incompatible in the kingdom Jesus taught and modeled.

Peace and Dialogue

Because conflicts often exist between Christians, efforts toward dialogue are necessary to overcome animosity. Dialogue helps to build relationships by openly expressing convictions in the hope of overcoming stereotypes that exist. So often our perceptions of others are guided by uninformed propaganda instead of first-hand information. Dialogue helps identify and understand the differences that exist, while dispelling preconceived notions that have no basis in reality. Dialogue also builds relationships with members of Christ's Church from different countries and different denominations, as well as provides an opportunity to break down harmful stereotypes of those from other religious backgrounds. Dialogue seeks open and honest conversation to increase mutual understanding and respect and a safe place for participants to describe their faith, how they live out that faith, and to clarify differences and uniting ideas. The main goal is to provide a human face to the religious "other."

Peace and Protest

A difficult task for Christian peacemakers is how to address injustice in wider society, i.e., how should the people of God interact with political figures and institutions? One could argue that the Church should be supportive of the state by using Jesus' words, "give back to Caesar what is Caesar's and give to God what is God's" (Mt. 22:21), or by using 1 Timothy's call to pray for all persons, including "kings and all who are in high places" (1 Tim. 2:1-2). These references have been used to deter Christian resistance in political affairs because God ordains the roles of kings and rulers. Missionaries often hold this view recognizing that civil disobedience in any form could bring dire consequences (e.g., visa denial or revocation). Other Christians, however, choose to take a stand against any government that acts unjustly and against the wishes of God. They see the value and purpose of prophetic confrontation (cf. Samuel admonishing Saul; Nathan calling out David; Jesus confronting the religious leaders). What should Christians do when they see political, social, or economic injustice?

Unfortunately, Christians are not of one mind on this issue. Yet, organized protest must remain a possibility when governments or institutions defy justice, lest we fail to learn from the legacy of Pastor Niemöller who, during the Third Reich, ignored the arrests of communists, trade unionists, and Jews until he became the next in line for imprisonment (Wistrich, 1995). As Jesus identified sources of injustice in his world, the Church must also do the same, offering accountability and hope through Jesus' invitation to receive forgiveness. Each local context demands that peace be interpreted individually and corporately so that the peace and love of God expressed through the life of Jesus may be known. Jesus met people where they were and addressed the need for healing and for forgiveness. We must meet people where they are so that God can address their physical and spiritual needs in the name of Jesus.

Summary

The gospel calls for Christ's church to address the spiritual and physical needs of those outside the church, with a holistic approach to ministry, following Christ's example (Mt. 9:35-38).

> [35] Jesus went through all the towns and villages, teaching in their synagogues, proclaiming the good news of the kingdom and healing every disease and sickness. [36] When he saw the crowds, he had compassion on them, because they were harassed and helpless, like sheep without a shepherd. [37] Then he said to his disciples, 'The harvest is plentiful but the workers are few. [38] Ask the Lord of the harvest, therefore, to send out workers into his harvest field."

Matthew records Jesus teaching, proclaiming, and healing as he traveled through the various towns and villages on his journey. The verbal proclamation of the kingdom of God was complemented with Jesus addressing the physical needs of persons he encountered. If this is the example Jesus modeled in ministry, why should the church today act any differently? Why do we choose between evangelism and serving the world by meeting the observed needs of others?

Secondly, Jesus' holistic ministry displays compassion for the crowds, whereas the disciples expressed a lack of patience with them. People often demand constant attention, draining significant energy from those who may become overwhelmed by the burden. Jesus viewed the masses as sheep lacking the devotion and courage of a shepherd, rather than an inexhaustible spiritual, emotional, physical and psychological drain upon him and his disciples. The compassion Jesus displayed reflects what W. O. Carver wrote more than a century ago, "The origin of missions is ultimately to be found in the heart of God" (Carver, 1909:12). The Mission of God begins with the mercy and love of God that led to the creation of humanity, then to entering into the world to reveal divine love, to demonstrating that love to the world by enduring the agony of the cross, and continuing to reveal love today through expressions of God's compassion. Love reveals God's motive for mission and the church is called to follow.

Next, Jesus claims the harvest is plentiful, but workers are few. One might interpret this as a call to expand the mission force sent to countries and regions around the world or it can be interpreted as a call to be engaged in the world. Notice, Jesus uses the term "workers" instead of "teachers" or "disciples." "Worker" implies one who is willing to serve. Jesus came to serve and he calls us to join him in the service of God's glorious kingdom.

Then, Jesus follows these words with an instruction to seek God's council. "Ask the Lord of the harvest … to send out workers into his harvest field." Too often, the first order of business is organization: planning a strategy, determining resources, and recruiting leaders. These are not misguided actions, but Jesus suggests that our first action is to seek out God. In doing so, Jesus promotes the understanding that the Church joins God in God's mission to establish his kingdom.

Finally, we see that Jesus employs strategic action when he sent out his disciples to "cast out impure spirits and heal every disease and sickness." These short verses provide a link between *missio Dei* and holistic ministry. What does this mean in terms of God's desire for us to be peacemakers in the world in which we live?

We know that Jesus addressed the physical needs of those he encountered throughout his ministry. Assisting people with their needs (e.g., clean water, adequate housing, food and the other basic necessities of life) is simply not an option that can be dismissed by a discerning Christian who looks to Jesus as a model of ministry. In addition to meeting the physical and spiritual needs of people, can we do this without addressing the institutions and individuals that have created the impoverished environment?

In conclusion, many people around the world yearn and pray for peace, though history records very few years when a war has not waged somewhere in the world. If we serve the Prince of Peace, are we not to be peacemakers and not just lovers of peace? Are we not to approach ministry inside and outside the church in the same holistic manner as Jesus taught and modeled? We should say, "May God's peace be yours," so that the world may know about the transforming power and unconditional love that emerges from the very character of God.

July 2011, Kuala
Lumpur, Malaysia

Bibliography

Bosch, David. *Transforming Mission: Paradigm Shifts in Theology of Mission*. Orbis. 1991.

Bowen, John. "Evangelism in the Augustine's Confessions: Ancient Light on a Contemporary Subject," *Academic Articles/One Comment*. The Institute of Evangelism, 8 March 2007.

Carver, William Owen. *Missions in the Plan of the Ages*. Revell. 1909.

Goodall, Norman, ed. *Missions under the Cross: Addresses delivered at the Enlarged Meeting of the Committee of the International Missionary Council at Willingen, 1952; with Statements issued by the Meeting*. Edinburgh House. 1953.

Engelsviken, Tormod. "Missio Dei: The Understanding and Misunderstanding of a Theological Concept in European Churches and Missiology." *International Review of Mission*. Vol. 92, No. 267. Oct. 2003.

Hoekendijk, Johannes Christian. "The Church in Missionary Thinking." *International Review of Mission*. Vol 41, No. 163. July 1952.

————————————————. *The Church Inside Out*. Isaac Rottenberg, trans. Westminster. 1964.

McIntoch, John A. "Missio Dei." *Evangelical Dictionary of World Missions*. Baker. 2000.

Scherer, James A., ed. *Gospel, Church and Kingdom: Comparative Studies in World Mission Theology*. Augsburg. 1987.

Swartley, Willard M. "The Relation of Justice/Righteousness to Shalom/Eirene." *Ex Auditu*. Vol. 22. 2006.

27 | Baptist Participation and Advocacy On Peace Issues In Our Global Context

Daniel L. Buttry

I'm honored to be here today addressing you as members of the Baptist World Alliance (BWA) Human Rights Advocacy Commission. Our advocacy for human rights goes deep in our Baptist DNA, for we were a movement born out of repression, a movement whose early members were prisoners of conscience. Those forbearers of faith shaped a vision of freedom, not just for us, but for all people in which the basic human rights, the freedom of religion, and the freedom of expression are respected.

I've been asked to take a global look at how we are carrying out that strategically important part of our Baptist mission in our current context. I believe I was asked to address this because of my special opportunity to serve International Ministries of the American Baptist Churches as their Global Consultant for Peace and Justice. In that capacity I've been able to visit many regions of the world and see the work of Baptists involved in issues of making peace, building justice, and advocating for human rights for those who are marginalized.

In doing this survey, I'd like to divide our work into three areas: a general look at the task from our particular vantage point at Baptist leaders, at the work within countries, and at the work globally.

First, what particular issues arise for us generally as Baptist leaders? I'd like to comment in two areas, one related to the nature of the gospel and the other to our sociological location.

We need to see the prophetic advocacy and the practical labor of peace-building as an integral part of our Christian witness in this world. Jesus said "Blessed are the peacemakers, for they shall be called the children of God." There is a witness to the very character of God in our peace work, a reflection that is also present in the unity we show amid all the diversity of our human family. I could spend the entire session talking about this, but I think that would be preaching to the choir. So let me just state that assumption, and if you want to question it later, that's fine.

We also have a special role to play because of our social placement. John Paul Lederach developed a pyramid to explore relationships in society related to peacemaking work. At the top are the chief leaders—those with high visibility. At the national level these are the presidents and prime ministers, the Pope and some archbishops or cardinals, and extremely wealthy business people. These are the people featured in most of the media news stories. At the bottom are the grassroots folks, the local communities with their leaders—pastors, school teachers, small non-governmental organizations (NGOs), public health workers, etc. In between are the middle-level leaders—those in national NGOs, academics and intellectuals, many business leaders, and most of us—church leaders in conventions and unions and ministries beyond the local church.

The people in the middle can play key roles in building peace because they can have relationships both to the top and to the grassroots. They are key connectors in society. If we can remain closely tuned to the experiences of those at the grassroots, hearing their cries and understanding their struggles, then we can be allies with them in amplifying their voices up to the top levels. We can also stand closer to those in power so that we can speak the messages of advocacy to them. Many times as peace processes develop, middle-level leaders become the ones that serve on peace commissions and do much of the practical work of giving shape to reconciliation.

So we don't have to wait for the top-level leaders to act. We may be standing right now at the most creative place for transformative leadership to be exercised. If we say we have no power, we are limiting ourselves and shutting off the wonderful works God might do through us.

I think we *must* make a witness for peace because of our gospel calling, and I think we *can* make a witness for peace because of our social placement as leaders.

So how might we make that witness within our home countries? We need to realize that as religious leaders we are both connected to significant groups of people, and that we also bring a particularly moral voice into the social and political context. Sometimes people will turn to that moral voice or be open to it for the facilitation of mediation in some capacity. If there is a civil war in a country, or different factions fighting in an ethnic group, to whom will they turn for help to negotiate a solution? Many times they don't want outside political groups, such as diplomats for other nations or even from the United Nations. Rather they turn to people within their own social groups they can trust. Religious leaders with their moral stature can be that trusted group, even if the religious leaders are not from the dominant group in that particular nation.

For example in the 1970s in Sudan's civil war, the parties, including the government, responded positively to the World Council of Churches and the All Africa Conference of Churches through their member body of the Presbyterian Church in Sudan. That launched a mediation process that ended that early civil war. The Sudanese mediation in the 1970s is fascinating because though most of those in the South were Christians, the dominant North was almost completely Muslim—yet Christian leaders were the mediators accepted by all.

In Liberia, the Council of Churches including key Liberian Baptists, were a major voice in advocating and driving the government and the rebels to the peace talks that ended their latest civil war. In Rwanda before the genocide, Baptist leader Eleazar Ziherembere and a Catholic bishop facilitated the peace process that brought the United Nations peacekeepers into the country. In Nagaland the Forum for Naga Reconciliation was launched with Wati Aier, a Baptist seminary principal, as the leading voice and advocate for peace. That process has achieved the signing of a Covenant of Reconciliation by all the Naga factions. In Myanmar, Baptist leader Saboi Jum has mediated a cease-fire between the military government and Kachin insurgents. He has also coordinated a group of Christian and Buddhist leaders who seek to mediate between the government and all the various ethnic insurgencies. The war in Nicaragua began moving to a settlement through the mediation of a group of Moravian leaders and the late Gustavo Parajón, former BWA Vice President and key Nicaraguan Baptist leader. There are probably many other examples I don't know about, especially from non-Baptist traditions.

The point is that religious leaders, if they lead from a place of moral integrity and the values of peace and respect for all, can be called upon to mediate in efforts to end violent conflicts. Some of these processes led to peace accords, some merely to ceasefires. All of them are problematic. Peace is messy in real conflicts, so each of these peacemakers has been critiqued by somebody—including me! But all of them, perhaps out of a pastoral heart for their people, out of courage and concern for their community, under the compulsion of the Holy Spirit entered into the places in the middle where most others were afraid to go. And I bless them for that! That's one critical peacemaking role that can be taken within a country.

Another role is even riskier—raising the advocating voice of the prophet. Just like Elijah confronted Ahab, or in the spirit of Amos or Jeremiah, speaking truth to power can be very challenging. Human rights advocacy, including issues of religious freedom, is often a direct challenge to the political powers. But people do that. Bishop Tutu did that in South Africa to the apartheid regime, and even since then to the majority government. Baptists also spoke out as part of the Speaking the Truth Campaign that helped lead to the release of Nelson Mandela.

It's one thing to speak prophetically from a position of social and religious strength. Tutu had that position in South Africa. Oscar Romero had that position as the Archbishop of El Salvador, a Catholic country. But as Romero's murder shows us, there may be no protection from martyrdom even for the most strongly positioned prophetic voice.

Still, voices get raised, and sometimes, from Baptists in vulnerable positions, from places at the margins. Socratez Sofyan Yoman in West Papua, a part of the island of New Guinea under Indonesian rule, has been a voice for human rights where the Papuans are experiencing a low-intensity genocide. He lives with great risk, yet he continues to speak boldly. In many countries in the Middle East, South Eastern Europe, and Central Asia, Baptists are tiny bodies. In the Republic of Georgia, Baptist Bishop Malkhaz Songulashvili has spoken out repeatedly for human rights including the rights of all religious minorities. I've heard non-believers refer to him as "our Malkhaz." Sometimes these prophetic pastors are arrested, and religious rights are denied despite constitutional provision. It's very hard to be a prophetic advocate for human rights when you are trying to survive at the margin in society.

There is yet a third way for peace advocacy to be carried out within countries, and that is through nonviolent struggle. Sometimes we can advocate for peace, for justice, for freedom, for human rights, not just with words but also with direct action to resist oppressive structures and even governments. This year is the 50th anniversary of the Freedom Rides in the Civil Rights Movement of the United States. Blacks and whites joined together to defy racist laws of segregation in buses and bus terminals throughout the U.S. South. At the front were some Baptist seminary students—John Lewis and Bernard Lafayette. They suffered severe beatings, but they led the way through their nonviolent action.

Recently we've seen fresh waves of nonviolent resistance for peace and freedom awakening in the Muslim and Arab world, often with Christians joining in side-by-side. It takes prophetic advocacy from the pulpit or the press to the streets and public squares. It moves from the bold visionary voice to the shared struggle of many people. It is a struggle to overcome evil with good, as Paul urges in Romans 12.

Mubarak Awad is a Palestinian Christian (not a Baptist, though his brother Alex is the pastor of the East Jerusalem Baptist Church). Mubarak shaped the strategy of nonviolence in the first Intifada. As Palestinian young people are now beginning to reject the violence of Hamas, they are turning afresh to a nonviolent voice from their own community. Among the Nagas, Wati Aier and many other nonviolent activists engaged in the "Journey of Conscience" in 2000, a nonviolent campaign that played a major role in shifting the Naga leadership from the guys with the guns to the civil society. Their nonviolent campaign also opened up sectors of Indian society to the idea of a negotiated settlement to the Indo-Naga conflict. In Orissa, India following the outbreak of violence against the Christian community by Hindu nationalist militants, Samaresh Nayak, General Secretary of the Bengal-Orissa-Bihar Baptist Churches Association, took to the streets in a protest march alongside sympathetic Hindus who were also appalled by the violence.

So within our countries I think we can see at least three specific ways we can engage in advocating and laboring for peace, justice, freedom and human rights: mediation, speaking prophetically, and engaging in nonviolent direct action.

But we are gathered here at the Baptist *World* Alliance. We are thinking globally, beyond the context of any particular country. Or we are thinking how we as a global community of faith and fellowship might help our brothers and sisters in particular countries with their struggles for peace, justice, freedom and human rights. As I think about these matters I see at least four areas for global work.

The first is in mediation. I mentioned the religious mediators that may be called upon within countries. Sometimes those mediators can benefit from partners outside their context who can join the mediation team.

John Paul Lederach is a Mennonite from the U.S. who joined with Gustavo Parajón and Moravian church leaders in the mediation effort that was the first step in ending the civil war in Nicaragua. I've worked directly with Saboi Jum in Burma during mediation efforts from 1989-1992. I also have worked with Wati Aier, along with John Sundquist of the American Baptists Churches, Ken Sehested of the Baptist Peace Fellowship of North America, Ron Kraybill of the Mennonites, and a team of British Quakers at various times and stages of the Naga mediation efforts.

Lederach talks about this partnership using terms to describe each role. There is the insider/partial role. This is the person within the country. They know the history, the context, the people, and the complexities of the conflict. They are partial in that their own lives have been shaped by the conflict and will be shaped by the outcome of the mediation process. The outsider/neutral role is complimentary. The outsider doesn't know as much about the situation but provides connection to outside networks for solidarity, resources, options, and stories of similar struggles. Outsiders are neutral in the sense that they aren't bound by the conflict and are able to leave at the end of the process (or earlier). This neutral role can give participants of the mediation some perspective that transcends the immediacy of the conflict and sometimes an urgency to accomplish something while the support is there.

As a global network, we can explore how to support both the mediators within each conflict situation and the mediators coming from outside to be parts of mediation teams.

The second area of global work is training. For those of us who are seminary trained, did you have any courses in peacemaking, mediation or nonviolence? Maybe you had a course in social ministry. We seldom get much about these matters in our theological education. Church leaders engaged in peacemaking have to pick up their skills from other sources. So Bible-based training in peace work can be a valuable contribution. About 70 percent of my ministry is doing such training. I was in Kyrgyzstan earlier this year doing conflict transformation training for church leaders—a context that has ethnic, political and religious conflicts brewing and at times exploding. One participant said afterward, "This is exactly what we needed." Other Baptists are engaged in training programs. I was involved with the Asian Pacific Baptist Federation's conflict resolution training in Chiang Mai in 1996. The Naga peace initiative was conceived at that event. When people are trained in the "things that make for peace," their imaginations can be fired up to envision new possibilities for their conflicts.

The third area is advocacy. I spoke about the prophetic voices raised within countries. Such voices can be raised from outside as well. We see global advocacy for human rights in groups like Amnesty International and Human Rights Watch. The BWA has taken on that role, especially on the issues of human rights and religious freedom. Almost every major conflict that makes world news and even conflicts that the rest of the world ignores has been the topic of official news releases and statements from the BWA. That's tremendous.

One of the big questions related to advocacy is when to speak and when to be silent, especially as outsiders. We can make bold pronouncements, but we who are outside do not have to pay the price for those pronouncements. Rather our Baptist and other Christian friends within the repressed context pay that price. In South Africa during the apartheid years we faced this struggle, especially over the matter of sanctions. Outsiders can make pronouncements and engage in sanctions at relatively low cost. But it was the prophets within the country, Desmond Tutu and others, who urged outsiders to engage in sanctions. The South Africans engaged in the struggle chose to take on the additional suffering caused by sanctions in the hope that this suffering would advance the collapse of that oppressive system. We need to listen carefully to our partners within the context and engage in supportive advocacy.

Advocacy can also be taken up in the other direction. For example, during the 1980s, Nicaragua suffered from a war in which the opposition Contra group was funded by the United States government. The Nicaraguan Baptist Convention issued a series of pastoral letters to churches in the U.S. saying that this war, and the U.S. funding, was crushing the dreams of their people. I was pastor of a local church that had a peacemakers group engaging in protests and acts of civil disobedience about the war. We put the text of one of the pastoral letters of a huge sheet and displayed it at the U.S. federal building in our city. We envisioned ourselves as a megaphone, amplifying the voice of our Nicaraguan sisters and brothers. Global advocacy can give national church leaders amplification of their cries for justice, freedom and peace.

In our advocacy, we also need to be careful that we are not made captive by any political agenda, particularly by the dominant powers in our world. Our moral voice must be politically transcendent. We must be rooted in values coming from God and elucidated by Scripture; but our advocacy must not be partisan. We don't want freedom, justice and peace only for folks who believe like us. In fact, as prophets we might have to speak directly against our own folks at times. Baptists are persecuted in many parts of the world, but I've also seen situations where Baptists have been part of restricting the rights of others. True prophetic advocates are captive only to God and God's values, not one's own national, ethnic or religious self-interest.

The fourth area of global engagement is support, specifically financial support, but also pastoral support and emotional support for the peacemakers. Exodus tells the story of Moses holding up the rod of God during the battle with the Amalekites. When the rod was raised, the Hebrews prevailed. But when he let it fall from fatigue, the tide of battle turned against them. So Hur and Aaron came alongside and held up his weary arms. Globally we need to be like Hur and Aaron holding up the arms of our peacemaking Baptists. We need to engage in the Baptist act of taking the offering to fund these ministries. So much money is poured into war-making, and countering that war-making with the works of peace is not cheap.

For every round of the Naga reconciliation talks we had to bring the international mediation team from the U.S. and U.K. That's a lot of expensive flights. Then we had to gather the Naga civil society team, and each of the factions had to send their representatives—more flights. Then we were all staying in the Chiang Mai YMCA for four or five nights, using their conference facilities and feeding as many as forty people. Add it all up, and that's a lot of money. Many of the groups paid their own ways, so those funds were provided by various organizational budgets, some of them mission budgets. But there were also the core costs that had to be raised. And that was just for one round of talks. Yet nothing would have happened without that investment of people, time and money. More people would be dying. Explosive situations would have raged out of control rather than being quickly extinguished. Peace is costly, but war is far more costly.

It's wonderful for me to see the growth of peacemaking work within the Baptist community. When Jesus came into Jerusalem on Palm Sunday, he wept over the city. As he wept he said, "Would that even today you knew the things that make for peace! But now they are hid from your eyes" (Lk. 19.42). I envision Jesus weeping today over so many of our nations and capital cities—oh, that we knew the things that make for peace! But if we in the Baptist World Alliance will learn those things that make for peace, teach those things that make for peace, fund those things that make for peace, and do those things that make for peace—I think we will be drying the tears of Jesus. Drying the tears of Jesus—what a precious thing to do!

28 | ADVOCACY FOR PEACE AS A MISSION OF THE CHURCH IN THE 21ST CENTURY

David Kerrigan

"I have no peace, no quietness; I have no rest, only turmoil" (Job 3:26).

"Peace I leave with you, my peace I give you" (Jn. 14:27).

Introduction

There is a compelling argument from scripture that we are called to be biblical peacemakers. As such, for some years, I have encouraged people within and beyond BMS to take peacemaking seriously for this is a matter of biblical discipleship, Christ himself affirmed the blessedness of those who dared to be peacemakers.

But we need to begin with a reality check. The absence of peace is all around us and the reasons are many:

War: Peace is If the 20th century was one of the bloodiest in history, our hopes that the 21st century might be better did not survive long. Over the last 10 years the insecurities of life have imprinted themselves on the psyche of our generation with profound impact. Following the murderous attacks of 9/11 a war against terrorism was invoked with the warning that it would last for years. So, wars began, some understandable, others less so, but all have led to catastrophic loss of life and all are surely regrettable.

For a whole generation, the world seems to be at its each other's throats. Iraq, Afghanistan, Chechnya, Pakistan, Sudan, Israel, Palestine, Sri Lanka, DR Congo, Yemen, Uganda, Libya, Somalia, Nepal… the list of conflicts goes on.

Migration: The world is restless. The globalisation from which we in the west have prospered drives migration in millions. People risk everything for the hope of finding a better life or simply a refuge in a different land. For those who make it, there is little welcome. Labels are taken out and dusted down. We distinguish between 'genuine' asylum seekers (a tiny minority – agreed?), 'economic migrants' (scroungers – yes?), illegal aliens and so on but in our hearts we know that few feel welcome, whatever description we use.

Internal strife: Further afield, we see large swathes of the church divided. We share the same faith but we disagree about our interpretations of faith to the point where we judge and condemn those who differ from us. We argue and separate over issues of property, leadership, power, money and sometimes even theology, and in gaining the illusion of doctrinal or ethical purity, we lose the very unity for which Christ himself prayed, which the world sorely needs, but which we consider of little value.

Structural imbalances: In a world where food is plentiful, famines persist. Life expectancy in many nations is pitifully low whilst infant mortality is shamefully high. The abuse of children and women is a stain on our very humanity. Whilst many struggle to live on a dollar or two a day, much of the world has binged itself on debt-fuelled excess. We have plundered the world's resources, abused the world's workers and come close to destroying the world's ecosystems.

This catalogue of events paints a bleak picture and it could be bleaker still. Each and every one of these circumstances robs us of peace.

But a different picture could also be painted, one that gave encouragement for the present and hope for the future. Tales could be told of peace efforts bearing fruit in Angola, Nepal and Northern Ireland. Baptists have been instrumental in peace initiatives, such as the meetings of the Baptist Union and Baptist Convention in South Africa in the late 1990s, the apology for the Transatlantic Slave Trade issued by the Council of the Baptist Union of Great Britain in November 2007, or the peace process amongst different warring factions in Nagaland from 2007-2010.

In times of great suffering, people respond generously. They give not only with their money but also with those things that cost so much more. Only the poor of Albania could have opened their hearts and homes to the less poor of Kosovo.

We see people of all faiths and none standing together in agreement that war must always be a last resort. And in recent months we have seen Christians protecting Muslims, and Muslims protecting Christians as each community worshipped God in Tahrir Square, Cairo.

These gestures indicate that a better way forward can be glimpsed, occasionally, and we could construct an encouraging catalogue of examples in which people work to create peace out of strife.

But one does not cancel out the other. War and peace co-exist. We cannot inhabit one world and ignore the other. We live in a fractured world, but look for help to construct an alternative. The question is 'where to start' or more sharply the question is "how do we start?' for as followers of Jesus Christ, his pronouncement 'Blessed are the peacemakers for they will be called children of God" (Matthew 5:9) can leave us in little doubt where to begin.

And so in this paper I want to explore four main areas:

- Firstly, and briefly, what does the Bible mean by peace?
- Secondly, what is the relationship between peace and justice and are there different models of justice on offer? Can any claim to be more biblical or Christ-like than others?
- Thirdly, we look to scripture to see if we can detect a significant strand of the narrative that focuses on peace and justice issues such that we might conclude this is part of God's unfolding mission in and for the world.
- Fourthly, I want to address the wider issue of conflict transformation and seek to address the relationship between peace & justice, and conflict transformation.

Shalom – The Goal We Seek

Shalom can be understood as right relationships in every area of life: with God, with neighbour, and with the cosmos. It means completeness, soundness and well-being. It can mean material prosperity (Ps, 73:3) or physical safety (Ps, 4:8) or spiritual well-being (Ps, 85:10, Isa, 48:18).

Leviticus 26:3-6 describes the comprehensive shalom which God will give to those who walk in obedient relationship to God. The earth will yield rich harvests, wild animals will not ravage the countryside, and the sword will be laid to rest. Shalom means not only the absence of war but also a land flowing with milk and honey. It also includes fair economic relationships with the neighbour. It means the fair division of land so that all families can earn their own way. It means the Jubilee and sabbatical release of debts so that great extremes of wealth and poverty do not develop among God's people.

Of course these are issues of justice, but the result of such justice, Isaiah says, is peace (32:16-17). And the psalmist reminds us that God desires that "righteousness and peace will kiss each other" (Ps. 85:10).

Against this backdrop, the Messiah was spoken of as the Prince of Peace (Isa. 9:6), and in the New Testament it was proclaimed that in Christ our peace has come (Lk. 1:79), by him peace is given (Mk. 5:34) and his disciples are its messengers (Lk. 10:5f; Acts 10:36). It is clear therefore that in both Old and New Testaments, the figure of Jesus is central to our understanding of peace. His life, death resurrection, ascension and his second coming are events loaded with significance for our understanding of the peace God seeks for all humankind.

At the heart of this narrative lies the event of crucifixion, destroying the barriers of sin and death that separate us from God. But the salvation that ensues is not just one of a personal relationship between God and self. The cross challenges all the divisions that threaten to divide humankind. Suddenly, the question of what peace means is taken into the area of gender (male/female), ethnicity (Jew/Greek) and even how our economies work (slave/free) as we see in Galatians 3:28. All who stand together as a result of God's grace are challenged to make *shalom* a living reality.

And when it works, the impact was and is profound. So visibly different was this new community of *shalom* that onlookers could only exclaim 'behold how they love one another'. "Their common life validated their gospel of peace."

Retributive v Restorative Justice

As we have seen, achieving peace demands that situations, structures and events are addressed where it is apparent that injustice prevails. Peace and Justice cannot be divided. If peace is to mean that network of healthy relationships that allow us to live our lives as God intended, in harmony with God, with humankind and with the cosmos, justice issues need to be addressed. I take justice to mean the processes by which grievances and hurts are addressed in such a way that all parties can attain and maintain a measure of peace.

But this is where we need to distinguish between retributive and restorative justice. For if we are to work for peace as a Gospel imperative, we need to be aware that justice comes in more than one shape and size.

Restorative justice is an approach to justice where offenders are encouraged to take responsibility for their actions and "to repair the harm they've done- by apologizing, returning stolen money, or (for example) doing community service". It can stand alone as an alternative to retributive justice or it can find an important role within or alongside retributive justice.

Perhaps a simple story will illuminate. Imagine I am peace with my neighbours. We probably agree on the important things in life, and we don't allow minor things to disrupt our relationships. We live with and tolerate our differences. I don't upset them by playing music so loud that my neighbours can't sleep at night. They don't aggravate me by throwing rubbish into my garden. But there is one problem we struggle with. A tree in my garden has grown tall, though not tall enough to be a problem in my opinion. Sadly they do not share my opinion! The tree was given to me as a gift so I love it. But it is overshadowing my neighbour's garden and they don't like it.

One day, my neighbours cut down the tree, and my peace is shattered. Their action is unlawful and resulted in the loss of something dear to me. So I take them to court and they're fined £1000. Justice has been done – retributive justice – they have been punished. But I still don't have my tree, and we never talk to each other again. It's not difficult to see that the so-called peace we now have is not the *shalom* we had before. It is not a peace that encourages trust and relationships to recover.

Imagine if someone had been able to talk to us both before we reached crisis point, the destruction of our relationship might have been avoided. And even in the aftermath of the destruction of the tree, could we envisage an approach to the problem that achieves more than simply punishing the perpetrator of the crime but actually helped us both to understand how the problem arose in the first place, and maybe brought us to a place of forgiveness and reconciliation.

The parable of the tree is not to suggest that retributive justice has no place. There *are* crimes that demand punishment. Rather, I am concerned that so much of what passes for justice in the public arena is retributive in nature such that we make the error of assuming it's the only show in town. A moment's thought will make us realise that we have many Alternative Dispute Resolution (ADR) practices available to us. In every society, family, home and relationship, conflict is primarily resolved through concession, mediation and arbitration, and not punitive measures.

The language in the table on page 319 may seem strange and quasi-legal, which it is, but apply the resolution of a dispute within family life, or between children, to the table below and we see more clearly how restorative justice works.

We do well to remember that in many ways the ministry of Jesus was restorative rather than retributive. "Who is this man who eats with sinners" is the view of someone who wants retribution against the tax collectors. It is not a question

Retributive Justice	Restorative Justice
Crime is an act against the state, a violation of a law, an abstract idea	Crime is an act against another person and the community
The criminal justice system controls crime	Crime control lies primarily in the community
Offender accountability defined as taking punishment	Accountability defined as assuming responsibility and taking action to repair harm
Crime is an individual act with individual responsibility	Crime has both individual and social dimensions of responsibility
Punishment is effective: Threats of punishment deter crime Punishment changes behavior	Punishment alone is not effective in changing behavior and is disruptive to community harmony and good relationships
Victims are peripheral to the process	Victims are central to the process of resolving a crime.
The offender is defined by deficits	The offender is defined by capacity to make reparation
Focus on establishing blame or guilt, on the past (did he/she do it?)	Focus on the problem solving, on liabilities/obligations, on the future (what should be done?)
Emphasis on adversarial relationship	Emphasis on dialogue and negotiation
Imposition of pain to punish and deter/prevent	Restitution as a means of restoring both parties; goal of reconciliation/restoration
Community on sideline, represented abstractly by state	Community as facilitator in restorative process
Response focused on offender's past behavior	Response focused on harmful consequences of offender's behavior; emphasis is on the future
Dependence upon proxy professionals	Direct involvement by participants

(Source: Conflict Solutions Centre)

that would come from the lips of one who sought reconciliation with their enemy. Similarly the woman caught in adultery resulted in a lynch-mob calling for retributive justice that involved stoning the woman to death. Jesus acted justly, turned away their hypocrisy, and told her to sin no more.

Restorative justice is seen to have advantages over retributive justice in many situations. In a paper presented at a meeting of the Organisation of Commonwealth Caribbean Bar Associations' in Nassau, Bahamas in May 2001, Judge McElrea, District Court and Youth Court Judge, New Zealand touched on these:

- Victims are more satisfied with the restorative justice system than the normal court sentencing process;

- Outcomes of restorative conferences are more imaginative than Court sentences;

- Because the parties are able to meet together and talk about what has happened there is a real possibility for reconciliation and healing to occur;

- Responsibility for offending is seen in a wider context in a restorative conference.

- Restitution is more likely to be paid if the offender has agreed to it than if it has been imposed by a Court;

- The dynamics of restorative conferences have a lot to do with empowering the primary stakeholders, who under "conventional" adversarial processes are largely in the control of professionals such as lawyers, judges, social workers or probation officers.

Now, before this paper becomes derailed into a discussion on the criminal justice systems in different countries, let me say the significance of mentioning restorative justice here is because many of the intractable disputes that bedevil our churches, unions, convention, tribal and ethnic groups and even nations do not lend themselves to a retributive approach to encouraging justice and peace.

Where two families have had a disagreement that has resulted in years of stony silence across the church, sending one of them to prison isn't an alternative. Similarly, when a Baptist convention splits over leadership dispute, it isn't a criminal offence therefore sending the person who, in your view, is guilty to the local jail isn't going to happen! And even at the highest levels, disputes between Catholics and Protestants in Northern Ireland involved criminality on both sides, for which retributive justice was dispensed. But peace only came about when a more nuanced process was pursued. The Truth and Reconciliation process in South Africa was another example, as are the Gacaca (Ga-cha-cha) courts of Rwanda. One example within our own mission work is a paralegal advisory service in Uganda which seeks to find non-court based resolutions for petty offenders being held without trial in police stations across Kampala.

The Quest for Peace as a Major Strand in Scripture

The presence or absence of peace, the search for peace, or the promise of peace, are not incidental themes in Scripture. From beginning to end, the biblical narrative is concerned with peace. As a result it's not hard to draw out examples of divine peacemaking.

For instance, God's promise to Abram in Genesis 12 to make him into a great nation was arguably a restorative response to the murder, wickedness and pride that had gone before: Adam and Eve had been expelled from the Garden of Eden; Cain had murdered Abel; the wickedness of the world had resulted in the flood; the arrogance of Babel had led to them being scattered; and Sarah's barrenness was a source of despair for Abram. Out of all this, God brings hope, healing and a new community through the birth of Isaac. God's calling of a people included two elements. First, "I will bless you," God said, "so that [second] you will be a blessing."

Further, it can be argued that God enacted restorative justice when he rescued the enslaved Israelites from Egypt and led them to a new land. He gave them the Torah which, in contrast to the Egyptian mentality of dominance and punishment, laid out a way to live a healthy, just and peaceful life. So it was that Aaron and Moses pronounced God's blessing to include the promise of shalom … if only they would follow God's commandments: "Worship the LORD your God, and his blessing will be on your food and water. I will take away sickness from among you, and none will miscarry or be barren in your land. I will give you a full life span" (Ex. 23:25-26).

Another example comes from the judges and kings who ruled over the tribes of Israel and reverted back to the unjust ruling system of the Egyptians. They created forced labour (1 Kgs. 5:14), gathered riches for themselves, worshipped other gods, and a society of rich and poor developed. The prophets continually pleaded with the people and their leaders to return to the Lord and the Torah, but God maintained his compassion and mercy (Hos. 11:8-9).

Jesus was the embodiment of peace itself. He proclaimed the kingdom of God, forgave people's sins and healed them. And his instruction to those he healed was to "Go in peace." The people who had received healing and forgiveness had been made whole – they had received peace.

But it wasn't just Jesus who could bring peace. He taught his followers to do likewise – "Blessed are the peacemakers, for they shall be called children of God" (Mt. 5:9; Lk. 6:20-49). These disciples would go on to heal sickness, to preach against injustice, to share their possessions, to be peacemakers.

In the Sermon on the Mount (Mt. 5-7) and the Sermon on the Plain (Lk. 6:20-49), we are taught to love our enemies and pray for our persecutors and not to resist evil violently. These are non-retributive, transforming initiatives for peace and reconciliation.

Jesus' ultimate act of peacemaking mission was his death upon the cross, referred to above. The final expression of complete peace will be when the new heaven and the new earth are established at the end times. Once the old order of things has passed away there will be no more death, mourning, crying or pain (Rev. 21). Isaiah's vision of that day when even the relationship between predator and prey would be transformed – the lion and the lamb of Isaiah 11 - is a foreshadowing of shalom, where danger, fear and vulnerability are replaced with safety, meekness and trust.

God's desire for justice (Mic. 6:8), Christ's call to peacemaking (Mt. 5:9), and the Spirit's reconciling work (Eph. 2:11-22) are amongst the key motifs for understanding God's presence in the world and his will for his people. As such, they should also be considered an integral part of the foundation of the mission for the Church today in the 21st century.

Conflict Transformation

When we recall that the Bible speaks clearly about the Kingdom of God on earth, it should remind us that as Christian, and especially Christian leaders, our remit extends far beyond the walls of our churches. The care of communities and nations are as much our concern and that certainly applies when we talk of peace and justice.

If God's desire is for peace in the whole world therefore, and not only in our faith communities, and if justice-processes embody the means by which that peace is attained and maintained, that leaves us with the question – what is the relationship between peace and justice and conflict transformation?

John-Paul Lederach is a leading voice in the area of conflict transformation. Lederach is a Mennonite and in his view peacemaking refers to mediation and is only part of the wider conflict transformation process. Again, there are many definitions, but this one from World Vision UK is helpful.

Conflict transformation is an ongoing process of changing relationships, behaviours, attitudes and structures, from the negative to the positive. It requires timely interventions, respect for cultural context, patience and persistence and a comprehensive understanding of the conflict. As conflict is dynamic and conflict transformation is an ongoing process, learning is a vital component (worldvision.org.uk).

Lederach states "I believe that the nature and characteristics of contemporary conflict suggest the need for a set of concepts and approaches that go beyond traditional statist diplomacy."

It can be a mistake to assume that national and international disputes are solely the business of governments. Lederach and others argue otherwise. Lederach's triangle has been published in various forms and describes those who can play an influential role in conflict transformation within different sectors of society. A key role for the Church in conflict transformation is to stimulate the voice of the grassroots to influence the other levels of society.

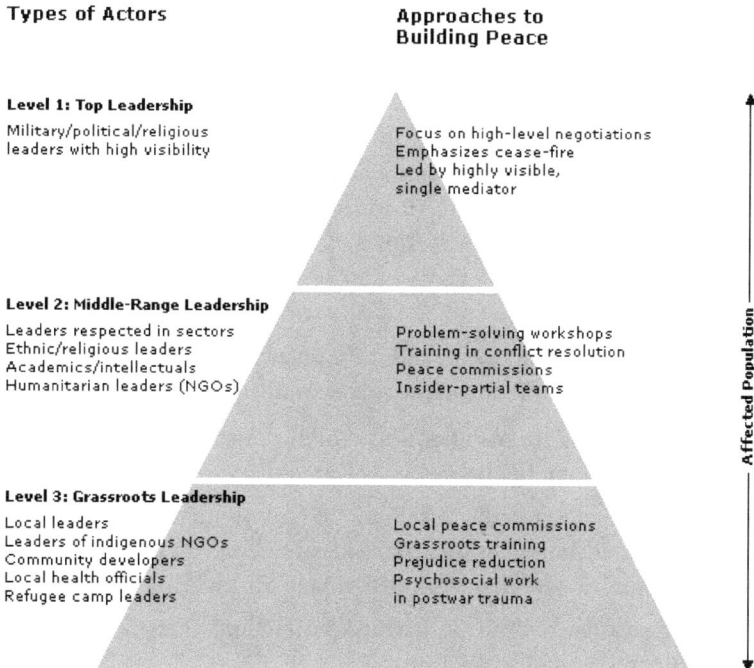

Types of Actors

Approaches to Building Peace

Level 1: Top Leadership

Military/political/religious leaders with high visibility

Focus on high-level negotiations
Emphasizes cease-fire
Led by highly visible, single mediator

Level 2: Middle-Range Leadership

Leaders respected in sectors
Ethnic/religious leaders
Academics/intellectuals
Humanitarian leaders (NGOs)

Problem-solving workshops
Training in conflict resolution
Peace commissions
Insider-partial teams

Level 3: Grassroots Leadership

Local leaders
Leaders of indigenous NGOs
Community developers
Local health officials
Refugee camp leaders

Local peace commissions
Grassroots training
Prejudice reduction
Psychosocial work in postwar trauma

Affected Population

Derived from John Paul Lederach, *Building Peace: Sustainable Reconciliation in Divided Societies* (Washington, D.C.: United States Institute of Peace Press, 1997), 39.

As Baptists, with a radical heritage of engagement with society, we should be well placed to exercise leadership within civil society and stimulate grass roots work for peace and reconciliation. Indeed through the Baptist World Alliance, we have millions of committed believers on the ground, access to those in power within many nations and have a significant measure of representation at the United Nations. Baptists are well placed to be a remarkable influence for peace in the world. This is all the more reason why we should at all times be aware that fractures among us damage our ability to strive for peace.

Conclusion

The gift of God *is* Peace and if we are messengers of good news, then we must be messengers of peace also. There is a pronounced strength and an oft-repeated occurrence to the message of peace in scripture, a message given to people whose worlds were far more uncertain than ours today. The hope of peace was a dream worth pursuing. It was the richest of ideals. It had personal, social and international implications. It had physical, emotional and spiritual dimensions. It was temporal and eternal. It was, in short, all that God had to offer. It was all that God saw we needed.

The church affirms the promise in its liturgy "Peace be with you" *"And also with you."*

But peace is not just declared, it is worked for. God's plan of salvation was the strategy for peace. It was fought for in the face of temptation and hostility. It was lived out in the face of sickness and sin. It persevered in spite of betrayal and denial. And all who have sought to follow the calling of God in successive generations have been called to walk this tortuous path. And that is the challenge for Christians today, including those of us who together are the Baptist World Alliance.

If the world is as we describe it, and if the gospel is indeed a message of peace, then in the years to come we must ask ourselves the questions such as:

- In what ways is it meaningful to talk of the role of peacemaking within BWA and its member bodies?
- What creative, symbolic, prophetic initiatives might BWA have taken in respect of tensions over Iraq, war in Sri Lanka, or in response to this year's events that we have come to call the Arab Spring?
- When partner bodies are divided by factions, are there peacemaking resources we could make available?

"Blessed are the peacemakers for they shall be called children of God" (Mt. 5:9).

Conclusion: Be the Voice of the Voiceless

Luis N. Rivera-Pagán

"Speak up for those who cannot speak for themselves, for the rights of all the destitute...defend the rights of the poor and needy"

(Prov. 31: 8-9).

Mission and social justice have been two historical pillars of the Baptist churches. William Carey (1731-1864), the British Baptist missionary, considered by many the "father of modern missions," represents the call to preach "the good news" to all the nations of the earth. Walter Rauschenbush (1861-1918), the North American Baptist theologian, perceived by many as the "father of the social gospel," embodies the biblical precept to be the "voice of the voiceless", in solidarity with the so many destitute human beings. Both, missionary proclamation and social justice, belong to the heart and kernel of Baptist history and tradition.

Despite the critiques that some of us might have regarding Carey's missionary perspectives or Rauschenbush's theological outlooks, they both represent with honor and distinction two essential dimensions of Baptist and Christian heritage: missionary proclamation and social justice. Carey sometimes may have attempted to westernize his missionary accomplishments and Rauschenbusch was always in the vicinity of marginalizing the vertical transcendent dimension of the Christian faith. Indeed, but they both represent two different but interrelated paradigms of our Baptist tradition that we should emulate and preserve: the indissoluble linkage between missionary proclamation and social justice.

The dichotomy and conflict that sometimes we hear in numerous ecclesiastical circles, including many Baptist congregations, between mission and liberation is erroneous. The Jesus that we find in the biblical Gospels incites us both to proclaim the gospel of repentance and forgiveness and to hope, pray and struggle for liberation and justice.

Obedience to Jesus' mandate at the end of the Gospel of Luke (Lk. 24:47f, i.e., to proclaim the gospel of repentance and forgiveness to all nations (*panta ta ethne*), as eminently exemplified by William Carey, has forged a Baptist global community—a worldwide community that preaches to all nations God's grace of radical personal and social transformation. The emphasis of that preaching lies in forgiveness and grace, not in judgment and condemnation, in the message of redemption and salvation, not in spiritual depreciation or degradation. The use of the Bible as an instrument of terror—so dazzlingly depicted by James Joyce in, *A Portrait of the Artist as a Young Man* (1916)—should never be considered a genuine missionary strategy. Baptist churches in Europe, North America, Latin America, the Caribbean, Africa, Asia, and Oceania, proclaim constantly the gospel of love and hope, redemption of evil and sin, as the authentic *telos* of all human endeavors and labors.

What does repentance (*metanoia*) mean? It signifies, first, that no culture and no national tradition are perfect and free from aberrations. Injustices abound everywhere and at all times. But in the authentic missionary kerygma hope prevails over despair, forgiveness over condemnation, grace over sinfulness. We must also remember that *metanoia* should likewise be a norm for the constant critical self-consciousness on the part of the churches. Too many churches, including Baptist congregations, have justified, in the name of God and quoting the Bible, unjust and oppressive social relations with tragic consequences for countless human beings. There have been frequent instances of iniquitous transformation of God into the Grand Inquisitor, when the God of grace has been infamously transmuted into the transcendent Source of racism, xenophobia, misogyny, or homophobia. But, always, and this is what I am striving to emphasize, the Spirit of Life has stirred tireless prophetic voices willing and able to defend and promote the rights of all destitute human brothers and sisters—those who might be considered, in Franz Fanon's famous terms, "the wretched of the earth," or, in Jesus' beautifully poetic language, "the least of these."

Several writers and historians have critically perceived the missionary expansion of Christianity as a central dimension of Western imperial and colonial expansion. Indeed, it has been so on many occasions, as dramatically depicted by the great Nigerian writer, Chinua Achebe, in his magisterial novel, *Things Fall Apart* (1958). But that is only the shadowy, secondary aspect of the missionary expansion. Baptist preachers here and there have also raised, clear and loud, their prophetic voices against all kinds of social injustice. They have dared to reenact the prophetic judgment, so central to our sacred scriptures, and have translated the gospel of grace and redemption into the demand of absolute respect to the rights of all human beings, whatever their nationality, ethnicity, cultural traditions, race, or gender identity. Many of them have been distinguished protagonists in the global struggles to sustain and nourish the perennial vision of a world devoid of subjugations, dispossessions or oppressions.

Baptist missionaries, ministers and laypeople have raised their voice to defend the cause of the poor, the needy, and the destitute. This Christian prophetic witness has been exceptionally depicted in the many testimonies, lectures, papers, round-tables, dialogues, reports, and homilies, staged during the recent annual meetings of the Baptist World Alliance in Malaysia (2011), Chile (2012), Jamaica (2013), and Turkey (2014), gathered together in this book. We are and should always be proud of these testimonies of faith and solidarity.

At a historical moment when critical voices as diverse as Pope Francis (*Evangelii gaudium*, 2013) and the French economist Thomas Piketty (*Capital in the Twenty-first Century*, 2014) warn us about the increase in social and economic gross inequalities, Christian prophets, of all denominations, once more dare to conjoin redemption and liberation, salvation and solidarity, peace and justice. To governments of all stripes they again reiterate the biblical commandment: "Defend the cause of the weak ... maintain the rights of the poor and oppressed.

Rescue the weak and needy; deliver them from the hand of the wicked" (Ps. 82:3f).

Jesus' proclamation mandate at the end of the Gospel of Luke should never be sundered from the prophetic words he uttered at the beginning of his ministry (Luke 4:18f), in the Nazareth synagogue: "The Spirit of the Lord is on me, because he has anointed me to proclaim good news to the poor. He has sent me to proclaim freedom for the prisoners and recovery of sight for the blind, to set the oppressed free, to proclaim the year of the Lord's favor."

These words, alluding to similar prophetic sentences uttered by the prophet Isaiah (Is. 61:1f), almost incited the audience to assassinate Jesus, in a paroxysm of public execution (Lk. 4:28-30). That initial conflictive drama would become the paradigm during the entire ministry of Jesus: the clash between the prophetic voice and the violent reaction by those satisfied with the things as they are. From Jesus to Martin Luther King, Jr., an African-American Baptist pastor, this would become the *via dolorosa* not to be spared by anybody willing and daring to envision and proclaim the Kingdom of God as the eschatological *telos* of human history.

This was the purpose of Walter Rauschenbush's theology. It was also the determination of many other distinguished Baptists, such as the ethicist, Glen Harold Stassen, recipient of the 2013 Baptist World Alliance Denton and Janice

Lotz Human Rights Award, who construed the unity of peace and justice as the relentless purpose of his numerous books, essays, lectures, and homilies. Inspired by the deeds and words of their Lord Jesus the Christ, Rauschenbush, Stassen and many other Baptist men and women proclaimed tirelessly the Kingdom of God as that eschatological culmination of human history in which "justice and peace have kissed each other" (Ps. 85:10).

This is the purpose of this book: to preserve the testimony of its many authors, men and women of faith, who in several annual meetings of the Baptist World Alliance, have done their best to express clearly, firmly, and coherently a vision of freedom, justice, and peace so eloquently expressed by the prophet Isaiah: "Then justice will dwell in the wilderness, and righteousness abide in the fruitful field. And the effect of justice will be peace, and the result of righteousness, quietness and trust for ever" (Is. 32:16f).

Contributors

Francisco Rodés González is a minister in the Fraternity of Baptist Churches in Cuba, professor at the Evangelical Theological Seminary in Matanzas and director of the Kairos Center for Arts, Liturgy and Social Service in Cuba.

Tony Peck is the general secretary of the European Baptist Federation.

Glen Harold Stassen was, until April 2014 when he died, Lewis B. Smedes Professor of Christian Ethics and executive director of the Just Peacemaking Initiative at Fuller Theological Seminary in California, USA.

A. Roy Medley is general secretary of American Baptist Churches, USA.

Amy Butler is senior pastor of The Riverside Church in New York in the USA.

Samuel Escobar is Professor Emeritus of Missiology at the Palmer Theological Seminary in Pennsylvania, USA, and professor at the Protestant School of Theology in Madrid, Spain.

Anaida Pascual Morán is a professor in the Graduate Studies Department of the Faculty of Education at the University of the University of Puerto Rico.

Mark Edward Greenwood is a missionary to Brazil serving with BMS World Mission.

Peter J. Paris is the Elmer G. Homrighausen Professor Emeritus of Christian Social Ethics of Princeton Theological Seminary.

Nancy Murphy is a clinical supervisor and licensed mental health counselor at Northwest Family Life Center in Seattle, Washington, in the United States of America.

Luis N. Rivera-Pagán is the former Henry Winters Luce Professor Emeritus of Ecumenics at Princeton Theological Seminary in New Jersey in the USA.

Lauran Bethell is and a global consultant for American Baptist International Ministries and founder of New Life Center in Chiang Mai, Thailand's.

Saw Wado is secretary of the Kawthoolei Karen Baptist Churches Youth Endeavor and tutor at the Kawthoolei Karen Baptist Bible School and College in the Maela Camp in Thailand.

Elsa Leo-Rhynie is a member of the Council of the University of Technology Professor Emerita of the University of the West Indies , where she was deputy principal (1996-2002) and principal (2006-2007).

Les Fussell is a former director of Baptist World Aid Australia.

Humberto Lagos Schuffeneger, a Chilean sociologist, lawyer and theologian, is the Director of the National Office of Religious Affairs of the Government of Chile.

Helle Liht is the assistant general secretary of the European Baptist Federation.

Paul Weller is professor of Inter-Religious Relations, Senior Research Fellow, and Head of Research and Commercial Development at the University of Derby, UK.

Edgar Palacios is associate pastor of Christian Education at the Calvary Baptist Church, Washington D.C. and a former executive director of the National Council of Churches in El Salvador.

B. Uche Enyioha is the former principal of the Baptist Theological Seminary in Kaduna, Nigeria.
Paul C. Hayes is senior pastor of Noank Baptist Church in Groton, Connecticut, USA.

Liliana Da Valle is adjunct professor of Ministerial Leadership at the American Baptist Seminary of the West in Berkeley, California, USA.

Kenneth L. Sehested is co-pastor of Circle of Mercy Congregation in North Carolina, USA, and a founding director of Baptist Peace Fellowship.

Samuel K. Roberts was a former dean at Virginia Union University and former

Professor of Theology and Ethics at the Union Presbyterian Seminary in Virginia, USA. He passed away on February 24, 2015

Donald L. Berry is professor of Religious Studies and director of the Global Missions Resource Center at Garner-Webb University in North Carolina in the United States.

Daniel L. Buttry is the Global Consultant for Peace and Justice for International Ministries, ABCUSA.

David Kerrigan is general director of BMS World mission.

Wati Aier is the Principal of Oriental Theological Seminary in Nagaland, India.

Appendix 1

Across-the-Board: Ipso Facto – Forum for Naga Reconciliation

Wati Aier

Prologue

The cultural and political history of the Naga people is unique as much as other peoples of the world. As such, while we respect the rights of others, we the Nagas have safeguarded our historical and political rights all these decades. Notwithstanding, forces from within and without have badly divided the Nagas. This division wedged into our history has left us with fierce confrontations leading to hate and anger, pain and hurt, wounds and scars, vengeance and bitterness, and memories unforgettable. In such a context the Naga national political parties, frontal organizations, the Church, civil societies have made a solemn commitment to "the process of genuine Reconciliation, Unity, and Peace among the Nagas … and there is no turning back" (Chiang Mai III).

Today, the voices for reconciliation and unity have grown into a force to be reckoned with. This is the truth! We are here, as God and the Naga people would want us to act, willing and daring.

The Forum for Naga Reconciliation (FNR) believes that reconciliation has begun. Nevertheless, it cannot come from sitting in our position. It cannot come from pre-conceived minds. It will never come, in our context, by pre-impositions from above. It will come only when Reconciliation can be given a sacrificial leap, a tough love, transcending all ill and mistrust of the past. To cling to the past is to be a victim in the present. In sacrificial leap and tough love reconciliation can be given a rightful opportunity by reciprocating in openness and willingness. But above all Naga reconciliation has to be based on the "historical and political rights of the Nagas." Time and again, all Naga political groups in principle have made commitments and have expressed the desire for Naga reconciliation based on the recognition of our inalienable rights.

Albeit, Nagas have detailed historical documentation of our rights, others may implicate a case of "historicism" to our interpretations. Therefore, despite our rich documentation, FNR today is putting into record that the "historical and political rights of the Nagas," unequivocal to the Nagas, are the following:

1. Naga People's Memorandum of 1929, known as the "Simon Commission," stating, "Nagas should be left alone to decide our own future." The twenty signatories on 10 January 1929, also attested to the fact all the Naga regions who are not signatories due to communication difficulties are also included. (We must bear in mind that in 1929, transportation as we see today was not possible and there was not a single telephone line in the Naga Hills).

2. The British India Act of 1935, declared "Naga Hills" as "Excluded Area" from India. It must be noted that the "whole of Naga areas were left as Naga Hills Excluded Area." It is also important to note that the British Government and the Queen of England authorized Sir Robert Reid to map the Excluded Naga country.

3. The Memorandum of Shri Akbar Hyderi, 26 June 1947, stating that the "Naga National council stands for the solidarity of all the Naga regions … (and) the Nagas right to self-determination."

4. Nagas declared 14 August 1947 as Naga Independence Day. In a solemn function at Mission Compound, Kohima, the Naga Flag was hoisted. The solemn function was attended by Mr. C R Pawsey, then Deputy Commissioner, Naga Hills district and Rev. Geo Supplee, USA Missionary.

5. The historic "Naga Plebiscite" of 16 May 1951, where an overwhelming majority of 99.9% of the Naga people mandated to be an independent nation.

The Present Naga Reconciliation: Ipso Facto

Since March 2008, the "Naga Political Groups" (now as Joint Working Group) and the FNR have achieved significant growth in the area of Naga Reconciliation. This is a matter of fact and open for all to see and witness. Contextually, the Naga Reconciliation has two levels:

The first level is the spiritual dimension on an individual and collective basis, before God and fellow beings. The reconciliation process has started and will go on as long as human history persists. Hence, reconciliation is dynamic.

Fallen humanity in a fallen world needs reminders that "All have sinned and have come short of the glory of God." Therefore none is righteous and perfect. Righteousness and perfection is of God. To look at others' mistakes and not admit one's own failure will always face people's judgment and above all God's displeasure.

The Journey of Common Hope calls for constant reminders that before God and his people we are all accountable.

The second level is the political dimension of reconciliation. Often, we are all faced with questions in this area. When will it happen? What are the conditions? And so on.

It must be noted that with the signing of the "Covenant of Reconciliation" by Brig (Retd) S Singnya, President, FNG/NNC, Mr. Isak Chishi Swu, Chairman, NSCN/GPRN, and Mr. SS Khaplang, Chairman, GPRN/NSCN, the "Naga Political Reconciliation" has already occurred in principle.

Thus, the Covenant of Reconciliation (COR) reads as follows:

> Having been deeply convicted by God's call in Christ, and the voice of the Naga people, for Reconciliation, we hereby solemnly commit before God to offer ourselves to Naga Reconciliation and forgiveness based on the historical and political rights of the Nagas. We resolve to continue to work together in the spirit of love, non-violence, peace, and respect to resolve outstanding issues amongst us.

Our leaders' commitment cannot be taken lightly.

Having reconciled, what is next? The answer lies in the COR: "We resolve to continue to work together in the spirit of love, non-violence, peace, and respect to resolve outstanding issues amongst us."

Across-the-Board: Ipso Facto

Since May 2008, Naga Reconciliation: A Journey of Common Hope has been at times, unpredictable and at other times, intentional. The signing of the "Covenant of Reconciliation" in June 2009 has been the cornerstone of unfolding a new era for the Nagas. It has opened vistas of access to free movement among the signatories of the covenant and this provided the avenue for free dialogue among them.

The Journey of Common Hope was taken to different districts of Naga areas by the JWG and the FNR under the goodwill of the respective Hohos, Unions and Councils.

Similarly, Mr. Th. Muivah, Hon'ble Ato Kilonser, NSCN/GPRN, heralded the message of Naga reconciliation during his goodwill mission to the Naga people. After everything has been said and done, one can reflect back and appreciate the journey to the hearts and minds of the Naga people by the Ato Kilonser. This very journey is a reminder to the Nagas that reconciliation is no one's monopoly but in often-remarkable ways fit into the jigsaw puzzle yet to complete.

The Monyakshu Conclave of 15 July 2010, between the GPRN/NSCN and the FGN/NNC is yet another one of those "unpredictable" happenings in the Journey of Common Hope. Nagas must appreciate the sacrificial leap and tough love these two groups had to wrestle within themselves in order to reach where they are today. This is also another remarkable event in our history.

Nevertheless, the GPRN/NSCN, FGN/NNC and the NSCN/GPRN understand that there awaits a final touch to the Naga reconciliation. Though, as stated above, "Nagas are reconciled in principle," yet the consummation has not occurred. This is the paradox! The undeniable consequence is simply this - all must converge onto the "historical and political rights of the Nagas," without any condition. Let us be reminded that this has been agreed upon by the signatories of the Covenant of Reconciliation and there is no turning back.

Consummation of the Naga Reconciliation: Ipso Facto

The FNR has given credit to the NSCN/GPRN for its achievement "between two political entities" at the highest – Prime Ministerial level. This achievement by the NSCN/GPRN is not their property alone but the common belongingness of the Nagas.

Notwithstanding the credit given, Naga political groups must be prepared for a dynamic paradigm shift. This requires a sacrificial leap and tough love. Today, we ought to opt by shifting from idealism to realism, from dogmatism to openness, and from "pick and choose" to inclusivity. This will require men and women of character willing to set free the self first before trying to set others free.

To consummate the Naga reconciliation, the FNR calls upon the signatories of the "Covenant of Reconciliation" to meet without delay, led by the highest-level leaders available, at a suitable locality. However, FNR reiterates that reconciliation must be for the above said purpose undermined by realism. Our purpose is to come together upholding the historical and political rights of the Nagas with the goal to solve our (Nagas) outstanding issues among us and work out the future together, even agreeing to disagree in solidarity.

Along this process, the FNR calls upon the signatories of the Covenant to include other Naga political groups who share the same vision.

Before building possible bridges across the river, it is suicidal to talk about defeat! Where will one acquire the materials? Who will supervise? What kind of bridges would we have? The ipso facto of the matter is let us first come and discuss what is possible and what is not.

For this task, the FNR appeals to all Christian denominations, and the NBCC in particular, who has been a stronghold of the FNR to organize prayer vigil throughout the Naga Churches at the earliest, and all Naga organizations to render their fullest support in their own capacity towards the consummation of Naga reconciliation.

Finally, in the coming days ahead, we all will be challenged to make space within ourselves by freeing our own selves on an individual level - so essential to all political leaders to be agents of true freedom. If one grasps this secret in a sense we are where we should be. As we decide to meet the others out of sacrificial leap and tough love, in a sense Nagas are already where they should be.

Throughout, Hohos, churches, students, women, and the public have played a role in placing a piece of the jigsaw puzzle of the Naga nation. Let us all pray and encourage the signatories of the Covenant of Reconciliation to complete the puzzle by picking up the final piece without delay.

It is heartening to note the recent Baptist World Alliance Congress in Hawaii acknowledging and welcoming the efforts of the Naga people towards "full reconciliation." This was stated by Dr. Neville Callam, General Secretary, BWA, on 31 July 2010, and a subsequent Press Release on the same day. This was affirmed and accepted by 87 nations.

Let us be grateful to the BWA and hearken to their appeal and support.

July 2011, Kuala
Lumpur, Malaysia

APPENDIX 2

Ethical Dimensions of Sustainability:
Religious and Educational Perspectives

June 17, 2012 at the Rio Convention Center (RioCentro), Room T-5, 9:30-11am
Rio de Janeiro, Brazil

RIO+20
United Nations
Conference on
Sustainable
Development

Summary of Recommendations

Since 1992, the United Nations has taken a series of initiatives on global environmental and development issues, which the United Nations Conference on Sustainable Development (Rio +20) will review under the theme *The Future We Want.*

Historic Process

The Rio+20 Conference in Rio de Janeiro is a great opportunity to reflect on what has been achieved in the last two decades and what present and future challenges need to be addressed. This conference joins the many UN-led global conferences that have developed norms and agreements on many pressing social issues that affect human beings and the planet. The timeline, in fact, dates back to four decades. when the nexus between human activity and its effects on the environment was addressed at the Stockholm Conference. The relevant conferences are:

1972: United Nations Conference on Human Environment (Stockholm, Sweden)
1992: United Nations Conference on Environment and Development ("Earth Summit" in Rio de Janeiro, Brazil)
2002: World Summit on Sustainable Development (Johannesburg, South Africa)
2012: United Nations Conference on Sustainable Development ("Rio+20" in Rio de Janeiro, Brazil)

As part of this historic process, the Rio+20 Conference gathered to discuss the "green economy" in the context of sustainable development and poverty eradication while working on a revised institutional framework for sustainable development. Conference delegates were charged with reviewing the "Rio Declaration" and the "Agenda 21" adopted in 1992 and agreeing on how approaches to "green economy" contribute to the goal of "sustainable development" at the local, national, regional, and international levels.

Participation of Civil Society: A Side Event on Religion and Education

Within the context of the Rio+20 Conference, the stakeholder participation mechanism defined in the "Agenda 21" provides for the representation of "Major Groups" that bring the perspectives of civil society and offer their recommendations to Conference negotiators. Thus, a side event was planned by the Baptist World Alliance and the General Board of Church and Society of The United Methodist Church. This side event highlighted the role of religious and educational communities in civil society and had the support of several international organizations, including the World Council of Churches, Maryknoll Office for Global Concerns, World Methodist Council, Church World Service, General Board of Higher Education and Ministry, United Methodist Women, Associação Brasileira de Instituições Evangélicas de Educação, Rede Metodista de Educação, the Instituto de Direitos Humanos do Mato Grosso do Sul, and A Rocha Brasil.

In this side event, participants started from the premise that discussions on sustainability are shifting so as to make political, economic, and scientific discourses inclusive of social, cultural, and spiritual considerations. Panel participants shared the view that this shift is due to fundamental ethical questions emerging in public debates at intersections between and among religion, culture, and education, but are often disregarded in political deliberations. Participants concluded, moreover, that although the version of the document *The Future We Want*, available at the time of the side event, has indicated how it values education (98-101), recognizes cultural diversity (16), and calls for a "holistic approach to sustainable development which will guide humanity to live in harmony with nature" (16), the document did not mention at all the ethical, cultural, and religious dimensions of sustainability.

The document also did not reflect the rich contribution and proposals on these matters of urgent ethical implications coming from the width and breath of civil society organizations which have robustly engaged the Rio+20 processes, both outside and within the framework of "Major Groups". Their perspectives, including those organizations that have offered ethical and religious perspectives, continue to be largely ignored in *The Future We Want*.

The side event also took note of the wider plurality of stakeholders encompassed within the concept of the "Major Groups" which participated in the international discussion on "green economy in the context of sustainable development and poverty eradication". Therefore, the document falls short of articulating one of its most important commitments: to "underscore that a fundamental prerequisite for the achievement of sustainable development is broad public participation in decision-making" which includes the broadest breath of civil society and non-governmental organizations. Especially, the organizations of women, children and youth, indigenous peoples, workers and trade unions, and farmers are articulating the voice and practice of what it takes to have a just, participatory, compassionate and sustainable communities based on the principles of human rights, peace and social justice. These principles are constitutive of global ethics whose references are lacking in the political statement of the Conference.

The political will exhibited by the conference statement is lukewarm at best. It is not strong in the way it indicates where accountability and responsibility lies in pursuing the identified goals and outcomes of the Rio+20 Conference and the previous conferences that were cited. Lamentably, the statement lacks political courage in putting forward a vision that addresses today's pressing concerns while ensuring rather than imperiling the sustainability of future generations.

Questions concerning ethical implications of sustainability

In view of these considerations and in dialogue with local communities around the world which have experienced the negative impacts of understanding and practicing *sustainability* and *development* solely in the narrow terms of "green economy", this side event addressed the issue of "ethical implications of sustainability" by exploring the following questions:

- What are the ethical implications of sustainability?
- How do religious and educational institutions address these challenges?
- What is the impact of religious and educational institutions on the global agenda for sustainability?
- What resources can religious and educational practices offer to a critical understanding of a "green society"?

Discussing how religious and educational communities promote ethical values and contribute to sustainable environmental action and practices on the ground at the local, national, regional, and international levels, the following speakers addressed the theme and the questions proposed by the panel, and from conversations with participants, they arrived at the consensual position expressed in this document: Rev. Liberato Bautista, Dr. Raimundo Barreto, Dr. Ann Marie Braudis, MM, Mr. David Weaver, Dr. Amos Nascimento, Dr. James Griffith, Dr. Mark Greenwood, Dr. Margaret Griesse, Rev. Ilkka Sipiläinen, and Dr. Gínia Bontempo.

Conclusions and Recommendations

The participants in the side event *Ethical Implications of Sustainability: Religious and Educational Perspectives* conclude that one of the priority goals defined in the statement *"The Future We Want"*, namely "to educate a new generation of students in the values, key disciplines and holistic, cross-disciplinary approaches essential to promoting sustainable development" (101), cannot be achieved without a serious consideration of the "ethical implications of sustainability," including perspectives expressed by religious and educational communities around the world.

The nexus between ethics and sustainability is provided in the *Charter of the United Nations* which expresses clear ethical imperatives: to save succeeding generations from the scourge of war; to reaffirm faith in fundamental human rights; to establish conditions under which justice and respect for the obligations arising from treaties and other sources of international law can be maintained; and to promote social progress and better standards of life in larger freedom.

Sustainability, based on these ethical perspectives, entails peace with justice and human security, development of peoples and communities, as well as responsibility of nations and states to uphold norms and standards of human rights. The allocation of funding to defense and military activities and the production of even more lethal instruments of violence over health, education, housing and so on, negates efforts to foster sustainability and human rights. Such human rights must take on a far greater scope than its current anthropocentric bent to one that is more cosmological so that we can truly live in harmony with the natural world.

The political statement presented at the Opening Plenary of the UN Conference on Sustainable Development (Rio+20) mutes and reneges on the above principles and mandates. If this statement remains unchanged the conference will not reflect the future that the peoples of the world want. In using the current financial crisis as an excuse for its timid proposals the statement has thus failed to critique the unbridled and unregulated pursuit of wealth and capital and the increased privatization of the production and distribution of public goods and services. The lifelines of the world's poor and marginalized to crucial social safety nets have been imperiled.

In its conclusion, this side event affirmed the need for a continuous consideration of "ethical implications of sustainability" which sheds light on a key strategic issue for Rio+20 UN Conference: the need to have innovative values and norms that translate the goals of sustainability at the local, national, and regional levels and promote "the integration and full participation of all stakeholders" (61).

Moreover, participants affirmed that such goals cannot be achieved by means of a reductionist and exclusivist "green economy". The political statement has privileged a market economy that has put premium to consumerism and greed over social equity, social justice and compassion. An ethic of solidarity and the empowerment of the moral agency of peoples are crucial in realizing wider, just, participatory, compassionate and sustainable communities that, in turn, constitute what might be called a "green society".

Rather than a harvest of words and more promises, the political statement of the Conference should point more to a harvest of food, access to water, the self-determination of peoples over their lands and resources, and the allocation of more funding for sustainable development goals aimed at the eradication of hunger and poverty. This, in the end, is the real Rio+20 agenda.

APPENDIX 3

MINISTERIAL ACCOMPANIMENT: A FRAMEWORK FOR COMMUNITY ENGAGEMENT

During our annual meeting in Izmir, Turkey 2014, the Commission on Peace (Commission) explored how the Commission on behalf of the Baptist World Alliance (BWA) and its member bodies may facilitate reconciliation and peace in situations of conflict and social injustice across the globe and do so in such a way that would empower local communities. Per our charge to offer and support peace efforts globally as a witness on behalf of worldwide Baptists we also find it compelling upon our engagement to ensure we do not drive the narrative of the proposed outcomes but instead support local communities in developing and sustaining narratives and programming that will organically promote and sustain peace and social justice. Therefore, we believe our assignment as ambassadors for Christ as well as our denomination to seek peace and social justice should begin with intentional conversations and planning for how we as a body engage, at what level we engage, and how do we intentionally perpetuate self-empowering experiences with communities/spaces of conflict and crisis. Candidly posing these questions allows us to reflect on our traditional understanding of engagement to ensure that the engagement empowers communities to take ownership and leadership in their resolution in order to promote a sustainable and empowering experience.

Therefore, we the Commission seek to develop a framework for engagement toward peace and social justice that empowers local communities and communities of faith through our engagement along side them. The engagement would seek to develop and/or share/nuance evidence-based problem solving strategies that resolve conflict and injustices while also supporting and promoting communities working collaboratively with faith-based institutions, local organizations, etc.

336

to bring about organic transformation for the good. This framework is what we define as Ministerial Accompaniment.

As a guide, per our discussions, the following is a draft of a potential framework for implementation of optimal and appropriate engagement by the Commission with communities/spaces of conflict and injustices. We do welcome any and all feedback that will assist us in ensuring that our engagement with communities is supportive of their organic ownership and leadership of strategies that will resolve issues of conflict and injustices.

The framework as in process:

I. ENGAGEMENT

Section A: Invitation

In writing to the BWA and Director of the Department of Freedom and Justice (DFJ), Bodies of Faith and/or Community Organizations, with particular priority to Baptist related communities, may request assistance and/or engagement of the Commission to assist in the investigation, development, and implementation of processes that brings about peaceful resolution of conflict(s) and/or injustice(ies).

Section B: Recommendation

In writing to the BWA and Director of the DFJ, BWA member Bodies, Organizations, and Entities and/or Commissioners of Peace may request assistance and/or engagement of the Commission to assist in the investigation, development, and implementation of processes that brings about peaceful resolution of conflict(s) and injustice(ies).

II. INVESTIGATION

Section A: Preliminary Data/Intelligence Collection

Director of the DFJ in consultation with the Chairperson of the Commission will assign staff personnel and/or a Commissioner to gather preliminary data and intelligence from the inviter/recommender as well as draw upon additional available information from resources to prepare a preliminary report about the conflict(s) and/or injustice(ies). The preliminary report will identify specific issue(s) of conflict(s) and/or injustice(ies) with recommendation(s) which will be submitted to the Director of the DFJ and the Chairperson of the Commission and subsequently to the Commission for a decision. The decision could be to either pursue potential engagement, refer to other appropriate entity(ies) or organization(s) for possible engagement, or decline engagement with stated reasons. Such recommendation is thus forwarded to the BWA Board for final decision. Whatever the final decision, the BWA will officially notify the inviter and/or recommender.

Section B: On-ground Data/Intelligence Collection

If approval is given to move forward, the Director of the DFJ in consultation with the Chairperson of the Commission will establish a Task Force, including but not limited to staff personnel, the assigned Commissioner who prepared the preliminary report, and a representative of the inviter/recommender.

The Task Force will schedule an on-ground investigation of the conflict(s) and/or injustice(s), including but not limited to overview and assessing of present realities on-ground, conduct a series of comprehensive community-oriented conversations, observe on-going work that seeks to resolve the conflict(s) and/or injustice(ies).

Upon the completion of the on-ground investigation the assigned Commissioner along with the Task Force will submit a report with recommendations to the BWA Board, Director of DFJ, and the Chairperson of the Commission with subsequent reporting to the Commission for further decision to either pursue potential engagement, refer to appropriate entity(ies) or organization(s) for possible engagement, or a decline of engagement with stated reasons.

Section C: Referral

The Commission on Peace shall keep an on-going Resource List of Entities, Organizations, and evidence-based problem solving strategies that address conflict(s) and/or injustice(ies) in order to refer or draw upon in our work.

When requests are made for engagement and the Commission believes that it cannot undertake such an engagement the Commission with BWA Board and Director of the DFJ can refer inviters/recommenders to other resources of assistance drawn from the Resource List. In addition, if the Commission, with the approval of the BWA Board and Director of the DFJ decides to engage, staff personnel and the assigned Commissioner and/or Task Force can access the Resource List for additional support in the investigation and/or engagement.

Section D: Notification

The BWA Board and the Director of the DFJ in consultation with the Chairperson of the Commission shall in writing formally respond to inviters/recommenders with the decision of the Commission to pursue potential engagement, refer and/ or connect them to appropriate entity(ies) or organizations(s), or decline the engagement with stated reasons.

III. MINISTERIAL ACCOMPANIMENT

Section A: Identification of Host(s) and Collaborative Partner(s)

The Director of the DFJ in consultation with the Chairperson of the Commission, staff personnel, and the assigned Commissioner and Task Force are to identify a host entity(ies), preferably a Baptist entity(ies), as well as other potential collaborative partner(s) for engagement.

Section B: Memorandum of Understanding

The Director of the DFJ in consultation with the Chairperson of the Commission and BWA Board approval will commission staff personnel, assigned Commissioner, and the Task Force to develop a Memorandum of Understanding (MOU), setting guidelines and boundaries of the engagement between BWA/ DFJ/Commission, the host site, and the collaborative partners(s). In addition, as the engagement proceeds and further negotiations are needed, the Director of the DFJ in consultation with the Chairperson, staff personnel and the assigned Commissioner are empowered to do so subject to BWA Board approval. The MOU will be the guiding principal for the engagement, however, may be adjusted as circumstances dictate with all parties agreeing. There will be no engagement without an operational MOU.

Section C: Plan of Implementation

The Director of the DFJ in consultation with the Chairperson, staff personnel, the assigned Commissioner, host representative(s), and representative(s) of collaborative partners will identify existing evidence-based problem solving strategies, if any, that would be appropriate to address the conflict(s) and/or injustice(ies) of the engagement. Further, it could require the nuancing of the selected strategy(ies) for the particular locale or may require the development of a new and appropriate strategy(ies) for engagement. Whatever strategy chosen to implement engagement should not exceed a three-year commitment unless the Commission with BWA Board and Director of the DFJ approval grants an extension.

Any strategy(ies) employed must empower the community of the engagement to own and sustain their own resolution. In addition, the community of the engagement must take the lead in the execution of any strategy(ies) employing a framework in which it operates for optimal comprehensive community participation and/or buy-in. Finally, there must be a clear and concise Action Plan, delineating responsibilities and timelines as well as a methodology of evaluation. The action plan will serve as an addendum to the MOU subject to BWA Board and Director of the DFJ approval.

Along with the identification and/or development of a strategy(ies) to resolve conflict(s) and/or injustice(ies), there must be an accompanying Budget/Financial Plan. The Budget/Financial Plan must clearly delineate expected expenses, available resources, and an Action Plan to secure potential resources to meet budget. In addition, the Budget/Financial Plan must delineate clearly responsibilities and timelines. The Budget/Financial Plan will serve as an addendum to the MOU subject to BWA Board and Director of the DFJ approval.

Section D: Reporting

The Director of the DFJ, staff personnel, and the assigned Commissioner on behalf of the working group (assigned Commissioner, host, and collaborative partners) will submit a quarterly report updating the status of the engagement with pros and cons and any further recommendations/adjustments/concerns, etc. to the BWA Board and the Chairperson and subsequently to the Commission. In addition, at the conclusion of the engagement the Director of the DFJ, staff personnel, and the assigned Commissioner are responsible for a full report including results of evaluation with measured outcomes for eventual publication, initially to the BWA Board and the Chairperson, subsequently to the Commission on Peace and then as BWA would dictate. Further, the Director of the DFJ, staff personnel, and the assigned Commissioner will prepare a protocol of engagement based on the particular conflict(s) and/or injustice(ies) for addition to the Commission's Resource List. Such protocol, at the direction of the BWA Board and the Director of the DFJ, may also be widely published as a tool of engagement.

Section E: Extension

All plans of engagement should be developed for a period not to exceed 3 years. If after three (3) years, upon recommendation of the Director of the DJF, staff personnel, the assigned Commissioner along with the working group, an extension may be granted for another one to two (1-2) years subject to the BWA Board approval.

IV. FINANCES

Section A: Host Financial Responsibility

If at all possible, the host site of the engagement is responsible for on-ground implementation of the plan unless otherwise agreed upon. The Commission shall not engage in Ministerial Accompaniment bearing the full financial burden of implementation and follow through.

Section B: Financial Officer

Director of the DFJ shall secure the services either through in-kind services of the BWA or independent individual/entity whose responsibility is the management, budgeting, disbursement, accounting, and reporting of all funds related to the work of engagement by the Commission subject to BWA Board approval. This individual/entity shall be known as the Financial Officer.

In consultation with the Director of the DFJ, the Financial Officer shall assist in the development of a Budget/Financial Plan for the engagement. In addition, as funds are generated to support the engagement, the Financial Officer shall work in conjunction with the assigned Commissioner to ensure all necessary financial reporting requirements are met to secure funding and the required reporting processes are followed subject to the BWA Board approval.

Section C: Financial Reporting

The Financial Officer shall report on the particular status of the budget monthly to Director of the DFJ and BWA Board. In addition, the Financial Officer share report quarterly, unless otherwise designated, to the Chairperson and subsequently to the Commission. And finally, at the conclusion of an engagement a full reporting of the finances of the engagement should be prepared for the BWA Board, Director of the DFJ, the Chairperson and subsequently the Commission. The final report will also include a sample budget for the implementation of the particular engagement plan as a reference for subsequent like engagements. The sample budget should be attached to the protocol and housed as a resource by the Commission.